The Sea of Identities

A Century of Baltic and
East European Experiences
with Nationality, Class, and Gender

Edited by
Norbert Götz

©The Authors

Södertörn University
SE-141 89 Huddinge

Cover image: Bundesarchiv, image 167-3916B, by Alfred Paulus
Cover: Jonathan Robson
Layout: Jonathan Robson and Per Lindblom

Printed by Elanders, Stockholm 2014

Södertörn Academic Studies 60
ISSN 1650-433X
Samtidshistoriska frågor 31
ISSN 1650-450X

ISBN 978-91-87843-00-6

In memory of our colleague

Åsa Casula Vifell
(1976–2014)

who was to be one of the
contributors to this book.

Contents

Abbreviations 7

1. Introduction: Collective Identities in Baltic and East Central Europe 11
Norbert Götz

Part 1: National Identities

2. Fluctuating Dynastic and National Affiliation: The Impact of War and Unrest on Bornholm, Åland, and Saaremaa 31
Janne Holmén

3. The Nordic Threat: Soviet Ethnic Cleansing on the Kola Peninsula 53
Andrej Kotljarchuk

4. An Unimaginable Community: The SS Idea of a 'Greater Germanic Reich' and the German Minority in Denmark 85
Steffen Werther

5. The Ambiguity of the West: Objectives of Polish Research Policy in the 1990s 109
Sofia Norling

Part 2: Labour Identities

6. Lost Worlds of Labour: Paul Olberg, the Jewish Labour Bund, and Menshevik Socialism 139
Håkan Blomqvist

7. From Fordism to High-Tech Capitalism: A Political Economy of the Labour Movement in the Baltic Sea Region 173
Werner Schmidt

8. Solidarity and Diplomacy: Sweden and the Democratisation of Poland, 1980–1989 193
Klaus Misgeld and Karl Molin

Part 3: Gendered Identities

9. Gender Equality Policies: Swedish and Lithuanian
Experiences of Nordic Ideas   225
Eva Blomberg, Ylva Waldemarson, and Alina Žvinklienė

10. Group-Work on Gender Equality in Transnational Cooperation:
Raising Feminist Consciousness or Diminishing Social Risks?   247
Yulia Gradskova

11. Young Moldovan Women at the Crossroads: Between
Patriarchy and Transnational Labour Markets   269
Kristina Abiala

Part 4: Environmental Awareness

12. Waves of Laws and Institutions: The Emergence of National
Awareness of Water Pollution and Protection in the
Baltic Sea Region over the Twentieth Century   293
Simo Laakkonen

List of Illustrations, Maps, and Tables   319

Contributors   323

Abbreviations

AFL-CIO	American Federation of Labor and Congress of Industrial Organizations
AIC	*Arbetarrörelsens internationella centrum* (International Centre of the Swedish Labour Movement) and its archives
ARAB	*Arbetarrörelsens arkiv och bibliotek* (Labour Movement's Archives and Library, Stockholm)
ÅSUB	*Ålands statistik och utredningsbyrå* (Åland Islands Statistical Agency)
Aug.	August
BA	Bund Archives
BSR	Baltic Sea region
ch.	chapter
CEEC	Central and Eastern European Countries
CIA	Central Intelligence Agency (USA)
Dec.	December
DGB	*Deutscher Gewerkschaftsbund* (Confederation of German Trade Unions)
DN	*Dagens Nyheter* (a Swedish daily newspaper)
DNSAP	*Danmarks National Socialistisk Arbejder Parti* (Denmark's National Socialist Workers' Party)
doc.	document
ESFA	*Essingeöarnas socialdemokratiska förenings arkiv* (Archives of the social democrats of Essinge islands in Stockholm)
EU	European Union
EUR	Euro (currency)
Feb.	February
FM	Foreign Ministry
FMG	Foreign Ministry of Germany (*Auswärtiges Amt*)

FRG	Federal Republic of Germany
GAMO	*Gosudarstvennyi arkhiv Murmanskoi oblasti* (State Archives of the Murmansk oblast)
GARF	*Gosudarstvennyi arkhiv Rossiiskoi Federatsii* (State Archives of the Russian Federation)
GDP	gross domestic product
GDR	German Democratic Republic
GF	*Grafiska fackförbundet* (Swedish Union of Graphical Workers)
ICFTU	International Confederation of Free Trade Unions
ILO	International Labour Organisation
IPA	Independent Polish Agency
ISB	International Socialist Bureau
ITS	International Trade Secretariats
Jan.	January
KBN	*Komitet Badań Naukowych* (Research Committee; Poland)
KOR	*Komitet Obrony Robotników* (Polish Workers' Defence Committee)
LAA	*Landsarkivet for Sønderjylland, Aabenraa* (Provincial Archives of Southern Jutland in Aabenraa)
LO	*Landsorganisationen* (Swedish Trade Union Confederation) and its archives
MDL	Moldovan leu (currency)
MID	Military Information Division (USA)
NAD	National Archives of Denmark (*Rigsarkivet*)
NAS	National Archives of Sweden (*Riksarkivet*)
NATO	North Atlantic Treaty Organization
NB 8	Nordic–Baltic 8
NEP	New Economic Policy (Soviet Union)
NGO(s)	non-governmental organisation(s)
NKVD	*Narodnyy Komissariat Vnutrennikh Del* (Soviet Secret Police)
Nov.	November
NSDAP-N	*Nationalsozialistische Deutsche Arbeiter Partei – Nordschleswig* (National Socialist German Workers' Party of North Schleswig)
Oct.	October
OPZZ	*Ogólnopolskie Porozumienie Związków Zawodowych* (All-

	Poland Alliance of Trade Unions)
p(p).	page(s)
PK	*Politikommandørens arkiv* (Archives of the Police Commander)
PDK	*Predel'no dopustimye koncentratsii* (Soviet maximum permissible concentration standards for water)
PKB	*Den parlamentariske kommissions beretning* (Report of the parliamentary commission [on Denmark under German occupation])
POA	Paul Olberg's archives
PZPR	*Polska Zjednoczona Partia Robotnicza* (Polish United Workers Party)
R&D	Research and development
RGAE	*Rossiiskii gosudarstvennyi arkhiv ekonomiki* (Russian State Archives of Economics)
RGASPI	*Rossiiskii gosudarstvennyi arkhiv sotsial'no-politicheskoi istorii* (Russian State Archive of Social-Political History)
RSFSR	Russian Soviet Federative Socialist Republic
RUB	Ruble (Russian currency)
SD	Sicherheitsdienst des Reichsführers-SS (Secret Service of the SS)
SEK	Swedish kronor (currency)
Sept.	September
SIKiS	*Solidaritets Informationskontor i Stockholm* (Solidarity's Information office in Stockholm)
SK	*Sturmkolonnen* (Para-military organisation of the North Schleswigian Nazis)
SKIF	*Sotsyalistishe Kinder Farband* (Socialist Children's Union)
SPD	*Sozialdemokratische Partei Deutschlands* (Social Democratic Party of Germany)
SS	*Schutzstaffel* (paramilitary organisation of the German Nazi party)
SvD	*Svenska Dagbladet* (a Swedish daily newspaper)
SYKE	*Suomen ympäristökeskus* (Finnish Environment Institute)
TCO	*Tjänstemännens Centralorganisation* (Swedish Confederation of Professional Employees)
TsUNKhU	*Tsentral'noye Upravleniye Narodno-Khozyaystvennogo Uchyota* (Soviet Central Statistical Office)
TV	Television

UN	United Nations
UNDP	United Nations Development Program
US(A)	United States (of America)
USPD	*Unabhängige Sozialdemokratische Partei Deutschlands* (Independent Social Democratic Party of Germany)
USSR	Union of Soviet Socialist Republics
VoMi	Volksdeutsche Mittelstelle (SS Ethnic German Liaison Office)
YAF	Yidisher Arbeter Froy (Women's organisation of the General Jewish Labour Bund in Lithuania, Poland and Russia)
YIVO	*Yidisher Visnshaftlekher Institut* (Institute for Jewish Research)
ZAGS	*Zapis Aktov Grazhdanskogo Sostoyaniya* (Soviet Civil Registry Office)

1. Introduction: Collective Identities in Baltic and East Central Europe

Norbert Götz

After a preoccupation with collective identities culminated in the mass destruction of the Second World War and the Holocaust, and after the postwar remapping and resettlement was enforced, ethnic identity was 'out' for many decades as a political vehicle or a proper topic of research.[1] The ideas of the behaviour of the individual and his or her gentle civilisation in the spirit of enlightenment took its place. Personal affiliation with a group was regarded as a functional piece in a greater puzzle of general progress; stronger types of identification that did not harmonise with the rationality of light bonds were believed to be doomed to vanish. Such modernism existed in a capitalist and a communist variety, with greater emphasis on the individual and the universal dimension respectively (in its communist version the universalism was a class-based projection). The suggestion that Sweden represents a 'third way', with a political culture that has been lauded as 'statist individualism' (Trägårdh 1997; see also Berggren and Trägårdh 2006), highlights the country's peculiar status at the time of the Cold War (see Bjereld, Johansson, and Molin 2008). The lack of independent societal forces has given rise to a conformist, single norm-oriented Nordic *Sonderweg* (Stenius 2013).

During the Cold War, both historical materialism and modernisation theory gave meaning to a bipolar world with its two competing universalisms aiming at humankind at large.[2] There was an intellectual distance,

---

[1] As a research concept, 'identity' was not in use until after the Second World War. Earlier, however, there was a widespread scholarly discourse that would now be associated with identity issues such as national character, race, profession and class status, or women's rights.

[2] On the affinity of modernisation theory and capitalism, see Thompson (1991: 267, 272).

even isolation, of scholarly communities. There was also a clash of ideas, the 'sacred drama' of a deliberative confrontation of different strands of thought at the United Nations (O'Brien and Topolski 1968; Götz 2011), and a number of proxy wars on the periphery. However, there was no actual clash of identities among the dominant cultures. The Baltic Sea, divided by the Iron Curtain with military forces stationed on either side, could appear as a 'Sea of Peace' in Soviet propaganda. Moreover, a convergence of the two types of political economy was anticipated not only in Marxist eschatology, but also by the champions of Western modernisation theory (e.g., Rostow 1960). Under the circumstances of prevailing universal ideologies and the nuclear-conditioned need for peaceful coexistence identity remained a non-issue.

Things changed in November 1989 after the fall of the Berlin Wall, an event I first witnessed in the neighbourhoods of Wedding and Prentzlauer Berg (see Götz 2012), and later when I became involved with its repercussions on the geographical imagination of the 1990s. It prompted the remaking of Scandinavian studies at Berlin universities from a philology dealing with Scandinavian languages and literatures to a broadly defined field of Northern European studies that reached out to the current affairs of the wider Baltic Sea area, including a dose of 'future studies' (see Götz, Hecker-Stampehl, and Schröder 2010). However, by 1989 Gorbachev's Perestroika had already stimulated independence movements in the Baltic Soviet Republics and political initiatives for an intensified cooperation across the Baltic Sea (Gerner and Hedlund 1993; Lieven 1993; Williams 2007). In Poland, which had exemplified the potential transformation of Eastern Europe throughout the 1980s, the independent trade union *Solidarność* (Solidarity) had been re-legalised in April 1989 (see the contribution by Misgeld and Molin in this volume; also Eriksson 2013). In the early 1990s forces that had been set in motion led to the dissolution of the Warsaw Pact and the Soviet Union, creating a radically new geopolitical situation.

In Sweden, with its history of a Baltic empire, long coastline, and central position at the Baltic Sea, but also its supposed neutrality and its own version of a blurred 'socialist' capitalism during the Cold War, the turbulence in the region was closely watched (Lundén and Nilsson 2008; Nilsson and Lundén 2010). In the field of academia the inception of the Foundation for Baltic and East European Studies (*Östersjöstiftelsen*) in 1994 and the creation of Södertörn University in 1996 were perhaps the most conspicuous developments (Konnander 1998; Gerdin and Johansson 2005).

1. INTRODUCTION: COLLECTIVE IDENTITIES

In this environment, the Swedish Institute of Contemporary History (*Samtidshistoriska Institutet*), established in 1999, was formed with a thoroughly international research profile. In addition it was commited to fulfilling its mission as a monitor of recent Swedish developments (Gerdin and Östberg 2004). In this the Institute differed from its sister institutions in other countries, which, by what appears to be a contemporary history paradox, often retain a stricter focus on their own nation than what other branches of history do. The current volume documents some of the international studies conducted by the Institute's researchers, with an emphasis on issues related to national identities, labour orientations, and gender perspectives.

The issue of identity reappeared as a driving force in the processes accompanying the end of the Cold War. Devout Catholicism and a political culture of romantic patriotism made Poland a natural starting point for questioning the matrix of Yalta (Davies 2001 [1984]). The native populations of Latvia, Estonia, and Lithuania opposed not only the political Sovietisation of their republics, but also the demographic Russification and environmental degradation to which they were exposed. They expressed their discontent in a 'singing revolution', mobilising cultural assets to reinvigorate national identity and ultimately independence (Vesilind, Tusty, and Tusty 2008; Škapars 2005). The East Germans went from shouting to their rulers *Wir sind das Volk* (We are the people) to being courted by the phrase *Wir sind ein Volk* (We are one people). The latter phrase was invented in Leipzig to persuade those in power not to resort to violence against demonstrators. Eventually the expression was reframed as a pan-German slogan suggesting the reunion with West Germany (Winkler 2000: 520, 558). In all these cases identity became an instrument for solving issues connected to the definition and the empowerment of a sovereign.

Not only did the Baltic Sea region become a space for the reconfiguration of national identities: it became much more of a contact zone than in previous decades, and was sometimes conceived of as a laboratory for the post-national forging of identities (Olesen 2012). There arose the question of what the lifting of the Iron Curtain meant for Nordic cooperation and whether the latter arena was to include countries like Estonia, Latvia, and Lithuania (Joenniemi 1997; Lehti and Smith 2003). An epistemic community of intellectuals working in think tanks and academia imagined the Baltic Sea region as an identity project in analogy to the nation building of the nineteenth century, although one to be achieved in a multi-layered 'neo-medievalist' fashion (Neumann 1994: 67; see Wæver 1991). Hence, an early attempt to draw on traditional layers of identity for Baltic Sea cooperation was its political promotion by the slogan *Neue Hanse* (New Hansa). One of the problems of this "neo-liberal double" (Stråth 2000: 204) of the notion of the 'Sea of Peace' was that in many places it was conceived of as referring to an epoch of German dominance. After all, the past of the area is perhaps most concisely encapsulated in the observation that "throughout history, the Baltic has been a sea of conflicts and dividing lines" (ibid. 199).

Although the claim is sometimes made that the cultural substrate for a common Baltic Sea identity exists as, for example, in its brick architecture (Henningsen 2008: 34), the question has frequently been answered in the negative with regard to whether such an identity was actually in place or whether it emerged after the Cold War (Wulff and Kerner 1994: 17; Reuter 2004; Engelen 2006: 89; Henningsen 2011). Nonetheless, the 'Balticness' project of the Latvian presidency in the Council of the Baltic Sea States (2007/08) and the journal published under the same name between 2008 and 2010 show that a Baltic Sea identity continues to be a current political issue. In accordance with the motto 'If it did not exist, it would have to be invented', there is interest in "BSR [Baltic Sea region] branding and identity building efforts" from a commercial, regional development point of view (*State of the Region Report*™ 2013: 76).

The discursive or at times nominalistic approach of the region builders is evinced in the perplexing assertion by a political scientist that the three Baltic republics were "very much the apex of identity" of the Baltic Sea region-at-large (Wæver 1992: 39). Ironically, as was stated by a local researcher a decade later, "the 'Baltic' identity of Estonia, Latvia and Lithuania is arguably the best known and the most politically significant, but also the least appreciated among the Baltic states themselves" (Paulauskas 2005: 52). The term 'Baltic' is mainly associated in these countries with a common history of subordination by Russia and the Soviet Union. The three republics were also similar as neighbouring small states with the shared aim of NATO and EU membership (Miniotaite 2003: 211–12; see also Brüggemann 2003). Another difficulty with the term 'Baltic' is its aura of "oligarchic 'regionalism'" due to its roots in the former German ruling class of what today are Estonia and Latvia (Rebas 1990: 415). The formal cooperation of the three Baltic republics – such as in the inter-parliamentary Baltic Assembly – was the outcome of incentives to copy Nordic cooperation and with the prospect of occasional collaboration in the '5 + 3' and, later, 'NB 8' framework; but this has only been a surrogate for full membership in Nordic bodies that has been the actual goal of the Balts.³ In this connection Estonians, both politicians and scholars, tend to dissociate themselves from their peers in Latvia and Lithuania as they regard themselves as having the strongest claim to membership in the 'Nordic club' for cultural and historical reasons (Piirimäe 2011; cf. Lagerspetz 2003).

The model for such a reframing comes from Finland. During the interwar years it was regarded together with Estonia, Latvia, and Lithuania as one of four Baltic states. Despite the attempt of Finnish politicians to distance their country from its southern neighbours and, in the second half of the 1930s, adopt a Nordic profile, Finland was still addressed as Baltic in the secret protocol to the Molotov–Ribbentrop pact. Finland's continued independence, its admission to the Nordic Council in 1955, and its de facto role as part of a 'Nordic balance' of Cold War security policy contributed to the Nordic profile Finland sought after the Second World War.

More promising than searching for a joint identity in the Baltic Sea area or among the three Baltic states is the prospect of acknowledging a plurality of identities within the larger regional perimeter, including hybrid and transmigrant identities. The same applies to an envisioned East European identity, a term so associated with backwardness that those to whom it is applied tend to reject it (Lemberg 1985; Wolff 1994). Thus, only upon accession to the European Union and NATO was the Estonian government willing to join the UN East European electoral group to which it belonged according to the current regional definition (Götz 2008: 360). Apart from Estonia and Latvia with their Northern European orientation, terms preferred by those living in large parts of the former Soviet hemisphere are 'Central Europe' and 'East Central Europe' (Kundera 1984; Szücs 1988 [1981]; Halecki 1952). These concepts are markers of distance from Eastern Europe, as well as umbrella identities in their own right. In Russia the concepts of Europe and Eurasia are also preferred over Eastern Europe (see Steiner 2010). The volatility of regional labels with far-reaching implications for understanding heritage and destiny illustrates that identity is a matter of choice, and that self-conceptions and images held by others may diverge. Evidently, any identity claim has to anticipate its assessment of plausibility.

---

³ In the 1990s, the operative formula for Nordic–Baltic cooperation was '5 + 3', meaning a collaboration of the collective of Denmark, Finland, Iceland, Norway, and Sweden on the one hand, and the group of Estonia, Latvia, and Lithuania on the other. Since 2000, the corresponding term is 'NB 8', the Nordic–Baltic 8. This terminological change suggests greater homogeneity and equality of partners. At the same time, the Balts continue to be kept at a distance, as the combination of Nordic and Baltic confirms the existing spatial division.

The geopolitical shift of 1989 was preceded by the cultural shift of 1968, a turning point symbolising the emergence of a post-materialist lifestyle with an emphasis on individual self-expression and its repertoire of autonomous contextual identities (Gassert and Klimke 2009; Inglehart 1977). Thus, the relatively coherent collective identities of the industrial age, such as the one provided by the labour movement, was displaced by more voluntaristic forms of identification and joint action (Beck 1983). Hippie-culture, 'new social movements', and environmentalism emerged, and the idea of assimilating minorities and immigrants was replaced by the vision of a multi-cultural society. For the first time, the gendered division of labour and its biased power relations was seriously called into question by the women's movement. Human rights issues came to the fore, were codified on the eastern side of the Iron Curtain through the 1975 Helsinki Final Act, and contributed to undermining the legitimacy of communist regimes among their citizens (Eckel and Moyn 2013; Saal 2014). Eastern European dissidents began to rediscover and cultivate the idea of civil society as an autonomous public sphere beyond the authority of the state (Keane 1988; Hackmann 2003).

By 1989, these identity-related developments together with processes of individualisation had been going on for two decades, undermining the bipolar world paradigm, and contributing to its ultimate demise. When the spell of the Cold War ended, it not only unleashed the issue of national and regional identities; rather, the patchwork of individual lifestyle preferences, identity choices, and 'othering' distinctions also gained significance. These processes were subject to such intersectional and socio-economic overlapping as that of gender, as well as Western versus post-communist backgrounds (Lindelöf 2010). In addition, civilisational and religious identities increasingly functioned as sources of meaning in a world that had recently been freed of its axiomatic conflict (Huntington 1996). The Baltic Sea region is today a meeting place or fracture site between the three main Christian denominations. There is potential for cooperation and conflict in the attempt to assume a joint Baltic Sea identity stemming from the mutual engagement of the Lutheran and Catholic worlds, with the exclusion of the Orthodox component (Kreslins 2003).

The belief that humanity would rise above particularistic identities in the spirit of modernity and tolerance was shown to be an illusion after the end of the Cold War. Neither had capitalism and communism converged to any considerable extent, nor did the 'homo oeconomicus' become the blueprint of human behaviour. Primordial identities were not phased out and voluntaristic identities did not become unalianable assets of the individual that were taken for granted. On the contrary, a new age of identity had begun in which traditional categories like distinctive nations, sex, and religion once again clashed with one another and with postmodern orientations including transnationalism, a variety of gender roles, and lifestyles. Collective and individual identities remained more relevant than ever for policy makers.

This book concentrates on national, labour, and gender identities. Each topic is represented by three to four chapters, and the volume concludes with a chapter on the development of environmental awareness. Identity and 'awareness' or 'consciousness' are related concepts (see Giesen 1991; Berding 1994; Bråkenhielm 2009), the former expressing conformity with an ideal type, and the latter referring to the acknowledgement of a problem. Hence, it is awareness that gives identity direction and turns it into a political force that merits attention. All contributions to this volume discuss identities correlated with different states of awareness and as factors in problem-solving processes. The period addressed is contemporary history since the 1930s, with a few excursions into earlier years and particular attention to the era since 1945. The span of years chosen shows that the Institute of Contemporary History stands for a wider approach than its own programmatic definition of the field as the era since 1945. Contemporary history is a moving target about which living historical witnesses may be consulted (for an international overview of the many attempts to delimitate contemporary history, see Metzler 2012).

While the Institute of Contemporary History was begun with a grant from the Bank of Sweden Tercentenary Foundation (*Riksbankens Jubileumsfond*) and is indebted to a number of funding institutions for its activities over the years, most contributions to this volume have resulted from projects supported by its present main sponsor, the Foundation for Baltic and East European Studies. This book is an expression of our gratitude for the generous on-going support they have given us. Unless stated otherwise, the contributions to this book and the projects mentioned in this introductory chapter are based on grants by the Foundation for Baltic and East European Studies.

The present chapter contains preliminary reflection on "Spaces of Expectation: Mental Mapping and Historical Imagination in the Baltic Sea and Mediterranean Region", a recently launched multi-disciplinary, bi-lateral project with our long-term cooperation partner Ca' Foscari University in Venice. It is scheduled to run from 2014 to 2018. The larger project analyses in six historical and political science case studies the meaning attached to the Baltic and the Mediterranean, investigates the mental maps correlated to historical representations, compares the imaginations of the two regions, and studies their involvement with each other. Our aim is an improved understanding of how historical trajectories have been attached to two maritime areas that are critical to European integration. Other researchers at Södertörn University engaged in the project are Janne Holmén, Jussi Kurunmäki, and Vasileios Petrogiannis; and Deborah Paci and Rolf Petri at Ca' Foscari University.

Chapter Two, Janne Holmén's "Fluctuating Dynastic and National Affiliation: The Impact of War and Unrest on Bornholm, Åland, and Saaremaa", shows that national identity is far from self-evident, as commonly believed. A counter-factual potential for national identification (or even independence) exists for all three Baltic islands that he examines. Holmén summarises aspects of the larger project "Islands of Identity: Identity Building on Bornholm, Gotland, Åland, Saaremaa and Hiiumaa, 1800–2000", which explored the connection between regional history writing and identity. It was conducted from 2010 to 2013 with the participation of Erik Axelsson and Samuel Edquist.

In the third chapter, entitled "The Nordic Threat: Soviet Ethnic Cleansing on the Kola Peninsula", Andrej Kotjarchuk discusses preliminary findings of his ongoing project "Soviet Nordic Minorities and Ethnic Cleansing on the Kola Peninsula". He analyses the politics of identity as a collective attribution by state agencies, including mapping the ambiguity of some early measures with emancipatory intentions and repressive potential. Drawing on genocide studies, Kotjarchuk reconstructs the process of violence from the registration of minorities through deportation and state-sanctioned killings to the politics of amnesia. Kotjarchuk's research, which will undoubtedly arouse interest beyond academic circles, began in 2013 and will run for three years.

Chapter Four, Steffen Werther's "An Unimaginable Community: The SS Idea of a 'Greater Germanic Reich' and the German Minority in Denmark", summarises some of the findings of his dissertation on the impact of Nazi ideology on the German-speakers of Southern Denmark during the Second World War (Werther 2012). It shows how national and racial policies diverged, disarraying the relation of the Reich with a German minority abroad. At the same time the article illustrates another way in which the Foundation for Baltic and East European Studies facilitates research at Södertörn University by financing the Baltic and East European Graduate School (BEEGS). The Foundation is one of the few Swedish research underwriters that continues to provide full funding for doctoral candidates, something gratefully acknowledged by all those interested in Södertörn University as an exciting site for 'young research'. This offers a window of opportunity for promising academic talent from the wider Baltic Sea region and elsewhere, and for the Swedish scientific community to become more actively engaged with perspectives from abroad.

Sofia Norling's chapter "The Ambiguity of the West: Objectives of Polish Research Policy in the 1990s" also draws on a doctoral dissertation, one that was based at the Institute of Contemporary History (see Norling 2014). It examines how science policy was remade from an instrument of societal progress under the communist regime to one recognising the autonomy of academia, and later reconfigured as a tool serving the development of the market economy and Poland's accession to the European Union. Her study was a part of Teresa Kulawik's project "Knowledge, Politics and the Public Sphere in the Baltic Sea Region".

The sixth chapter, "Lost Worlds of Labour: Paul Olberg, the Jewish Labour Bund, and Menshevik Socialism" by Håkan Blomqvist, explores the rich biography of a Swedish social democratic publicist with a background in Tsarist Latvia, revolutionary Russia, Weimar Germany, and the Jewish labour movement. This mosaic of formative experiences, identity anchors, and contemporary responses to world events from the Bolshevik revolution up to 1960 goes beyond the scope of Blomqvist's 'larger' project "Bund in Sweden 1946–1954: A Jewish Labour Movement at the Crossroads", which has been underway since 2013 and will conclude in 2015.

The seventh chapter, "From Fordism to High-Tech Capitalism: A Political Economy of the Labour Movement in the Baltic Sea Region" by Werner Schmidt, shows how working-class awareness eroded, giving way to a strategic paralysation and competitive corporatism in the 1970s. It explains the macro-economic shift behind this development – which led also to the breakdown of the Soviet system – in the light of regulation theory and a neo-Gramscian perspective. The article is the initial outcome of the third part of "The Labour Movement in the Baltic Sea Region", the longest running research endeavour at the Institute of Contemporary History. The project was started in 1997, making it older than its host institution. The third and concluding part of this project is subtitled "A New World of Crises and Insecurity (1970–2010)". Other scholars exploring this topic between 2013 and 2015 are Kjell Östberg, Lars Ekdahl, and Håkan Blomqvist.

Klaus Misgeld and Karl Molin are co-authors of the article "Solidarity and Diplomacy: Sweden and the Democratisation of Poland, 1980–1989".

They show how working class solidarity led to the engagement of Swedish civil society and officials in the Polish struggle for democracy in the 1980s. This development was at odds with the Swedish Cold War profile of acting, on the one hand, as a 'world conscience', and, on the other, of pussyfooting on issues involving nearby dictatorships. Paradoxically, this profile and the formal policy of neutrality enabled Sweden to get more actively involved than might otherwise have been the case. Thus, Misgeld and Molin's study illustrates at various levels, including those of unintended consequences, the formative power that particular identities may have for political action. The article describes the outcomes of the project "Sweden and the Polish Democratic Movement, 1980–1989" that was financed from 2007 to 2010 and also involved Paweł Jaworski and Stefan Ekecrantz, the latter being the Institute of Contemporary History's first PhD (see Ekecrantz 2003).

Chapter Nine by Eva Blomberg, Ylva Waldemarson, and Alina Žvinklienė, "Gender Equality Policies: Swedish and Lithuanian Experiences of Nordic Ideas", analyses how the linkage of human rights and gender equality has altered the normative parameters of policy making, and how international organisations such as the Nordic Council and the Nordic Council of Ministers use the 'Nordic gender equality model' for branding purposes. Moreover, the article deals with the institutionalisation of the equal opportunities ombudsman in Sweden and Lithuania. It results from the project "*Mourning Becomes Electra*: Gender Discrimination and Human Rights", which has been conducted since 2010 with grants from the Swedish Research Council (*Vetenskapsrådet*) and the Foundation for Baltic and East European Studies.[4]

Another outcome of the *Mourning Becomes Electra* project (its Swedish Research Council-branch) is Yulia Gradskova's chapter "Group-Work on Gender Equality in Transnational Cooperation: Raising Feminist Consciousness or Diminishing Social Risks?" In analysing a trilateral cooperation between Finnish, Lithuanian, and Russian organisations from 2006 to 2012 that aimed at improving gender equality education through group

---

[4] Technically speaking, these are two independent projects, both entitled "*Mourning Becomes Electra*: Gender Discrimination and Human Rights". They have a slight variation in their English second subtitle "Altered Relations among International Organs, *States*, Collectives and Individuals from a Nordic and Eastern European Perspective 1980–2009". The italicised word is not part of the subtitle of the project supported by the Swedish Research Council. Whereas the work of Eva Blomberg (in addition to that of Yulia Gradskova) has been funded by the Swedish Research Council, Ylva Waldemarson and Alina Žvinklienė have been grantees of the Foundation for Baltic and East European Studies.

work, the article provides insights into the dynamics of transnational networks. While gender equality was the common denominator of the three collaborators and the funding institution, each organisation combined its engagement with different side-issues that were at variance with the overarching goal.

Kristina Abiala's chapter "Young Moldovan Women at the Crossroads: Between Patriarchy and Transnational Labour Markets" is an interview-based sociological study of attitudes and experiences toward gender inequality, and of personal dreams about the future among school and university students. The article explores the ways in which various determinants have an effect on the negotiation of a gendered identity in a society with traditional values. It identifies openings for change, especially with regard to women's participation in higher education, and in migration as an option with repercussions on the Moldovan home country. Abiala's study is the result of a research project entitled "Global Capitalism and Everyday Resistance at the Intersection of East and West", which she conducted from 2007 to 2013 in collaboration with ethnologists Mats Lindqvist and Beatriz Lindqvist.

The book concludes with a chapter on "Waves of Laws and Institutions: The Emergence of National Awareness of Water Pollution and Protection in the Baltic Sea Region" by Simo Laakonen, a chapter the completion of which was also supported by the Helsinki University Centre for Environment (HENVI). Showing how urban-industrial water pollution has been discussed and handled in Sweden, Finland, the Soviet Union, and Poland from the late nineteenth century to the end of the Cold War, the study challenges the prevailing assumption that environmental awareness only emerged in the 1960s. The article is an outcome of "Driving Forces for Environmental Policy-Making and Capacity Building in the Baltic Sea Region", a project that began in 2011 and will continue until 2015, and also involved Åsa Casula Vifell.

The projects represented in this book are not the only ones at the Institute of Contemporary History relevant to its topic. Members of the project "The Sea of Peace in the Shadow of Threats" were preoccupied with finalising major monographs and were therefore unable to contribute to the present volume. Project members Fredrik L. Eriksson, Piotr Wawrzeniuk, and Johan Eellend have worked together from 2009 to the present, studying the security situation in the Baltic Sea region in the interwar period, particularly the self-image and threat perceptions among the Swedish, Polish, and Estonian armed forces.

The recent projects, "The Roma Genocide in Ukraine 1941–44: History, Memories and Representations" and "The Moral Economy of Global Civil Society: A History of Voluntary Food Aid", were still in their early stages and not ready to present their findings when this book was made. The Genocide Project with researchers Piotr Wawrzeniuk, Andrej Kotljarchuk, and David Gaunt studies Nazi policies towards the Roma in the Ukraine during the Second World War, and examines the memory work of the Roma, on the one hand, and official commemoration policies, on the other. The Food Aid Project is funded by the Swedish Research Council and includes Norbert Götz, Steffen Werther, Katarina Friberg, and Georgina Brewis. Werther's study on relief to the Ukraine in the famine of 1921/22 focuses on Eastern Europe, although the scope of the project as a whole is wider. The project is also interested in identities and seeks to develop the concept 'moral economy' as a tool in their analysis.

'Internationalisation' has become a buzzword in Swedish academia over the past decade. At Södertörn University and at the Institute of Contemporary History we practice an internalised form of 'internationality' on a daily basis. It arises from a genuine academic interest, a way of looking at things, and as a matter of multinational social and scholarly backgrounds. This may be seen in the topics addressed and the researchers involved in the present volume. About half of the staff of the Institute of Contemporary History have Swedish roots; the other half represents a smorgasbord of German, Finnish, Belorussian, and Polish-Ukrainian backgrounds. In addition, the institute's projects employ British, Italian, Lithuanian, Russian, and US scholars. What collaborative work on the basis of such different experiences means for the identity of the Institute may be summarised by the term 'Swedish-Baltic cosmopolitanism'.

In 2014 the Institute of Contemporary History celebrates its fifteenth anniversary. The present anthology combines the task of presenting current Baltic and East European studies conducted in Södertörn University's strong research environment with the scholarly ambition of using case studies to explore how identities and the awareness of a spectrum of problems have influenced political choices. The political history of the Baltic Sea region and Eastern Europe is congenial with the twentieth century as an 'age of extremes', making it a fruitful region in which to study identities and their impact on political solutions.

Above: The Berlin Wall at Zimmerstraße, 25 June 1984 (Bundesarchiv, Bild 210-0506 / Photographer: Philipp J. Bösel and Burkhard Maus)

Left: Police from West- and East-Berlin at the Berlin Wall, improvised border crossing point at Potsdamer Platz, 15 Nov. 1989 (Bundesarchiv, B 145 Bild-00008581 / Photographer: Klaus Lehnartz)

References

Beck, U. (1983) "Jenseits von Stand und Klasse? Soziale Ungleichheiten, gesellschaftliche Individualisierungsprozesse und die Entstehung neuer Formationen und Identitäten." *Soziale Ungleichheiten*, ed. by Kreckel, R. Göttingen: Schwartz, 35–74.

Berding, H., ed. (1994) *Nationales Bewußtsein und kollektive Identität*. Frankfurt/Main: Suhrkamp.

Berggren, H. and Trägårdh, L. (2006) *Är svensken människa? Gemenskap och oberoende i det moderna Sverige*. Stockholm: Norstedt.

Bjereld, U., Johansson, A.W., and Molin, K. (2008) *Sveriges säkerhet och världens fred: Svensk utrikespolitik under kalla kriget*. Stockholm: Santérus.

Bråkenhielm, C.R. (2009) *Linnaeus and Homo Religiosus: Biological Roots of Religious Awareness and Human Identity*. Uppsala: University.

Brüggemann, K. (2003) "Leaving the 'Baltic' States and 'Welcome to Estonia': Re-Regionalising Estonian Identity." *European Review of History* 10 (2), 343–60.

Davies, N. (2001 [1984]) *Heart of Europe: The Past in Poland's Present*. Oxford: University Press.

Eckel, J. and Moyn, S., eds (2013) *The Breakthrough: Human Rights in the 1970s*. Philadelphia: University of Pennsylvania Press.

Ekecrantz, S. (2003) *Hemlig utrikespolitik: Kalla kriget, utrikesnämnden och regeringen 1946–1959*. Stockholm: Santérus.

Engelen, H. (2006) "Die Konstruktion der Ostseeregion: Akteure, mentale Landkarten und ihr Einfluss auf die Entstehung einer Region. "*Die Ordnung des Raums: Mentale Landkarten in der Ostseeregion*, ed. by Götz, N., Hackmann, J., and Hecker-Stampehl, J. Berlin: Wissenschafts-Verlag, 60–90.

Eriksson, F., ed. (2013) *Det började i Polen: Sverige och Solidaritet 1980–1981*. Huddinge: Södertörn University.

Gassert, Ph. and Klimke, M., eds (2009) *1968: Memories and Legacies of a Global Revolt*. Washington: German Historical Institute.

Gerdin, M. and Johansson, A.W. (2005) *En högskola av en ny typ? Två seminarier kring Södertörns högskolas tillkomst och utveckling*. Huddinge: Södertörn University.

Gerdin, M. and Östberg, K. (2004) "Samtiden som kulturarv: Några anteckningar kring Samtidshistoriska Institutets tillkomst." *Samtidshistoria och politik: Vänbok till Karl Molin*, ed. by Björk, R. and Johansson, A.W. Stockholm: Hjalmarson & Högberg, 114–22.

Gerner, K. and Hedlund, S. (1993) *The Baltic States and the End of the Soviet Empire*. London: Routledge.

Giesen, B., ed. (1991) *Nationale und kulturelle Identität: Studien zur Entwicklung des kollektiven Bewußtseins in der Neuzeit*. Frankfurt/Main: Suhrkamp.

Götz, N. (2008) "Western Europeans and Others: The Making of Europe at the United Nations." *Alternatives* 33 (3), 359–81.

Götz, N. (2011) *Deliberative Diplomacy: The Nordic Approach to Global Governance and Societal Representation at the United Nations*. Dordrecht: Republic of Letters.

Götz, N. (2012) "Norbert Götz: Professor i samtidshistoria." *Akademisk högtid med doktorspromotion och professorsinstallation*. Huddinge: Södertörn University, 24–25.

Götz, N., Hecker-Stampehl, J., and Schröder, S.M. (2010) "Wahlverwandtschaft mit dem Norden oder Die Skandinavistik als politische Wissenschaft: Bernd Henningsen zum 65. Geburtstag." *Vom alten Norden zum neuen Europa: Politische Kultur im Ostseeraum*, ed. by Götz, N., Hecker-Stampehl, J., and Schröder, S.M. Berlin: Wissenschafts-Verlag, 19–33.

Hackmann, J. (2003) "Civil Society against the State? Historical Experiences of Eastern Europe." *Civil Society in the Baltic Sea Region*, ed. by Götz, N. and Hackmann, J. Aldershot: Ashgate, 49–62.

Halecki, O. (1952) *Borderlands of Western Civilization: A History of East Central Europe*. New York: Ronald.

Henningsen, B. (2008). "A Model Region: The Baltic Sea." *Baltic Worlds* 1 (1), 30–4.

Henningsen, B. (2011) *On Identity – No Identity: An Essay on the Constructions, Possibilities and Necessities for Understanding a European Macro Region: The Baltic Sea*. Copenhagen: Baltic Development Forum.

Huntington, S.P. (1996) *The Clash of Civilizations and the Remaking of World Order*. New York: Simon & Schuster.

Inglehart, R. (1977) *The Silent Revolution: Changing Values and Political Styles Among Western Publics*. Princeton: University Press.

Joenniemi, P. (1997) "Norden as a Post-Nationalist Construction." *Neo-Nationalism or Regionality: The Restructuring of Political Space Around the Baltic Rim*, ed. by Joenniemi, P. Stockholm: NordREFO, 181–234.

Keane, J., ed. (1988) *Civil Society and the State: New European Perspectives*. London: Verso, 1988.

Konnander, B. (1998) *En ny högskola på Södertörn*. Huddinge: Södertörn University.

Kundera, M. (1984) "The Tragedy of Central Europe." *New York Review of Books* 31 (7): 33–8.

Lagerspetz, M. (2003) "How Many Nordic Countries? Possibilities and Limits of Geopolitical Identity Construction." *Cooperation and Conflict* 38 (1), 49–61.

Lehti, M. and Smith, D.J., eds (2003) *Post-Cold War Identity Politics: Northern and Baltic Experiences*. London: Cass.

Lemberg, H. (1985) "Zur Entstehung des Osteuropabegriffes im 19. Jahrhundert: Vom 'Norden' zum 'Osten' Europas." *Jahrbücher für die Geschichte Osteuropas* 33 (1), 48–91.

Lieven, A. (1993) *The Baltic Revolution: Estonia, Latvia, Lithuania and the Path to Independence*. New Haven: Yale University Press.

Lindelöf, K.S. (2010) "Not Yet Equal: Reflections on East/West and Female/Male in a Polish Context." *Baltic Worlds* 3 (4), 22–7.

Lundén, Th. and Nilsson, T., eds (2008) *Sverige och Baltikums frigörelse: Två vittnesseminarier om storpolitik kring Östersjön 1989–1994*. Huddinge: Södertörn University.

Metzler, G. (2012) "Zeitgeschichte – Begriff – Disziplin – Problem." *Zeitgeschichte: Konzepte und Methoden*, ed. by Bösch, F. and Danyel, J. Göttingen: Vandenhoeck & Ruprecht, 22–46.

Miniotaite, G. (2003) "Convergent Geography and Divergent Identities: A Decade of Transformation in the Baltic States." *Cambridge Review of International Affairs* 16 (2), 209–22.

Neumann, I.B. (1994) "A Region-Building Approach to Northern Europe." *Review of International Studies* 20 (1), 53–74.

Nilsson, T. and Lundén, Th., eds (2010) *1989 med svenska ögon: Vittnesseminarium 22 oktober 2009*. Huddinge: Södertörn University.

Norling, S. (2014) *Mot väst: Om vetenskap, politik och transformation i Polen*. Huddinge: Södertörn University.

O'Brien, C.C. and Topolski, F. (1968) *The United Nations: Sacred Drama*. London: Hutchinson.

Olesen, J.E. (2012) "History of the Baltic Sea Region." *Baltic Rim Economies* 9 (2), 39.

Paulauskas, K. (2005) "The Baltic States: Picking Regions, Shedding Myths, Decoding Acronyms." *Lithuanian Foreign Policy Review* (No. 1–2), 51–64.

Piirimäe, P. (2011) "The Idea of 'Yule Land'." *Baltic Worlds* 4 (4), 36–9.

Rebas, H. (1990) "'Baltic Regionalism'?" *Regional Identity under Soviet Rule: The Case of the Baltic States*, ed. by Loeber, D.A., Kitching, L.P., and Vardys, S.V. Hackettstown, NJ: AABS, 413–28.

Reuter, M. (2004) "Fear of the Other and the Emergence of Regional Identity in the Baltic Sea Area." *Perceptions of Loss, Decline and Doom in the Baltic Sea Region*, ed. by Hecker-Stampehl, J., Bannwart, A., Brekenfeld, D., and Plath, U. Berlin: Wissenschafts-Verlag, 343–53.

Rostow, W.W. (1960) *The Stages of Economic Growth: A Non-Communist Manifesto*. Cambridge: University Press.

Saal, Y. v. (2014) *KSZE-Prozess und Perestroika in der Sowjetunion: Demokratisierung, Werteumbruch und Auflösung 1985-1991*. Munich: Oldenbourg.

Škapars, J., ed. (2005) *The Baltic Way to Freedom: Non-violent Struggle of the Baltic States in a Global Context*. Riga: Zelta grauds.

State of the Region Report™ (2013) *State of the Region Report™ 2013: The Top of Europe – Plowing Ahead in the Shadows of a Fractured Global Economy*. Copenhagen: Baltic Development Forum. Available from http://www.bsr2013.eu/wp-content/uploads/BDF_SotRR_2013_web.pdf [16 Feb. 2014].

Steiner, H. (2010) "'Russia in Europe': A Historical and Topical Debate." *New Europe: Growth to Limits?*, ed. by Eliaeson, S. and Georgieva, N. Oxford: Bardwell, 81–9.

Stenius, H. (2013) "A Nordic Conceptual Universe." *Multi-Layered Historicity of the Present: Approaches to Social Science History*, ed. by Haggrén, H., Rainio-Niemi, J., and Vauhkonen, J. Helsinki: University, 93–104.

Stråth, B. (2000) "The Baltic as Image and Illusion: The Construction of a Region between Europe and the Nation." *Myth and Memory in the Construction of Community: Historical Patterns in Europe and Beyond*, ed. by Stråth, B. Brussels: Lang, 199–214.

Szücs, J. (1988 [1981]) "Three Historical Regions of Europe." *Civil Society and the State: New European Perspectives*, ed. by Keane, J. London: Verso, 291–332.

Thompson, E.P. (1991) "The Moral Economy Reviewed." *Customs in Common*. London: Merlin, 259–351.

Trägårdh, L. (1997) "Statist Individualism: On the Culturality of the Nordic Welfare State." *The Cultural Construction of Norden*, ed. by Sørensen, Ø. and Stråth, B. Oslo: Scandinavian University Press, 253–85.

Vesilind, P., Tusty, J., and Tusty, M. (2008) *The Singing Revolution: How Culture Saved a Nation*. Tallinn: Varrak.

Wæver, O. (1991) "Culture and Identity in the Baltic Sea Region." *Co-operation in the Baltic Sea Region: Needs and Prospects*, ed. by Joenniemi, P. Tampere: TAPRI, 79–111.

Wæver, O. (1992) "From Nordism to Baltism." *The Baltic Sea Area: A Region in the Making*, ed. by Jervell, S., Kukk, M., and Joenniemi, P. Oslo: Europa-programmet, 26–38.

Werther, S. (2012) *SS-Vision und Grenzland-Realität: Vom Umgang dänischer und 'volksdeutscher' Nationalsozialisten in Sønderjylland mit der 'großgermanischen' Ideologie der SS*. Stockholm: ACTA.

Williams, L.-K. (2007) *Zur Konstruktion einer Region: Die Entstehung der Ostseekooperation zwischen 1988 und 1992*. Berlin: Wissenschafts-Verlag.

Winkler, H.A. (2000) *Der lange Weg nach Westen, vol. 2: Deutsche Geschichte vom 'Dritten Reich' bis zur Wiedervereinigung*. Munich: Beck.

Wolff, L. (1994) *Inventing Eastern Europe: The Map of Civilization on the Mind of the Enlightenment*. Stanford: University Press.

Wulff, R. and Kerner, M. (1994) *Die Neue Hanse*. Berlin: Freie Universität.

Part 1: National Identities

2. Fluctuating Dynastic and National Affiliation: The Impact of War and Unrest on Bornholm, Åland, and Saaremaa

Janne Holmén

Experiences of war and foreign occupation have often been used to strengthen national identity, both during the actual conflict and in later history writing. This chapter illustrates how the geographic location and insularity of three islands in the Baltic Sea – Bornholm, Åland, and Saaremaa – have caused the islanders to experience the conflicts of the nineteenth and twentieth century differently from the populations in the main parts of the states to which they today belong: Denmark, Finland, and Estonia. The islanders' isolation and their particular experience of history have contributed to making the construction of national identity and its relationship to regional identity problematic. Because of specific geographic, historical, and political preconditions, this issue has been handled differently on each island. However, in all cases, the construction of identity has been characterised by an underlying quest for security.

Scholars have argued that islands are ideal geographic locations for the formation of a common identity among their inhabitants. Geographers, anthropologists, and social scientists have maintained that island populations share a feeling of belonging and affinity that is a consequence of 'islandness', the specific characteristics of islands – isolation and boundedness (e.g. White 1995: 4; Olausson 2007: 29; Hay 2006: 22; Royle 2001: 11; Baldacchino 2004: 272f). Islandness is often used as an alternative to the negatively connoted term 'insularity'.

However, the sea does not only function as a natural delimiter, it is also a means of communication and transport. Today it is a common assumption that "connectedness describes the island condition better than isolation" (Hay 2006: 4f). Their small hinterlands forces islands to trade in order to gain access to vital goods; the smaller the islands are, the more dependent they tend to be upon trade. The extent to which an island is isolated or connected is not exclusively a consequence of geographical factors. Political and historical circumstances influence the balance between the separating and the connective properties of the surrounding sea. Border changes, custom regulations, and developments in shipping affect the islanders' possibility and propensity to interconnect with the surrounding world.

War is perhaps the factor that has the greatest potential to disrupt and alter existing patterns of trade and communication. During periods of war and unrest islands have often become more secluded from the mainland – due, for example, to piracy and privateering, travel restrictions, or minefields. The geographical situation makes the islanders' experience of war different from that of the mainlanders. Fortifications, foreign occupations, and a great influx or outflow of refugees have affected islands in particular ways. These experiences have played a vital role in the formation of regional identities on the islands.

It has been claimed that small island states are exceptionally vulnerable to unconventional security threats; there are several examples of islands that have been captured by a few dozen mercenary soldiers (Bartmann 2007: 300). However, small military forces on islands are equally vulnerable to popular uprisings, and such uprisings have, in turn, affected the formation of regional identities.

This chapter investigates how war and unrest have contributed to the formation of regional identities and how they have affected the relationship between regional and national identity in the three Baltic island regions of Bornholm, Åland, and Saaremaa. Referring to the islands as regions emphasises that they constitute – or have until recently constituted – provinces or counties, units of administration directly under the state. The method of research used is an investigation of regional history writing from the three islands, that is, of publications either written by an inhabitant or former inhabitant of the island, or published with the help of an institution on the island. Regarding content, regional history writing is understood as publications that cover the history of the entire island region, rather than only single municipalities or secondary islands. This selection of sources provides a picture of how leading groups and individuals on the islands perceive their history and use it to construct a regional identity.

Bornholm

Bornholm is part of Denmark, and with a few interruptions has been so ever since the late tenth century, although this contention has been highly contested. In the Middle Ages, Bornholm was the scene of a power struggle between the Danish kings and the archbishops of Lund in Scania. From 1525 until 1575 the island was leased to Lübeck, and in 1658 it was ceded to Sweden. An uprising in December that year brought the island back under the control of the Danish king. Scania and the rest of eastern Denmark, however, were permanently lost to Sweden, which meant that Bornholm became situated far (135 km) from Denmark, while Sweden was only 35 km away. From 1940 to 1945, the island, like the rest of Denmark, was under German occupation. In contrast to the rest of the country, Bornholm also experienced a year of Soviet occupation from May 1945 until April 1946. In 2012 the total population of the island was 41,000, and it is steadily shrinking (Statistics Denmark). Bornholm was a Danish county (*amt*) until 1 January 2007, when it became part of *Region Hovedstaden*, which comprises Copenhagen and parts of Sjælland.

Regional history writing on Bornholm portrays the islanders as a breed of devout Danes, who have repeatedly been let down by the Danish crown in times of crisis. In 1525 Frederick I leased the island for 50 years to Lübeck, which in return promised to leave Gotland that it had invaded in an attempt to remove Christian II from the Danish throne. In the opinion of the Bornholmian physician and amateur historian Marius Kofoed Zahrtmann, who published an extensive history of the island in 1934–35, this meant that Fredrik I traded Danish Bornholm for Swedish Gotland, thus selling the islanders to their worst enemy. During the peace negotiations in Brömsebro, 1645 Christian IV was faced with a similar dilemma. The Danish Council was in favour of ceding Bornholm to Sweden, and Carl Gustaf Wrangel of Sweden invaded the island in order to increase the pressure. However, the Danish king preferred to cede some Norwegian counties and the two "un-Danish" islands of Gotland and Saaremaa rather than Bornholm, according to Zahrtmann (1934: 111–14, 237–9, 251). His eagerness to differentiate between Bornholm and un-Danish areas within the Danish realm was fuelled by his conviction that for long Bornholm had mistakenly not been considered part of Denmark proper.

In the treaty of Roskilde in 1658, Denmark ceded Bornholm to Sweden. The peace did not last long as the Swedish king Charles X Gustav attacked Denmark again later that year. The Bornholmians remained loyal to their new masters until the Danish king encouraged them to attempt an uprising. A conspiracy to kidnap the Swedish governor, Johan Printzenskiöld, failed as Pritzenskiöld was shot in the head while trying to escape. This forced the conspirators to launch a full rebellion, and 9 December 1658 the Swedish garrison of 60 soldiers at the medieval castle Hammershus capitulated (Rasmussen 2000: 97, 102f, 116, 121).

When the Bornholmians were in control of their island they sent a delegation to Copenhagen to formally return it to the Danish king. This is one of the most central points of regional Bornholmian history writing: the islanders were Danes by their own choice and efforts, and they were therefore the most Danish of all Danes (e.g. Jørgensen 1900: 255; Zahrtmann 1934: 298; Rasmussen 2000: 125; Bøggild 2004: 140). Since the Danish king promised the Bornholmians never to hand over their island to Sweden and promised the Swedes never to give it to any foreign power, Zahrtmann (1934: 299f) concluded that the uprising in 1658 forever tied Bornholm to Denmark. The confidence in Denmark's willingness and ability to defend Bornholm that Zahrtmann displayed in 1934, however, was soon to be shaken.

The most important difference between the Bornholmian authors who wrote before the Second World War and the ones active after it is that the latter group continuously repeat that Denmark abandoned Bornholm, a tendency which has been exacerbated in the last decades. Both the journalist Hansaage Bøggild and the teacher Ebbe Gert Rasmussen, who had written a doctoral dissertation on the uprising, lamented that Denmark at the turn of the millennium withdrew all military from Bornholm, which they describe as the most Danish and defence-friendly part of Denmark. To Rasmussen, 1658 was not the year when Bornholm was forever tied to Denmark. Instead he stressed that the generation of 1658 knew Bornholm could manage itself, and acted accordingly. In his book about the 1658 uprising, Rasmussen also mentions the Russian bombings in 1945 as an example of how Denmark again turned its back to the island (Bøggild 2004: 42f; Rasmussen 2000: 159–61). The bombings seem to have meant the end to the enthusiastic patriotism and faith in 300-year old royal promises expressed by Zahrtmann and his contemporaries.

Bornholmian history writing has for centuries elaborated upon the privileges which the Danish king Christian IV granted as reward for the successful uprising. Only in the late 1900s did Ebbe Gert Rasmussen (1982: 274) complement this picture with the notion that the king also used the opportunity to establish autocracy on the island two years earlier than in the rest of Denmark. According to Rasmussen, the Bornholmians did not understand the implication of the fact that they had given Bornholm to the king as a personal, hereditary gift.

Another problem with the privileges was that Christian IV did not specify their exact nature, or whether they should apply to all islanders or only to active participants in the uprising. This led to centuries of disputes between the monarchy and the islanders until the last remnants of the privileges disappeared in 1867. In 1770, the Bornholmians' refusal to pay taxes almost prompted the Council in Copenhagen to send armed forces against the islanders (Zahrtmann 1935: 180f).

The most important privileges were the reductions on certain taxes and the right of Bornholmians to do military service on their home island. The latter meant that the islanders became members of the Bornholmian militia, which was supposed to defend the island and could not be forced to fight elsewhere. As a consequence, the Schleswig Wars in 1848–51 and in 1864, which were major events in Danish history and became important constituents of Danish national consciousness, involved Bornholm only tangentially. Nationalist Bornholmian history writers highlighted, however, the Bornholmian volunteers, primarily the war hero Johan Ancher, and used their actions as proof that the Bornholmians supported the Danish war effort (Jørgensen 1901: 282–4; Zahrtmann 1935: 238; Klindt-Jensen 1957: 315).

After the Bornholmian militia was dissolved in 1867, the islanders received military instruction in central Denmark. Bornholmian history writers who witnessed this change were quite positive towards its effects; Zahrtmann believed it brought the island closer to the motherland, while the teacher and amateur archaeologist J.A. Jørgensen (1901: 306) claimed it allowed the islanders to widen their horizons. He was of the opinion that the militia's officers understood the need for military training, and that the end of absolute monarchy brought enlightenment, something that made the Bornholmians willing to accept the change rather than referring to Bornholm's privileges, as had always been the case in the past. According to Zahrtmann (1935: 238f) a more Danish and less Bornholmian generation grew up on the island after 1867. Between the Schleswig Wars and the Second World War Bornholmian history writing was more permeated by Danish nationalism than at any other time. During this period it was evidently believed that greater integration with Denmark could alleviate the negative effects of the isolation from which the island had suffered.

A consequence of the Bornholmian uprising in 1658 was that it had increased the island's isolation and made it a distant outpost of the Danish realm. The island is situated close to Scania, which together with Blekinge and Halland had formed Eastern Denmark from the early middle Ages. It was to these areas the island had its strongest economic and cultural ties. But while these areas were permanently conquered by Sweden in the wars of the mid-1600s, the Bornholmian rebellion against Swedish power made the island a last remnant of Eastern Denmark, detached from the rest of the Danish kingdom.

This isolation contributed to the fact that the Second World War in many respects became a different experience for the islanders than for most Danes. The Germans on Bornholm were not under the same command as the troops in Denmark, and Bornholm was not included when the German forces in Denmark capitulated on 4 May 1945. The island's strategic location was vital in the German attempts to rescue their refugees from the eastern front, and therefore leading officers on the islands were instructed to keep up resistance against Soviet troops for as long as possible. This led to the Soviet bombings of Bornholm on 8 and 9 May 1945, after which almost a year of Soviet occupation followed. Research in Soviet archives after the end of the Cold War has revealed that the occupation was motivated by political considerations and the strategic location of the island (Jensen 2000).

The fact that Bornholm was bombed while the rest of Denmark celebrated the end of the war – and particularly the fact that the local resistance movement was unable to get the ministers in Copenhagen to answer the telephone while bombs were falling over Rønne and Nexø – led to strong feelings of abandonment on the island. Considering that regional history writing, in general, stresses the island's Danish patriotism, the depictions of the 1945 bombings illustrate how rapidly dramatic events of war might affect expressions of affinity and identity. Several history writers state that the islanders were so disappointed with the Danish government's inability to help during the Soviet bombings and occupation of the island that they were contemplating joining Sweden. This brief shift of sentiment was influenced by the fear that Bornholm would become permanently occupied by the Soviet Union (Kure 1981: 17; Barfod 1976: 327).

The memory of the uprising in 1658 was used by both the underground resistance and the regional authorities during the Second World War. The illegal newspaper, *Pro Patria*, first published in January 1944, featured a seventeenth century freedom fighter on its front page. In March 1945, Bornholm's *amtmand* (governor), Paul Christian Stemann, admonished the German commander Gerhard von Kamptz to handle the local population gently, as the islanders had once shot a Swedish commander (Barfod 1976: 237).

Still today, regional history writers describe Bornholmians as the most Danish of all Danes, but nonetheless easily forgotten by Denmark due to their geographic location. They use the traditional model to interpret what they perceive as new errors of neglect by Copenhagen, and continue to maintain that Denmark neither understands nor cares about the needs of Bornholm. One example cited is transportation, an area claimed to be handled without understanding by the Danish authorities (Bøggild 2004: 16f, 41f; Rasmussen 2000: 159).

Åland

Åland is an autonomous province (*landskap*) in Finland. The main island is situated 70 km from the Finnish mainland, and 36 km from the Swedish. However, the main island of Åland is connected to mainland Finland by an archipelago with the highest density of islands found anywhere in the world (Depraetre and Dahl 2007: 71). The Åland islands are composed of nearly 7000 islands larger than 0.25 ha, 60 of which are populated. If even the smaller islets and skerries are counted, Åland has around 27,000 islands, with a total land area of 1552 square kilometres. Åland had 28,500 inhabitants 31 December 2012. Åland and Finland were integrated parts of Sweden until 1809, when they came under Russian sovereignty. In 1921, Åland became an autonomous province of the now independent Finland, and this autonomy has since been extended on several occasions. The official language on Åland is Swedish, the mother tongue of 90 per cent of Åland's population, but spoken by only 5 per cent of mainland Finns (ÅSUB 2012).

The past two centuries of Åland's history have been dominated by international conflicts brought on by the island's strategic location. However, in the seventeenth century, Åland was located at the centre of the Swedish realm, was not subject to hostilities, and did not occupy a particularly important strategic position. The efforts of Czar Peter I to transform Russia into a maritime power made Åland accessible to Russian galleys, which advanced through the archipelago. The majority of Åland's population fled to mainland Sweden between 1714 and 1718, when the island was occupied by Russian troops. During the war between Sweden and Russia in 1742–43, the pattern was repeated, but the number of inhabitants that fled was smaller.

In the winter of 1808, Åland was again occupied by Russian troops. This time it was not Russian galleys that conquered the island, but army units who crossed the ice between Finland and Åland. In spring, the ice generally melts earlier over the open waters between Sweden and Åland than in the archipelago between Åland and Finland. In the days before motorised shipping there was a period in spring when Åland could be reached by boat from Sweden while melting ice still obstructed travel to Finland. When the Russian troops realised this in April 1808, they feared that they might be attacked by the Swedish navy without hope of escape or assistance. They ordered the population to hand over their boats and clear the ice in the harbours within 24 hours – or their ears would be cut off and they would be sent so Siberia. According to Bomansson, an Ålander who later wrote Finland's first doctoral dissertation in archaeology and would become the first head of the Finnish national archives, the islanders took the threats literally, although the Russians had probably intended them only as a scare tactic. The fact that the Russians ordered the islanders to gather in the harbours made it easy to organise an uprising (Bomansson 1852: 44–9). Many Russians were caught by a surprise attack. The rest were defeated in one battle on the main island of Åland and one in the Archipelago, with small Swedish naval ships aiding the insurgents in the latter battle.

In the twentieth century the 1808 uprising was claimed to be a manifestation of the Ålanders' Swedish patriotism. However, during recent decades, local identity on autonomous Åland has developed in the direction of a national identity, which has been paralleled by a more Ålandic and less Swedish interpretation. The 1808 uprising is now seen as an example of the islanders' preparedness to take their destiny in their own hands (Hakala 2006; Holmén 2009b: 34).

During the Crimean War, French and British troops destroyed the Russian fortress in Bomarsund on Åland, and the islands became demilitarised. This was the first time the Åland islands achieved any form of exceptional status. The demilitarisation was confirmed in later peace treaties in the twentieth century and was complemented by a declaration of neutrality. As a consequence of Åland's law of autonomy, military service is not mandatory for the islanders. Since military service has been an important vehicle for promoting nationalism, this exception has probably made it more difficult for Finnish nationalism to gain a foothold on Åland. In the twentieth century, especially in the late 1930s when there were plans to fortify Åland, regional political leaders used anti-militaristic rhetoric. Their major fear, however, was that an influx of Finnish military personnel would threaten the islands' monolingual Swedish status, which was the *raison d'être* for Åland's autonomy (e.g. Eriksson and Virgin 1961: 83). However, since the 1980s, demilitarisation has become more ideologically and symbolically significant on Åland (e.g. Eriksson, Johansson and Sundback 2006: 108 f).

According to the Swedish historian, Martin Hårdstedt, who was assigned to author part of the volume about the nineteenth century in the series, *Det åländska folkets historia* (History of the Ålandic People), the island's strategic location was a curse, and he claimed that disputes about what state Åland should belong to have been a characteristic trait of Åland's history in the past 200 years. From having been located at the centre of the Swedish kingdom, in 1809 the islands became the western outpost of the Russian empire. On the Finnish mainland, the separation from Sweden caused debates about language, but these debates did not initially greatly affect Åland where the transition manifested itself mainly with regard to the housing of Russian troops and the construction of the fortress of Bomarsund (Kuvaja, Hårdstedt, and Hakala 2006: 140–2, 207). The large military presence was heavily taxing on the local population, and according to Martin Isaksson, an Ålandic politician and amateur historian, this was the reason why demilitarisation after the Crimean War was perceived as such a relief. Isaksson (1981: 213) is of the opinion that it is impossible to understand *åländskhet* (Ålandicness) without taking this into consideration.

The most important war for the formation of Ålandic identity was arguably the First World War, which led to the revolutions that ended the Russian empire. On 6 December 1918 Finland declared independence from Russia. However, Åland had been isolated from the developments on the mainland during the war, and even earlier that autumn, leading Ålanders had initiated a process to reunite the islands with Sweden. It is believed that it was not until the winter of 1918 that the majority of Åland's population came to support the thought of reunification with Sweden (Högman 1986: 126–8). An important factor behind this shift of loyalty was that the regional newspaper *Åland* had switched from espousing Finnish nationalism, and now took a pro-Swedish stance. A dispute over Åland between Sweden and Finland followed, with each side claiming that the islands had historically been considered part of its country. However, since what is now independent Finland had been a fully integrated part of Sweden until 1809, the question was anachronistic, a fact pointed out already by contemporary historians such as Harald Hjärne (Nordman 1986: 154f).

To appease the Ålanders, Finland offered the island autonomy, something the population initially refused to accept. However, in 1921, the League of Nations granted Finland sovereignty over Åland, on condition that the language and culture of the inhabitants would be protected. The islands were thus granted autonomy in line with the earlier Finnish proposal.

The few Ålanders who had written history before the First World War, such as Bomansson and Reinhold Hausen, had done so from a Finnish nationalist point of view. Some members of the provincial government that was formed on Åland realised the importance of history writing in shaping the identity of the islanders. As a consequence of this, in the early 1930s, the regional authorities hired an archaeologist, Matts Dreijer, who came to have a profound influence on Ålandic history writing in the twentieth century. Initially, he portrayed Åland as a province closely tied to Sweden, in line with the arguments put forward by Swedish historians in the struggle for Åland in 1918–21. After the Second World War, when hopes of reunification with Sweden finally disappeared and local politicians started to focus on developing Ålandic autonomy, Dreijer began to accord Åland in the Viking and Middle Ages a more significant and independent role. He downplayed Åland's ties to ancient Sweden, and suggested that Åland had been a base for Danish crusades to Finland in the twelfth century. His theories were fully developed in the first volume of *Det åländska folkets historia* (Dreijer 1979). In recent decades regional history writers have distanced themselves from Dreijers' attempts to construct an ancient foundation for Åland's present autonomy, as they maintain his grandiose interpretation of scarce historical and archaeological sources has damaged the reputation of Ålandic history writing. (Holmén 2009a: 313f, 319f). The latest volume of *Det åländska folkets historia*, the multi volume work that was initiated by Dreijer, is also critical of his perspective (Kuvaja, Hårdstedt, and Hakala 2006).

During the period of the peace movement in the 1980s, some writers saw Åland's demilitarisation and neutrality as something more than just a means of protecting the island's autonomy and monolingual status. For example, Salminen (1979: 181) claimed that pacifism had become second nature to the Ålanders, while Eriksson, Johansson, and Sundback (2006: 78) considered the settlement of Åland's status by the League of Nations an example of successful conflict resolution that should be exported to other disputed zones. The Åland Island Peace Institute, the publisher behind Eriksson, Johansson, and Sundback's book, indeed tries to export "the Åland example", for example by hosting visitors who want to study Åland's autonomy, demilitarisation, and neutralisation. This line of thought is connected to a relatively positive view of Åland's relationship to Finland.

Such interpretations implied a break with then dominant hegemonic perception, which still prevails, that Åland's gains were the result of a hard, continuous struggle against the reluctant, and sometimes hostile, parliament in Helsinki. In the late 1990s, politicians who held a negative view of Finnish attitudes towards Åland founded a party that favours complete independence. This party, *Ålands framtid* (Future of Åland), however, has failed to garner more than 11 per cent of votes in regional elections, and all other parties are in support of continued autonomy as part of Finland.

Saaremaa

Saaremaa is an Estonian county (*maakond*) with a surface area of 2922 square kilometres and a population of 34,527, down from around 40,000 in the early 1990s. The county constitutes 6.5 per cent of Estonia's land area and is home to 2.6 per cent of the population of that country. This makes it the island in this study with the largest area relative to the total area of the state to which it belongs. Prior to the Second World War, 60,000 persons, representing 5 per cent of the country's total population, lived on Saaremaa. In addition to main Saaremaa and adjacent small islands, the county consists of the sizeable island of Muhu and more distant Ruhnu in the Bay of Riga. Kuressaare is situated on the southern coast of Saaremaa and has had good connections to Riga, which was the centre of Livonia. The distance from the southern tip of Sõrve peninsula on Saaremaa to Latvia is less than 30 km. Today 98 per cent speak Estonian on Saaremaa, but German was common until the Second World War. It was the language of the landed aristocracy and of the merchants in Arensburg (modern day Kuressaare). Ruhnu had a Swedish speaking population that deserted the island for Sweden during the Second World War.[1]

Saaremaa was invaded by German crusaders in 1227, and the island, like Hiiumaa, was divided between the Brothers of the Sword (known as the Livonian Order after 1237) and the bishopric of Oesel-Wiek, which also comprised present day Läänemaa on the mainland. In 1559, Saaremaa became tied to Denmark, which handed the island over to Sweden in 1645. In 1710, Russian troops gained control over the island, and it remained part of the Russian Empire until the end of the First World War, when Estonia gained independence.

---

[1] The population statistics for Saaremaa and Hiiumaa have been determined by searches of the of Statistics Estonia database (http://pub.stat.ee) for 2012.

While successful rebellions play an important role in Bornholm's and Åland's regional history writing, the historians of Saaremaa tell a tale of uprisings that have been bloodily put down. Due to its geographic location, Saaremaa was the last Estonian province to be conquered by German crusaders. In the Middle Ages there were several uprisings, such as the Great Uprising in 1343, which left the island in the hands of the rebels for almost a year. History on Saaremaa in the nineteenth century was written by Baltic Germans like Pastor Martin Körber who saw these rebellions as something indicative of the freedom-loving islanders, whom he considered superior to the Estonians and Livonians on the mainland (Körber 1885: 54). However, twentieth century professional Estonian historians, such as Enn Tarvel (2007: 96–8), instead stressed the island's links to mainland Estonia. For example, they considered the Great Uprising on Saaremaa as part of a larger uprising on the Estonian mainland.

In the sixteenth century, the Estonian and Livonian mainland was ravaged by wars that involved Polish-Lithuanian and Russian troops. During the battles between these land-based powers, Saaremaa functioned as a refuge at sea, and the influx of refugees fuelled the development of a town around Arensburg castle.

Saaremaa then underwent periods of Danish, Swedish, and Russian rule. As a consequence of developments on the Eastern Front during the First World War, the island was invaded by German forces in October 1917. According to Kersti Lust's article in the post-Soviet anthology, *Saaremaa 2*, the Germans restricted personal liberty and stressed the importance of the German language in schools. The pupils were educated to revere the ruling German class and the German army. The Baltic German nobility on Saaremaa wanted to tie the island to Germany as soon as possible, and after the Treaty of Brest-Litovsk the Livonian nobility tried to join Germany as an independent duchy. This caused the animosity on Saaremaa against the Germans, which was further increased by the quartering of troops, in particular as the harvest of 1918 had failed (Lust 2007: 239–40). The combination of these factors caused an explosive situation on the island.

The new Estonian government tried to conscript troops to fight the Red Army, whose advance westwards was perceived as a serious threat against the young country's independence. In February 1919, a rebellion broke out on Muhu among men from Saaremaa drafted for military service. They marched towards Saaremaa's main city, Kuressaare, recruiting followers primarily from Muhu and eastern Saaremaa. However, since it was February and the straits were frozen, the government in Tallinn managed to send troops over the ice. They massacred the rebels to ease their entry into Kuressaare.

Before the First World War, all regional history writing on Saaremaa had been penned in German by members of the Baltic German elite. The most prominent Baltic German history writers were Johan Wilhelm Ludvig von Luce, Peter Wilhelm von Buxhöwden, Jean Baptiste Holzmeyer, and Martin Körber. After Estonia's first independence, the regional authorities became dominated by ethnic Estonians, but it took some time before this resulted in Estonian-minded regional history writing on Saaremaa. The only major work from the inter-war period was the volume about Saaremaa in the monumental series *Eesti*, which covered entire Estonia. There the uprising was mentioned very briefly (Luha, Blumfeldt, and Tammekann 1934: 348–9), probably because this conflict between Estonians was difficult to harmonise with the nation-building intentions of the work. In 1940 Estonia was annexed by the Soviet Union, which lost it to Germany in 1941 but regained it in 1944. In the 1950s, a new strand of regional history writing started to emerge, in which the 1919 uprising was used to illustrate the revolutionary spirit of the islanders. In exile, Baltic Germans and nationalist Estonians gave different versions of the event. Thus, there exist three fundamentally different interpretations of the uprising: the Communist perspective, the most prolific proponent of which was Vassili Riis, the Baltic German perspective of Baron Oscar von Buxhoeveden, and the national Estonian perspective adopted by writers in exile during the Soviet era and at home during Estonia's periods of independence. Riis and von Buxhoeveden lived on Saaremaa as children at the time of the uprising. Riis's father was among the insurgents and two members of the Buxhoeveden family were among the first to be killed by the rebels. Riis was a leading figure in the local secret police (NKVD) during the Soviet occupation of 1940–41, and was responsible for the mass executions committed towards the end of this period, while von Buxhoeveden lived most of his life in Germany (G. Buxhoeveden 2009; *Postimees*; *Saaremaa ülestoust* 1919: 210).

Riis was of the opinion that the uprising was directed against German landlords and capitalists, and that bourgeois Estonia was the successor of the Germans. According to von Buxhoeveden, this version of history was a deliberate falsification intended to place blame on the Baltic Germans. He saw the uprising as a premeditated Communist attempt to create a Soviet republic, and believed it was enabled by the lack of communication between the Baltic Germans and the Estonian authorities, as well as by problems caused by the rapidity with which new Estonian institutions replaced the old institutions of the nobility. According to the Saaremaa Defence League's (*Kaitseliit*) history writing, the rebellion broke out when a drunken crowd from the most unstable parts of the island came under the influence of agitators. In his article in the post-Soviet anthology, *Saaremaa 2*,[2] Jüri Ant argued that sailors and soldiers who had returned from the war were unwilling to be mobilised again; they had seen great empires collapse and had difficulties believing in the feasibility of Estonian statehood (Buxhoeveden 1969: 91f, 94, 102; Riis 1960: 43, 54, 121, 138–40, 184, 308; *Kaitseliidu* 1998: 11–13, Ant 2007: 268–9).

The latest and most detailed study of the uprising, Piret Hiie's *1919: Aasta mäss Muhu- ja Saaremaal*, based on her Masters' thesis, claims that the lack of land reform on Saaremaa was a major reason for the rebellion. Hiie (2010: 49, 112–14), however, also believes that the economic problems following the German occupation, and the weakness of the regional government contributed to the uprising, as did Bolshevik agitation and the island's isolation from the mainland, which resulted in a lack of accurate information.

The uprising of 1919 has been a highly divisive issue. Buxhoeveden and Riis were writing from the respective viewpoints of the Baltic Germans and the rebels. The Defence League's account from 1998 was closely tied to another one of the parties in the conflict, the Estonian government. In the book, *Saaremaa 2*, published in 2007, and in Hiie's work in 2010, the parties were no longer portrayed as heroes or villains. Instead, the whole course of events is described as a terrible accident brought on by extreme circumstances. This is similar to how the event is portrayed by Blumfeldt (Luha, Blumfeldt, and Tammekann 1934: 348–9) and by the ethnologist Gustav Ränk (1979: 223–37). This strand of moderate national history writing, however, is also supportive of the Estonian government's version. The supposition that the islanders rebelled due to having received incorrect information implies that had they only been correctly informed they would have acted as good patriots. National identity is thus still seen as a natural, rather than a constructed, phenomenon.

In 1939 the Estonian government was forced to permit Soviet military bases in Estonia, including on Saaremaa. When Germany attacked the Soviet Union in 1941 and approached Estonia, the Soviet authorities started mass executions of political prisoners. These killings continued longer on

---

[2] Like *Saaremaa* from 1934, the two post-Soviet volumes, *Saaremaa 1* and *Saaremaa 2* were written and published through a combination of regional and national efforts.

Saaremaa than on the mainland, since it took time for the Germans to conquer the island, in part because their naval ships were too large to navigate the surrounding shallow waters. Among the units that eventually liberated the island was a Finnish motor boat expedition. In 1941, Finland reconquered territory it had lost in the Winter War 1939–40 and occupied additional land in Karelia. Circles among the extreme right in Finland had for decades nurtured ideas of a 'Greater Finland' that would include territories outside the country's borders. Some of these plans also included Estonia. The advance of Finnish troops in 1941 made the idea of a Greater Finland seem more realistic.

This idea was not without support on Saaremaa. A secret society named *Suur-Soome Riik* had been organised already in the spring of 1941 (*Saaremaa 1940–1941* 1996: 5). The German police estimated that one to two per cent of the island's population supported a Communist society, while three to five per cent was in favour of a union with Greater Germany. However, 80 per cent of the islanders were estimated to support joining Greater Finland (Meripuu 2007: 324–5).

The idea had surfaced earlier under similar political circumstances. Gustav Ränk (1979: 216) recalled in his memoirs that his father heard talk about a merger between Estonia and Finland during the German occupation in 1917–18. As illustrated by Zetterberg (1984: 519), these plans were associated with the idea that a union with Finland was the only alternative for Estonia to achieve independence without tying the country to Germany or Russia.

In a time when great powers repeatedly overran smaller nations, the relative security provided by a supposedly strong Greater Finland seemed attractive. Unlike the brief Bornholmian flirt with the thought of joining Sweden in 1945, and the Ålandic quest for reunification with Sweden, the attraction of Greater Finland on Saaremaa was probably not unique to the island but shared by many mainlanders as well. At least German leaders were worried that Finnish propaganda would affect the Estonians (Werther 2012: 139).

Conclusions

The memory of how islanders through collective action liberated and briefly took control over their own islands has played an important role in the construction of regional identity on Åland and Bornholm. It has been used as a manifestation of the islanders' patriotism and their self-determination.

In contrast, the uprising on Saaremaa in 1919 is today considered to have been a tragic accident. During the period of Soviet rule, however, Communist history writing used the incident to illustrate the revolutionary spirit of the islanders, and interpreted it as a result of their identification with fellow peasants and workers in the Soviet Union.

The comparison between the three islands illustrates how feelings of loyalty towards a nation-state might be altered in times of war, if that state seems incapable of providing security. When Finland seemed to be slipping into civil war and Bolshevism, Ålanders turned their eyes to Sweden, as some Bornholmians did when Danish authorities seemed to have abandoned the island during the bombings in 1945. After Estonia was erased from the map in 1940, Greater Finland seemed attractive to many on Saaremaa. Of these shifts in allegiance, only the Swedish orientation on Åland had permanent consequences. The most important explanation for this is no doubt Åland's acquisition of autonomy within Finland in 1921. Although autonomy was forced upon the Ålanders against their will at the time, as most were in favour of joining Sweden, it did create regional authorities with some real influence. The elected members of these political bodies attempted to defend Åland's autonomy by developing the islanders' regional identity, and they intentionally used history writing as a means to this end. Through this processes, the sentiments of 1918 – and the view of history with which they were associated – became firmly rooted in Ålandic society.

Åland's intermediary position between Sweden and Finland has contributed to its acquisition of autonomy. An interpretation close at hand is that the autonomy is a result of the fact that Ålanders, contrary to what is the case on other islands in the Baltic Sea, speak a language different from that spoken by the majority population on the mainland. However, it was rather the strategic aspect of Åland's location that aroused the attention of the European powers who decided the island's fate in the League of Nations in 1921. They legitimised their decision in the Wilsonian principles of national self-determination, which was then the prevailing ideology. The initially unwanted autonomy gradually developed into the backbone of Ålandic identity, no doubt aided by the fact that it has helped Åland avoid the negative economic and demographic developments experienced by other islands in the Baltic Sea. Since this autonomy was devised as a protection of an ethnic minority, Ålandic history writers have supported it by emphasising the islanders' cultural and linguistic Swedishness.

Bornholm, Åland, and Saaremaa, due to their strategic locations, have been fortified in times of war. During the First World War, Åland and Saaremaa were isolated from the mainland due to travel restrictions imposed by the military. It is possible that this relative isolation during the nationally formative period that preceded the Finnish and Estonian declarations of independence might have contributed to the fact that islanders from Åland and Saaremaa found themselves on a collision course with the new national governments in Helsinki and Tallinn, respectively. The stress caused by the quartering of troops has been raised as an important factor in the development of Ålandic identity, as well as an underlying cause of the 1919 uprising on Saaremaa.

On Åland and Bornholm, exemption from military service (and on Bornholm, reintegration into the national military in 1867) has affected regional and national identity. Resentment towards military service also played an important role in the outbreak of the uprising on Saaremaa in 1919.

The military history of these three islands in the Baltic Sea illustrates how identity has been formed in interplay between geographic and political factors. Although identity on the islands is influenced by their insularity – which has imposed a certain isolation that has been heightened in times of war – identity is by no means static. Expressions of identity and national affiliation have been heavily influenced by the islanders' shifting security concerns. Bornholmian history writers have applied a dual strategy. On one hand, they refer to the islanders' patriotism in order to garner increased support from Denmark, while on the other hand, they remind the Bornholmians that through their history, they have repeatedly been forced to take responsibility for their own island in times of crises. Ålandic history writers underwent several shifts of national identity in the twentieth century, abandoning Finnish nationalism in favour of Swedish nationalism, when the Russian Revolution and the Finnish Civil War raised concerns about the island's security as a part of Finland. After the Second World War, Swedish nationalism was replaced by a more independent Ålandic interpretation of history, which is ripening into a kind of Ålandic nationalism. After the end of the Cold War, when the security threats in the Baltic Sea appeared smaller than for centuries, some Ålanders even started to advocate independence, denouncing the idea that their islands needed any support from a larger nation state.

While Ålandic and Bornholmian history writing have their own character and have developed on somewhat different paths as compared to mainland history writing, on Saaremaa the development of history writing in the twentieth century has followed the same pattern as on the mainland. A Baltic German interpretation of history was succeeded by a national Estonian, Soviet Age and then a second wave of national Estonian, history writing, just as on the mainland. This is probably partially a result of the fact that Saaremaa predominantly shares its experience of twentieth century history with the Estonian mainland, although the island's slightly detached position has delayed or exacerbated certain trends and events. The greatest anomaly, the 1919 uprising, was swiftly resolved, aided by the island's relative proximity to the mainland. However, the locations of Åland and Bornholm as strategic outposts in relative proximity to other nation states have resulted in experiences of war that are qualitatively different from the national commemoration of the same events – as the feeling of abandonment that the bombings of Bornholm caused and the international interventions that gave Åland autonomy and demilitarisation. Since integrating these events into the larger Danish or Finnish national historical narratives is associated with insurmountable difficulties, Bornholmian and Ålandic history writing have acquired an independent characteristic – something that, in turn, has most likely contributed to a strengthened regional identity.

The Baltic Sea and its islands (Image: base map from Wikimedia Commons, edited by Janne Holmén)

References

Ant, J. (2007) "Saaremaa poliitiline elu 1918–1940." *Saaremaa 2: Ajalugu, majandus, kultuur,* ed. by Jänes-Kapp, K., Randma, E. and Soosaar, M. Tallinn: Koolibri, 264–89.

ÅSUB (2012): *Åland in Figures.* Mariehamn: Åland Islands Statistical Agency. Available from http://www.asub.ax/files/alsiff2012_en.pdf [2 Dec. 2013].

Baldacchino, G. (2004) "The Coming of Age of Island Studies." *Tijdschrift voor economische en sociale geografie* 95 (3), 273–83.

Barfod, J. H. (1976) *Et centrum i periferien: Modstandsbevægelsen på Bornholm.* Rønne: Bornholms historiske samfund.

Bartmann, B. (2007) "War and Security." *A World of Islands: An Island Studies Reader,* ed. by Baldacchino, G. Charlottetown: Institute of Island Studies, 295–322.

Bomansson, K. A. (1852) *Skildring af folkrörelsen på Åland, 1808: En scen ur Suomis sista strid: Med en öfversigt af Åland i allmänhet.* Stockholm: Bonniers.

Buxhoeveden, G. von (2009) Personal email (20 Oct.).

Buxhoeveden, O. (1969) "Der Kommunistenaufstand auf Oesel im Februar 1919 aus deutsch-baltischer Sicht." *Baltische Hefte* 15, 90–102.

Bøggild, H. (2004) *Gyldendals bog om Bornholm.* Copenhagen: Gyldendals.

Depraetere, C., and Dahl, A. L. (2007) "Locations and Classifications." *A World of Islands: An Island Studies Reader,* ed. by Baldacchino, G. Charlottetown: Institute of Island Studies, 57–106.

Dreijer, M. (1979) *Det åländska folkets historia, vol. I:1: Från stenåldern till Gustav Vasa.* Mariehamn: Ålands kulturstiftelse.

Eriksson, J., and Wirgin, W. (1961) *Ålandsfrågan 1917–1921: Minnen och upplevelser.* Stockholm: Hörsta.

Eriksson, S., Johansson, L. I., and Sundback, B. (2006) *Fredens öar: Ålands självstyrelse, demilitarisering och neutralisering.* Mariehamn: Ålands fredsinstitut.

Hakala, P. (2006) "Trohet mot det svenska fäderneslandet – folkresningen 1808 i åländsk historieskrivning." *Åländska identiteter,* ed. by Holm, S. et al. Helsinki: Historicus.

Hay, P. (2006) "A Phenomenology of Islands." *Island Studies Journal* 1 (1), 19–42.

Hiie, P. (2010) *1919: Aasta mäss Muhu ja Saaremaal.* Kuressaare: Saaremaa muuseum.

Holmén, J. (2009a) "Vikingatid och medeltid i åländsk historieskrivning." *Tankar om ursprung: Forntiden och medeltiden i nordisk historieanvändning*, ed. by Edquist, S., Hermanson, L., and Johansson, S. Stockholm: The Museum of National Antiquities.

Holmén, J. (2009b): "Historiens roll i byggandet av en åländsk nationell identitet." *Tiedepolitiikka* (4), 31–5.

Isaksson, M. (1981) *Kring Bomarsund: Tio försök att skildra åländska verkligheter åren 1808–1856*. Helsinki: Söderströms.

Jensen, B. (2000) "Soviet Occupation of a New Type: The Long Liberation of the Danish Island of Bornholm 1944–1946." *Scandinavian Journal of History* 25 (3), 219–37.

Jørgensen, J. A. (1900) *Bornholms historie, vol. I: Fra Oldtiden til 1660*. Rønne: Sørensen.

Jørgensen, J. A. (1901) *Bornholms historie, vol. II: Fra 1660 til nutiden*. Rønne: Sørensen.

Kaitseliidu Saaremaa maleva arengulugu (1999). Kuressaare: Kaitseliidu Saaremaa maleva ajalootoimkond.

Klindt-Jensen, J. (1957): "Urolige tider." *Bogen om Bornholm*, ed. by Nielsen, R. and Sørensen, T. Haderslev: Danskerens forlag.

Kure, B. (1981) *En ø i krig: Bornholms besættelses-historie baseret på en række avisartikler i dagbladet Bornholmeren i 1980*. Rønne: Bornholmeren.

Kuvaja, C., Hårdstedt, M., and Hakala, P. (2008) *Det åländska folkets historia, vol. IV: Från finska kriget till Ålandsrörelsen 1808–1920*. Mariehamn: Ålands kulturstiftelse.

Körber, M. (1885) *Bausteine zu einer Geschichte Oesels: Fünf Jahrhunderte, von der heidnischen Vorzeit bis zum Frieden von Nystädt*. Arensburg: Wochenblatt.

Luha, A., Blumfeldt, E., and Tammekann, A., eds (1934) *Saaremaa: Maateaduslik, majanduslik ja ajalooline kirjeldus*. Tartu: Eesti Kirjanduse Seltsi kirjastus.

Lust, K. (2007) "Saaremaa Vene impeeriumi koosseisus 18. sajandi lõpust 1918. aastani." *Saaremaa 2: Ajalugu, majandus, kultuur*, ed. by Jänes-Kapp, K., Randma, E. and Soosaar, M. Tallinn: Koolibri, 216–63.

Meripuu, M. (2007) "II Maailmasõda ja Saaremaa." *Saaremaa 2: Ajalugu, majandus, kultuur*, ed. by Jänes-Kapp, K., Randma, E. and Soosaar, M. Tallinn: Koolibri, 290–304.

Nordman, D. (1986) "Historiker kämpar om Åland: Om de svenska och finländska historikernas argumentering i Ålandsfrågan 1917–1921." *Väster om Skiftet: Uppsatser ur Ålands historia*, ed. by Jungar, S. and Villstrand, N. E. Turku: Åbo Akademi, 139–58.

Olausson, P. M. (2007) *Autonomy and Islands: A Global Study of the Factors that Determine Island Autonomy.* Turku: Åbo Akademi University Press.

Postimees [online]. Available from http://www.postimees.ee/leht/96/05/04/krimi.htm [2 Dec. 2013].

Rasmussen, E. G. (1982) *Dette gavebrev: Det politiske spil omkring den bornholmske opstand og Peder Olsens indsats i løsrivelseverket 1658–59.* Rønne: Bornholms historiske samfund.

Rasmussen, E. G. (2000) *Skuddet: En bog om Villum Clausen og de dramatiske hændelser under den bornholmske opstand i 1658.* Nexø: Editio.

Riis, V. (1960) *Kolmandat teed ei ole.* Tallinn: Eesti Riiklik Kirjastus.

Royle, S. A. (2001) *A Geography of Islands: Small Island Insularity.* London: Routledge.

Ränk, G. (1979) *Sest ümmargusest maailmast.* Stockholm: Välis-Eesti and EMP.

Salminen, J. (1979) *Ålandskungen.* Stockhom: Rabén och Sjögren.

Saaremaa 1940–1941: Punavõimu tulek, selle likvideerimine, vol. 2. (1996). Kuressaare: Kaitseliidu Saaremaa Malev.

Saaremaa ülestous 1919 (1989). Tallinn: Eesti raamat.

Statistics Denmark. Available from http://www.dst.dk/en/Statistik/emner/befolkning-og-befolkningsfremskrivning/folketal.aspx [2 Dec. 2013].

Statistics Estonia. Available from http://pub.stat.ee [2 Dec. 2013].

Tarvel, E. (2007) "Piiskopi- ja orduaeg 1227–1572." *Saaremaa 2: Ajalugu, majandus, kultuur,* ed. by Jänes-Kapp, K., Randma, E. and Soosaar, M. Tallinn: Koolibri, 77–142.

Werther, S. (2012) *SS-Vision und Grenzland-Realität: Vom Umgang dänischer und "volksdeutscher" Nationalsozialisten in Sønderjylland mit der "großgermanischen" Ideologie der SS.* Stockholm: Acta Universitatis Stockholmiensis.

White, G. M. (1995) *Identity through History: Living Stories in a Solomon Islands Society.* Cambridge: Cambridge University Press.

Zahrtmann, M. K. (1934) *Borringholmerens historiebog: Første og anden bog.* Rønne: Colberg.

Zahrtmann, M. K. (1935) *Borringholmerens historiebog: Tredje og fjerde bog.* Rønne: Colberg.

Zetterberg, S. (1984) "Die finnisch–estnischen Unionspläne 1917–1919."*Jahrbücher für Geschichte Osteuropas* 32, 517–40.

3. The Nordic Threat:
Soviet Ethnic Cleansing on the Kola Peninsula

Andrej Kotljarchuk

> It's the hidden enemy, whom we don't know, who is dangerous.
> We know all the people [in this report] and have files on them.
> The day will come when we'll settle accounts with them.
> Stalin (cited in Bazhanov 1990: 93)

Access to previously unavailable sources from Soviet archives has brought to light a little-known history, namely 'national operations' of the Soviet secret police (NKVD) and the deportation of minorities, one of the central features of Stalinist repression (Samuelson and Sorokin 2007: 739–56). Local studies have already provided a deeper understanding of the nature and mechanism of this repression (Vatlin 2004; Kotljarchuk 2012a). However, most previous studies have been concerned with large minority groups (Iwanow 1991; Mann 2005; Dönninghaus 2009) or with the deportation of minorities during the Second World War (Nekrich 1978; Sword 1994; Poljan 2004). This chapter focuses on the inter-related phases and dimensions of state-run violence in a short-term and long-term perspective and on a case uncharted by previous research. Investigating local material in the broader context, it examines Soviet large-scale violence towards Nordic minorities of the Polar area as a gradual process of ethnic cleansing. It also reconsiders the ways in which the Soviet state dramatically changed the population structure of the Kola Peninsula and fully integrated this region into the 'pure' Russian context.

Historians have put forward many explanations for the mass repression of various ethnic groups committed by the Soviet Union; two approaches are particularly relevant. Most scholars focus on the security dilemma in the border area, suggesting the need to secure the ethnic integrity of Soviet space vis-à-vis neighbouring capitalistic enemy states. They stress the role of international relations and believe that representatives of 'western minorities' were killed not because of their ethnicity, but rather because of their connection to countries hostile to the USSR and the fear of disloyalty in case of an invasion (Werth 2003: 215–39; Mann 2005: 318–28; Kuromiya 2007: 141–3). Other scholars argue that the Soviet terror against minorities was actually genocide based on ethnic criteria (Nekrich 1978; Nahaylo and Swoboda 1990: 79–80; Kostiainen 1996: 332–41; Naimark 2010; Snyder 2010: 92–108). However, previous historiography usually analyses the Great Terror, deportations during the Second World War, administrative and cultural discrimination, and the cleansing of cultural landscapes separately.

The main idea in the present study is the use of the theoretical framework of Holocaust and genocide studies for analysing Soviet state-run repression on the Kola Peninsula and examining this as a continuing process, with a particular concern for ethnic violence. As Norman Naimark (2010: 11) has pointed out, "implicit in any evaluation of Stalin's mass killing of the 1930s is our knowledge and understanding of the horrors of the Holocaust". The theoretical model developed by the author for this study is based on the ethnic violence approach – the investigation of different phases and dimensions of genocidal strategy (Chapman 1994; Martin 1998; Dulić 2005; Naimark 2001; Jones 2011). This model sees ethnic violence as a gradual political process that is divided into the following phases and dimensions:

Diagram 1: Phases of ethnic violence

Phase 1: Preparation and conceptualisation of mass violence	•Registration of members and mapping of minority •Isolation •Propaganda of hatred
Phase 2: Implementation	•Organised massacre •Forced deportation •Destroying of economic, cultural, and religious life •Prevention of normal family life and reproduction
Phase 3: Cleansing of cultural traces	•Intentional destruction of native heritage •Cleansing of cultural landscape •Memory politics of forgetting

The first phase concerns the preparation and conceptualisation of state-run mass violence. The crucial question is how an ideology of hatred is formulated by the political leadership and then mediated to the local authorities and the broader public through official documentation and mass media. The second phase relates to the technology and short-term effects of mass killing and deportation. The last phase bears on the long-term results of the destruction, the cleansing of cultural landscapes, the official politics of forgetting and its consequence for the affected ethnic community. The present article covers phases one and two.

Historical background

The Kola Peninsula has long had strategic importance for the Nordic countries and is historically considered a part of Norden (Skogan 1992). The natural resources and the demographic and socio-economic structures of the western part of the Kola Peninsula were similar to the Norwegian *Finnmark* and Swedish *Norrland* in the beginning of the twentieth century. Here Sami reindeer herders coexisted with Finnish, Norwegian, and Swedish farmers, fishermen, and hunters of Barents Sea animals. A relatively mild northern climate created possibilities for agriculture and milk production.

The Peninsula's indigenous Sami population has roots that date back to medieval times. In 1868, the imperial government in St. Petersburg decided to invite to Russian Lapland new settlers from neighbouring Sweden-Norway and the Grand Duchy of Finland. This decision led to a rapid Scandinavian colonisation of the Peninsula (Shrader 2005). In the late nineteenth century, there were more than 1000 settlers from Sweden-Norway, making up 8 per cent of the population of the Kola Peninsula (Thorsen and Thorsen 1991:14). Colonists founded a dozen Finnish settlements, Norwegian (Tsipnavolok, Kildin, and Terebirka) and Swedish (Murmasjö, Kovda, and Kosoi vorot) colonies, and several settlements of Northern Sami. The Nordic newcomers chose an isolated lifestyle and usually preferred not to mix with the local Russian population (Volens 1926: 11–13; Saeter 1992; Carlbäck 2000: 75–6; Leinonen 2008; Orekhova 2009).

Unlike many European countries where ethnic minorities faced discrimination, the Soviet Union proclaimed a policy of support of cultural and linguistic rights for all ethnic minorities. In the 1920s, the Bolsheviks systematically promoted the national consciousness of minorities (Martin

2001). In the Russian North, the historical experiment of multinationalism included the establishment of dozens of autonomous territories, the training of native cadres and the introduction of a native system of education (Slezkine 1994).

The Soviet administrative rebuilding of Russia was prepared by the collection of data on nationalities.[1] The first all-Soviet census of 1926 counted 1919 Finns, 1708 Sami, 715 Komi, 168 Norwegians, 108 Nenets, and 12 Swedes living in the Murmansk region.[2] 148 residents were foreign citizens, most probably immigrants from Sweden and Norway. The total population on the peninsula at that time was 22,858 persons. Therefore Nordic minorities (without foreign citizens, Finno-Ugric Komi, and Uralic Nenets) made up approximately 16.7 per cent of the entire population and about 29 per cent of the rural population of the Murmansk region.

A number of national units were created on the Kola Peninsula with native-language media and schools. In 1930, a Finnish national district with Polarnyi as the centre was founded, including the Norwegian national council of Tsipnavolok. The same year Sami autonomy with its centre in Jokanga and a Lappish national district with its centre in Kola were established (Routsala 2005). About 44.6 per cent of the population of the Polarnyi district at that time were Finns. Together with Sami, Norwegians, and Swedes, they made up the majority – 57 per cent of the population (Orekhova 2009: 208).

The Nordic settlements on the Kola Peninsula played an important role in Soviet propaganda abroad. The Kremlin sponsored the emigration of Nordic workers to the Polar area (Gustafson 2006; Kotljarchuk 2012a). The legal communist press in Norway and Sweden described the successes of the Soviet nationalities policy towards Scandinavian minorities (Wretling 1931: 18–19; cf. Jentoft 2001: 87–114; Kotljarchuk 2012a: 78–99).

---

[1] The statistical data of the present chapter is based on the official results of the 1926 and 1939 Soviet censuses and on published or digital databases on the victims of Soviet terror, where ethnicity and place of residence are mandatory criteria. Among them are the *Kniga pamiati* (Memory Book: List of the Names of Persecuted People on the Kola Peninsula, 1997), the database of Memorial with over 2.6 million names of victims of the Stalinist terror, the regional database of North-Western Russia "Recovered Names" and the database "Repressed Russia" with over 1.4 million names.

[2] The real number of Swedish immigrants was probably higher. Many settlers from the northern part of Sweden declared their Finnish ethnicity in the 1926 census. In 1938, the Swedish colony of Kovda (previously in Karelia) was included in the Murmansk region. The number of Swedish citizens increased in the 1930s as a result of the emigration of Swedish leftists and workers (the so called *Kirunasvenskar*) to the Soviet Union.

Nordic threat: A case of continuity?

Fifteen years after the start of Nordic colonisation, the government of imperial Russia raised the alarm. In 1881, the Ministry of Internal Affairs prepared a secret report "Materials for the Solutions Related to the North of Russia, Murmansk, and the White Sea Ports". The government recognised that emigrants from Sweden-Norway and the Grand Duchy of Finland had built within a short period of time a prosperous economic zone in the tundra. However, the 100-page document regarded the Finnish-Swedish-Norwegian colonisation of the Murmansk coast a huge political mistake, resulting in "the peaceful conquest of our West coast" (Materialy dla razrabotki voprosov 1881: 43). A number of countermeasures were proposed: administrative reform (elimination of the special colonist district), development of infrastructure in order to reorient the colonists from Sweden-Norway to Russia, attracting native Russians to settle at the Barents Sea coast, and finally Russification of the colonists (ibid. 41–53). As Jens Petter Nielsen points out "this process was motivated less by a desire to Russify than by the wish to preserve the unity and integrity of the Russian state" (Nielsen 2005: 22).

Imperial authorities noted that the second generation of Nordic colonists and Sami did not study the Russian language. In order "to Russianise the younger generation of colonists and Lapps" a special boarding school was established in Aleksandrovsk/Polarnyi where all subjects including the Lutheran religion were taught in Russian (Obshchezhitie dla detei kolonistov 1902).

The Soviet regime on the Kola Peninsula was established in 1920 after three years of civil war. The remote Northern periphery was *terra incognita* to the Soviet leadership, whose personal experience was urban and linked to the industrial milieu (Toulouze 2005: 140–1). The Soviet nationalities policy was based on the contradistinction between the past Empire of the Romanovs and modern Soviet Russia (Kotljarchuk 2012a: 24–30). Lenin and his party stressed that imperial Russia had been a "prison of nations" where an "exhaustive suppression of national minorities" prevailed (Drabkina 1930; Natsionalnye menshinstva 1929: 35–61; Lenin 1962: 69). Therefore, with the help of a favourable policy of 'indigenisation', the Bolsheviks aimed to attract people like the Nordic colonists and Sami to take their side (Kotljarchuk 2012b).

The concepts of the nationalities policies of the Russian empire and Soviet Russia were entirely different. Tsarist Russia decided on cultural

Russification; the Soviet state declared full support for minority rights and administrative autonomy. The Bolsheviks anticipated, in line with the Marxist doctrine, that Nordic colonists belonging to the poorer farmers and fishermen would be loyal to the new nationalities and socio-economic policy (Bogatstva Murmanskogo kraya 1934: 99). The government regarded reindeer herders of the North in a positive way as "primitive communistic groups" (Slezkine 1994: 220–1; Leete 2004: 28–30; Kotljarchuk 2012b). The main aim of the nationalities policy towards the Sami was "the elimination of the age-old backwardness", that is, to help them catch up with other, "more advanced" minorities, but at the same time to reinforce their ethnic identity (Natsionalnye menshinstva Leningradskoi oblasti 1929: 35–6). The positive class evaluation of the Kola-Nordic communities gave an additional confidence to the authorities in the attainability of the goals of the new nationalities policy. However, not all local Bolsheviks believed in the progress of indigenisation. In 1929, the planning commission of Murmansk district discussing the future demographic development of the region made the following analysis:

> Murman was largely colonised not by Russians, but by Finns and Norwegians, something that certainly has a negative effect, in particular it was one of the reasons for the ceding to Finland in 1920 a part of our territory of the Western Murman.[3]

Therefore, the Murmansk planning commission proposed to move 2000 households of ethnic Russian fishermen to the Barents coast. Local Soviet authorities perceived Nordic settlements as a security problem.

Registration

The all-Soviet census of 1926 – the first complete census in Soviet history – included 188 ethnic categories classified around numerous linguistic groups. Alongside this census, the government initiated a special Polar census in which a highly detailed survey of indigenous groups and minorities of the Barents Sea area was collected (Thorvaldsen 2011). One of the

---

[3] Докладная записка Мурманской окружной плановой комиссии "О переселении в 1930-1931 гг. 2000 семейств рыбаков колонистов на мурманское побережье Баренцева моря". State Archives of Murmansk oblast (GAMO), fond R-132, opis' 1, delo 322, pp. 28–9. According to the 1920 Treaty of Tartu, Soviet Russia ceded the Petsamo area to Finland. In the years 1584–1919, this territory had been a part of the Arkhangelsk region of Russia.

official aims was "solving the national question" by mapping compact minority areas and producing scientific grounds for establishing national autonomy (Blum and Mespoulet 2003: 204-11). While part of the authorities used the collected data for the support of minority rights and facilitating social-economic transformation, the secret police analysed the same data for surveillance of different social groups that were considered suspicious (Holquist 2001).

The Soviet secret police was involved in the activity of the Central Statistical Office (TsUNKhU). The chief staff at the central and regional level were approved by the secret police and each branch of TsUNKhU had at least one police officer posted for duty. On the request of the secret police, the Central Statistical Office reported statistical data (Zhiromskaya 1999: 148-52). The NKVD had a special eighth department of statistics with detachments in every region that counted members of various suspicious social groups from foreign citizens to former White army soldiers (Tinchenko 2011-12). In 1934, the Civil Registry Office (ZAGS) was integrated into the Soviet secret police.

In 1925, by the initiative of Felix Dzerzhinsky, the Research Institute of the North (*Institut Izucheniya Severa*) was founded and already by the following year scholars from this institute published a socio-demographic investigation of colonists of Western Murman (Volens 1926). In 1927, an ethnographic map of the Murmansk region was prepared at the Soviet Academy of Sciences with description of the settlements of Sami, Finns, and Norwegians.

The role of Soviet scholars in the mapping of the Russian North and in collecting ethnic data has been discussed in previous studies (Eidlitz Kuoljok 1985; Kuropiatnik 1999). In his book on ethnographic knowledge and the making of the Soviet Union, Francine Hirsch drew attention to the role of statistical and anthropological mapping of minorities in the Soviet terror (Hirsch 2005: 273-308). Holocaust studies show the significance of anthropology and eugenics in the mapping of potential victims (Müller-Hill 1998; Gretchen 2004). Nevertheless, the link between Soviet anthropologic and demographic research and preparation of national operations of the NKVD is largely understudied.

In 1929, the Murmansk branch of the Central Statistical Office prepared a statistical report of the region, based on the all-Soviet and Polar census. It contained details on the ethnicity of the population of the Kola Peninsula, with data for all settlements. The survey included information on the "dominant ethnicity" of inhabitants, the number of their families, and certain ethnic groups' share of the village population (Murmanskii okrug 1929).

During the 'national operations' and deportations, the collected ethnic data was supposed to help identify suspicious nationalities (Blum and Mespoulet 2003: 219). The 1940 NKVD secret order on the "Resettlement of foreign nationalities from Murmansk and the Murmansk region" was based on the precise knowledge of citizens to be deported, their place of residence, gender, professional, and age profile (Kisilev 2008: 118–22). As Peter Holquist (2001: 133) noted, "with macabre precision the Soviet state indicated region-by-region target victims". Unfortunately, the limited access to internal documents of the NKVD in Russian archives is an obstacle to gaining more thorough knowledge on the role of registration in the preparation of the Great Terror and Soviet deportations.

Isolation as instrument of covert policing actions

Studies of the Holocaust have shown that segregation and the international isolation of the German-Jewish population played a crucial role in the first steps towards genocide (Longerich 2007: 29–129). The question is, therefore, whether socio-geographic and international isolation facilitated the mass operations of the NKVD on the Kola Peninsula. On the eve of the Great Terror, all leaks abroad were unwanted. Reactions of the Scandinavian and Finnish press and diplomatic intervention would have significantly complicated the NKVD practice of mass repression. The illegal escape of potential victims was also an issue in the sparsely populated Soviet–Finnish–Norwegian borderland. One of the first steps of the government in isolating Nordic colonists and citizens was to limit their access to diplomatic missions. By 1937–38, Scandinavian diplomats worked under tremendous pressure. For example, the Soviet side denied visas to newly appointed Swedish diplomats, violated the principle of inviolability of the diplomatic bag, and arrested Soviet citizens belonging to the technical staff of Scandinavian missions. The NKVD also secretly installed listening devices in diplomatic apartments. These actions paralysed the consular service (Ken, Rupasov, and Samuelsson 2005: 114 note 87).

The next step was the liquidation of all diplomatic representation outside Moscow. The vice-consulate of Sweden in Arkhangelsk was closed in 1935, with the interests of Sweden in the Barents Sea region being represented by Norway after that. However, in 1937, the NKVD conducted the mass arrests of "persons affiliated and associated with the Norwegian consulate" in

Arkhangelsk, the latter being accused of being "a nest of espionage". During the special operation, 63 individuals were arrested (including a Kola Norwegian merchant venture, Martin Ulsen), the consulate was closed, and Norwegian consul Albert Viklund who had grown up in Russia was forced to leave the Soviet Union (Ovsiannikov 1994). The Norwegian consulate in Arkhangelsk had been a traditional place for asking for help among Kola Norwegians and Swedes (Jentoft 2001: 110). In autumn 1937, the Soviet government demanded the closure of the Swedish consulate in Leningrad. At that time, the Murmansk district was a part of the Leningrad region. After the preparatory work and the evacuation of the property in January 1938, the consulate ceased to exist. In December 1937, at the request of the Soviet government, the consulate of Finland in Leningrad was likewise closed. Therefore, by January 1938, not a single representative of the Nordic states was based in north-western Russia.

On 28 October 1937, at the height of the 'national operations', the NKVD issued order 00698 "On combating counter-revolutionary espionage, terrorist, subversive activities of the staff of embassies and consulates of Germany, Japan, Italy, and Poland". The order created a new concept in the Soviet repressive dictionary, namely, 'consular ties', which meant the criminalisation of any contact between Soviet residents and diplomatic missions. The order did not define the punishment, thereby opening the opportunity for mass violence. A new NKVD directive from 1 February 1938 equated 'consular ties' to other crimes of espionage, something that in practice implied the death penalty. The 00698 order also covered the embassies of Nordic countries. Paragraph 7 provided for the intensification of "surveillance of the other missions, through which the Japanese, German, Italian, and Polish intelligence services conduct counter-revolutionary work in the Soviet Union, namely Finnish, Austrian, Balkan and Scandinavian" (Bilokin 2000: 27). The diplomatic corps in Moscow discussed the shocking arrests of embassy visitors provided by the Soviet government. The Swedish Ambassador William Winter informed Foreign Minister Rickard Sandler of the impotence of diplomatic missions of the Nordic countries to help their compatriots.[4]

---

[4] "Den främlingsfientliga rörelsen i Sovjetunionen." Winther to Sandler, 26 May 1938. National Archives of Sweden (*Riksarkivet*, henceforth NAS), Kungl. Utrikesdepartementet (henceforth FM), HP 514, vol. 62.

Strengthening of border control

The demarcation made as result of the 1920 Tartu Treaty between Finland and Soviet Russia divided Scandinavia and the Kola Peninsula with a 300-kilometres straight-line boundary under Finnish and Soviet control. For the first time in history, a well-guarded border between two hostile states isolated Russian subjects in the High North from their western kinsmen.

The new border broke family ties. In tsarist Russia, Kola Norwegians and Finns had free contact with residents of nearby Norway and the Grand Duchy of Finland (which was still under Russian control). The port of Aleksandrovsk and the Norwegian town of Vardø were connected by a regular ferry. In Vardø, Kola Norwegians, Finns, and Swedes usually baptised and confirmed their children and bought necessary goods, including fishing equipment, boats, and coffee (Volens 1926: 20). The Sami people moved freely in the tundra between Finnish and Russian Lapland. However, in the mid-1920s Soviet authorities imposed a ban on the output of the Kola colonists to the port of Vardø and tightened their control over meetings between Russian and Finnish Sami.

Starting in the 1920s, a special 'border zone' was erected (Martin 1998: 830), dividing the Nordic colonists and Sami of the Kola Peninsula from Finland and Norway with a 22-kilometre wide border strip. Every Soviet citizen, including locals, were required to have a special NKVD-border guard permission in order to enter the border zone. Entering the territory of the zone without identification documents was forbidden.

In 1934, fortified border areas were introduced and starting in 1935 a special programme to create a politically reliable squad within the population of the border area was realised. NKVD officers were ordered to deport to the inland all unreliable individuals and every village council in the border area was to have a police officer. The local party organisations were instructed to increase the number of communists and *Komsomol* members (Ramanava 2007). As a result, by 1937, the local party branch in the Norwegian colony Tsipnavolok included 12 members (Jentoft and Goncharova 2008: 94), among them no Norwegians.

Increasing economic restrictions made smuggling a survival strategy of the colonists and Sami. The centre of smuggling was the Rybachy Peninsula (Fiskarhalvøya/Kalastajasaarento). Before the Second World War, this peninsula was divided between Soviet Russia and Finland. On the eastern shore of the peninsula were Tsipnavolok, as well as some Finnish farms and settlements of Norwegian Sami. On the west coast of the peninsula close to the Soviet border, the Finnish village of Vaidaguba was situated. As a result of strict border control, colonists had to meet their compatriots illegally during fishing and hunting sea animals in the Barents Sea. However, the establishment in 1933 of the Soviet Northern Navy and of the base of the maritime border guard in Polarnyi led to a significant limitation of the meetings on the sea and in the tundra.

Propaganda of hatred

Unprecedented in Soviet history, state-run terror demanded mass propaganda of hatred. Genocide Studies show that the Holocaust was prepared through a governmental campaign that was filtered to society through mass media (Glass 1997: 129–45; Herf 2006: 17–49; Jones 2011: 487–98). As Leo Kuper has shown, it is not the social conditions within a society that cause genocide, but rather a situation where the powerful make the decision to exterminate a group of people (Kuper 1982: 40–56).

The ideological orchestration of 'national operations' included two main aspects. First was the concept of the new round of mass repressions directed this time against suspicious nationalities, then the conceptualisation of terror and its implementation in society. At the end of March 1937, the newspaper *Pravda* published a speech Stalin gave at the Plenum of the Central Committee of the Communist Party on 3 March 1937, titled "On the errors of party work and further steps to eliminate the Trotskyite and other hypocrites". The full text appeared as a separate edition and was reprinted by the local press. In this speech, Stalin formulated the "essential facts" that laid the ideological foundation of the Great Terror. If in the beginning of the 1930s repressions were directed against certain social groups (i.e., kulaks and priests), now the dictator warned about the total cleansing of Soviet Union. According to Stalin "sabotage and subversive spy work of agents of foreign states hit the Soviet state and our organisations from top to bottom" (Stalin 1997: 151). Nevertheless, Stalin announced a thesis of the permanent nature of class struggle in the USSR. In 1937, the media dictionary of Soviet newspeak was enriched by a number of new terms (Pöppel 2007). The formula of 'capitalist encirclement' meant a dramatic turn of Soviet domestic and foreign politics. For the first time, Stalin did not make any exception and all the neighbouring countries entered the list of enemies (Stalin 1997: 151–73). The idea of international solidarity with the working class and Western communism was abandoned in favour of the isolation and distrust of foreigners. In the orders to the

NKVD, Stalin and the party leadership emphasised that the mass operations against Poles, Latvians, Germans, Estonians, Finns, Greeks, Iranians, Chinese, and Romanians applied to both foreign and Soviet citizens.[5]

In the summer of 1937, publications on the activities of foreign intelligence agents were one of the hot topics in Soviet press. On 11 July 1937, the chief of the fourth secret political department of the NKVD for the Leningrad and Murmansk areas, Petr Korkin, published in *Leningradskaya Pravda* an article titled "On the subversive activities of foreign intelligence services in the rural area". The author claimed that even the remote areas of northern Russia had become "an active field of intelligence services of capitalist encirclement" (Kotljarchuk 2012a: 122–34). A number of prints published in hundreds of thousands copies were talking about the destructive espionage of capitalistic states against the Soviet Union and their internal agents. The publications were addressed to all groups of society: from the NKVD officers and party officials to kolkhoz propagandists, librarians, and pioneer leaders (see Zakovskii 1937; *Shpionam i izmennikam 1937; Shpionazh i razvedka 1937*; Zilver 1938). As Oleg Khlevnyuk (1992: 170) has pointed out, Soviet writers and journalists produced easily recognisable stories during the Great Terror suggesting that mass purges were justified and that the country was full of spies.

The Soviet Union had stable diplomatic, economic, and political relations with Sweden and Norway. Unlike Finland, these neutral countries were not on the list of primary Soviet enemies. The Kremlin evaluated the relationship with these Scandinavian countries as always correct (Chubar'ian and Riste 1997: no. 191, Ken, Rupasov, and Samuelsson 2005: 33–4). For the Kremlin leadership, it was significant that unlike in Finland the Communist parties in Sweden and Norway acted legally. The fact that these countries did not have a common borderline at that time with the Soviet Union also played a role. However, the spiral of the Great Terror changed this positive image and from 1937 numerous articles were published depicting Norway and Sweden as the main bases of espionage against the Soviet Union (see Hôtes inopportuns 1937; Tarle 1937; Norvezhskaya diplomaticheskaya 1937; Gribov 1938). Soviet publications

---

[5] Постановление ЦК ВКП (б) от 31 января 1938 года "О продлении до 15 апреля 1938 года операций по разгрому шпионско-диверсионных контингентов из поляков, латышей, немцев, эстонцев, финн, греков, иранцев, харбинцев, китайцев и румын, как иностранных граждан, так и советских поданных, согласно существующих приказов НКВД СССР." Russian State Archive of Social-Political History (RGASPI), fond 17, opis' 166, delo 585, p. 27.

became a matter of great concern for Swedish diplomats in Moscow who realised that the Kremlin consciously built a negative image of Sweden.[6]

The thesis of active espionage suggested a wide network of domestic agents, and according to the Soviet press, the agents were members of numerous minorities. In 1937, the readers of *Polarnaya Pravda*, the leading official newspaper of the Murmansk region, learned that local Soviet cadres of the Polar district were "Finnish nationalists who despise the Russian language, incite enmity between Finns and Russians, and undermine the Soviet kolkhoz system" (Razgromit' burzhuaznykh 1937). The newspaper of the national Polar district "Polarnoin kollektivisti / Polarnyi kollektivist", which appeared both in Finnish and Russian published a series of articles against "Finnish bourgeois nationalists who usurped the political power in the district" (Paikallisesta nationalismista 1937; see also Mitä tekee 1937; Natsionalisticheskie nastroeniya 1937; Otkazalas' razgovarivat' 1937; and Bystree likvidirovat' 1937).

Many publications were about meetings at which the workers of the country unanimously supported the elimination of ordinary spies and saboteurs (Edinstvenno spravedlivyi 1937). The judgment of the state was presented as a verdict on behalf of the entire society. The largest children's daily newspaper *Pionerskaya Pravda* published a number of articles about foreign countries' espionage and children helping the police to catch the spies. The article "Exposing the conspiracy" was about the arrest of a spy at the door to a Norwegian consulate (Pionerskaya Pravda 1937: 20).

Through propaganda, the population and local authorities were prepared for the mass cleansing of certain minorities. This was important for two reasons. First, the national operations and the deportation of minorities were secret; their progress was not reported by the Soviet media (unlike the Moscow trials). Second, to hide mass arrests in rural areas was not possible, and the exact number of captured people became known next day. The state-organised propaganda campaign reached its goals. NKVD documents of 1937–38 show that the simple reference to the 'foreign origin' of an arrested individual convinced witnesses of the guilt of the accused person. For provincial policemen, the official newspapers served also as information sources that helped to elaborate the design of 'national operations' (Vatlin 2004: 49).

---

[6] "Med artikel över Sverige." Eric Gyllenstierna to Sandler, 14 Oct. 1937. NAS, FM, HP 514, vol. 61; Nils Lindh to Hans Beck-Friis, 15 Nov. 1938, ibid., vol. 62.

Organised massacre

In July 1933, Stalin visited the Kola Peninsula together with the head of the Leningrad region Sergei Kirov and defence minister (*people's commissar for military and navy affairs*) Kliment Voroshilov. Stalin was the first leader of Russia and the USSR to visit this region. By a Politburo decision, the Northern Navy with 12,000 military personnel was established in the centre of the Finnish national district of Polarnyi.[7] Industrial development was promoted in conjunction with further militarisation of the peninsula. Geological exploration, which started in the 1920s, led to the development of a number of mines. According to the second five-year plan for the Soviet economy, a number of large strategically important factories and facilities were built on the peninsula. Thus, over a short period of time the Kola Peninsula transformed from a nature reserve into an area of high military significance (Shashkov 2000; Mikoliuk 2003; Kotljarchuk 2012b).

The new strategic importance of the Kola Peninsula for the totalitarian regime turned the Nordic minorities into a perceived threat. In 1937, the NKVD started top-secret mass operations in order to execute members of several ethnic minorities (Werth 2003; Savin 2012). At a meeting of the Politburo on 20 July 1937, Stalin initiated the first operation by writing "a proposal" that "all Germans working in our military, semi-military, and chemical plants, and in electrical power stations and building sites, in every region, are to be arrested" (Repressii protiv sovetskikh nemtsev 1999: 35). In all, 56,787 Germans were arrested, 41,898 of whom were shot. Only 820 of them were citizens of the Reich (Okhotin and Roginskii 1999: 70–4). The second operation was "Polish", leading to the arrest of 139,815 Soviet Poles and the execution of 111,071 of them (Repressii protiv polakov 1997). A number of other operations were organised after these models, concerning, for example, people of Greek, Latvian, Iranian, Afghan, Bulgarian, and Finnish nationality. According to official statistics, altogether 335,513 people were arrested in these 'national operations', 247,157 of whom were shot (Werth 2003: 232; Savin 2012: 43).

Sami, Norwegians, and Swedes were not officially covered by these campaigns and therefore not included into the official data. However, the state-run violence against them was designed in accordance with the principles of other 'national operations' (Kotljarchuk 2012b). In 1937–38, the NKVD fabricated a number of 'underground organisations' on the Kola

---

[7] Протокол Политбюро ВКП (б) № 139 от 15 июня 1933 года. RGASPI, fond 17, opis' 3, delo 924, p. 18.

Peninsula. Kola Norwegians were accused of spying for Norway and Germany as members of a fictitious espionage organisation, the "Blue Cross or the Order of Rosicrucians".[8] Finns were supposed to be agents of Finland's General Staff and the Petsamo bureau of the Finnish secret police *Valpo* (Mikaliuk 2003: 101–2; Savilova 2008). Dozens of Sami were accused of being members of an underground rebel organisation, the alleged aim of which was to establish an independent Sami state (Kotljarchuk 2012b).

The Sami underground rebel organisation was a falsification of the NKVD and already in 1940 a number of policemen were arrested and sentenced to prison for "violations of socialist legality during the investigation of the Sami case" (Kiselev 1999). Einar Laidinen and Sergey Verigin (2004: 168–9) found the names of 179 actual agents of Finland, of whom 89 were natives of the Karelian and Kola borderlands, but among whom were no Sami. Among those arrested in the course of the Nordic operations were also ethnic Russians. For example, Vasiliy Alymov, the director of the Murmansk museum and a leading researcher of Sami culture, was accused of being the designated president of a future Sami state. His wife and adult son were also arrested and shot. The NKVD used the correspondence of Alymov with Swedish, Norwegian, and Finnish scholars regarding the Sami as "evidence of the international network of a Sami underground organization" (Kotljarchuk 2012b).

Altogether, 694 Finns, 68 Sami, 23 Norwegians, and 6 Swedes were arrested in the Murmansk area in 1937–38, approximately one fifth of the adult population belonging to these nationalities (Mikaliuk 2003: 62–3; Kotljarchuk 2012b). Most of the victims were shot. The executions were decided by a so-called *troika* – a three-man meeting of the local police chief, the local prosecutor, and the party secretary. The death rate of the arrested during the Great Terror among Kola Norwegians was 77 per cent, a higher figure than the 73.8 per cent average for all victim groups of the NKVD's 'national operations'. The death rate of the arrested Sami was 64.7 per cent (Kotljarchuk 2012b: 69). Many of those who had been sentenced during the Great Terror by *a troika* to "ten years incommunicado" were also murdered. Thus, the final number of Nordic victims might be even higher.

The Great Terror and mass arrests caused a deep economic crisis of previously prosperous Finnish, Norwegian, and Sami kolkhozes. In January 1939 the local government of the Polar district stated that the production

---

[8] Дело контрреволюционной шпионско-повстанческой организации "Голубые кресты или Орден Розенкрейцеров", 1938 год. GAMO, fond P-140, opis' 3, delo 3153.

plan of 1938 was fulfilled by only 20 per cent and that most of the fishing boats were not staffed (K lovu 1939).

A number of features distinguish the 'national operations' from other parts of the Great Terror, making them similar to genocide. The murders were conducted secretly on a mass scale. The suspicious ethnicity was one of the determining criterions for most of the arrests. The victims were killed under cover of night and buried en masse in unmarked places. Large-scale places, for example in Levashovo, were guarded by the secret police until the time of perestroika.[9] In many other smaller places, the NKVD sought to conceal all traces of mass murder. The arrested people disappeared and relatives did not get to know what really happened to them until the fall of the Soviet Union. Among the victims – supposed members of Nordic and Sami 'nationalistic' organisations – were also people of other ethnic backgrounds (Russians, Komi, Latvians, etc.). This is one of the differences between the Soviet mass murder and the Holocaust. However, all those arrested by the Murmansk police were connected in some way to Scandinavia and Finland, or had close personal relations with Nordic families. Another difference as compared to the Holocaust is that the direct victims of the Great Terror were adults only.

Deportation

An argument for the Soviet regime to use mass violence against Nordic minorities in order to secure the Murmansk region was the Winter War. In January 1940, the Soviet Foreign Office accused Sweden and Norway of supporting Finland and planning a large-scale war against the Soviet Union (Vneshniya politika SSSR 1946: no. 395). In his speech at the Supreme Soviet on 29 March 1940, the head of government and Foreign Minister Viacheslav Molotov explained for the Soviet elite the reasons for the Winter War and blamed Great Britain, France, and Sweden for supporting Finland against the USSR. According to Molotov, the Great Powers intended to use Finland, Sweden, and Norway as a springboard for a future war. Therefore, he claimed, the Soviet occupation of the Petsamo area aimed to protect the Murmansk region and railroad (Shestaya sessia Verkhovnogo 1940: 26–37).

---

[9] The Levashovo forest in the neighborhood of St. Petersburg is the largest mass grave of the victims of the Great Terror in Russia. Here many of Kola Finns, Sami, Norwegians, and Swedes were murdered in 1937–38. In 1989, the mass graves of Levashovo were opened to the public. Since that time, dozens of memorials have been erected to the memory of different ethnic groups, among them Finns, Norwegians, Estonians, Poles, Germans, Italians, Lithuanians, and Assyrians.

As a result of the Winter War, the Soviet Union occupied Finland's Petsamo area, which until 1920 had been a part of Russia. Finland lost its access to the Arctic Ocean and a new state border between the USSR and Norway emerged. In addition to this, large border territories in middle and southern Finland were incorporated into the USSR.

In the course of preparation for the Winter War, on 16 September 1939, Murmansk was given a special status as a closed city. As part of this decision, the Politburo ordered the NKVD to deport from the city "500–700 suspicious people, especially Finns and Estonians".[10] To protect the new state border, 10 NKVD border guard regiments were sent to the Karelian and Murmansk sector, totalling 7000 soldiers. Like in eastern Poland, the NKVD began to 'cleanse' the new territory of former citizens. However, 312 Finnish citizens of the Petsamo area were repatriated to Finland, and not deported and interned like the Poles (Savilova 2008: 142–3). That this was not seen as a solution to the security dilemma is evident from the order of NKVD's chief Lavrentiy Beria in July 1940 that all Finns, Norwegians, Northern Sami, and Swedes of the Murmansk region be deported. The deportation included 6973 Finns, Norwegians, and Swedes living on the Kola Peninsula as well as a small number of Balts who were forcibly relocated from the Kola Peninsula to the inland of north-western Russia.[11] Russian Sami were not included in this list. Those of them who lived in the borderland had already been forcibly resettled by decision of the local government in February 1940 to the inland of the Peninsula (Stepanenko 2002).

Unlike, for example, the deportation of Soviet Koreans from the Far East, which was justified with reference to Japanese espionage (Gelb 1995), the regulations and instructions of the Murmansk deportation do not contain any reasons for the resettlement. The threat of the Nazi German advance to the Russian Arctic after the occupation of Norway in May of 1940 was not reflected in official documents because the USSR and Nazi Germany had to act as allies after the Molotov–Ribbentrop pact.

---

[10] Постановление политбюро ЦК ВКП (6) " О переводе города Мурманска на режимное положение", 16 September 1939. RGASPI, fond 17, opis' 162, delo 26, p. 5.
[11] Приказ народного комиссара внутренних дел СССР [Л. П. Берия] № 00761 "О переселении из гор. Мурманска и Мурманской области граждан инонациональностей". 23 June 1940. State Archives of Russian Federation (GARF), fond R-9401, opis' 2, delo 1, pp. 207–09; Инструкция народного комиссара внутренних дел СССР [Л. П. Берия] "О порядке переселения граждан иностранных национальностей из города Мурманска и Мурманской области". 23 June 1940. Ibid., pp. 210–12.

Another reason was the new dimension of violence during the Second World War that resulted in the transition from terror to large-scale deportations of certain minorities. Starting in January 1940, the NKVD carried out extensive deportations of Poles from western Belarus and Ukraine. On 5 March 1940, the Politburo under the chairmanship of Stalin adopted a secret resolution on the execution of all Polish soldiers and officials captured in 1939. As a result, at least 21,736 Polish nationals were killed in the Katyn forest and other places of the Soviet Union.

Destruction of economic, cultural, religious and family life

The radical change of nationalities policy resulted also in the abolition of all Nordic autonomous territories on the Kola Peninsula and the abolition of the native (Finnish, Norwegian, and Sami) school system in 1938. This was justified by the Kremlin and local authorities in terms of the threat, for example, that national territories "were established by bourgeois nationalists" and had become "a base for numerous spies" (Gatagova 2005: no. 132). Minority schools on the Kola Peninsula were said to have "become an arena of anti-Soviet bourgeois influence on children" where the "Russian language was ignored and discriminated against" (Gatagova 2005: no. 136). Moreover, native newspapers and libraries on the Kola Peninsula were closed, and textbooks in native languages were confiscated and destroyed or moved to the so-called 'special deposit' (*spetskhran*). On 17 January 1938 the last issue of *Polarnoin kollektivisti* appeared in Finnish language. The liquidation of the native system of education and press, and the linguistic Russification policy was explained by the local authorities as serving the colonists and their children's future (Ivanov 1938). The 1940 deportation led to the economic collapse of the western area of the Kola Peninsula. On 5 August 1940, the local government of Murmansk reported to the central government in Moscow that because of the "relocation of foreign nationalities, many territories of our region, especially the Kola and Polar districts, remained entirely without labour".[12] The deportation was followed by the expropriation of property and destruction of material objects. The Lutheran churches that had existed on the Peninsula since the end of the nineteenth

---

[12] Докладная записка исполнительного комитета Мурманского областного совета в Совнарком Союза ССР "О переселении в Мурманскую область 286 хозяйств из других областей Союза ССР." 5 Aug. 1940. Russian State Archives of Economics (RGAE), fond 5675, opis' 1, delo 330, pp. 46–7.

century and dozens of Sami Orthodox churches were destroyed (Berdieva 2000: 85).

After the Second World War, the Kola Peninsula as a Soviet borderland to the NATO alliance became the most militarised and high-security area of the country. Deported Nordic groups never returned. A number of deported nations were rehabilitated on a collective base and their national autonomies were re-established after Stalin's death. The case of Kola Nordic groups is similar to Volga-Germans, Soviet Koreans, and Poles, who did not receive permission after the war to return home and did not regain autonomy. The punishment of these groups was collective, no matter what the post-Stalinist rehabilitation offered on the individual level.

The Sami case is unique in Soviet history. Not only was Sami national autonomy, which existed on the Kola Peninsula in the 1930s, never restored, the forcible deportation of the Sami population continued until the 1960s. By 1965, almost all reindeer herders had been concentrated in the four kolkhozes of Lovozero (Gutsol 2007). As a result, the Sami people lost their indigenous rights to their nomadic lifestyle, along with most of grazing lands and water resources in Russian Lapland. The balance between use of natural resources and suitable development was destroyed (Kozlov 2008: 21–3). Population pressure led to the depletion of grazing lands and the ecological destruction of the tundra. The population of reindeer declined from 40,000 animals in 1964 to 25,000 animals in 2001. Unemployment and alcoholism became spread among the Russian Sami and many of them left their homes for major cities in north-western Russia (Kozlov 2008: 23–4).

The Nordic colonies and Sami settlements on the Kola Peninsula were small with a fragile cultural heritage that could easily be destroyed. Today most of the former Nordic villages have no indication of previous human habitation, though on some of them military installations have been built. The cultural landscape created during a century of Nordic colonisation has been eradicated.

In 1995, the Norwegian government introduced a special repatriation programme for Kola-Norwegians and their descents who had immigrated to Russia and could not return after 1917. Through this programme, approximately 150 people came back to their historic homeland. Finland has a special individual programme of repatriation for Russian citizens of Finnish and Ingrian descent.

The Great Terror on the Kola Peninsula had a disproportional impact on men. The brunt of repression was directed against men of the age of sexual reproduction (20–45 years old), something that contributed to the vulnerability of the population. The terror also had a great impact on men in the age group of 46–72 years. This cohort reached adulthood before the October revolution and was, as it was regarded as belonging to *l'ancien régime*, seen as populated by potential enemies of the Soviet government. The age profile of these victims also reflects the fact that elders who traditionally occupied the leading position in the local communities suffered most from the terror (Kotljarchuk 2012b).

The forced deportation of Nordic minorities in 1940 also contributed to the prevention of a normal reproductive and family life. Deported people were placed in special settlements under the direct control of the NKVD. The food supply and economic situation in special settlements were often worse than in the Gulag. Unlike the Gulag camps, the contingent of special settlements (*spetsial'nye poseleniya*) was based on the family structure. This contributed to the high mortality rate of children (Kotljarchuk 2011). The special settlers (*spetsposelentsy*) were interned until 1954 and did not get permission to return home afterwards. After the Second World War, the Murmansk area remained a special regime area where former 'criminals' were not allowed to reside. As a result of this, the Nordic colonists were spread over the entire Soviet Union and lost their connectedness.

Conclusion

There are several interacting links between the different phases of this ethnic violence. Mass arrests and the disappearance of people in 1937/38 created an atmosphere of fear that helped the authorities in 1938/39 to destroy without protest the administrative and cultural autonomy of minorities and the native system of education. The Great Terror contributed to the lack of collective resistance in the course of the forced deportation of 1940. The deportation of Nordic minorities led to the economic collapse of the western part of the Kola Peninsula and provides evidence for Michel Foucault's claim that it is meaningless to look for logically structured economic purposes in the activities of political regimes that prefer violence over dialogue and do not care about economic consequences (Nilsson 2008: 83–91).

The present study confirms Alain Blum's and Martine Mespoulet's (2003: 204–25) observation that, in the course of censuses and statistical investigations, the Soviet government constructed different ethnic categories that were not only used for the support of minorities, but also for cruel mass violence towards certain groups. The secret police collected ethnic data for the domestic surveillance of citizens in many interwar states. The U.S. military intelligence service (MID) used the New York City registration data in order to keep track of immigrant groups (foreign-born Jews) who, according to the MID, created a counter-intelligence problem (Bendersky 2000: 158–282, 337–93). However, while such policies led to unlawful surveillance and discrimination of minorities in democratic states, it was a starting point for mass killing and ethnic cleansing under totalitarian regimes.

After having isolated the Kola-Nordic population from Scandinavia, the Soviet authorities executed their repressive mass operations in silence and avoided international protests. The changed nature of Soviet nationalities policy remained unknown in Norden and for many Scandinavians, the Soviet Union continued to be an inspiring example of a positive nationalities policy and a functional planned economy (Wråkberg 2013).

The main contributions of propaganda in the course of the Soviet terror were the following: (1) creating a negative image of the at-risk groups, (2) claiming that the members of certain national groups did not belong to the loyal part of society, (3) creation of an atmosphere of uncertainty, fear, and suspicion in the national districts, (4) creation of general fear of certain ethnic minorities, (5) explanation of mass arrests, (6) glorification of informers and their collaboration with the secret police, and (7) neutralisation of bystanders in order to change their behaviour to active or passive cooperation with the NKVD and non-resistance to on-going mass violence.

Like in Nazi Germany (Friedlander 1980), the Soviet bureaucracy manipulated formal language in order to make its communication incomprehensible to bystanders. The NKVD orders, for example, used the following definitions: 'contingent' (*kontingent*) for arrested jailed and deported people, 'first category' (*pervaia kategoriya*) for those who were to be murdered and 'second category' (*vtoraia kategoriya*) for those to be sent to the Gulag. Instead of deportation (*deportatsiya*) or forcible relocation (*vyselenie*), the party and NKVD edicts preferred to speak about 'resettlement' (*pereselenie*). Such a use of language contributed to the dehumanisation of the victims.

The founder of the Soviet state, Vladimir Lenin, had believed that instead of the capitalist state that he defined as "an apparatus of suppression" the Bolsheviks would build a classless global community (Lenin 1969: 90–1). This utopia turned to the nightmare of mass killings and the destruction of dozens of Soviet minorities.

Dividing the analysis of Soviet mass violence into different but inter-related phases and dimensions makes it possible to investigate state-run violence against minorities as a continuous political process. Future research should investigate additional similarities and differences between Soviet crimes against humanity and other genocides.

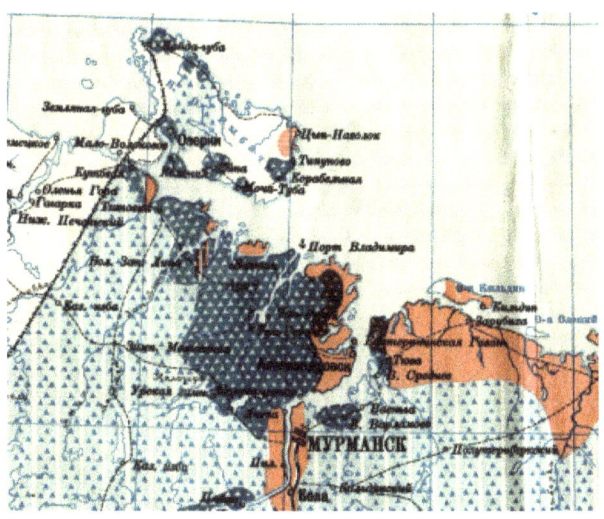

Top: Map of Russian Lappland, St. Petersburg, 1745 (Photographer: Andrej Kotljarchuk)

Bottom: Ethnographic map of the Murmansk region. Blue – Sami; deep blue – Finns; striped red – Norwegians; red – Russians (Photographer: Andrej Kotljarchuk)

Front page of the Finnish-language newspaper Polarnoin kollektivisti, no. 92, 17 Dec. 1937 (Courtesy of Russian National Library in St. Petersburg / Photographer: Andrej Kotljarchuk)

Mourning ribbon in the Sami language over Petr G. Chaporov (executed in 1937 by the NKVD in Leningrad), Levashovo Memorial Cemetery, St. Petersburg 2000 (Photographer: Aleksandr Stepanenko)

References

Bazhanov, B. (1990) *Bazhanov and the Damnation of Stalin*. Athens, Ohio: Ohio University Press.

Bendersky, J.W. (2000) *The 'Jewish Threat': Anti-Semitic Politics of the U.S. Army*. New York: Basic Books.

Berdieva, Y. P. (2000) *Gosudarstvenno-tserkovnye otnosheniia na Kol'skom poluostrove v pervoi treti XX veka*. Murmansk: State Pedagogical University. Diss.

Bilokin, S. (2000) *Mekhanizm bolshevistskogo nasiliia*. Kiev: [DMP 'Polimed'].

Blum, A. and Mespoulet, M. (2003) *L'anarchie bureaucratique: Pouvoir et statistique sous Staline*. Paris: Découverte.

Bogatstva Murmanskogo kraya: Itogi i perspektivy khoziaistvennogo razvitiya Kol'skogo poluostrova (1934). Moscow, Leningrad: Ogiz.

"Bystree likvidirovat' ostatki vreditel'skoi raboty v rayone" (1937) *Polarnyi kollektivist* (17 Oct.).

Carlbäck, H. (2000) "Svenskar i Ryssland – svenskt i Ryssland." *Människan i historien och samtiden: Festskrift till Alf W Johansson*, ed. by Björk, R. and Björklund, F. Stockholm: Hjalmarson & Högberg, 62–81.

Chapman, J. (1994) "Destruction of a Common Heritage: The Archaeology of War in Croatia, Bosnia and Hercegovina." *Antiquity* 68 (258), 120–6.

Chubar'ian, A. and Riste, O., eds (1997) *Sovetsko-Norvezhskie otnosheniia 1917–1955: Sbornik dokumentov*. Moscow: Russian Academy of Sciences.

Dönninghaus, V. (2009) *Minderheiten in Bedrängnis: Sowjetische Politik gegenüber Deutschen, Polen und anderen Diaspora-Nationalitäten 1917–1938*. Munich: Oldenbourg.

Drabkina, E. A. (1930) *Natsionalnyi i kolonialnyi vopros v tsarskoi Rossii*. Moscow: Izdatel'stvo Kommunisticheskoi akademii.

Dulić, T. (2005) *Utopias of Nation: Local Mass Killing in Bosnia and Herzegovina 1941–42*. Uppsala: University.

Eidlitz Kuoljok, K. (1985) *The Revolution in the North: Soviet Ethnography and Nationality Policy*. Stockholm: Almqvist och Wiksell.

Friedlander, H. (1980) "The Manipulation of Language." *The Holocaust: Ideology, Bureaucracy, and Genocide*, ed. by Friedlander, H. and Milton, S. Millwood, NY: Kraus International, 103–13.

Gatagova, L. S. (2005) *TsK RKP(b) – VKP(b) i natsionalnyi vopros, 1933–1945*. Moscow: Rosspen.

Gelb, M. (1995) "An Early Soviet Ethnic Deportation: The Far-Eastern Koreans." *Russian Review* 54, 389–412.

Glass, J. M. (1997) "Against the Indifference Hypothesis: The Holocaust and the Enthusiasts for Murder." *Political Psychology* 18 (1), 129–45.

Gretchen, S. (2004) *From Racism to Genocide: Anthropology in the Third Reich.* Urbana: University of Illinois Press.

Gribov, G. (1938) "Neitralitet na sluzhbe agressorov." *Pravda* (7 Sept.).

Gustafson, A. (2006) *Svenska sovjetemigranter: Om de svenska kommunisterna och emigrationen till Sovjetunionen på 1920- och 1930-talen.* Linköping: Nixon.

Gutsol, N.N., Vinogradova, S.N., and Samurokova, A.G. (2007) *Pereselennye gruppy kol'skikh saamov. Kola Sami Relocated Groups.* Apatity: Kola Research Center Press.

Herf, J. (2006) *The Jewish Enemy: Nazi Propaganda during World War II and the Holocaust.* Cambridge, Mass: Harvard University Press.

Hirsch, F. (2005) *Empire of Nations: Ethnographic Knowledge and the Making of the Soviet Union.* Ithaca: Cornell University Press.

Holquist, P. (2001) "To Count, to Extract, and to Exterminate: Population Statistics and Population Politics in Late Imperial and Soviet Russia." *A State of Nations: Empire and Nation-Making in the Age of Lenin and Stalin,* ed. by Suny, R. and Martin, T. Oxford: Oxford University Press, 111–44.

"Hôtes inopportuns et indésirables conseillers (lettre de Stockholm)." (1937) *Journal de Moscou* (12 Oct.).

Ivanov, N. "Hôtes Za izuchenie russkogo yazyka" (1938) *Polarnyi kollektivist* (1 Feb.).

Iwanow, M. (1991) *Pierwszy naród ukarany: Polacy w Związku Radzieckim w latach 1921-1939.* Warsaw, Wrocław: Państwowe Wydawnictwo Naukowe.

Jentoft, M. (2001) *De som dro østover: Kola-nordmennenes historie.* Oslo: Gyldendal.

Jentoft, M. and Goncharova, E. (2008) "Norvezhtsy i GULAG." *Almanakh Astes* 5, 91–129.

Jones, A. (2011) *Genocide: A Comprehensive Introduction,* 2nd edn. London: Routledge.

"K lovu ne gotoviatsia" (1939) *Polarnyi kollektivist* (2 Jan.).

Ken, O., Rupasov, A., and Samuelsson, L. (2005) *Shvetsiia v politike Moskvy 1930-1950.* Moscow: Rosspen.

Khlevnyuk, O. (1992) *1937: Stalin, NKVD i sovetskoe obshchestvo.* Moscow: Respublika.

Kisilev, A. (1999) "Saamskii zagovor." *Zhivaya Arktika* 3-4, 58–60.

Kostiainen, A. (1996) "Genocide in Soviet Karelia: Stalin's Terror and the Finns of Soviet Karelia." *Scandinavian Journal of History* 21 (4), 332–41.

Kotljarchuk, A. (2011) "Ukrainasvenskar i Gulagarkipelagen: Tvångsnormaliseringens teknik och kollektivt motstånd." *Historisk Tidskrift* 131 (1), 3–24.

Kotljarchuk, A. (2012a) *Shvedskie kolonisty Ukrainy v totalitarnykh experimentakh XX veka*. Moscow: Rosspen.

Kotljarchuk, A. (2012b) "Kola Sami in the Stalinist Terror: A Quantitative Analysis." *Journal of Northern Studies* 6 (2), 59–82.

Kozlov, A.I., ed. (2008) *Kolskie saamy v meniaushchimsia mire*. Moscow: Institut Naslediya.

Kuper, L. (1982) *Genocide: Its Political Use in the Twentieth Century*. New Haven: Yale University Press.

Kuromiya, H. (2007) *The Voices of the Dead: Stalin's Great Terror in the 1930s*. New Haven: Yale University Press.

Kuropiatnik, M. (1999) "Expeditions to Sami Territories: A History of the Studies of the Kola Sami in the 1920s–1930s." *Acta Borealia* 16 (1), 117–25.

Laine, A. (2001) "Deportation of Finns from the Murmansk Region to Soviet Karelia in 1940." *Aspects of Arctic and Sub-Arctic History: Proceedings of the International Congress on the History of the Arctic and Sub-Arctic Region*, ed. by Sigurðsson, I. and Skaptason, J. Reykjavík: University of Iceland Press, 155–64.

Leinonen, M. (2008) "The Filmans: Nomads at a Dead End." *Journal of Northern Studies* 2 (2), 51–75.

Lenin, V. (1962) "K voprosu o natsional'noi politike." *Polnoe sobranie sochinenii*, vol. 25. 5th edn. Moscow: Izdatel'stvo politicheskoi literatury.

Lenin, V. (1969) "Gosudarstvo i revolutsiya." *Polnoe sobranie sochinenii*, vol. 33. 5th edn. Moscow: Izdatel'stvo politicheskoi literatury.

Longerich, P. (2007) *Holocaust: The Nazi Persecution and Murder of the Jews*. Oxford: Oxford University Press.

Mann, M. (2005) *The Dark Side of Democracy: Explaining Ethnic Cleansing*. New York: Cambridge University Press.

Martin, T. (1998) "The Origins of Soviet Ethnic Cleansing." *The Journal of Modern History* 70 (4), 813–61.

Martin, T. (2001). *The Affirmative Action Empire: Nations and Nationalism in the Soviet Union, 1923–1939*. Ithaca: Cornell University Press.

Mikoliuk, O. V. (2003) *Politicheskie repressii na Murmane v 30-ye gody XX veka*. Murmansk: State Pedagogical University. Diss.

"Mitä tekee Tujunen?" (1937) *Polarnoin kollektivisti* (17 May).

Müller-Hill, B. (1998). *Murderous Science: Elimination by Scientific Selection of Jews, Gypsies, and Others in Germany, 1933-1945*. Plainview, New York: Cold Spring Harbor Laboratory Press.

Murmanskii okrug: Statistiko-ekonomicheskoe opisanie (1929). Murmansk: Izdatel'stvo Murmanskogo okruzhnogo ispolkoma.

Nahaylo, B. and Swoboda, V. (1990) *Soviet Disunion: A History of the Nationalities Problem in the USSR*. London: Hamilton.

Naimark, N.M. (2001) *Fires of Hatred: Ethnic Cleansing in Twentieth-Century Europe*. Cambridge, Mass.: Harvard University Press.

Naimark, N.M. (2010) *Stalin's Genocides*. Princeton: Princeton University Press.

"Natsionalisticheskie nastroeniya v Zapadnoi Litse" (1937) *Polarnyi kollektivist* (16 Sept.).

Nekrich, A. (1978) *The Punished Peoples: The Deportation and Fate of Soviet Minorities at the End of the Second World War*. New York: W.W. Norton.

Nielsen, J. P. (2005) "The Murman Coast and Russian Northern Policies ca. 1855-1917." In *the North My Nest is Made: Studies in the History of the Murman Colonization 1860-1940*, ed. by Iurchenko, A. and Nielsen, J. St. Petersburg: European University, 10-27.

Nilsson, R. (2008). *Foucault: En introduktion*. Malmö: Égalité.

"Norvezhskaya diplomaticheskaya missiya v Madride." (1937) *Pravda* (7 Jan.).

Obshchezhitie dla detei kolonistov Murmanskogo berega (1902). Arkhangelsk: Gubernskaya tipografiia.

Okhotin, N. and Roginskii, A. (1999) "Iz istorii 'nemetskoi operatsii' NKVD 1937-1938." *Repressii protiv sovetskikh nemtsev: Nakazannyi narod*. Moscow: Zven'ia, 35-74.

Orekhova, E. (2009) *Kolonizatsiya Murmanskogo berega Kolskogo poluostrova vo vtoroi polovine XIX - pervoi treti XX veka*. St. Petersburg: University Press.

"Otkazalas' razgovarivat'" (1937) *Polarnyi kollektivist* (4 Sept.).

Ovsiannikov, E. "Delo norvezhskogo kunsula Viklunda" (1994) *Pravda Severa* (13 July).

"Paikallisesta nationalismista ja kulttuuri-joukkotyön puuttumisesta oserkossa Kolhoosi Rajkastaja" (1937) *Polarnoin kollektivisti* (17 May).

Pobol, N.L. and Poljan, P.M. (2005) *Stalinskie deportatsii 1928-1953*. Moscow: Mezhdunarodnyi fond Demokratiya.

Poljan, P. (2004) *Against Their Will: The History and Geography of Forced Migrations in the USSR*. Budapest: Central European University Press.

Pöppel, L. (2007) *The Rhetoric of Pravda Editorials: A Diachronic Study of a Political Genre*. Stockholm: University.

Ramanava, I. (2007) "Zhytsio va umovakh savetskaha pahranichcha." *Pogranicza Białorusi w perspektywie interdyscyplinarnej*. Warsaw: Wydawnictwo DiG, 73–101.

"Razgromit' burzhuaznykh natsionalistov do kontsa" (1937) *Polarnaya Pravda* (16 Oct.).

"Razooblachennye zagovory." (1937) *Pionerskaya Pravda* (20 Dec.).

Repressii protiv polakov i polskikh grazhdan (1997). Moscow: Zven'ia.

Repressii protiv sovetskikh nemtsev. Nakazannyi narod (1999). Moscow: Zven'ia.

Samuelson, L. and Sorokin, A. (2007) "Den ryska 'arkivrevolutionen': Källvolymer belyser sovjetepokens mörka sidor." *Historisk Tidskrift* 127 (4), 739–56.

Savilova, S. (2008) "Politicheskie repressii protiv kol'skikh finnov." *Almanakh Astes* 5, 130–49.

Savin, A. (2012) "Etnizatsiya stalinisma? Natsionalnye i kulatskaya operatsii NKVD: Sravnitel'nyi aspekt." *Rossiya* 21 (3), 40–61.

Shashkov, V.Y. (2000) *Repressi v SSSR protiv krestyan i sud´by pereselentsev Karelo-Murmanskogo kraya*. Murmansk: State Pedagogical Institute.

Shestaya sessia Verkhovnogo soveta SSSR 29 marta – 4 aprelia 1940 goda: Stenograficheskii otchet (1940). Moscow: Izdatel'stvo Verkhovnogo soveta.

Shpionam i izmennikam rodiny ne budet pochshady: V pomochsh' bibliotekariam (1937). Leningrad: Leningradskoe gosudarstvennoe izdatel'stvo.

Shpionazh i razvedka kapitalisticheskikh gosudarstv: V pomochsh' propagandistu i besedchiku (1937). Leningrad: Leningradskoe gosudarstvennoe izdatel'stvo.

Shrader, T. (2005) "Legislative Aspects of Norwegian Colonization of Murman, 1860–1915." *In the North My Nest is Made: Studies in the History of the Murman Colonization 1860–1940*, ed. by Iurchenko, A. and Nielsen, J. St. Petersburg: European University, 61–85.

Skogan, J. (1992) *Norge, Russland og betydningen av Kola-halvøya i historisk lys*. Oslo: Norsk Utenrikspolitisk Institut.

Slezkine, Y. (1994) *Arctic Mirrors: Russia and the Small Peoples of the North*. Ithaca: Cornell University Press.

Stalin, I. (1997) *Sochineniya*, vol. 14. Moscow: Pisatel'.

Sword, K. (1994) *Deportation and Exile: Poles in the Soviet Union, 1939–48*. Basingstoke: Palgrave Macmillan.

Tarle, E. (1937) "Uroki istorii." *Izvestia* (22 Feb.).

Thorsen, L. and Thorsen, T. (1991) *Russland via Vardø: Nordmenn på Murmankysten*. Bodø: Skutvik.

Thorvaldsen, G. (2011) "Household Structure in the Multiethnic Barents Region: A Local Case Study." *The 1926/27 Soviet Polar Census Expeditions*, ed. by Anderson, D. New York: Berghahn Books, 117–32.

Tinchenko, Y., ed. (2011–12) *Kniga ucheta lits, sostoyavshikh na osobom uchete byvshikh belykh ofitserov v organakh GPU Ukrainy*, vol. 1–4. Kharkiv: Sluzhba bezopasntosti Ukrainy.

Vatlin, A. (2004) *Terror rayonnogo mashtaba: Massovye operatsii NKVD v Kuntsevskom rayone Moskovskoi oblasti v 1937–1938 godakh*. Moscow: Rosspen.

Vneshniya politika SSSR: Sbornik dokumentov (1946), vol. 4: *1935–1941*. Moscow: Izdatel'stvo gazety Pravda.

Volens, N.V., ed. (1926) *Kolonisty Murmana i ikh khoziaistvo: Materialy statistico-ekonomicheskogo issledovaniya 1921–1922*. Moscow: Nauchno-tekhnicheskii otdel Instituta po izucheniiu severa.

Werth, N. (2003) "The Mechanism of a Mass Crime: The Great Terror in the Soviet Union, 1937–38." *The Specter of Genocide: Mass Murder in Historical Perspective*, ed. by Gellately, R. and Kiernan, B. Cambridge: Cambridge University Press, 215–39.

Wråkberg, U. (2013) "Science and Industry in Northern Russia from a Nordic Perspective." *Science, Geopolitics and Culture in the Polar Region: Norden beyond Borders*, ed. by Sverker, S. Farnham: Ashgate, 195–219.

Wretling, A. (1931) *Tvångsarbete i Sovjetunionen?* Stockholm: Arbetarkultur.

Zakovskii, L.M. (1937) *Shpionov, diversnatov i vreditelei unichtozhim do kontsa*. Moscow: Partizdat.

Zhiromskaya, V. (1991) "Statistika 1930-kh godov v sisteme gosudarstvennoi vlasti." *Vlast' i obshchestvo v SSSR politika repressii*. Moscow: Russian Academy of Scienses, 146–63.

Zilver, L. S. (1938) *Byt' nacheku: V pomochsh' pionervozhatomu: Besedy v pionerskom lagere*. Moscow: Izdatel'stvo TsK VLKSM Molodaya gvardiia.

4. An Unimaginable Community: The SS Idea of a 'Greater Germanic Reich' and the German Minority in Denmark

Steffen Werther

During the early decades of the twentieth century, the emergence of scientific racial theory combined with the German Reich's general enthusiasm for everything Germanic and Nordic contributed to what in Germany was termed the 'Nordic Idea' (*Nordischer Gedanke*). The concept included the notion that the *Völker* of the 'Nordic Race' shared a community of fate. Leading National Socialists such as Heinrich Himmler, Alfred Rosenberg, and Walther Darré seized upon the idea and developed it further. Himmler transformed the SS into the most influential and consistent advocate of the resultant 'Greater Germanic Idea' (*großgermanische Idee*). The creation of a Reich of 'Germanic *Völker*' was among its primary goals. This became a problem for the populations of countries which the Germans, and, by extension, the SS occupied, not least because of Himmler's determination to recruit and educate other 'Germanics' in, for example, Scandinavia, for his international *Waffen-SS* (Wegner 2006).

In terms of practical implementation the ideology was dependent on the idea of 'race' as the unifying ground for the Greater Germanic commonwealth. But the Greater Germanic Reich ran aground on the contradiction between two fundamental national-socialist constructions: that of 'race' (*Rasse*), and that of the (national) sovereignty of a 'people' (*Volk*). Many groups and parties in what were seen as Germanic countries found national-socialist ideas attractive, but were worried about the Greater Germanic Idea's threat to national sovereignty. The supra-national aspect of the project often led them to reject the offer of racial unification. They were wary of what they saw as camouflaged German imperialism, a threat to their nation's independence.

This chapter examines the antagonism between *Volk* sovereignty and racial community. However, the focus is not on the main subjects of this idea, that is, the Norwegians and Danes – and first and foremost, Norwegian and Danish Nazis – but on the only German minority group living in Scandinavia: that of Denmark's North Schleswig.[1] This minority, finding themselves on the 'wrong' side of the German–Danish border after the Versailles plebiscite in 1920, had long sought for a border revision – that is, to move the border north again, allowing them to reunite with the Reich. Ironically, the occupation of Denmark by the German army did little to advance their cause. On the contrary: they were called on to suppress this, their key demand. No revision of the border was made, even after the German occupation in 1940.

The primary sources for this study are so-called *Schulungsbriefe* (a sort of in-house didactic pamphlet) published between 1940 and 1945 by the German minority's National Socialist German Workers' Party of North Schleswig (*Nationalsozialistische Deutsche Arbeiter Partei – Nordschleswig* or NSDAP-N). The NSDAP-N, which was the minority's only political party, was led by veterinarian Jens Möller. The *Schulungsbriefe* contained guidelines for the training and education of full party members. Such (re)education had become necessary because some of the German minority organisation's fundamental political positions, such as those concerning relations to the Danish National Socialists and the issue of border revision, were being criticised by authorities in Germany. The German minority leadership had been instructed by the local representative of the German Foreign Office (*Auswärtiges Amt*) and the SS Ethnic German Liaison Office (*Volksdeutsche Mittelstelle,* VoMi) that the NSDAP-N would have to induce its member base to follow a new political course – otherwise, there would be serious complications.

In this article, I analyse how the German minority leadership read, challenged, and manipulated the SS's concept of the Greater German Community, with particular attention to the use of the concepts race and *Volk*. My thesis is that Denmark's German minority was, in fact, placed in a politically and ideologically difficult situation when the Germans occupied Denmark and it became necessary to cooperate with the SS. Paradoxically, the SS's celebration of Germanic racial identity posed a threat to the minority leadership's political goals, to the minority's identity, and, in the end, to the minority's existence. Minority leaders sought to maintain what

---

[1] The Danish term for North Schleswig is *Sønderjylland* (South Jutland).

could be called a *völkisch* line, that is, a 'we are *Germans* and because of that, where *we* live is part of Germany – and should be within German state borders'. This was the only attitude that would not alienate their followers. However, they were in no position to refuse outright the demands and requests for alternative attitudes emanating from the SS. They had, as a result, to show a certain amount of ideological and political flexibility.

The period of German occupation has always been a focal point of Danish history-writing (for comprehensive overviews see, e.g., Poulsen 2002; Christensen, Lund, Olesen, and Sørensen 2005). The role played by the German minority, including the matters mentioned above, has received its share of attention. My source material, however, makes possible a more detailed understanding of and hence provides insights into the close links between, on one side, National Socialism's political praxis and ideology and, on the other, the very specific manner in how this relationship was handled in the region.

In his pioneer study of the German minority and German border policy between 1933 and 1939 Sven Tägil (1970) stressed that the National Socialist ideal of 'Nordic race' affected the border policy. Because of this ideal, Schleswig was treated as something of a special case, which made it difficult for the ethnic-nationalist confrontation course preferred by the German minority to assert itself. According to Tägil, ideological considerations played a role here. So did the German Foreign Office, which, entirely focused on foreign relations, was concerned with preventing a deterioration of Germany's relationship to Denmark, a rift of which England could take advantage.

In a seminal text, Henrik Skov Kristensen (2004), who concentrates on the border question in the days following the German occupation of Denmark, tries to answer why the border had not been changed. He points out that the German acceptance of the otherwise despised 'Versailles border' had been guaranteed in a German memorandum of 9 April 1940. In this memorandum, accepted "under protest" by the Danish government, Germany promised to respect Denmark's territorial integrity in return for the Danish capitulation. Kristensen has also published a biographical article on the German minority leader Jens Möller, in which he discusses, among other things, Möller's inner conflict – torn between wanting to pursue active border-revision politics while being duty-bound to obey instructions to the contrary emanating from Germany and especially the SS (Kristensen 2008; for the political organisation of the minority, see Becker-Christensen 2003).

In his classic work on the history of the minority during the German occupation of 1940–45, Johan Peter Noack (1974) also discusses the Greater Germanic Idea. Noack claims that in fact there was sporadic evidence of 'Greater Germanic' fantasies on German decision-making, but that these were limited to the period between New Year 1939 and Autumn 1940. Noack assumes that the Greater Germanic Idea was, after the occupation of Denmark and Norway, primarily used to obscure the power-political violation. However, Noack does not underestimate the influence of the Greater Germanic Idea when it comes to the SS. On the contrary, he identifies this idea as key for recruitment of Danes to the Waffen-SS. Noack believes that because the SS depended on the Danish Nazi party for its Danish recruits, it often attempted to interfere in the politics of the minority leaders. Again, the German minority might feel frustrated as its *völkisch* border-revision policy, which would have harmed the SS's cooperation with the Danish Nazis, was routinely suppressed.

Background: The 'Nordic minority'

In the plebiscite of 1920, codified in the Versailles treaty, 75 per cent of the population of North Schleswig had voted for accession to Denmark. As a consequence, about 30,000 German North Schleswigians became a minority in Denmark. The highest goal of this group's interest organisations was to safe-guard 'German culture', German real estate (*Boden*), and to bring about a border revision.

After 1933 the German Nazis had important political and military reasons for not acting on this issue, but there were also ideological factors inherent in the Greater Germanic ideology. From the perspective of race, as defined by Nazi thinkers, the German border to Denmark was the only Versailles border that divided two Germanic territories, and North Schleswig held the only German minority living inside a 'Germanic' country. In Poland, Alsace-Lorraine and Czechoslovakia, Nazi propaganda spoke of 'foreign domination'. There, the German minorities (the so-called *Volksdeutsche*, that is, ethnic Germans living outside of the Reich) were surrounded by racial aliens. In Denmark, by contrast, the minority lived among 'racial brothers'. National economist and later National Socialist Karl C. Thalheim had already 1931 written, in his work on the *Grenzlandsdeutschtum* (border-land Germans) that:

> The special character upon which the problem of *Grenzlandsdeutschtum* in North Schleswig is founded – in contrast to the questions arising

concerning our east and west borders – is the fact that the German *Volkstum* stands, here, in a border-struggle with a same-tribe, Germanic *Volkstum* (Thalheim 1931: 41).[2]

This 'special character' at least partially explains why North Schleswig, alone among the parts of former Germany lost at the end of the First World War via plebiscite or decree, was never re-annexed or re-united with the Reich, despite the fact that the annulment of the Versailles treaty was the second point of the Nazi Party's programme. In the eyes of the SS, in particular, the German–Danish border constituted not a dividing line but a surface of contact between two Germanic people, the Germans and the Danes. It was a bridge to the North – destined, it was thought, to play a special role in the development of the Germanic Reich.

Shortly after the German forces had marched into Denmark, the SS instigated cooperation with two Danish parties: Denmark's National Socialist Workers' Party (*Danmarks National Socialistisk Arbejder Parti*, DNSAP) and the German minority's NSDAP-N. Both were National Socialist; both competed for rather small memberships; both had their organisational point of gravity in North Schleswig (Tägil 1970: 133; Rasmussen 2004: 141; Djursaa 1981: 59).[3] On one point, however, they differed fundamentally: While DNSAP found its supporters among those with Danish sympathies, the NSDAP-N voters were members of the German minority in Denmark.

The two parties had been in opposition since the early 1930s. The bone of contention was the conflict between Danish and German minority ethnic-national – in German *völkisch* – aspirations (Werther 2012: 69–127). The leader of Denmark's National Socialist Party, Frits Clausen, was a native of the region. As a nationalist he supported the Danish view in issues of borderland conflict, rebuffing the German minority's demands for a border revision (on the DNSAP see Lauridsen 2002). As a counter-move, he made use of, among other things, the Nazis' propaganda on behalf of the Nordic Idea, according to which, he argued, no border revision would be necessary: the German minority was already living in a Germanic country.

---

[2] *Volkstum* is untranslatable, meaning, roughly the physical and cultural essence and character of a given people.
[3] In 1939 the NSDAP-N received 15.9 percent, or 15,500 votes, in the Danish province Sønderjylland (i.e., North Schleswig). The DNSAP received 4.3 percent of the total vote in Sønderjylland (and 1.3 percent in the rest of the country, 31,000 votes in total).

The Waffen-SS began to recruit volunteers from both Danish and German minority nazi groups directly after the occupation in April 1940. They propagated the Greater Germanic Idea among both the DNSAP, the Danish National Socialists, and among the 'ethnically German' (*volksdeutsche*) minority's NSDAP-N. This is a significant difference in recruitment when compared to East Europe. In the latter area, the Waffen-SS recruited *Volksdeutsche* – that is, Germans living in foreign countries – primarily on ethnic bases. In Denmark, to the disgust of the German minority, they were recruited as Germanics – that is, not as Germans, but as representing a pure Nordic racial type – a categorisation which put the minority on par with the despised Danes who were considered as equally racially pure. A Foreign Office statement mandated that the SS's recruitment in North Schleswig "should have nothing to do with *Volkstum*". Rather, Himmler tried to recruit especially "racially pure Nordic types" for the Waffen-SS.[4]

After the occupation, North Schleswig's 'racial' particularity was declared a guiding principle in German minority politics, not only by the SS Head office (*SS-Hauptamt*) and the SS's VoMi, but also by the German Foreign Office. The closing remarks of a conference between the VoMi and the Foreign Office are a good example:

> Unlike the battle of *Völker* [*Volkstumskampf*] of south-eastern Europe, the *Volksdeutsche* of North Schleswig face a racially and culturally equal opponent. [...] In attempting the overall settlement of *volksdeutsche* matters in North Schleswig, one cannot proceed from local considerations [that is, from what the German minority wanted], but must take into account top-level political, especially Greater Germanic goals.[5]

This policy left the minority-German actors little leeway. NSDAP-N leader Jens Möller tried to push border revision by arguing that SS's much-treasured designation of North Schleswig as a bridge between Germany and Scandinavia was possible only if the 'Schleswig issue' (of border revision) was resolved. Only as "one Schleswig under German leadership would this country again finally serve its real purpose: to be a bridge to the North".[6] Möller thus tried to make the achievement of the SS's idea of a general reconciliation between all Germanics, North Schleswig as the bridge

---

[4] Note from Foreign Office on the planned recruitment for the Waffen-SS in Denmark, 16 May1939 (PKB 1953: doc. 262).
[5] Report from a *volkspolitische Tagung* of the Foreign Office and by representatives of the VoMi, 1 Oct. 1941.
[6] Report by Möller, 21 Oct. 1940 (PKB 1953: doc. 59, p. 687).

between "South Germanics and North Germanics", conditional upon a border revision. Soon, this strategy would be elaborated in the NSDAP-N's *Schulungsbriefe*.

In the meantime, until Autumn 1940, the party leadership of NSDAP-N either opposed or ignored the Greater Germanic Idea. The fact that the SS's Greater Germanic propaganda was largely directed to Scandinavians, not Germans, complicated the situation further. Few in the German minority were attracted to the SS's idea of Nordic racial supremacy, seeing that it meant that they, who had German *Volksangehörigkeit*, would have to content themselves with being Danish citizens living in a Germanic country. On the contrary: as a 'ethnic group' or *Volksgruppe*, they feared that the Greater Germanic Idea would supplant the notion, very important to them, of having special status, even in Germanic Denmark, as part of the German *Volksgemeinschaft* (people's community). After all, the only reason the SS gave for telling the NSDAP-N to actively support a Greater Germanic line was that by doing so the NSDAP-N would serve the 'interest of the Reich'.

Finally, the NSDAP-N leadership found itself forced to take a formal stance on the Greater Germanic Idea. It was not possible to staunchly refuse to cooperate, but NSDAP-N leaders could propose their own reading. As the SS ideology was quite vague in its formulation, there was room for interpretation (Werther 2012: 128–173). The NSDAP-N's reinterpretation was particularly clear in the party's *Schulungsbriefe*, which were produced in order to communicate the new ideological line to the party's followers, not least by making 'Germanic' more digestible. Their interpretations of the Greater Germanic Idea served, on the one hand, as arguments to use against the SS's unwanted demands, and, on the other, to pacify their own supporters, who were deeply disappointed by the non-occurrence of a border revision.

The Schulungsbriefe of the NSDAP-N

Starting in the fall of 1940, the NSDP-N *Schulungsbriefe* appeared at regular intervals of about every one to two months. Spanning four to six printed pages, they were meant for internal use, for making known the current party position on various questions, and for recruiting to the party. The publication was not, however, directed towards individual party members. Rather, the *Schulungsbriefe* served the party's propagandists, its local leaders, speakers and educational leaders as an instruction manual for teaching party members party ideology. Certain *Schulungsbriefe* also provided concrete didactic remarks and instructions.

By issuing such *Schulungsbriefe*, the leaders of the German minority wished to impose a homogeneous political and ideological direction upon the NSDAP-N, so that party members would, in the future, act in concert, at least on the most important issues, and so that conflicts with agencies of the German Reich could be avoided. Through this "inner securing" of the party, an "outer expansion" of the German minority group was to be achieved.[7] Referring to talks with the VoMi in December 1940, the party leadership formulated the goals as follows:

> The political instruction serves a double purpose. It shall give party comrades a weapon in their hands for the fight for their *Heimat*. Secondly, it will open their eyes to the great tasks of a new Germanic future and for the place of the Nordic neighbour *Volk* in this field of action.[8]

The term 'fight for the *Heimat*' is a veiled allusion to border revision. Locals – but hopefully not the SS – would know what was meant. Intimations, circumlocutions, and metaphors were important means of getting around the proscription against alluding to the border question.

Like the party, the *Schulungsbriefe* were very concerned with the Greater Germanic Idea. It was seen, at first, as an obstacle to a border revision. In time, however, it was treated more sympathetically, in that it increasingly served as a vehicle for actually advocating border revision in the teeth of disapproval by the occupying German forces.

The author of the *Schulungsbriefe* was Asmus Wilhelm Jürgensen (1902– 72), who claimed the title *Landesschulungsleiter* (County Educational Leader) and who as of Autumn 1940 was head of the Educational Bureau (*Schulungsamt*) of the NSDAP-N. In 1943, Jürgensen took over the party's Bureau for Press and Propaganda. He was also active in Waffen-SS recruitment in North Schleswig. Jürgensen came from South Schleswig; a German citizen, he had moved to North Schleswig in 1930 as a teacher. Here he began to write articles on border policy issues for the newspaper *Nordschleswigsche Zeitung*, and participated actively in the political organ-

---

[7] Quotes from a report of the German consulate on the *Leergebietstätigkeit der deutschen Volksgruppe*. Lanwer to Gesandtschaft, 19 June 1941 (PKB 1953: doc. 72, pp. 708–9).
[8] Report by the German minority North Schleswig dated Feb. 1941, National Archives of Denmark (Rigsarkivet, henceforth NAD), Danica, Tyske arkivalier om Danmark, Auswärtiges Amt (Foreign Ministry of Germany, henceforth FMG), 388.

isations of the German minority. His declared goal was a border revision; his view of Danes was hostile enough to earn him not only the hatred of Danes but the reprimands of German occupational forces.⁹

After the war, Jürgensen claimed that he had been entirely free to decide on the content of the *Schulungsbriefe*, that he had not had to submit them to the Party Council Meetings, and that only in isolated cases did he even "familiarise" party leader Möller with the contents. This is questionable.¹⁰ After all, the contents of the *Schulungsbriefe* were meant to present the party's opinion on significant and sensitive issues, issues that could decide the future of the German minority as *Volksgruppe*. However, even if Jürgensen had acted entirely on his own, the party leadership never expressed criticism of the *Schulungsbriefe*, and so probably approved of their content, at least after the fact.

The first positions taken

The first *Schulungsbrief der NSDAP-N* appeared in Autumn 1940. This debut issue was entitled "Our Schleswig and the Germanic Work of Adolf Hitler", and explicitly discussed the Greater Germanic Idea.¹¹

By the summer of 1940, experience had shown the minority leadership that the Greater Germanic Idea was being taken more seriously than ever in Germany. The leaders were also informed of, and very much worried about, the Danish National Socialists' cooperation with German agencies, such as Foreign Office and the SS. After all, they knew all too well that the Danish National Socialist leader, Frits Clausen, was hostile to border revision, and therefore feared lest he gain power and influence. Possibly, the minority leadership was also familiar with the content of a report by DNSAP-friendly representative of the SS Secret Service (SD), Eberhard Löw, and Foreign Office representative Gustav Meissner. This report had rejected a "territorial reintegration of North Schleswig" as a death blow to "Germanic

---

⁹ Statement during interrogation by Larsen and Stehr, 21 Dec. 1945 (PKB 1953, doc. 174, pp. 233–4); Lanwer to Kassler, 26 Nov. 1941 (ibid., doc. 77, p. 715); Lanwer to Kassler, 17 Dec. 1941 (ibid., doc. 78, pp. 716–7) and statement by Lanwer, 1 Oct. 1946 (ibid., doc. 175, pp. 234–5).

¹⁰ Statement by Jürgensen during interrogation, 20 March 1946. Landsarkivet for Sønderjylland Aabenraa (LAA, Provincial Archives of Southern Jutland), Politikommandørens arkiv (PK, Archives of the Police Commander), 221.

¹¹ *Schulungsbrief der NSDAP-N*, no. 1, "Unser Schleswig und das germanische Werk Adolf Hitlers." Undated, but appearing before 21 Nov. 1940 (see Noack 1975: 59, footnote 2). LAA, PK 324 (earlier 313) and PK 308 (published, in part, in PKB 1953: doc. 69, pp. 701–2).

policy"; it would bring to naught the work of German-friendly groups. In the report, Löw and Meissner state that "a great task of the future" awaited the German minority "from inside the Danish border".[12] Indeed, that autumn, a NSDAP-N regional leader had openly campaigned for the German minority's conciliation with the Danish National Socialists (see Paysen 1941). He had used the Greater Germanic Idea to justify his actions, and furthermore did so with the support of the SS. It was clearly time for the NSDAP-N to give its own interpretation to the Greater Germanic Idea, before the political damage became egregious.

The Autumn 1940 *Schulungsbrief*, accordingly, opened by emphasising the self-evident leadership of Germany in the "new Europe" and the "Germanic space" – referring to what was termed *Großraumtheorie* (see Kletzin 2002: 41; Herbert 2001: 271–98; Blindow 1999: 58–62). This is a theory of geopolitical spheres of influence and interests developed by Carl Schmitt before the war and picked up by National Socialist ideologues. It explicitly contained a "right of *Völker*" and a "right for intervention on behalf of *Völker*", that is, intervention on behalf of members of one's *Volk* living abroad.

Schmitt's theory could be used as a basis for advancing a Greater *German* Reich based on *völkisch* rather than racial community (Blindow 1999: 58). We can see this in the *Schulungsbriefe* that show elements plucked from the *Großraumtheorie*, not least as the concept was further developed by SS member Werner Best (as *völkische Großraumordnung*, see Herbert 2001: 277). These theories not only legitimised Germany's but also the minority *Volksgruppe*'s claim to leadership in the region, as part of not a race, but a *Volk*.

The "new Europe", so said the Autumn 1940 *Schulungsbrief*, was an "organic whole under the leadership of Germany" in which other *Völker* would be "integrated". "The old cant of equality and equal rights of different *Völker*" was thus a thing of the past, the writer argued: As each *Volk* would be positioned differently, in the new order, according to its abilities and merit – as are individuals within a human community – "unfailingly, in the new great *Völkergemeinschaften* that arise there will be leaders and followers". Germans, unsurprisingly, were identified as the "leader *Volk*" in Germanic space. Germany was "the largest Germanic unit in the new Greater Germanic space. The right to leadership comes to Germany because of its size and merit". The

---

[12] Note from Meissner and Löw on the political situation in Denmark, 10 July 1940 (PKB 1954: doc. 63, pp. 126ff).

word "integrated" combined with the entitlement to "leadership" made it clear that in the eyes of the German minority, the future ought to entail a subordination of other "Germanic *Völker*" to Germany.

After having settled the question of leadership in Europe, the *Schulungsbrief* devoted itself to the *Heimat* – that is, the region in which the German minority lived – noting that the party comrades had a dual task: As German North Schleswigians they had to "fight for a German *Heimat*" while as German National Socialists they also had "to contribute to the remaking of the Greater Germanic Empire".

> At first, it might seem that fulfilment of one task would exclude the fulfilment of the other. Whoever fights for a German North Schleswig steps into a battle position against the Danes and thereby harms the Greater Germanic efforts. Whoever, on the other hand, takes a position for the Greater Germanic idea must withdraw as a national adversary of Danes in the border land.[13]

This astute analysis of the situation was, however, immediately repudiated. The text continued: "This conception is fundamentally erroneous. It can only be argued by someone who does not know our *Heimat*". In that sentence, the NSDAP-N *Schulungsbrief* rejected the judgment of any outside powers (including the SS) on the irreconcilability of these two ideas, for it held that outsiders lacked the knowledge necessary to appraise the North Schleswig situation. The *Schulungsbrief* went on to emphasise that each minority leader had obligations towards the German North Schleswigians, "whose whole longing and whose whole hope [was] the Reich", that is, for a border revision. This, one could not deprive them of. At the same time, however, there were obligations to the *Führer*. As his followers, one must keep in sight and fight for the "great task of our time" (that is, the Greater Germanic Reich).

The obvious impossibility of fighting both for making North Schleswig a part of Germany and the "creation of the Greater Germanic Reich" was vehemently denied. On the contrary, the writer claimed, "the fulfilment of the one task is necessary in order to fulfil the second", for the "road to the North [...] always [has gone] through Schleswig, never around Schleswig". The *Schulungsbrief* writer followed SS doctrine in describing the military occupation of Denmark as necessitating a further ideological conquest:

---

[13] "Unser Schleswig und das germanische Werk Adolf Hitlers" (note 11).

If the Greater Germanic community under German leadership is to come into existence, then this world view must be victorious also in the North. It is no use to integrate these *Völker* merely on the surface; they must also be won over inwardly.[14]

The necessity of executing a border revision before going on to the Greater Germanic community was justified by arguing that the 'Schleswig Question' poisoned the relationship between Germans and Danes. In the *Schulungsbrief* it was argued, that only if a solution to this problem was found – and here, only a "German solution" (border revision) was conceivable – could the North be brought to believe in a "Germanic community". North Schleswig had always been a "bridge between the Germanic south and the Germanic north", the *Schulungsbrief* continued, and if it was to fulfil this function again, a border revision was mandatory. The *völkische* work of the German minority was therefore, the author claimed, in fact, "in a great measure a service to the Greater Germanic Reich of Adolf Hitler".

There was, thus, no attempt to launch a complete rejection of the Greater Germanic Idea. Instead, the NSDAP-N tried to portray itself as an advocate of the idea while imbuing it with its own political goals. In order not to be forced to give up the demand for a border revision, the *Schulungsbriefe* redefined the German minority's ultimate goal, claiming that border revision was only an (unavoidable) way-station towards the Greater Germanic Reich. The party could thus keep its original goal, yet still appear as openly faithful, Germanic-thinking National Socialists striving for Greater Germanic fulfilment.

In a subsequent *Schulungsbrief*, the party rank and file was appeased with the promise that the NSDAP-N would not lose sight of the role of what it termed the "every-day German *völkisch* detail work in the border land" despite "larger political contexts". This alludes to the German minority's self-defined role as the protector of Germanness (*Deutschtum*) in the border region. It was even understandable, it was emphasised, if, "in light of the general situation" the man-in-the-street *Volksgruppe* member often had difficulty understanding the leadership's position. But the writer was adamant on one thing: the new direction was "no about-turn". Rather, the party was "placing an old task within [the scope of] a greater, far-reaching responsibility. We revive the old German task within a greater project". The NSDAP-N-leadership had, it was claimed, merely "raised the narrow

[14] Ibid.

Schleswig question to the breadth of future Europe", thus uniting "the development of our own position [...] with cooperation for the creation of a community of fate that included all German *Völker*". The *Volksgruppe* would not shirk this greater, double task.[15]

This is a clear example of how party publicists attempted to reconcile SS policy with the party's own goals, and justify a political-ideological shift in position to party supporters. After the war, a former NSDAP-N official stated that what he now called his "policy of reconciliation" had, in fact, led to "a rather fierce [negative] reaction within the minority". He had, indeed, been forced to explain himself at various party educational evenings, the so-called *Schulungsabende*.[16]

'Völkisch hierarchy' rather than 'Germanic equality'

With the slogan "without [border] revision, no German–Danish understanding", the *Schulungsbriefe* made a clear qualitative distinction between *Volk* and race. This distinction they turned into a rhetorical tool, repeatedly emphasising that, although the Danes were indeed the Germans' racial equals, they were still inferior as a *Volk*. It is probably because of their investment in the distinction between *Volk* and race that the NSDAP-N neither publicly, nor in its communications with the SS, took advantage of being the only German minority that also had a 'Nordic affiliation', and thus a very high racial status. Perhaps an open endorsement of the SS racial theory's description of them as a 'Nordic minority' might have brought them substantial benefits. After all, the maps of the SS racial scientists showed a high concentration of 'Nordic blood' in North Schleswig, which confirmed the racial superiority of the minority not only over many so-called *Volksgenossen* from the Reich, but also and especially over German minorities in east and south-east Europe.

Of course, the NSDAP-N also brought up 'race' and 'racial equality'. After all, the concepts were essential to the Greater Germanic Idea. Each time the term occurred, however, the *Schulungsbriefe* would immediately tack on an explicit reference to the category of *Völker*. This was, in fact, the minority's ideological last-ditch position. Not even the SS could breach its ramparts. The *Schulungbriefe* thus advanced the *Volksgemeinschaft* to counter the SS's (imagined) racial Germanic community. Only this would

---

[15] *Schulungsbrief* 2nd Series, no. 1, "Die Revolution der Grenzlandhaltung." LAA, PK 221.
[16] Statement during interrogation by Jürgensen, 20 March 1946. LAA, PK 221.

allow them, as Germans, to escape the embrace of the hated racial confreres, the borderland Danes.

Accordingly, *Volk* appears again and again. As a key NSDAP-N formulation puts it, "National socialism is the natural recognition of the *Volksgemeinschaft*". The latter was defined as a "God-given unity"[17] and the "cornerstone of a new world order".[18] A later *Schulungsbrief* even speaks of a "*völkischen* era", in which the "*Volk* [...] is the first and decisive factor".[19] By declaring the primacy of the *Volk*, further, the NSDAP-writer could explain why, despite the demands of the SS, when it came to the "German task in North Schleswig [...] nothing [has] changed".[20] For this task meant, above all, holding fast to the position of *Deutschtum*. According to the author, the victory and breakthrough of National Socialism was dependent on the strength of the German *Volk*. For this reason, no "position must be lost, even vis-à-vis a blood-related *Volk*" (i.e., the Danes). The German minority was, in short, to continue its *völkisch* crusade. This would have to be done, the author claimed, as long as Greater Germanic unity was not yet "reality" – that is, not in the foreseeable future.[21] In the meantime, according to NSDAP-N:

> Humans as individuals are equal. Germans and Danes have the same blood in their veins. What made them distinctive, today, in terms of value, as well, is the [relative] strength of the *völkischen* community to which they belong.[22]

In *Schulungsbrief* no. 2, which has the title "Volkstum als tragende Kraft" (The Fundamental Power of *Volkstum*), the NSDAP-N position is expressed with exceptional clarity.[23] The *Schulungsbrief* took up other areas reconquered and formally re-annexed by the Germans, such as the Saarland, Sudetenland, Memelland, and Danzig. All of these were seen as models for North Schleswig. In these areas, although re-annexation lay with Hitler, the ground had been laid by the extensive efforts of the local German minorities, the writer claimed. "The German minority prepares for the de-

---

[17] *Schulungsbrief der NSDAP-N*, no. 2, ca. Dec. 1940, "Das Volkstum als tragende Kraft." LAA, PK 308.
[18] "Die Revolution der Grenzlandhaltung" (note 15).
[19] *Schulungsbrief* 2nd series, no. 9, "Zwischen Winter und Sommer." LAA, PK 308.
[20] "Die Revolution der Grenzlandhaltung" (note 15).
[21] "Die Revolution der Grenzlandhaltung" (note 15).
[22] *Schulungsbrief* no. 7, "Das deutsch-dänische Verhältnis", undated, appeared in mid-1941.
[23] "Das Volkstum als tragende Kraft" (note 17).

cision through their *völkischen* efforts, the *Führer* makes the decision". It was "therefore idle to talk" – at least, at present – "about border-revision plans and border-moving deadlines". Rather, the North-Schleswig problem had to be brought to a state of *"völkischer Reife"* (*völkisch* ripeness). The task of the German minority was therefore to "consolidate and carry forward our *Volkstum*". In this, unsurprisingly, the party was to function as the "externally tautly organised and internally unified and aligned elite troop" of the German minority.

The hope for a border revision was thus explicitly nourished ("the fight for Schleswig goes on") and tied to party discipline ("obedience toward the party leader"). If this could be made to sound convincing, even those who disliked the Greater Germanic Idea would stay with the NSDAP-N – indeed, party leaders hoped to expand party membership.

The relationship to the Danish national socialists

The next step for this second *Schulungsbrief* was to deal with the notion, inherent in the Greater Germanic Idea, that the NSDAP-N should cooperate with the Danish National Socialists. Here, the writer continued to emphasise the differences between 'race' (which would put Danes on par with Germans) and *Volk* (which would not), again claiming that borderland leadership fell naturally to the German minority.

> Our struggle is for all the people living in our [North Schleswig] *Heimat*. They are all of the same blood. The theory of [different] German and Danish blood is a fairytale. There is no such thing as German and Danish blood. We are racially alike and therefore equal in value. *The equality thus refers to race, not to Volk.* As *Volk* we are superior to the Danish *Volk*. Our *Volksgemeinschaft* is greater, younger, more vigorous, and has more growth potential, that cannot be denied. Our relationship to the Danish National Socialists is thus given.[24]

It was given, this means, that the German minority NSDAP-N could never simply join the ranks of Scandinavian Nazi parties. Supposed racial equality was overridden by a hierarchy of *Völker*. This was, in fact, an entirely 'un-Germanic' interpretation of SS ideology; the SS held that common race was exactly what would overcome traditional ethnic and national conflicts between all Germanic tribes. Nor could the SS support the claim to *völkisch*

---

[24] "Das Volkstum als tragende Kraft" (note 17), italics in the original.

superiority; it would end any Danish attraction to the glamour of the SS idea of a single Greater Germanic Reich (and also, incidentally, end the recruitment of Danes to the Waffen-SS).

However, the NSDAP-N's idea of a leading position for Germans within the Germanic Reich had, in fact, wide currency. Even within the SS, Germany and the Germans were often visualised as being, at least, a sort of 'nucleus' of the Greater Germanic Reich. This idea recurred in later *Schulungsbriefe*, which explicitly argued that the German minority in North Schleswig should take a clear leadership position.[25]

As the author of the second *Schulungsbrief* put it, a *völkische* distinction, even within National Socialist movements, between Danes, Norwegians, Germans, etc., would always remain.

> There is no international National Socialism. National Socialism is *völkisch*-specific. It [National Socialism] is indeed possible, even necessary, for all Germanic *Völker*. But each *Volk* will then shape National Socialism as political reality according to its own *völkisch* characteristics. That is, there will then be [distinctive] German, Danish, Dutch National Socialist *Volksgemeinschaften*, each with its own *völkisch* imprint.[26]

Here, the writer establishes the existence of '*völkisch* variations' within National Socialism, a distinction entirely consistent with the above quote's definition of the relationship between National Socialism and *Volk*. From this it follows, in turn, that the various Germanic National Socialist *Volksgemeinschaften* are far from equal in value or status: "They [the other *Völker*] are in a Germanic space under the leadership of Germany. The German National Socialist *Volk* is the *Führervolk* in the Greater Germanic space." At this point, finally, a reference was made to North Schleswig: "To this National Socialist German *Volk* we belong." "Who," the writer concludes, would, under these circumstances, "give up their place among the *Führervolk* in order to be integrated in the ranks of a *Volk* that marches as a follower of us." The omission of a question mark at the end of this sentence anticipates the answer. No member of the *Führervolk* would ever desert ranks to join Frits Clausen's Danish Nazi party. Quite the contrary: "The

---

[25] See, in this context, *Schulungsbrief der NSDAP-N*, no. 3, "Der Norden und Wir" (undated, probably published Feb. 1941), LAA, PK 308. For dates, see the "Bericht der deutschen Volksgruppe North Schleswig", Feb. 1941, NAD, FMG 388.

[26] "Das Volkstum als tragende Kraft" (note 17).

stronger had the right to lead" and "strength comes not from the numbers, but depends on *völkisch* power and vigour".²⁷

The quality trumps quantity argument was, of course, particularly useful to Germans living in North Schleswig. They were, after all, a very small minority. Germany's leadership role in the Greater Germanic Reich had been justified (by the same author) by references to, amongst other things, "the size of its *Volksgemeinschaft*". But in North Schleswig, quality was what mattered:

> All Germanic National Socialists who with us and through us fight for a new Europe are our comrades. We reach out our hand to them for common fight and victory. But we do not thereby forget that we are part of the *Führervolk*.²⁸

The degeneration of the North

The innate, qualitative superiority of the German minority to the Danes was explained, not only by referring to the high-quality *völkisch* essence of the minority, but to the degeneration from an earlier Germanic high-mark status by the Danes, as well. An alleged "Germanic alienation" had taken place in Denmark. The entire North had come "under the influence of the liberal West" and lost "its Germanic face". This is why so many Scandinavians – so lectured a *Schulungsbrief* – fallaciously held that "Nordic character and democracy were one and the same thing", thus disclaiming the "real Nordic world". As a result, there was a "battle between liberal-Jewish influence of the West and the real Germanic North". The German minority, part, evidently, of the "real Germanic North", was fighting the Danish "democratic leaders" because these were "knowingly hindering the reshaping of the Germanic space". While the "degenerative Jewish forces were allowed official advantage" north of the German border, "the vigorous powers of the Germanic space" found a refuge and *Heimat* in Germany.²⁹ A minority Waffen-SS volunteer wrote in a reader's letter to the minority magazine *Der SK-Mann* that "certainly the soldier spirit is anchored in the blood of the Germanic *Völker*, but the example of our Danish neighbours clearly shows that it perishes if it is not cared for" (Ein Brief 1943).

---

²⁷ "Das Volkstum als tragende Kraft" (note 17).
²⁸ "Das Volkstum als tragende Kraft" (note 17).
²⁹ "Der Norden und Wir" (note 25).

Now the "North's Moment of Fate" had come, as the title of yet another *Schulungsbrief* put it.[30] Denmark must follow the example shown by Norway's Quisling, turn away from England and abandon pan-Scandinavianism. The latter was a failed movement, degenerate not least because it excluded Germany. "In the storm of the present day, the pale shadow of a 150-year-old Scandinavianism is wiped out." Thus, the German minority's battle of *Völker*, the *Volkstumskampf* against the Danes, was vindicated even from a Greater Germanic point-of-view. The very willingness of Germans to accept the idea of a Greater Germanic community showed their *völkisch* superiority to their blood brothers.

The Danes considered minority *Deutschtum* as "artificially fostered" (according to the *Schulungsbrief* entitled "The North and Us").[31] The Germans, by contrast, were willing to accept the fact that

> the two *Volkstum*, divided for more than a thousand years, have grown on Germanic-common land. Germans and Danes are thus, with respect to race and history, equal and have equal rights to the Schleswig land.

The Germans' ability to propagate this, it was argued, showed "the great moral superiority of the German position". Even when working against Danes in the "battle for the [North Schleswig] *Heimat*", the German minority was conscious of the "common history of all Germanics". Thus, they admitted to "equal racial rights", but at the same time – and here a central thesis is repeated – claimed, by dint of that very admission, "great *völkisch* superiority".[32]

The Danes had, as a *Schulungsbrief* put it, continually sabotaged German attempts to raise German–Danish competition to a dignified, chivalrous level, a struggle between near-equals. Long before the German occupation, the author claimed, younger men among the German minority had advanced the idea of equal rights between Danes and Germans, attempting to raise the tone and nature of the border contest to the level of a "knightly contest". But the Danes had, according to the writer, ignored these overtures. As a result, blame could not fall on the German minority for the Danish–German divisions within the North Schleswig *Heimat*.[33]

---

[30] *Schulungsbrief der NSDAP-N*, no. 12, "Die Schicksalsstunde des Nordens", LAA, PK 308.
[31] See note 25.
[32] "Der Norden und Wir" (note 25).
[33] "Die Revolution der Grenzlandhaltung" (note 15).

In this manner, three birds were shot with one logical arrow. First, the *völkische* superiority of German minority North Schleswigians could be derived from its alleged Germanic attitude and the Germanic ideology. Second, the accusation that the minority had divided the *Heimat* was not only repudiated, but turned back against the accusers. Third, the *Volkstumskampf* was legitimised. It was, perhaps, fought against Germanics, but against degenerate Germanics who did not act in a Germanic manner. The minority, by contrast, had made the Germanic Idea into a guiding "principle for their practical conduct": they had "abandoned any discussion of the border" and instead "concentrated on the inner [spiritual, cultural] work". They had started "a free cultural competition between the two *Völker*". By contrast, the Danes' *Volkstumspolitik* was wholly "negative", its objective "absorption" of the German minority – that is, "elimination by finer means".[34]

The high culture of the 'real' Germanics was further elaborated. Unlike the Danes, for instance, the German minority had always possessed the "secure anchor in their *völkische* identity" necessary to appreciate, for example, really valuable Northern contributions, such as books by Knut Hamsun. It was the minority that had held open the "door to the North" despite conflicts in the *Heimat*. The German North Schleswigian, it was claimed, acknowledged "as a matter of course, the racial equality of the opponents and thus the Germanic blood brotherhood".[35] Possessing "the broader outlook and finer sense of responsibility", the minority was equal to taking on the burden of leadership in the border land.[36] This was not a question of tyranny; rather, the rule of the sage, who reaches out and cares for his spiritually backwards brother, showing him the way: "we do not wish to repress our Germanic brother nations in the North, but rather to have them ascend with us to new tasks and new grandeur."[37]

Conclusion: The 'unimaginable community'

In a new edition of his classic work, in an added chapter on the interpretation of the National-Socialist state, Ian Kershaw brings up the fact that recent scholars take National Socialist racial ideology seriously as a major driving force. He sees this is as the most important paradigm-change in

---

[34] "Die Revolution der Grenzlandhaltung" (note 15).
[35] "Der Norden und Wir" (note 25).
[36] "Die Revolution der Grenzlandhaltung" (note 15).
[37] "Der Norden und Wir" (note 25).

research on the Nazis (Kershaw 1999: 394). This 'primacy of ideology' view had already been advanced in the case of various parts of the SS (Wildt 2003: 863; Heinemann 2003: 18). Despite its absurdities and contradictions the Greater Germanic Idea and the efforts to implement it cannot be relegated to the land of fantasies. Michael Salewski admonishes us not to give in to the impulse to ridicule: all this had, in fact, "deadly" impact (Salewski 1991: 203).

In fact, in National Socialist praxis, the logic of racism, and the primacy of racial ideology often successfully challenged the dictates of 'political rationality'. Racial ideology lay behind arguments for forced labour and wars of extermination. Yet it did not suffice to convince a German minority of the "historic necessity" of the Germanic racial community, even though this minority in other respects willingly conformed to, or internalised, the German Third Reich's values and wishes.

The examples and analyses discussed above show why this might be; and shows, as well, the creativity exhibited by minority ideologues when pursuing their oppositional goals. The result was the elaboration of a new ideological minority orientation which could conform to German demands without giving up their fundamental commitment to border revision.

Politically, Himmler's supranational Greater Germanic visions placed the minority party in a dilemma, as national identity – that is, reunification with Germany – was a constituent of their members' self conception. The supranational element of the Greater Germanic Idea was also the main cause of resistance on the part of the minority-German National Socialists, who refused the SS's efforts to re-make them as Germanic – or worse still, as Danish.

In contrast to Germans living in Germany, the minority was actually forced to choose between *Volk* and race (this is at least how they experienced it); indeed, a large part of the conflict between the German minority and the SS was caused by a clash between an established imagined people's community (*Volksgemeinschaft*) and the imposed imagined racial community (*Rassengemeinschaft*). The nationalist devil could, it turned out, not be driven out by the Germanic Beelzebub. The construct of a Greater Germanic Reich was, for the *Volksdeutsche* of North Schleswig, in a reformulation of Benedict Anderson's (1983) famous phrase – an 'unimaginable community'.

Eftner F2 (2)

Schulungsbrief

der

NSDAP Nordschleswig

2. Folge. Nr. 1

Die Revolution der Grenzlandhaltung

Eine klare Trennung der Völker gibt es fast an keiner Stelle, wo sich Völker begegnen. Staaten kann man durch Steine und Schlagbäume abgrenzen. Aber Völker sind nicht wie Staaten durch Verträge geordnete Gebilde, sie sind lebendige Einheiten, denen man keine Grenzen stecken kann. Darum ist dort, wo sich zwei Völker begegnen, fast immer ein Uebergangsgebiet vorhanden, in dem die beiden Völker ineinander gewachsen sind. **In diesem Gebiet, dem eigentlichen Grenzland, ist eine Auseinandersetzung zwischen den lebendigen Kräften beider Völker unausbleiblich.** Man kann dem Leben keine Ruhe gebieten, wo sich ebenbürtiges, gleichwertiges Leben gegenüber tritt. Selbst wenn man durch künstliche Maßnahmen die Völker reinlich scheiden würde, möchte das immer nur vorübergehend einen Zustand der Ruhe herbeiführen. Die Völker würden infolge ihrer Lebenskraft wieder ineinander wachsen.

Damit wird die Grenze zu einer dauernden Kraftprobe der sich hier begegnenden Völker und damit zu einem Zeugnis der völkischen Lebenskraft. Dieser Prüfung kann kein Volk entlaufen, sie ist durch die ...

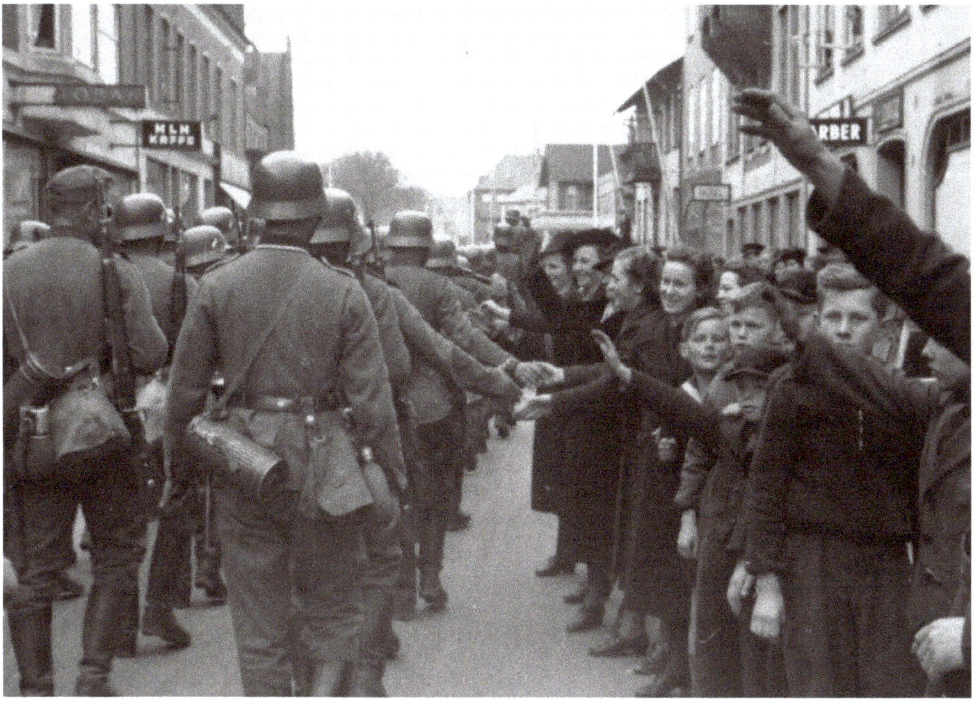

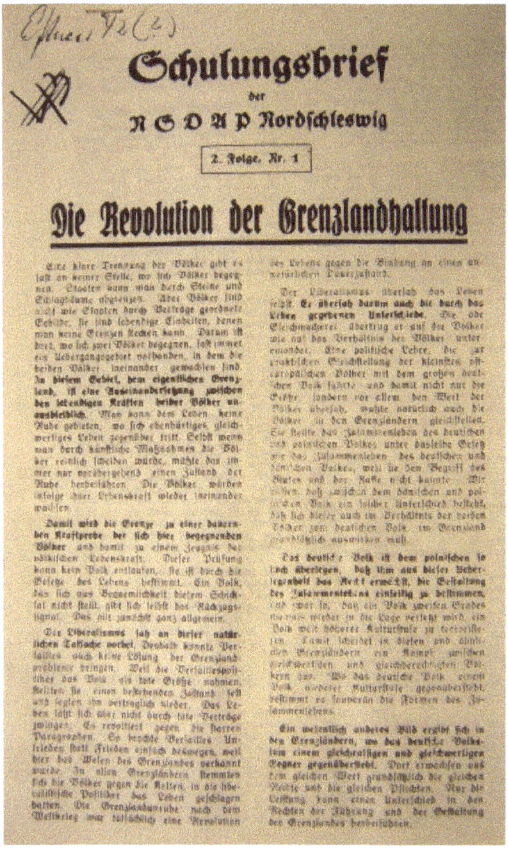

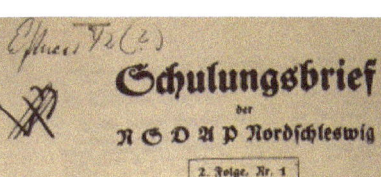

(Above) German solders passing hailing bystanders in the city of Aabenraa, Denmark, 12 April 1940 (Photo: Museum Sønderjylland, ISL / Photographer: Ludwig von Münchow)

(Left) Publications of the German minority in Denmark: The "Schulungsbrief" (Photographer: Steffen Werther)

Publications of the German minority in Denmark: "Der Nationalsozialismus … im Grenzland" (Photographer: Steffen Werther)

References

Anderson, B. (1983) *Imagined Communities: Reflections on the Origin and Spread of Nationalism*. London and New York: Verso.

Becker-Christensen, H. (2003) "NSDAP-N og Slesvigs Parti: Det tyske mindretals virke under besættelsen." *Partie under press – demokratiet under besættelse*, ed. by Lund, J. Copenhagen: Gyldendal, 328-44.

Blindow, F. (1999) *Carl Schmitts Reichsordnung: Strategie für einen europäischen Großraum*. Berlin: Akademie Verlag.

Christensen, C., Lund, J., Olesen, N., and Sørensen, J. (2005) *Danmark besat: Krig og hverdag 1940-1945*. Copenhagen: Høst & Søn.

Djursaa, M. (1981) *DNSAP – Danske Nazister 1930-45*. Copenhagen: Gyldendal.

"Ein Brief an den SK-Mann." (1943) *Der SK-Mann* 2 (11/12).

Elvert, J. (1999) *Mitteleuropa! Deutsche Pläne zur europäischen Neuordnung (1918-1945)*. Stuttgart: Franz Steiner Verlag.

Hansen. H. (2001) "Mindretal og flertal i Nordslesvig omkring 1940." *Nationale mindretal i det dansk-tyske grænseland 1933-45*, ed. by Bohn, R., Danker, U., and Kühl, J. Aabenraa: Institut for Graenseregionsforskning, 122-41.

Heinemann, I. (2003) *Rasse, Siedlung, deutsches Blut: Das Rasse- und Siedlungshauptamt der SS und die rassenpolitische Neuordnung Europas*. Göttingen: Wallstein Verlag.

Herbert, U. (2001) *Best – Biographische Studien über Radikalismus, Weltanschauung und Vernunft 1903-1989*. Bonn: Dietz.

Kershaw, I. (1999) *Der NS-Staat: Geschichtsinterpretationen und Kontroversen im Überblick*. Reinbek: Rohwohlt.

Kletzin, B. (2002) *Europa aus Rasse und Raum: Die nationalsozialistische Idee der Neuen Ordnung*. Münster: LIT Verlag.

Kristensen, H. (2004) "Der 9. April 1940." *Demokratische Geschichte: Jahrbuch für Schleswig-Holstein* 16, 155-69.

Kristensen, H. (2008) "Zwischen Hitler und Heimat, Volksgruppenführer Jens Möller." *Demokratische Geschichte: Jahrbuch für Schleswig-Holstein* 19, 41-69.

Lauridsen, J. (2002) *Dansk Nazisme 1930-45 – og derefter*. Copenhagen: Gyldendal.

Lund, A. (1995) *Germanenideologie im Nationalsozialismus: Zur Rezeption der 'Germania' des Tacitus im 'Dritten Reich'*. Heidelberg: Universitätsverlag C. Winter.

Noack, J. (1975) *Det tyske mindretal i Nordslesvig under besættelsen*. Copenhagen: Munksgaard.

Paysen, C. (1941) *Der Nationalsozialismus als Weltanschauung im Grenzland: Eine Darstellung der Verhältnisse in Nordschleswig.* Tondern: Buchdruckerei Andresen.

PKB (1953) *Den parlamentariske kommissions beretning, vol. 14: Det tyske mindretal under besættelsen.* Copenhagen: J.H. Schultz.

PKB (1954) *Den parlamentariske kommissions beretning, vol. 13: Besættelsen – set med tyske øjne.* Copenhagen: J.H. Schultz.

Poulsen, H. (2002) *Besættelsesårene 1940–45.* Aarhus: Aarhus Universitetsforlag.

Rasmussen, R. (2004) "Die dänischen Nationalsozialisten in Nordschleswig 1930–45." *Demokratische Geschichte: Jahrbuch für Schleswig-Holstein* 16, 135–53.

Salewski, M. (1991) "Die Perversion der Einheit: Die nationalsozialistischen Ideen." *Historische Mitteilungen der Ranke-Gesellschaft* 4, 200–11.

Thalheim, K. (1931) *Das Grenzlanddeutschtum: Mit besonderer Berücksichtigung seines Wirtschafts- und Soziallebens.* Berlin/Leipzig: De Gruyter & Co.

Tägil, S. (1970) *Deutschland und die deutsche Minderheit in Nordschleswig: Eine Studie zur deutschen Grenzpolitik 1933–1939.* Lund: Svenska Bokförlaget.

Wegner, B. (2006) *Hitlers politischen Soldaten: Die Waffen SS 1933–1945: Studien zu Leitbild, Struktur und Funktion einer nationalsozialistischen Elite.* 7th edn. Paderborn: Schöningh.

Werther, S. (2012) *SS-Vision und Grenzland-Realität: Vom Umgang dänischer und 'volksdeutscher' Nationalsozialisten in Sønderjylland mit der 'großgermanischen' Ideologie der SS.* Stockholm: ACTA.

Wildt, M. (2003) *Generation des Unbedingten: Das Führungskorps des Reichssicherheitshauptamtes.* Hamburg: Hamburger Edition – Institut für Sozialforschung.

5. The Ambiguity of the West: Objectives of Polish Research Policy in the 1990s

Sofia Norling

For the part of Europe that was enclosed by the so-called Iron Curtain, the autumn of 1989 represents the beginning of sweeping political changes. During the 1980s the Soviet Union had adopted a liberalising approach under the leadership of Mikhail Gorbachev, and subsequent political developments meant that after four decades of authoritarian rule and planned economy, the former state socialist Central and Eastern European Countries (CEEC), altered their course towards democracy and capitalism. The surge of liberalisation culminated in the dissolution of the Soviet Union in 1991, and the definitive fall of the Iron Curtain.

One of the policy fields where these sweeping changes became visible was research policy. The role of science and research for society had to be renegotiated and the relationship between politics and science to be redefined. According to the Soviet model that had been adopted in the state socialist CEEC, scientific activities depended on political protection. Both applied research (technological self-sufficiency) and basic research (which was meant to support ideological convictions) were seen as building blocks in the state socialist body politic. Science historian Konstantin Ivanov (2002: 319) describes the basic principle for the model as "the requirement that the production of scientific knowledge be closely linked to the industrial and economic needs of the society".

One of the countries where such a research ideal was strongly implemented and practised during the period of state socialism, was Poland. However, the Polish transformation of research policy differs in a number of ways from the rest of the CEEC. The reasons for these differences have been discussed in the light of the country's political history (Norling 2014: 88). A crucial aspect is the specific heritage of ideas on science and the role of research in society. Many social science studies understand this heritage as a consequence of Poland's chequered political history.

The Polish state, even though established as early as the tenth century, lost its independence in 1795 and was not re-established until 1918, subsequently becoming a Soviet vassal state after the Second World War. The country has thus endured long periods with a lack of full sovereignty. This has in turn contributed to civil society and citizens being conceptualised in opposition to the government and the state administration. The Polish political culture is therefore characterised by an attitude to state power as being 'external', 'foreign', and 'unauthorised', without legitimacy anchored in civil society (Gerner 2009: 221). Instead legitimacy was vested in a social class called the intelligentsia (*inteligencja*), that is, a group of individuals that possess social characteristics associated with higher education. The intelligentsia played a crucial role in the formulation and defence of the national identity and the creation of cultural, political, and scientific values beyond state authority (Kennedy 1991: 238).

An important part of the philosophical tradition of the Polish intelligentsia concerning science and research before the Second World War was formulated according to the Humboldtian liberal model with its emphasis on scientific freedom and independence of politics (Herczyński 2008: 15–17). During the years following the end of the First World War, the Polish research system and research policy were, to the extent they were formulated, in line with a tradition of that kind (Kozłowski 1998: 90). Consequently, when the Soviet model of research policy was introduced, it went against the research ideal of the intelligentsia. However, when research policy was reorganised after 1989, the intelligentsia's ideal of the role of science in society again became an important starting point for political practice (Connelly 2000: 78), implying a break with the policy that had been formulated by the Polish communist party PZPR (*Polska Zjednoczona Partia Robotnicza*) in line with the Soviet model.

During the roundtable discussions held in connection with the transition from state socialism to democracy in 1989, scientific autonomy and the greatest possible freedom from political control were emphasised as part of the framing of the new politics between the *Solidarność* trade union and PZPR (Jabłecka 2009: 84–5). The scientific faction responsible for this issue at the time formulated a policy model for research that was almost opposite to the Soviet model. The ideal of scientific freedom and self-autonomy, and the separation of politics from science were then realised in Poland. The formulation of the role of science and research no longer lay in the hands of politicians but with academics themselves, not unlike the model envisioned by the intelligentsia in the inter-war years.

In practice this development meant that The State Committee for Scientific Research (*Komitet Badań Naukowych*, KBN) became responsible for the formulation of the new research policy and the organisation of the research system. KBN was to function as a more or less autonomous body in relation to the Polish government, and it not only dealt with research grants but was also responsible for research policy at macro level in order to safeguard the freedom of science from political control. This solution was in several ways unique compared with how research systems and research policy were structured in the other CEEC after the fall of state socialism. Nowhere was the idea of scientific autonomy incorporated so clearly into political practice as in Poland. The scientific production of knowledge thus rapidly moved from resting on an ideal of societal utility to one that acknowledged the intrinsic value of science. This ideal was also strongly rooted in Polish political history, research policy traditions, and the culture of the intelligentsia.

However, modifications of the new Polish research policy soon started to take shape. The early 1990s were a time of crumbling economy, the need for mobilisation of public resources for building up the market economy was perceived as urgent, and subsequently the country's entry into the EU had to be prepared. All this contributed to comprehensive renegotiations and reinterpretations of the anti-politics oriented model with academic self-organisation as a basic choice (Norling 2014: 11–12).

This chapter examines these comprehensive renegotiations and reinterpretations, mainly by analysing Polish research policy discussions in the journal *Sprawy Nauki* during the 1990s. The study uses the concepts of 'boundary-work' and 'demarcations' regarding science as introduced by American sociologist Thomas F. Gieryn (1999), along with concepts of critical transformation theory. Epistemologically the approach is a social constructionist one, assuming that ideas about science and its demarcations are historically, socially, culturally, and politically conditioned. The question of what constitutes science is therefore seen as an empirical issue, not one to be answered in general. By using concepts of critical transformation theory, a strand of thought that has emanated from postcolonial studies, emphasis will be given to the analysis of symbolic geographical positions for the boundary-work. The study thus examines the notion characteristic of European history and the present day of a 'Western European' identity that is superior to other imagined symbolic European identities such as an

'Eastern European' or 'Southern European' one in terms of 'modernity' and 'development' (Andrén 2001: 35–7).

There is a significant difference between studies of a symbolic Eastern European identity position in relation to a Western European one and the 'Orientalism' discourse examined by postcolonial studies. Here, rather than studying an identity completely 'beyond' the symbolic Western European identity, the research concerns an imagined 'not really there' identity, that is, an identity that can 'almost' be likened to the symbolic Western European, but which does not quite succeed – socially, culturally, economically, or politically (Lindelöf 2006: 72–4).

There are several explanatory models for how an East European symbolic 'almost identity' of this kind arose. For example, sociologist Klaus Eder emphasises (2006: 264) that the geographical proximity to 'the other' – in the form of tsarist Russia and later the Soviet Union – played a crucial role in the relationship between the imagined East and West. Another explanatory model discussed by the Hungarian historian György Péteri is that the Iron Curtain contributed to a kind of de-Europeanisation of the now post-state socialist countries, which characterised both notions of the East in the West, and of the East in the East (Péteri 2010: 2). Again, however, this is not about a symbolic identity position that completely ends up in the unknown 'other', but that instead means something in between, both included in the Western European norm, and at the same time outside of it. Both Eder and Péteri, therefore, call this position the telling 'second other'.

A designation that, like 'the second other', is used to describe the imagined distinction between 'East' and 'West', is 'semiperiphery', as opposed to the 'core'. Instead of periphery, the symbolic geographical identity position of the CEEC is here to be understood as something between the periphery and the core. Like the identity position 'second other' it is thus about an exclusion that is not complete (Blagojević 2010: 186). The discussion on symbolic geographical identity positions that informs the present study contributes to analysing the boundary-work in a more initiated way. Concepts such as 'semiperiphery' and 'core' help to distinguish and understand what forms of linguistic representation were possible and viable for use in the boundary-work, as opposed to what forms were not.

An autonomous research policy is realised

January 1991 saw the launch of KBN, officially the actual basis for the new autonomous Polish research policy model, according to *Ustawa z 12 stycznia 1991 r. o Komitetcie Badań Naukowych* (The Act of 12 January on the State Committee for Scientific Research). At that time KBN consisted of two units (commissions), one for basic research and one for applied research. These became more clearly defined and formed part of a structure of a number of special committees that were to be the guardians, each within their own field, of the autonomy that would from then onwards characterise scientific endeavours. Generally committee members were academics, often professors with special knowledge in their particular field. Those elected could also be replaced every six months in line with the idea of openness and transparency in the new formulation of research policy. This would mean that autonomy would always be assured and the research world would have considerable influence on political developments concerning research.

KBN was thus initially given the role of a guardian of the autonomous scientific community. A new law was enacted by parliament that established that KBN was to function as the highest authority regarding research policy, and that its chairperson would not simply be of ministerial rank but would also be a valid member of the government (*Ustawa* 1991). It also stated that KBN's tasks would include,

> Providing the government and parliament with guidelines for Poland's research policy, including proposals for the proportion of GDP that should go to R&D
>
> Providing the government with proposals for plans and budget for R&D
>
> Defining the focus of R&D
>
> Distributing budgeted funds to institutions and research teams, and following up on their use
>
> Initiating and overseeing legislation and financial proposals regarding research and technological progress
>
> Signing international agreements on cooperation in technology and research (ibid).

KBN had almost the entirety of the state research budget at its disposal, and would fund all research activity and research institutions in the country. In this way two roles were combined: that of a research ministry with duties concerning strategic planning and activities and executive duties; and responsibility for funding all research. KBN's management team consisted at that time of five ministers who represented the government, twelve researchers, elected by the research community, and two representatives of the subcommissions for applied and basic research. All decisions were made based on a voting procedure, and KBN's chairperson had a veto whatever the issue (Jabłecka 2009: 88-9).

The reason for such a drastic reorganisation, giving KBN a status that was decision-making rather than advisory, and eliminating "politicians from the entire decision-making process", as well as holding the entire budget for funding research, can, according to science historian Jan Kozłowski (1998: 94), be understood in the light of the fact that,

> In the Polish reform, creating a new path and rejecting the past resulted in a denial of every organizational and political principle, even if some of these principles, such as research funding by various sectoral departments or the involvement of politicians in science policy formulations, are common in democratic countries.

This new, almost utopian, research policy model, in which science in its entirety was governed by representatives from their own sphere, is remarkable, not least in consideration of the research policy development Western Europe went through during the same period. There the situation was instead characterised by a change process dominated by an ever greater management spirit and a move towards centralised budgeting and planning processes. The EU's common research policy gained in significance, with institutional arrangements in the form of research councils, new framework programmes, and the Lisbon Convention, not least as an effect of the then increasing management and control of the public sector. The Polish case was thus detached from the trend towards increasing research policy control in Western Europe during the period in question, despite the fact that during the roundtable discussions the Poles had expressed their wish to be included in the 'Western European' community.

Research policy reforms after 1989

The political situation immediately after the roundtable discussions of 1989 and the creation of KBN meant that General Jaruzelski occupied the post of president of Poland and PZPR was still guaranteed a monopoly of authority up until the first free presidential elections since the end of the Second World War, in 1990. Lech Wałęsa took over the post of president after Jaruzelski, and in the parliamentary elections the following year 29 parties entered the Sejm. The political situation was characterised by rapid political upheavals and instability, with constant changes of prime minister during the first post-communist years (Raciborski 2003). Lena Kolarska-Bobińska (2003: 91–8) has described this period as a time when new coalitions, parties, and political leaders replace each other in a rapid stream, and democracy was more imaginary than real. It is also in this political context that the formulation of the new post-state socialist research policy took place, that is, in a political landscape characterised by the transformation process's first, and largely chaotic, phase. Whereas they initially ensured a relative distance from state policy events as a result of the requirement for autonomy during the roundtable negotiations, the action plan at the start of the 1990s was oriented around the fulfilment of the first strategic research policy document prepared by KBN, "Principles for the Acts of Legislation Concerning the Field of Science, Higher Education, and Research and Development Activities", which went into force 1991 and was published in 1993 (hereafter called *Principles*).

However, it soon became necessary to define in greater detail the somewhat vague guidelines in this document. Another strategy document was therefore compiled by KBN on behalf of the new left-leaning government, *Założenia Polityki Naukowej i Naukowo Technicznej Państwa* (The Basis for the National Science and Technology Policy, hereafter called *Basis*). The document was drawn up by a group of experts within KBN, and the text stated that the research policy should result in the short term in making social and economic development in the country easier, and in the long term ensure financial growth and social development, through these areas being given as much as possible of the resources set aside for research. Here the two overall tasks of research are also described as to "acquire unique and important results from the most attractive research fields in the world" and to "acquire unique and important technologies and exploit their use in technical collaboration within Poland and between Poland and the rest of the world" (*Basis* 1993: 68–9).

The total scientific freedom, which in *Principles* had an almost utopian nature, both for applied research and basic research, thus began in the practical context of the reforms to be renegotiated, and the demarcations surrounding science were reworked. This primarily affected applied research, which in the document is ascribed a need for increased management towards a social benefit-oriented context (through getting closer to state policy and the business world). Science is ascribed other values, partly through the introduction of *Basis*, and the most urgent task for research policy is described as renewing and changing legal regulations for applied research so that it matches the country's economic development. This becomes even more significant in a clarification of the priorities, which states,

> (a) that research in Poland must be on a high level, comparable with a global standard; (b) that the results of research must have a crucial importance and a meaningful effect on other research areas; (c) that it must apply to fields that have an indisputable significance for civilisation and the culture of society and the country; (d) that there must be a measurable likelihood that the results will be useful and that they will form the basis for adapted or new technology (*Basis* 1993: 66).

Although the positions in *Basis* differ considerably in terms of scientific autonomy from what people had originally seen ahead of them when *Solidarność's* scientific faction sat down to negotiate with the communist party about research policy in democratic Poland, it is clear how careful KBN's group of experts was about defined frameworks for what science is to devote itself to. The discussions concerning the boundaries between science and politics in this phase are thus to a great extent still about maintaining a continued separation of spheres in line with the ideals of the roundtable discussions, although the beginnings of a relaxation can be discerned. An inclosure to the document also states that research area priorities should be updated regularly with regard to research that is essential for the country's administration to function, living standards to be raised, the development of the economy and competitiveness of goods and services, and the strengthening of democracy and the "social acceptance of a free market economy" (*Basis* 1993: 70). Thus a certain displacement with regard to ideas and expectations of, and requirements for, the role of science is brewing in the reforms, where more benefit-oriented ideas get a foothold in the document.

Apart from this inclosure, two kinds of prioritised programmes are also written into the document. The first of these, *Strategic Government Programmes* (SPR), involved prioritising research of which the result was important for the country and the other, *Special Programmes and Research Equipment* (SPUB), was a research programme that formed part of international programmes, and where equipment costs were high. These programmes hurried development on towards more comprehensive renegotiations and reinterpretations of the autonomous research policy model. However, this only applies to applied research, which was now clearly defined as the engineering and architectural sciences, the chemical and technical sciences, electricity and power measurement studies, and transport studies (which had their home in KBN's subcommission on applied research). Basic research, which was classified as the humanities, jurisprudence, mathematics, physics and astronomy, the biological and environmental sciences, medical sciences and agricultural and forestry research, was thus still outside the priority framework.

This distinction, which had previously not been as significant, was a milestone for the continued development of Polish research policy. There was still a surprising amount of freedom in science's relationship with politics, as well as with the business world, while at the same time the renegotiations concerning applied research began to take off. Applied research was seen more and more as being in need of politicisation, and thus clearly distinct from basic research, which was still given a freer rein. The total state budget for research during the first part of the 1990s was between 0.57 and 0.76 per cent of GNP, in relation to 1.3 per cent in 1989, and the non-state portion of the funding was still very low. In the budget of 1993 about 45 per cent of the funds were used for the statutory activity of research institutions, 18 per cent for grants, 13 per cent for targeted projects, and the rest for miscellaneous items. Of the statutory funding, 60 per cent was expended by the Committee for Applied Research and 40 per cent by the Committee for Basic Research (Jabłecka 2009: 84–5).

However, the research policy scenario for basic research and its as yet unmanaged nature soon came under pressure, in connection with the ever stronger political demands for international cooperation, especially in consideration of the Polish government's ambitions in regard to European integration.

Increased international cooperation

In the mid to late 1990s political development in Poland rested largely on adaptations with a view to membership of the EC (EU) and NATO, which created conditions for an increasing retreat from the initially prepared research policy model in *Principles*. Back in 1990 the EC parliament had adopted a resolution on cooperation with the CEEC with regard to R&D, and the EC's *Third Framework Programme* opened up the possibility of funding new networks between its member states and these countries (Framework 3C). Adjustments needed to be made before these changes, which became clear fairly soon after publication of *Basis*. The almost utopian approach to scientific freedom was renegotiated and reinterpreted in the reforms. The public investigation in connection with the issue of EU membership and research policy ordered by KBN and the government's

European integration group (prepared by KBN-active academics and published in the series *White Paper, Poland – The European Union*) states, for example, that,

> For developed countries, a typical strategy is to concentrate on high-tech production or even on information processing technologies to maintain the dominant role on increasingly globalized markets; such a concentration is possible only if the level of education increases in the society. Thus science, education and technology become vital elements of development strategies at the beginning of the 21st century; these elements will decide who will join highly developed countries and which countries will be left on the periphery (Wierzbicki 1997: 2).

Thus here the comparison with the Western way of running research policy is realised, and in consideration of the measures demanded, the concept was articulated in relation to a new kind of view as to how the spheres of science and politics in particular should relate to one another. During the round-table discussions, the striving to be like the 'West', or the desire to be absorbed into the 'core', was actually only a kind of symbolic opposition to state socialism models. Instead of in relation to the ideal of freedom and the idea of a self-governing intelligentsia, the West was now loaded with values associated with more control and strategic prioritisation of research, that is, a less clear demarcation between science and other spheres. This type of approach to the 'West' in Polish research policy after 1989 was a highly important element in the assertion of epistemic authority and crucial for the results of the associated boundary-work. This is the most important component in the repertoire that constitutes resources for the actors taking part in the boundary-work.

Preparation in various social areas in a bid for EU membership, which often required scientific expertise, meant that a number of state programmes for prioritised research were initiated. In relation to integration into the EU, *Basis* was therefore not by a long stretch a sufficiently clear document for directives on research policy strategies and efforts. Instead, therefore, the document *Dodatkowe Założenia polityki naukowej i naukowo-technicznej państwa* (The Supplement to The Basis for the National Science and Technology Policy, hereafter called *Supplement*) was produced to remedy the deficiencies in *Basis*. In concrete terms *Supplement* meant that a greater and more clearly defined focus on research and research orientations that concerned innovations within the country's economic sphere were to be adopted (*Supplement* 1997: 2). The introduction to the document states that the starting point for choosing prioritised orientations for research has been,

> – development of the economy, particularly the increase of innovativeness and competitiveness of products and services, as well as their adaptation to international standards, especially to those obligatory in the European Union,
> – increase of well-being and security of people, as well as the increase of environmental protection, maintenance and bringing up to date information connected with the technological security,
> – correct functioning of the State (its institutions and authorities, as well as civil services (ibid. 2–4).

In this way the prioritised research areas now became clear, and compared with *Basis,* where they were still open to interpretation, far better defined. Each prioritised field was specified and explained, and rather than suggesting there was one kind of science with uniform activity characterised by 'scientific freedom' a clear boundary between applied research and basic research was drawn. The role of science was interpreted as a means of social development and state benefit. *Supplement* was in this way also a turning point for the ideas and expectations of, and requirements for, science in the continuing reforms of Polish research policy.

Research policy discussion

In parallel with the reforms and the associated renegotiation and reinterpretation of demarcations surrounding science, throughout that period there was a research policy discussion in the journal *Sprawy Nauki* (Science Issues, during the initial period *Bulietyn Komitetu Badań Naukowych*, Bulletin of the State Committee for Scientific Research), which in line with what was described in *Principles* was to become an important element of the new, transparent research policy activities within KBN. This would feature detailed reports of research policy initiatives, decisions, proposed programmes, and any other information that could conceivably be produced from activities within KBN, alongside discussions on development, in which academics, politicians, and other stakeholders would be able to have their say. It is therefore also in this journal that the first discussions concerning a renegotiation and reinterpretation of the demarcation that preceded the reforms in post-state socialist Poland came to be held.

As early as in the first few issues, it is clear that the journal played a major role in the discussions on the organisation of the new research policy. These discussions were conducted in connection with workshops, conferences, and meetings led by KBN and were characterised by a Humboldtian approach to the issue, in terms of autonomy and scientific freedom from interference from political or commercial interests. It became important to position oneself in the discussions in relation to the state socialist regime's outlook on science, and ideas concerning a closer relationship between science and politics were presented with great caution.

The boundary-work's linguistic representations thus dealt with a clear distinction primarily between science and politics, and a defence of what had been established during the roundtable discussions. A telling example of this in *Sprawy Nauki* was when Prime Minister Jan Krzysztof Bielecki, together with members of the Sejm and Senate, were invited to attempt, together with KBN's academics, to define a continued line for research policy based on *Principles*. In a speech that was published in the journal, Bielecki stressed the importance of maintaining a dialogue between politics and science with regard to both applied and basic research, with the emphasis on the fact that academics should almost be allowed to themselves determine the future of research policy regarding the relationship between science and politics,

> We want to participate in our development as an at least partially [*srednio*] industrialised country. Western countries have developed quickly through investing at a medium level in both improvement [*przetworzenia*] and research. I assume that these issues ought to interest research. I, being responsible for the government, should have asked you long before this for a dialogue and a formulation of questions such as this. It is extremely important for there to be a bridge between those who hold political power and those who have to set the best basic policy conditions. I do not know if we can do anything about that, or if everything has already been done, and that it is simply the case that we have not had time to achieve a consensus on these issues? Communication has not been at its best. Not least, this is about securing broad and active participation from scientists in Poland's transformation process (Bielicki 1991: 16).

In this statement science becomes a sphere whose right to self-determination seems inviolable, and it seems almost as if there hardly existed any communication between politicians and politically-active academics within

KBN during the first years of the transformation. At the same time Bielicki's statement can be interpreted as a hint of the importance of maintaining trust between academics and politicians and not sticking firmly to the autonomous position of the roundtable discussions, in order to be able to get closer to the industrialised core.

The caution expressed by Bielicki did, however, soon become increasingly rare in the discussions. This development was initiated by the meeting between the new research policy and the practical circumstances in the form of a national economic crisis and, as a consequence, the fact that the funds initially promised by the government for KBN's use were cut drastically. It is also in connection with this that the tone of the journal changed and actors who expressed themselves there to an increasing extent began to devote themselves to arguing for a renegotiation of the earlier demarcations surrounding science. The research funding system demanded, perhaps more than anything else in the formulation of the first framework of the new research policy model, a meeting between politics and science. Soon also the advertising of research funds according to the model created in the light of the roundtable discussions' maxim on total scientific freedom marked the start of the more critical discussions surrounding the idea of independent intellectual and autonomous thought. This criticism originated in the requirements for greater efficiency when the ideas of free applications came to nothing as a result of advertising funds where there were no instructions as to what research should be focused on. A chaotic situation (not unlike the general political situation) broke out when no practical options were found for performing the work of checking the thousands of applications that came streaming in. According to historian Antoni Kukliński (1992: 10), at that time a newly-appointed KBN member, the first application processes were characterised by the fact that,

> The procedure was very important, intensively discussed and difficult to prepare in document. It was to introduce principles of competition in a community, which hardly knew the idea of competitiveness. Moreover, the idea of financing of individual scientists had to be incorporated into the system which for decades served as an instrument of constraint of individual entrepreneurship. It had to be expected that numerous traps would show up in the process of the first research grants competition – from organizational and administrative problems to various conflicts of interest, which could easily undermine credibility of the results.

Thus the striving for scientific autonomy suddenly collided with such things as economic requirements, and the newly-won academic freedom ran into obstacles. The shortage of computers, inability to employ a large number of administrators, or simply the lack of copying equipment, paper, faxes, etcetera also quickly became an acute problem, which contributed to the gap between idea and reality. Kukliński (1992: 14–15) continues,

> One week before deadline there were only few hundreds of applications received. However, during the last days they were delivered literally on trucks and piled high up in three rooms. Finally 9524 applications were received in 48000 copies. The Committee had not had enough office cabinets [...] finally the committee received around 16000 reviews (average 1.7 reviews per project).

This situation gave rise to a more critical discussion in *Sprawy Nauki* concerning possibilities for realising the sought-after autonomy. It is also in this context that the documents that came to replace *Principles* were drawn up, and the continuing discussion and work on the boundaries surrounding science took place. In *Sprawy Nauki* it now becomes clear that a greater acceptance of politicisation, primarily in terms of drawing up strategies and prioritising fields (mainly for applied research), begins to take off. The roundtable discussion model was cautiously questioned (initially), and one of the participants in the discussion, economics professor Cezary Ambroziak (1992: 6), who was appointed to head the international cooperative effort on behalf of KBN, gave his opinion in an article that is representative of this type of argument,

> I would not turn my back to problems of scientific policy. One of the tasks is to find the answer to the question, whether the state, providing funds for scientific activity, should define priorities and if so where they should be introduced. Right now I will say I opt for priorities although I know that many would speak against them. I should like to emphasize, however, that in my understanding of this question priorities do not mean dispositions who should do what. There are not only topical priorities, but also others, for example structural priorities which mean preference given to some forms of cooperation between scientists, research establishments and users of results of scientific research. There are priorities at different levels – strategic, political, and operational.

This quotation illustrates how a re-evaluation and reinterpretation of how to pursue and talk about research policy and views on demarcations surrounding science were in the making, although Ambroziak discusses the prioritised research fields in rather vague terms. A cautious rhetoric aimed at dismantling the roundtable discussions' autonomous ideal can thus be discerned, although the statement implies that there is still support for the requirement to maintain the boundaries between science and politics in particular, in line with the roundtable discussions' demarcations. This type of argument becomes even more significant when Ambroziak goes on to state:

> I am aware that defining priorities is a very complicated, difficult and sensitive matter. However no government, especially the one operating in the time of economic crisis, can afford distribution of money, even for scientific research without at least an attempt to define in which areas the technological, social and economic progress is most desirable. Having limited financial resources at our disposal we would make serious mistake if we had not indicated priorities. Even the richest government of the United States has limited resources compared to the possible scope and range of research (Space Programme, AIDS prevention, SSA). No matter if we want it or not, the real setting of priorities begins in the phase of general distribution of the total amount allocated for research: for domestic research, for international scientific co-operation, building investment and so on. Often those distributions and proportions have been and are set up arbitrarily and mechanically (Ambroziak 1992: 6).

Here Ambroziak uses arguments concerning the handling of research policy in the Western world to defend politicisation of the research funding issue. He also makes it clear how the politicisation and coupling together of social benefit and science suddenly, and in contrast to the initial approach KBN took to the relationship between politics and science, becomes part of what is regarded as free, the Western, or American way of pursuing research policy with implications for boundary-work. When Ambroziak (1992: 7) continues, this becomes even clearer:

> In Poland at present, besides the idea of privatization of industry, the Government has no other clear policy regarding selection of priorities in industry and agriculture, being the main basis for economic development and the source of national income. Unless having no policy is the policy. However this is not a secret that in highly developed countries among priorities there are alternative energy sources, energy preservation, microelectronics, new materials and biotechnology. All of them, more or less, should be developed in Poland. At present the problem of priorities is being discussed in depth within KBN bodies and

before the next contest for research grants the priorities will be announced.

Pointing out what is the norm in highly developed countries becomes in Ambroziak's text yet another method for equating political control of science with a sensible way of pursuing research policy. That the Western, developed way had previously been at least partially equated with autonomy and scientific self-governance then lost currency, through the statement that Poland was attempting,

> to follow the model (or rather one of the models) of research financing that has proven its efficiency in the Western countries. In the West, however, each foundation defines precisely its policy and topical preferences while in our case we have committed a sin of childhood advertising the contest in which everyone could present any application for research grant, without any limitations and priorities being set up (Ambroziak 1992: 7–8).

It is clear that Ambroziak considers East to be a category not worth striving for. He thus himself reproduces Poland's position in the semiperiphery, and the West as the core. Equality between the concepts of development and a Western research policy model with greater political control of science, as well as the characterisation of the current Polish system as childish, also indicate that the struggle for credibility on the view of the boundaries between science and politics is now present in the discussion. The boundary-work Ambroziak performs is thus part of this struggle, with clear signs of attempts to both assert epistemic authority through the argument about the West, and discredit the former demarcations.

A number of articles from this period make similar arguments as Ambroziak's, and it becomes ever clearer how the change in tenor with regard to values ascribed to the West is gaining ground. In the boundary-work, the spatial concept thus functions as a tool for argument rather than as a static idea. On the one hand, the West can thus be interpreted as only synonymous with a break from state socialism, and characterised by anti-statism, and in that sense used by advocates of an ideal that lies closer to the roundtable discussions. On the other, the West is equated with greater control in the research policy context and becomes part of the argument for modernisation, and the dismantling of the roundtable discussions' demarcations. The invoking of the West thus also functions, whatever the standpoint, as a way of reproducing the notion of the East's semiperipheral position.

During 1992 the struggle for credibility in the boundary-work that takes place among the actors becomes ever clearer. The issue of scientific freedom and autonomy in relation to political control is discussed with emphasis in *Sprawy Nauki*, and almost every text in the journal relates to the issue of demarcations between science and politics. Despite the criticisms described above, cautiously formulated by Ambroziak and others against the round-table discussions' ideas, the latter still come up to a relatively large extent, although it is possible to discern a certain shift in the arguments. One of several examples is when professor of history Henryk Samsonowicz (1992: 8), who had just been appointed chairperson of the commission's basic research section, responded to the question of how he sees the research policy and scientific reform process so far:

> I am satisfied that the system proposed by the scientific community a long time ago has finally been put into operation. This was one of the demands expressed by scientific societies during debates at the 'round table' and even earlier. Administering the science by not always competent officers and not by scientists themselves has always been causing a lot of controversies, as far as the structure of science is concerned. Personally, being in favor of the idea of scientists administrating science, I have always thought that we should at least try to make this idea alive. The most difficult problem we are facing is connected with troubles shared by the whole country, i.e. with very limited financial capabilities.

The wording Samsonowicz uses indicates a somewhat more subdued hope that a research policy in the sense people saw before them during the roundtable discussions would be realised. In the debate it is far from obvious that the state, or the economy for that matter, would be able to control the research community and the orientation of research. Samsonowicz (1992: 9) points this out by explaining,

> The fate of science in Poland in this difficult period stays in hands of the members of the Committee and its groups – elected representatives of the scientific community, hundreds of members of branch sections and few thousand reviewers. The best Polish scientists, including members of Scientific Committees of the Polish Academy of Sciences are among them. Science is a elitarian profession, where the best have the right. It's true, we all have the same size stomachs, but it does not apply to our heads. Even a favourable budget for science will not permit rational

> financing of more than half of our scientific base. It's a duty of the State Committee for Scientific Research to exercise all possibilities to assure that this better and more needed half will be preserved.

It is remarkable how autonomous Polish research policy still was, and how utopian it seemed in relation to research policy in Western Europe during this period. This becomes clear in a characteristic article published by Krzysztof Frąckowiak, in which he brings up the need to introduce regulation of funding to an increasing extent, but at the same time calls for caution when the demarcations surrounding science begin to change:

> Financing, and not administration is an instrument of the scientific policy of the Committee. However a large part of the scientific community expect more detailed recommendations than a simple statement that the basic research should have high standards, and the applied research should be justified by prospective users of their results. Some clearly demand that areas of concentration of research should be determined, although very few seem to be aware that they might find themselves beyond such areas. [...] We can only suggest, that when reductions of the scientific potential are unavoidable, it's better to select directions of research than to apply so-called 'horizontal cuts' [...] I wish to warn clearly against sometimes observed misled interpretation of un-reiterated principles adopted by the Committee (Frąckowiak 1992: 17).

Advancing positions

Soon, however, the more cautious tone, primarily on the issue of drawing up strategies and prioritised research fields, began to disappear. This discussion was then, in terms of time, in line with the framing of *Basis*. A defence of greater regulation and the necessity for it gained ground. As a result of this, international cooperation and comparisons with research policy guidelines of EU countries also became something discussed to an increasing extent in *Sprawy Nauki*. The whole time, however, the issue of scientific self-governance and autonomy emerged as a constant theme, often in references to informal debates, which illustrates the struggle for credibility in the boundary-work between actors during the period. One of several such examples is an article in which professor of biochemistry Stefan Nawiakowski (1993: 6) asserts that the closer relationships between science, politics, and the business community are problematic:

Often cooperation between research and industry falls between two stools when it comes to scientific checks, and is instead checked by administrators and lawyers. We must remember the difficulties of recruiting doctoral students in a situation where educational levels are constantly sinking.

The implementation of *Basis* did not, however, lead to any comprehensive critical discussion, and the cautious deviation from the roundtable discussions' demarcations surrounding science was soon subject to less and less comment. This is remarkable, particularly when the free competition that at the start had been so promising now became limited through the government's prioritised programmes. At the same time, the reforms drawn up were completely in line with a scientific common sense, according to which applied research should primarily serve the interests of society. There was thus often a considerable consensus among the actors during the late 1990s, and the dismantling of the demarcations in the reforms during that period was in general met with cautious confidence.

One of many telling examples of this is the ideas of chemist Marek Borowiak in his article *Nauka jako biznes* ("Science as business"). He suggested that the trend toward increased investment in, and control of, applied research, and inclusion of market forces in the scientific world, was in the interest of both the country and science, since more funds could be obtained from private sources, thus strengthening the Polish scientific sphere in terms of knowledge, while at the same time the state won competition points on the international market. In his argument, the new approach thus became by extension an asset for all academics, including those from the sphere of basic research, which in the article's summing up resulted in a desire for "scientific business" to be managed macropolitically as a resource, and thus invested in further (Borowiak 1993: 14–15). Ascribing to science a utility value rather than, as before, an intrinsic value, was thus now almost universal, and constituted a tool in the dismantling of the roundtable discussions' demarcations.

The turn in the discussion towards prioritised investments and control, technical innovations, and the use of concepts such as social benefit and closer relationships between science, politics, and the business world were also often described by authors of articles as almost a natural stage of development. Nevertheless in *Sprawy Nauki* the invocation of the need for scientific freedom was also set in relation to the impossible in a research policy based on a kind of apolitical scientific republic. It was claimed that anyone who wants to be modern cannot persist with autonomy. In this way the rhetoric was characterised by avoiding being part of the semiperiphery and wishing to be accepted into the Western core. Now, in connection with the political strivings to become a member of the EU, the significance of what this West was began to shift away from meaning some kind of whole that included late-capitalist countries in general, to Western Europe.

This argument was also clear in texts in a short series of publications entitled *KBN – Science and Government Series*, in which active KBN members and academics who were not linked to the political ruling process documented the ongoing trend. Among other things, this became clear when Kukliński (1991: 1) in his foreword to the first issue started by writing about how important it is to defend autonomy, to then continue with the following argument:

> The autonomy of the scientific community should not accept the ivory tower approaches. The development of science takes place in the changing environment of political, social, economic, and cultural needs of the society which, *inter alia*, are more or less efficiently and correctly expressed by the government and its agencies. In turn, the majority of governments in modern countries recognize that there is no development without important contributions generated by innovative science [...] The science policy must be formulated in the pragmatic field situated between the Scylla of irrational and overextended governmental intervention and the Charybdis of the XIX-century *laissez faire* approaches.

As scientific autonomy has been such a sensitive issue in Poland, it had to be mentioned and handled cautiously by all parties concerned. Pointing out the social representativity of the state, or even of the political sphere, opened up the possibility of a more politicisation-friendly approach, and an argument consistent with the dismantling work. Here the state and its political agenda became an inevitable requirement for the practice of good research policy, with the best interests of society in mind. The boundary-work was now based to an increasing extent on the spheres becoming closer rather than on separation, with the help of arguments that the duty of science now also encompassed social development and social benefit.

The work of dismantling the demarcations surrounding science becomes clearer the closer we come to the initial preparations for Polish membership of the EU, and the creation of the document known as *Supplement*. Prior to implementation of the new strategies set out in this, the boundary-work of the increasingly large group of dismantling-friendly actors became, in the discussion, argumentatively focused on emphasising the need for internationalisation (often referred to as modernisation) of research policy, according to the maxim 'if you want to be able to compete with Western European countries and become valid EU members'. The striving to be accepted into the core was in this way still predominant, and also became a rhetorical tool that aimed to convince the government to make major economic investments in research generally. One example of this is when professor of computer science, Kazimierz Kowalski (1995: 10) wrote that,

> The changes in Polish science seem to be moving in the right direction, although distressingly slowly. If we will be able to become more open to the world than we are now and will succeed in traducing a policy ensuring competition and elimination of inefficient teams, then the financial means which must be found for science will be used to full advantage and only then we will enter the road leading us to the European Science.

Another example is KBN member and science historian Jan Kozłowski's thoughts on the extent to which effective competition in relation to the Western world is today due to higher technological skills. According to him, a lack of focus in these areas concerning applied research in terms of state investment and prioritisation would become apparent in the future, and investment in research should not be seen as anything other than an investment. Research policy investments should therefore aim at the creation of "scientific islands of high-tech research" (Kozłowski 1995: 54). He concluded his argument by summarising, in two points, which science policy targets prior to entry into the EU ought to apply, namely knowledge development that links firms, scientific institutions, and state laboratories, and encouragement of innovations in society. Now the cautious line had moved forward somewhat, and increasingly close relationships between primarily science, politics, and the business community were asserted by the actors to be worth striving for. Yet another clear example of this was when Kozłowski (2000: 111) wrote a few years later that the EU and OECD countries "have reached the stage of social and economic development where omnipresence of innovations together with their R&D components is the key driver of their civilization advancement". Political control of primarily applied research can, according to his argument, be interpreted as an element of modernisation and the good Western Europeanisation of research policy, a political control that just a few years previously was, on the contrary, part of a state socialist, criticised view of science. A dismantling of the boundaries is thus again, but in a somewhat sharper argument, given credibility through reference to "best practices" (ibid.) of modern developed countries.

Conclusions

The general political trend in Poland in the early 1990s was strongly characterised by the almost chaotic context arising from the initial phase of the transformation process. For the research policy sphere, this period particularly involved major reorganisations, restructuring and a 'detox' from the country's state socialist heritage. The boundaries between state, industry, and academia were in the research policy spotlight, and the clear emphasis on autonomy that had been the guiding principle during the roundtable negotiations, had a significant impact on how research policy was organised.

Soon, however, there began a renegotiation and reinterpretation of the roundtable discussions' demarcations regarding science, partly as an effect of the rapid awakening following the 'shock therapy' for the country's economy, when the need for public resources for building up the market economy made itself felt. The earlier, almost utopian attitude in accordance with the Humboldtian research ideal of the Polish intelligentsia was increasingly called into question, and ambiguity arose. One of the areas where this process became clear was the discussion on research policy in *Sprawy Nauki*. The boundary-work done there was charactarised by the will to modify the distinct demarcation between the scientific and political sphere that had been established in connection with the roundtable discussion. The visions promoted leaned towards a social needs-oriented formulation of priorities and strategies for the Polish research policy. It is obvious that the rhetorical tools these actors used to promote the change of the roundtable ideals were based on the attractiveness of the symbolic West. The dichotomy between East and West runs right through the discussions, where a 'Western European' orientation stood for what was worth striving for, and an 'Eastern European' orientation for what was to be abandoned. The West did not represent any static value, but it was used, depending on the actors' aims for the boundary-work, to improve the impact of different arguments.

With the help of this rhetorical tool the adovcates of the approach seeking to dismantle the autonomy of science were able to renegotiate and reinterpret the demarcations regarding science in discussions on Polish research policy in *Sprawy Nauki*. As the discussants also were the ones in charge of research policy, their framing had impact on the formulation of innovation-oriented strategic programmes, a closer relationship between industry and research in policy formulations, and increasing focus on applicable research in steering documents. This is evident in connection with the publication of *Basis* and *Supplement* with their increasingly emphasised distinction of applied research and basic research, two fields that were previously clumped together as one kind of research demanding freedom and autonomy.

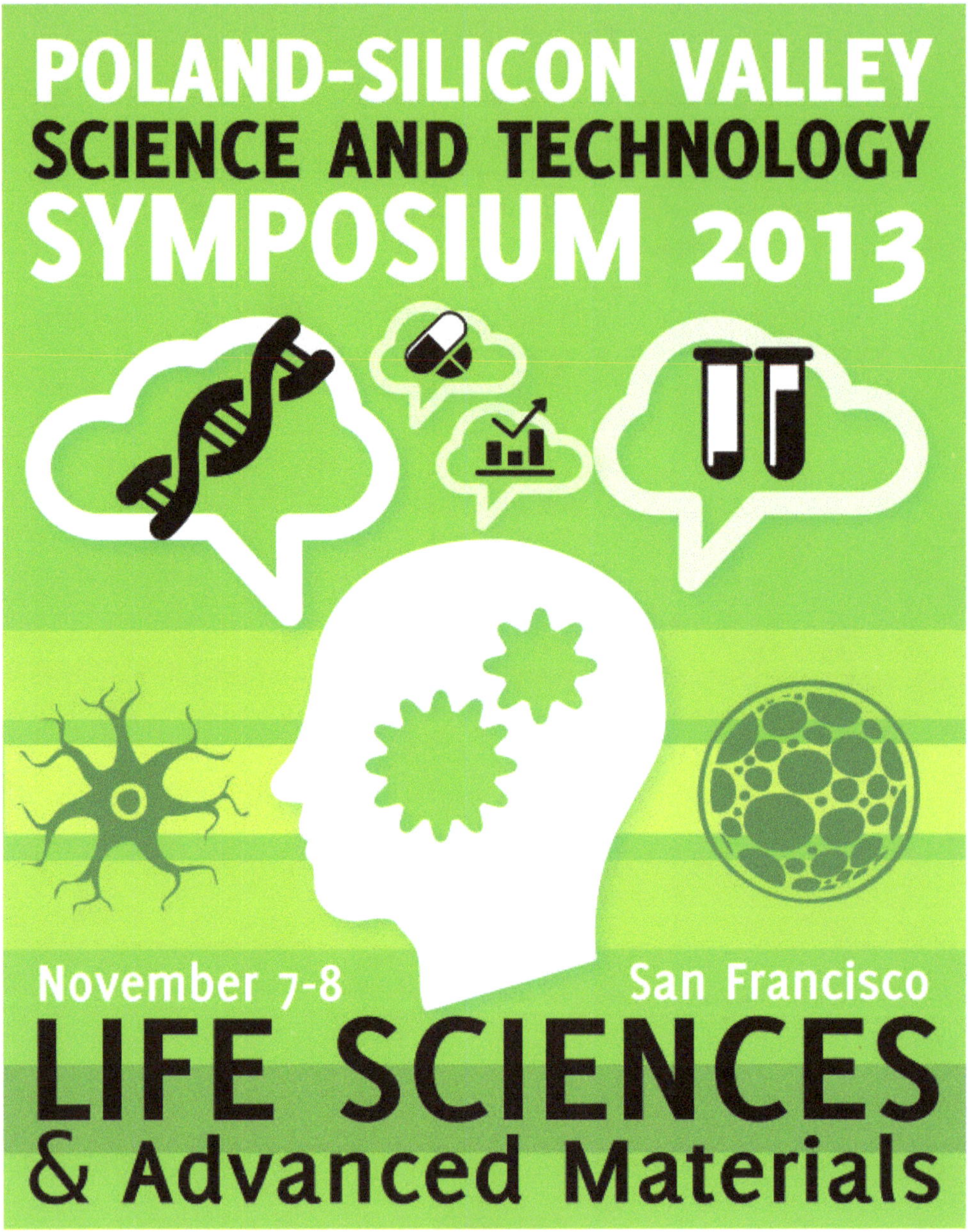

Poster for the Polish science event in San Francisco, 7–8 Nov. 2013 (© USPTC)

References

Ambroziak, C. (1992) "After Two Months in the KBN." *Bulletin of the State Committee for Scientific Research* (no. 1), 7–9.

Andrén, M. (2001) *Att frambringa det uthärdliga: Studier till idén om Centraleuropa.* Hedemora: Gidlund.

[Basis] "Założenia polityki naukowej i naukowo technicznej państwa: Cele, priorytety, finansowanie" (1993) *Przeglad Rzadowy* 8, 66–75.

Bielecki, J. K. (1991) "Wystąpienie premiera Jana Krzysztofa Bieleckiego na posiedzeniu komitetu badań naukowych." *Bulletin of the State Committee for Scientific Research* (no. 1), 16–19.

Blagojević, M. (2010) "Non-'White' Whites, Non-European Europeans and Gendered Non-Citizens: On a Possible Epistemic Strategy from the Semiperiphery of Europe." *Gender Knowledge and Knowledge Networks in International Political Economy*, ed. by Young, B. and Scherrer, Ch. Baden-Baden: Nomos, 183–97.

Borowiak, M. (1993) "Nauka jako biznes." *Bulletin of the State Committee for Scientific Research* (no. 4), 14–15.

Connelly, J. (2000) *Captive University: The Sovietization of East Germany, Czech, and Polish Higher Education 1945–1956.* Chapel Hill: The University of North Carolina Press.

Eder, K. (2006) "Europe's Borders: The Narrative Construction of the Boundaries of Europe." *European Journal of Social Theory* 9 (2), 255–71.

Frąckowiak, J. K. (1992) "Research Grants: New System of Science Financing in Poland." *Bulletin of the State Committee for Scientific Research* (no. 1), 4–5.

Framework 3C. Framework Programme of Community Activities in the Field of Research and Technological Development 1990–1994. Record Number: L 117 Retrieved: 1990-05-08, no. 164. CORDIS, European Comission.

Gerner, K. (2009) "Polen: Från motstånd i Gdansk till EU-medlemskap." *Det nya Östeuropa: Stat och nation i förändring*, ed. by Björklund, F. and Rodin, J. Lund: Studentlitteratur, 219–44.

Gieryn, T. F. (1999) *Cultural Boundaries of Science: Credibility on the Line.* Chicago: University of Chicago Press.

Herczyński, R. (2008) *Spętana nauka: Opozycja intelektualna w Polsce 1945–1970.* Warsaw: Semper.

Ivanov, K. (2002) "Science after Stalin." *Science in Context* 15 (2), 317–38.

Jabłecka, J. (2009) *Finansowanie badań ze źrodeł publicznych.* Warsaw: Centrum Badań Polityki Naukowej i Szkolnictwa Wyższego.

Kennedy, M. (1991) *Professionals, Power and Solidarity in Poland: A Critical Sociology of Soviet-Type Society.* Cambridge: Cambridge University Press.

Kolarska-Bobińska, B. (2003) "The EU Accesion and Strenghtening of Institutions in East Central Europe: The Case of Poland." *East European Politics and Societies* 17 (1), 91–8.

Kozłowski, J. (1995) "Polityka naukowa: Polityka innowacyjna." *Sprawy Nauki* (no. 3), 54–6.

Kozłowski, J. (1998) "Institutional Transformation of the STS in Poland." *Transforming Science and Technology Systems: The Endless Transition*, ed. by Meske, W. Amsterdam: IOS Press, 90–7.

Kozłowski, J. (2000) "Research Administrations in Central and Eastern European Countries under the Burden of the Past." *The Knowledge-Based Economy: The European Challenges of the 21st Century*, ed. by Kukliński, A. Warsaw: KBN, 107–14.

Kukliński, A., ed. (1991) *Transformation of Science in Poland.* Warsaw: SCSRRP.

Kukliński, A. (1992) "Polish Science: Experiences and Perspectives." *Bulletin of the State Committee for Scientific Research* (no. 1), 10–11.

Kowalski, K. (1995) "Polish Science and European Challenge." *Sprawy Nauki* (no. 1), 10–11.

Lindelöf, K. (2006) *Om vi nu ska bli som Europa: Könsskapande och normalitet bland unga kvinnor i transitionens Polen.* Gothenburg: Makadam.

Nawiakowski, S. (1993) "Nie ma idealnego system." *Bulletin of the State Committee for Scientific Research* (no. 6), 5–7.

Norling, S. (2014) *Mot "väst": Vetenskap, politik och transformation i Polen 1989–2011.* Huddinge: Södertörn University.

Péteri, G. (2010) *Imagining the West in Eastern Europe and the Soviet Union.* Pittsburgh: University of Pittsburgh Press.

[Principles] "Założenia do aktów prawnych dotyczących obszaru nauki, szkolnictwa wyższego i działalności badawczo-rozwojowej" (1993[1991]). *Nauka Polska, Jej Potrzeby, Organizacja i Rozwój 2.*

Raciborski, J. (2003) "System rządów w Polsce: Między semiprezydencjalizmem a systemem parlamentarno-gabinetowym." *Demokracja Polska 1989–2003*, ed. by Wiatr, J. Warsaw: Scholar, 75–97.

Samsonowicz, H. (1992) "After Two Months in the KBN." *Bulletin of the State Committee for Scientific Research* (no. 1), 8–9.

The Supplement to The Basis for the National Science and Technology Policy (1997) [title of the Polish original: Dodatkowe Założenia polityki naukowej i naukowo-technicznej państwa: Cele, priorytety, finansowanie]. Warsaw: KBN.

"Ustawa z 12 stycznia 1991 r.o Komitetcie Badań Naukowych" (1991) *Dziennik Ustaw* (no. 33) poz. 389.

Wierzbicki, A., ed. (1997) *Science & Technology*. White Paper, Poland – the European Union. Warsaw: Institute of Control and Computation Engineering WUT.

Part 2: Labour Identities

6. Lost Worlds of Labour: Paul Olberg, the Jewish Labour Bund, and Menshevik Socialism

Håkan Blomqvist[1]

> One of the darker sides of getting older, I feel, is that of having to outlive so many people one has known. Even here in Rome or in Milan, or wherever I happen to be, I recall those who no longer exist. Ever more seldom does one meet those people to whom one can say: Do you remember?

These words of the elderly Ukrainian Jewish socialist, Angelica Balabanoff in Italy, were read out by Ture Nerman at the interment in Skogskyrkogården's Jewish burial ground in Stockholm, one day in May 1960.[2] Paul Olberg was dead. He had been honoured from near and far with telegrams and flowers of condolence. "In the socialist world we feel deep sorrow and loss", explained the Party Secretary of Sweden's Social Democrats, Sven Aspling. But in particular, continued Aspling, it was Swedish Social Democracy that owed a debt of gratitude to Olberg, for his unfailing contributions to the socialist movement "in the country that was finally to become his homeland".[3] It was here, in Sweden, through his loyal membership of the party, that he became a dynamic participant in its activities and information

---

[1] I would like to thank Dr Paul Glasser for the translations of YIVO-documents from Yiddish and Nadezda Petrusenko for help with translations from Russian.
[2] "Vid gravsättningen av Paul Olbergs aska den 29 maj 1960", manuscript of Ture Nerman, Arbetarrörelsens Arkiv och Bibliotek in Stockholm (Stockholm Labour Archive and Library, hereafter ARAB), Paul Olberg's personal archive 435 (hereafter POA), vol. 25.
[3] Graveside address on burial of Olberg, by the party secretary S. Aspling, May 1960, manuscript of T. Lindbom, ARAB, POA, vol. 19.

work, by way of his numerous articles written for the labour movement press and the lectures given over the years.

Swedish Social Democracy was on its way to reaching its zenith, with record years of economic growth and the building of the welfare society (the so-called People's Home). But the praise from Balabanoff and others did not come in the first place from successful welfare-builders and pillars of state, but from the increasingly rare living memories of another cosmos, from radical socialist movements which had long been crushed in the vice of opposing forces – Soviet communism and capitalism, east and west – and then diffused in exile milieux the world over.

To this lost world belonged remnants of Russian Menshevism which had striven to survive as influential elements in the great social democratic mass parties in the West, in the inter-war and post-war periods. They comprised an aged and shrinking generation of orthodox Marxist social democrats from the period before 1917. In the funeral cortege at Skogskyrkogården, an observer noticed an almost exotic feature: Paul Olberg was followed to his final resting place by his fellow members of the Jewish Labour Bund (Paul Olberg död 1960). The same Bund – the once so powerful Jewish labour movement – that in 1905 shook Tsarism in Russia to its foundations and, through the uprising in the Warsaw Ghetto in 1943, showed the world that the Jews would not go like lambs to the slaughter. Paul Olberg, Menshevik and member of the Bund, through his long political life can help us now to illuminate the socialist world that disappeared in the east between 1917 and 1945 as well as the varied political destiny of the remnants.

The purpose of this chapter is, by way of certain main features in Paul Olberg's biography, to sketch out a political landscape in the labour movement that, once upon a time, was of great significance and that can contribute to our understanding of ideological influences within Social Democracy during the inter-war and early post-war years.

Olberg as Menshevik

Paul, or Pavel Karlovitj, Olberg was born in 1878 into a Jewish family in the Latvian town of Jakobstadt (nowadays Jekabpils) within the Russian empire. As a seventeen-year old, he joined the growing Jewish labour movement which in 1897 in Vilnius founded the Bund – or *Der algemeyner yidisher arbeter bund in Lite, Poyln un Rusland* – as the name was in Yiddish (*Lite* for Lithuania was added in 1901).[4] The Bund was among the instigators of the formation of the Russian Social Democratic Labour Party the following year. Olberg himself already had several years behind him of illegal activities as participant in the underground *kruzhki* – worker circles – smuggling Marxist literature during nighttime in the moorland tracts around Pinsk.[5] On account of this activity he was seized and imprisoned when twenty-one years old. Like so many other radicals, the year in prison became, in Olberg's own words, his "literary faculty" (75-årige 1953). With Marx, Engels, Lassalle, and Plekhanov in his intellectual baggage, he resumed his activities after his release, participated in the first Russian Revolution in 1905, moved between different places in the Russian Empire, and wrote for the socialist press.

With the split in the Russian Social Democrats in 1903, Olberg adopted a position in support of Pavel Axelrod's and Julius Martov's Menshevik faction. It was on the same occasion that the Bund also broke with the social democratic Bolshevik majority when the Bund's position as independent Jewish organisation was questioned. On the reunification of Russian Social Democracy, three years later in Stockholm, the Bund rejoined once more. In the division that occurred between Bolshevists and Mensheviks the members of the Bund, in general and after some hesitation, came subsequently to belong to the Menshevik side (Wolin 1974: 251, 272, 286, 311; Sapir 1974: 375; Liebich 1997: 40; Minczeles 1999: 114).

Olberg belonged to the Russian Marxist exile milieu in Switzerland after the defeat of the first Russian revolution and his first son, Valentin Pavlovich, was born in Zürich 1907.[6] Two years later his second son, Pavel Pavlovich, was born in Helsinki where Olberg, among other things, participated in the Finnish cooperative movement. Via this movement he came into contact with the Swedish Cooperative Union (KF) and contributed to

---

[4] Biographical information in print on Olberg's life occurs in newspaper articles concerning birthdays and in death notices. Here the information has been obtained from the articles: 75-årige 1953; Iz Partii 1958; En flyktingarnas vän 1958; Paul Olberg: Zum 1958; Paul Olberg 80 1958; Paul Olberg gestorben 1960; Paul Olberg död 1958; Pavel Karlovich Olberg 1960; Old Yiddish 1960. Paul Olberg's personal archive (ARAB, POA) includes his passport, press cards, and correspondence that contributes to his life story. Biographical information is to be found in S. Aspling's graveside address (see footnote 3) as well as in F.M. Olberg's handwritten fragmentary and anecdotal biographical details "Kogda moi muzj inogda raskazyval ...", ARAB, POA, vol. 30.
[5] F.M. Olberg "Kogda moi muzj inogda raskazyval ...", ARAB, POA, vol. 30.
[6] His wife writes in her biographical notes that Olberg went to Geneva already before the Russian Revolution in 1905 to study historical materialism on behalf of the pioneer of Russian Marxism, G. Plekhanov, see F.M. Olberg "Kogda moi muzj inogda raskazyval ...", ARAB, POA, vol. 30.

the publication *Kooperatören* with articles on cooperativism and economic conditions in Russia.[7]

In the wake of the Russian February Revolution in 1917, Olberg assisted, through the Russian support committee, those political emigrants in Stockholm returning home, the onward transportation of the Russian exile milieu who, from different corners of Europe, headed back to Russia via Sweden (Björkegren 1985: 251). He also took part, together with Axelrod, in the work of establishing an information bureau in Stockholm for the Russian Petrograd Soviet which at this time was dominated by the Mensheviks (Kan 2005: 128–9). Amongst the group of comrades in Stockholm was the Menshevik Bernard Mehr, a Swedish version of the name Bejnes Meyerowich. Like Olberg, his contemporary, Mehr originated from a Jewish family in Latvia where he was involved with the emerging social democratic labour movement but succeeded in reaching Sweden in 1905, having escaped from political imprisonment (Elmbrant 2010: 18–20).

In Sweden, Bernhard met and married the young Bund follower Sara Matles who, at about the same time, had fled from the city of Grodno (now in Belarus) when Tsardom crushed the rebellious strike wave in 1905 (ibid. 15–18). Bernhard and Sara Mehr constituted a hub in the support work for Russian political migrants during the stormy revolutionary periods around 1905 and 1917. Much later, in another era, Paul Olberg and Sara Mehr were to meet up again, this time in connection with a new help effort for refugees from the east.

Together with Axelrod, Olberg participated during the spring of 1917 in the preparations for the Stockholm Peace Conference, a failed attempt of the International Socialist Bureau (ISB), through a Dutch–Scandinavian working group to reconcile the different attitudes of European Social Democracy on the peace question (Sitzung 1917; Ascher 1972: 325–33). In a series of articles in *Social-Demokraten* Olberg defended the plans in response to the criticism of the Russian Bolshevists and the Swedish Social Democratic Left Party (Olberg 1917; Kan 2005: 131). Olberg belonged to the Russian Menshevik milieu in Stockholm which, to begin with, did not adopt a position in respect of the split in the ranks of the Swedish Social Democrats the same spring.

---

[7] Letter of recommendation by A. Gjöres, head of KF's organisation department and T. Odhe, editor of the periodical *Kooperatören*, Stockholm 28 May 1938, ARAB, POA, vol. 1. In the letter it is stated that Olberg in 1916 was recommended to the management of Sweden's KF publications by the Finnish cooperative movement's representative, Professor H. Gebhard.

Not only the Bolsheviks but also the Mensheviks sent fraternal greetings to the newly formed Social Democratic Left Party of Sweden on the occasion of its first congress in May 1917. During these spring months, with food riots occurring even in Sweden, the different wings of Swedish Social Democracy sought to bring clarity to the question of who represented what amongst the currents of Russian socialism, whereas the Russian socialists, conversely, sought to position themselves in response to the Swedish movement.

Through Stockholm, which for a time became the meeting place of international socialism, there flowed a stream of revolutionaries and reformists, internationalists and social patriots, pacifists and Leninists.

Here, Olberg not only belonged to the Menshevik circle but came into contact with the leading figures of Swedish Social Democracy such as Hjalmar Branting, Gustav Möller, and Arthur Engberg as well as figures of the Social Democratic Left Party such as Fredrik Ström, Zeth Höglund, and Ture Nerman. He got to know Angelica Balabanoff of the Zimmerwald movement who, a couple of years later, joined the Communist International, as well as many other prominent personalities of these revolutionary years. However, he also developed contacts with wider circles who were interested in developments in Russia.[8]

From the summer of 1917, Olberg was Stockholm correspondent for the Menshevik newspaper *Novaja Zhizn* in Petrograd, with Maxim Gorky as its most widely known writer (Kan 2005: 128).[9] The newspaper was banned by the Russian Provisional Government in September 1917 – that is to say, during the stormy days when Kornilov's troops marched on Petrograd to suffocate the ever stronger Soviet power base in the Russian capital. The publication of the paper was resumed from Moscow where, however, it was finally stopped by the new Bolshevik proletarian dictatorship in July 1918.

It was also during the year 1918 that Olberg returned to Russia and Petrograd for a time. In three articles for the Swedish *Social-Demokraten*, in the autumn of 1919, on the subject "Soviet Russia in reality", he criticised the Bolshevik terror, corruption, misrule, and food shortages (Olberg 1919a). Bolshevism had, believed Olberg, established a regime "with which

---

[8] From October 1917 to August 1918, he served for a period as editorial secretary for the publication *Shvedskii Eksport* which was issued in Russian by the Swedish Export Association (Sveriges Allmänna Exportförening), see letter of recommendation by Bengt Ljungberger, Stockholm 19 Nov. 1919, ARAB, POA, vol. 26.

[9] P. Olberg, press card for *Novaja Zhizn*, Petrograd 7 July 1917 in "Handlingar rörande Maxim Gorkis tidning", ARAB, POA, vol. 1.

the darkest times of Tsarism seem to pale in comparison." This was not the dictatorship of the proletariat but a dictatorship "over the proletariat" where all the freedoms of the working class are repressed and the regime could only rely on bayonets. "Time's wheel has rolled backwards", was Olberg's (1919a I) conclusion. The strongly Bolshevik-critical article series was inspired by his diary-like *Briefe aus Sowjet-Russland* (Letters from Soviet Russia) which was issued in pamphlet form in Germany the same year (Olberg 1919b).

The articles were valuable for Swedish Social Democracy which, in 1919, was under pressure from the Soviet Russian example. They were published at the same time as Swedish Social Democracy was forced to meet the challenge from the Communist International – the Comintern – which had been formed the same spring and counted the newly formed Swedish Social Democratic Left Party among its first member organisations. The large Branting meeting in the Auditorium in autumn 1919, convened to declare the social democratic rejection of the Bolshevik dictatorship of the proletariat (Demokrati 1919), coincided with the publication of Olberg's articles. It was during the time when Yudenich's military offensive had started against Petrograd and bourgeois opinion nurtured hopes that Bolshevik power was near its end. For the Swedish Left Socialists, the circumstances demonstrated how the Menshevik Olberg, who during his time in Russia "enjoyed all privileges", had now come to exalt Tsarism and as an "old, experienced newspaper man" knew how to write to "the full satisfaction of Soviet Russia's enemies" (M. 1919).

For Olberg, on the contrary, Branting's hard line against Bolshevism was proof that Swedish Social Democracy had risen to the challenge just as the Mensheviks themselves had. Paul Olberg's knowledge and documentation from within the Russian revolution and the development of the crisis became highly valued ammunition against the left leaning critics in the Swedish labour movement that were drawn to the Comintern. Already during the revolutionary year of 1917 and in the immediate post-war years Paul Olberg thus became a contributor to the Swedish Social Democratic press with a significant personal contact network amongst leading Swedish Social Democrats as a consequence.

The Mensheviks in exile

It was some time towards the end of 1918 that Paul Olberg left Russia and travelled to Berlin, the city that was in the throes of the German Revolution and the Spartacist Uprising in January 1919. An identity card, issued by the Workers' and Soldiers' Council in Berlin in November 1918, indicates that Olberg is in their service.[10] He was, already at that time, a man of experience and a political writer who, forty years old, had witnessed the Russian workers' movement birth and growth with all its ideological and political conflicts, the Russian revolutions of 1905 and 1917, the seizure of power by the Bolsheviks and the start of the Civil War. He had a wide network of contacts in the Russian, Swedish, and European social democratic parties and a wealth of experience as a socialist writer in several countries.

In the Berlin which he came to, the Social Democratic Party (SPD) had split apart and not only owing to the revolutionary surge of Spartacism. In the Independent Social Democratic Party (USPD), which was formed by the opponents of war within German Social Democracy in spring 1917, there were also party legends such as the 'father of revisionism' Eduard Bernstein and the interpreter of orthodox Marxism, Karl Kautsky. For Olberg, his wife Frida Markovna recalls, the articles he wrote for the German workers' press were literally "worth gold" and not just in political terms. "For the first article in the party newspaper *Vorwärts* he received two gold coins of 20 marks from Karl Kautsky."[11] As a writer for the German Social Democratic press and its leading organ *Vorwärts*, Olberg was able to get to know many of the key figures; he stayed for a period with Bernstein and served as Kautsky's secretary during his trip to Georgia in autumn 1920, before the Red Army invaded the country. The friendship with Kautsky and his family would last all his life.[12]

When the majority in the USPD decided to affiliate to the Communist International in 1920 the way back to the Social Democratic Party opened up for those who opposed the Bolshevik dictatorship. Even the Russian Mensheviks who identified with the USPD were to rejoin the SPD. It was during the period 1921–22, after the end of the Civil War, when the leading Mensheviks in Russia were forced to choose between banishment to Siberia or going into exile. The party had joined the Bolshevik side in the Civil War and operated legally in the new Soviet institutions but was subsequently faced by an ultimatum to join the ruling party or be declared illegal. The

---

[10] The card states that Herr Olberg "steht im Dienst des Arbeiter- und Soldatenrats. Berlin, November 1918." It was issued by "Der Ausschuß für öffentliche Sicherheit", ARAB, POA, vol. 1.
[11] F.M. Olberg "Kogda moi muzj inogda raskazyval …", ARAB, POA, vol. 30.
[12] For Olberg's extensive correspondence with Kautsky and his family, see ARAB, POA, vol. 23; correspondence with Bernstein in ARAB, POA, vol. 20.

party leader, Julius Martov, had left for Berlin in 1920 and, in the emerging Menshevik exile milieu, started the newspaper *Sotsialistitcheskii vestnik* – the Socialist Courier – commonly called *Vestnik*. Under the leadership of Martov and Rafael Abramovitch, in the Menshevik party's evolving foreign bureau, *Vestnik* was to form a mouthpiece for the Mensheviks, in practice the party leadership, for thirty years and continued to appear for a further decade. After Martov's death in 1923, Fyodor Dan was appointed the party leader while Abramovitch continued as Editor-in-Chief, right up to the last edition of *Vestnik* in 1963. By then, the newspaper and party had moved steadily westwards, both geographically and politically, from Berlin to Paris in connection with Hitler's accession to power, and from Paris to New York on the German occupation of France in 1940.[13]

It was in the Russian Menshevik exile milieu in Berlin, as well as in German and Latvian Social Democratic circles, that Paul Olberg was mainly active during the 1920s. The Russian Menshevik Party rejected from the start any plans to build up a new party in exile. Membership of the party's foreign organisation was only open to those who had joined before the seizure of power by the Bolsheviks in November 1917, whether the person was active illegally in Soviet Russia or in exile (Wolin 1997: 320-1). The party's members in exile during the 1920s may have numbered only a few hundred, of whom a small number were from the former party leadership of the years in Russia. Olberg never belonged to this leadership but had been a member ever since the foundation congress of the Russian Social Democratic Labour Party in 1898 and his background within the Latvian Social Democratic movement was significant in this case.

During the Latvian independence process in 1918, a new Social Democratic party under Menshevik leadership was formed; this party was to occupy a strong position in inter-war Latvia, up to the coup d'état in 1934, when it was banned. Through the Latvian Mensheviks, among others, the leadership in exile was able to establish close contact with supporters in Soviet Russia for intelligence and sharing of information (Liebich 1997: 106, 128). *Vestnik* could thereby include detailed knowledge about the Soviet developments that Olberg and other writers then communicated to social democratic circles in Europe.

The strategy for the Mensheviks in exile was, after their attempt to participate in the building of international cooperation through the so-

---

[13] For a complete overview of *Sotsialistitcheskii Vestnik's* publication, articles, and writers down the years, see Liebich (1992).

called Vienna International in the early 1920s, to become members of the mass membership social democratic parties in the West (Liebich 1997: 157–63). There they could contribute knowledge about the Russian experience and ideologically uphold what they saw as a Marxian perspective. As representatives of the Russian Social Democratic Workers Party, they were also represented in the re-established Socialist International leadership.

Menshevism regarded itself, through its central interpreters in the persons of Pavel Axelrod, Julius Martov, and his successor Fyodor Dan, as orthodox Marxist revolutionaries in contrast to what they saw as the utopian, voluntarian, and terroristic Bolshevism (Ascher 1972). Socialism was, as they saw it, an unavoidable historical consequence of capitalism's development, but which could only come about, as Marx explained, when capitalism's productive forces broke the old shackles holding back the forces of production. It was in the western world, where capitalistic industrial development had come furthest, and where proletarian wage work was predominant, that the prospects were to be found for a socialist transformation, not in backward Russia. Russian peasant society must first undergo its industrial modernisation before the preconditions even existed for the socialist phase. The task for Marxists in Russia, therefore, was, through the revolution, to establish a parliamentary democracy where the productive forces could be developed, an emerging labour movement strengthened and the conditions prepared for social reforms and the future socialist transformation (Sapir 1974: 364–89).

The Mensheviks believed that Bolshevism turned Marx upside down; their proletarian dictatorship was a despotic camouflage for archaic hierarchies and backward economic conditions. An expression for this viewpoint was the Menshevik criticism during the 1920s of the Soviet so-called New Economic Policy (NEP) where they maintained that the Bolshevik-led power of the Soviets was not in any way a proletarian dictatorship but, in social terms, appeared to be developing towards a bureaucratic state capitalist dictatorship (Wolin 1974: 245–9).

For Paul Olberg, therefore, his activities as journalist in Menshevik exile circles and, above all, on behalf of German, Latvian, and Swedish Social Democracy were central during his years in Berlin. But the personal networks within Russian Menshevism and European Social Democracy which, on that day in May 1960, would be reflected in the bouquets and telegrams that accompanied him to his final resting place, also included another dimension: the Jewish Labour Bund.

The Bund

The Bund, after its formation in 1897, had developed into a Jewish labour movement without peer in areas of Jewish settlement in the Russian empire; from Vilnius in the north-west and down across Belarusian, Polish, and Ukrainian communities where a Jewish proletariat emerged in the early years of the twentieth century. The organisation built its movement into a proletarian Jewish cosmos, based around a secular and socialist Yiddish culture in the form of political clubs and trade union sections, children and youth organisations, schools and orphanages, theatrical and cultural activities, sporting organisations and self-defence groups (Blatman 2003; Jacobs 2001; Minczeles 1999; Slucki 2012; Traverso 1997; Weinstock 2002).

Ideologically, the Bund differentiated itself both from the Marxists – Bolsheviks as well as Mensheviks – who favoured Jewish assimilation under the banner of universalism, and from the Zionist movement which was born in Basel the same year that the Bund was formed. Through its ideologues, with Arkady Kremer and Vladimir Medem as leading figures, the Bund developed a view of the national dimension and national rights that lay near the theoretical currents of Austro-Marxism, mainly formulated through Karl Renner and Otto Bauer.[14] In contrast to what was seen as Zionism's unrealistic utopianism and bourgeois nationalism, the Bund propagated the message of *doykait*; that the Jewish working people should struggle for their rights 'in situ' where they lived, 'here and now'. Through Jewish cultural autonomy within democratic civic states, the foundations would be laid for mankind's socialist liberation without the need for repression and subjection.

Like the Austro-Marxists, the Bund developed its perspective in a multi-ethnic empire and did not conceive that the liberation of the proletariat would be achieved through separation into new national states. Here the Bund was ideologically closer to the radical, more cosmopolitan Marxism which, in the figure of Rosa Luxemburg and others repudiated all merely national solutions (Hudis and Anderson 2004). However, unlike this current which in the name of internationalism also rejected the building of Jewish identity, the Bund was active in asserting, strengthening, and developing such an identity on the basis of socialist ideals. Yiddish as a linguistic

---

[14] Renner (1870–1950) and Bauer (1881–1938) were leading Austrian Social Democrats and Marxists. Bauer (1907) outlined his strategy in *Die Nationalitätenfrage und die Sozialdemokratie*. For Austro-Marxim, see Olausson (1987).

and cultural, secular and socialist community came to emerge as the distinguishing feature of the Bund.

The Russian revolution of 1905 coincided with the Bund's first heyday. The second could have been the Russian February revolution in 1917 but the movement was already then weakened by repression, ethnic cleansing, and the downfall of the Russian empire. With the seizure of power by Bolshevism, the Bund was subsequently brought face-to-face, like the Mensheviks, with an ultimatum of being repressed or merging with the victorious Bolshevik party. During the Russian Civil War, parts of the movement like the Jewish population otherwise, had joined the Red Army and the Soviets in self-defence against the 'White' side's anti-semitic mass pogroms. Under the designation *Kombund* elements of the Russian Bund were absorbed in the Communist Party's Jewish sections, *jevsektsii* (Gitelman 1972; Minczeles 1999: 260–2, 265–70, Weinstock 2002: 181–90, 233–8).

As part of Russian Social Democracy's organisational sphere, the Bund was to split apart during the Russian Revolution. While certain of the movement's leaders and elements followed Bolshevism, others came to regard themselves as part of the Menshevik-led bloc which was driven into exile. Among these was Paul Olberg and, as a Jewish socialist, he was far from alone. Almost the entire leadership group in the foreign bureau of the Mensheviks comprised intellectuals with a Jewish background (Liebich 1997: 12). But like so many other Russian and Polish Jewish Marxists – from Leo Trotsky to Rosa Luxemburg – the majority did not cultivate any Jewish identity *per se* but rather saw themselves as global revolutionaries in the service of humanity. They opposed both nationalist, as well as what we today would call ethnic oppression; they saw themselves as serving a greater cause than merely being champions of the Jewish proletariat, and they did not use the Jewish issue as a campaign banner. For supporters of the Jewish Bund, however, matters were rather different.

Rafael Abramovitch was one of the historic leaders of the Bund who, since the reunification of Russian Social Democracy in 1906, had represented the movement in the reunited party's central committee. With the split in the Russian Bund, Abramovitch and other Bund members followed the path of the Mensheviks and went into exile (Minczeles 1999: 266–7). Even though the Bund in Russia had been dissolved, Abramovitch remained in the Russian Menshevik exile leadership and, as an experienced publisher of Bund newspapers, became the editor of the newly started *Vestnik*. Abramovitch was always a Bundist, above all else, according to André Liebich in his history of Russian Menshevism in exile (1997: 26).

As writer for the Yiddish language *Forverts* in New York, the newspaper intended for the growing Jewish working class in the United States, Abramovitch represented, since the time prior to the Russian Revolution of 1905, a Socialist *Yiddishkeit*, a Jewish cultural identity on socialist foundations. One could say that Abramovitch, in an ideological sense, acted as a kind of shadow representative for the dissolved Russian Bund in the Mensheviks' exile leadership in Berlin, Paris, and New York during both the inter-war and the immediate post-war period after 1945.

In a similar way, Paul Olberg belonged to the network of the dissolved Russian Bund and was in close contact with Abramovitch and other exile Bund members throughout his life.[15] With the emergence of Nazism, the new World War and the Holocaust, an exceptional role change took place in this socialist exile milieu. From individual Russian Bund members belonging to the small Menshevik party in exile, they – as Mensheviks – now belonged to the much larger Bundist world movement that was established in the wake of the massive refugee flows arising from the World War.

It was outside Soviet Russia, in the newly independent Poland that broke away from the former Russian Empire, that the Bund not only lived on in the 1920s but gained increased influence in a growing Jewish working class (Blatman 2003; Minczeles 1999: 271–330, Weinstock 2002: 205–25). With union organisations for Jewish workers, the youth movement *Tskunft*, its self-defence militia *Tsukunft shturem* (Future Storm) and the sports movement *Morgnshtern*, together with the children's organisation SKIF (*Sotsyalistishe Kinder Farband*), and the women's organisation YAF (*Yiddisher Arbeter Froy*), the Bund created a world of Jewish, Socialist mass organisations. Further to this, there was the building up of the secular Jewish school system *Tsysho*, *Kultur Liges*, Yiddish theatre, artists and authors, and a network of social arrangements such as camping activities, kindergarten, and the famous, Bund-run Medem Sanatorium for the treatment of Jewish children and youngsters suffering from tuberculosis. In the Polish municipal elections in 1938, the Bund was the largest Jewish party, gaining over 60 per cent of the Jewish votes in Warsaw (Minczeles 1999: 313–4).

---

[15] An extensive correspondence between Olberg, Abramovitch, the Bund's central figure during and after the war E. Nowogrodsky, the movement's historian B. Nicolaevsky, S. Schwarz, and others is found in ARAB, POA, vols 20 and 22, and in YIVO (*Yiddisher Visnshaftlekher Institut*, i.e., Institute for Jewish Research), 1400 Bund Archives (in the following BA), ME 17, vol. 22 "Paul Olberg" and YIVO, BA, ME 18, vols 206–16 "Bund in Sweden. Jewish Socialist. Workers Party in Sweden".

In the struggle for the loyalties of the labour movement between Social Democracy and Communism, the Polish Bund long chose to remain outside both the Communist International and the Socialist International, re-established after the First World War. After its entry into the Socialist International in 1930, the movement constituted an extremely radical component, as well as an opponent to both what was considered a much too pragmatic, establishment socialism and to Labour Zionism's *Poale Zion* which, it was believed, represented a bourgeois nationalism (Minczeles 1999: 297–8).

Outside Poland, the Bund did not exist as a party but only in the form of a network and support groups in the different countries to which Jewish socialists, in the first place those with a Russian background, had gone (Slucki 2012). The individual Bundists normally joined up to the social democratic parties, in particular after the affiliation to the Socialist International. To be, for example, a German or French Social Democrat, a Bundist and, at the same time, to belong to the Menshevik exile milieu was, therefore, no contradiction. The Bund members in the USA were long the leading power in the textile workers' trade union organisations, as well as in the American umbrella organisation, the Jewish Labour Committee, which at the end of the Second World War encompassed over half a million members.

With the German invasion of Poland in 1939 and the new World War the main element of the Bund in Europe was destroyed. During the Soviet occupation of eastern Poland 1939–41 parts of the organisation's leadership were liquidated, of whom Henryk Erlich and Wiktor Alter, executed in 1943, were the most well-known representatives. During the Holocaust, the movement's mass base was pitilessly crushed. The uprising in the Warsaw Jewish Ghetto in 1943 under the leadership of the Bundist Marek Edelman, among others, constituted the movement's ultimate great struggle in Europe (Blatman 2003: 90–120).

Olberg in Sweden again

On Hitler's accession to power in 1933, Olberg together with his wife Frida Markovna came to Sweden with the support of Swedish Social Democrats. This was the year following the Social Democrats' great election victory, with the launch of the crisis programme which would change the direction of Swedish politics, and with the growing influence of the popular movements in the development of society. After initially staying at different addresses, and subject to provisional arrangements during the war, the couple moved to a bedsit in the working class district of Stockholm's Lilla Essingen.[16]

As Menshevik socialist it was given for Olberg to join the social democratic party wherever he happened to live. From being a member of the German SPD during the 1920s, already on his arrival in Sweden in 1933 he joined the Social Democratic Party where he developed contacts with leading party members.[17] Here he met up again with Anders Örne, a leading figure in the cooperative movement, who had managed to become both a member of the *Riksdag* and director-general of the Swedish postal service. Gustav Möller had been appointed Minister for Social Affairs after the election of 1932 while Arthur Engberg led the Ministry of Ecclesiastical Affairs. The Left Socialists Zeth Höglund and Fredrik Ström, who for a time had led the Swedish Communist Party, had now returned to the social democratic fold. Höglund, at the time of Olberg's arrival, was chairman of Stockholm's Social Democratic party organisation (labour commune) and Ström Editor-in-Chief for the daily *Social-Demokraten*. Olberg's contact network in Swedish Social Democracy extended to leadership levels in both the press and the government.[18] Through decision of the Social Democratic Party, Olberg immediately became engaged in organising the Labour Movement's Refugee Relief. He was however soon forced to leave the mission after a scandal with a Gestapo agent who managed to infiltrate the organisation.[19]

With the move to Lilla Essingen, he joined the district association of the Social Democrats in Stockholm. He maintained his membership for almost twenty years but occurs only exceptionally in the discussion minutes and as opening speaker at only one recorded meeting.[20] Instead, it was as a writer for Swedish and international Social Democracy that he appeared on the political stage. He contributed on a regular basis to the party press: *Social-*

---

[16] The first lease on Lilla Essingen dates from 1942, ARAB, POA, vol. 30.
[17] Olberg's first membership card of Stockholm's labour commune is from 1933, ARAB, POA, vol. 1.
[18] Among those sending congratulations on his sixtieth birthday in 1938, according to *Social-Demokraten* 24 Nov. 1938, were G. Möller, Z. Höglund, F. Ström, the party treasurer E. Wallin, and party secretary A. Nilsson, the lawyer G. Branting, the school principal G. Hammar, and the social democratic priest B. Mogård, ARAB, POA, vol. 1.
[19] Letter from the board of the Swedish Social Democratic Party to the board of Landsorganisationen (the Swedish trade union confederation) 14 May 1933, introducing the project and Olberg as its director, ARAB, SAP, E.I.II, utg skrivelser 1933. For the scandal: Fult streck 1934, Nazistspionen 1934, Socialdemokratiska flyktingskommittén 1934.
[20] Olberg gave a speech on 12 Oct. 1943 about "Poland and the Second World War", Annual Report 1 Feb. 1943 – 21 Jan. 1944, ARAB, Essinge Islands (Stockholm) Social Democratic Association archive no. 1036, in the following ESFA.

Demokraten and later *Morgon-Tidningen, Tiden, Frihet, Kooperatören, Folket i Bild*, and the Swedish trade union confederation (LO) journal *Fackföreningsrörelsen*. His contribution to the LO series of articles examined the role of the trade unions in the Soviet Union and the trade union policy of the Communist International (Olberg 1928; German edition 1930).

To the German Social Democratic press was added the Swiss press also. This Switzerland where he belonged to the Menshevik exile milieu, where his first son was born and his mother buried, in some sense was his second homeland and he saw the neutrality, the militia system for national defence, and local democracy as models. As Menshevik, he contributed to *Vestnik* and as Bundist to the Yiddish *Unser Stimme* published in Paris. Together with his writing activities, his extensive correspondence on political and ideological issues, with influential international socialists, provides insights in both the development of the Menshevik exile milieu and the Bund. Here, Olberg belonged to social democrats with a strong socialist conviction that through radical reforms it would be possible to abolish capitalism. At the same time he strongly rejected Soviet communism.

"There was a melancholic, white-haired man in Stockholm called Paul Olberg who had a past with connections to the Jewish Bund and German Social Democracy", wrote the Social Democrat Kaj Björk in his memories from the 1930s (1984: 134). "For a few kronor I translated his long articles for *Social-Demokraten*, where he eulogised old Kautsky's ideas on war and attacked the Soviet Union" (ibid.). At that time Björk himself, despite his social democratic critique, regarded the Soviet Union as a positive factor in world developments. For Olberg, however, there remained nothing of value in the Soviet example, in fact quite the contrary. Ever since 1917, he had warned about what he saw as Bolshevism's tyranny. He was now obliged to experience how everything he had fought for, since he was young, and associated with socialism – his party, comrades, and ideals – were swept away by the dictatorship.

During the terror of the Stalinist period his personal loss became immeasurable also. "He practically never wrote or spoke about the frightful misfortune that afflicted his family during the Yezhov era", wrote *Vestnik* in its obituary notice for Olberg (Pavel Karlovich Olberg 1960). Olberg's two sons had been drawn into the communist movement in Germany and Czechoslovakia and had been recruited by the Soviet security service, the NKVD. Having sought to infiltrate the Trotskyist opposition the elder brother, Valentin Olberg moved to Soviet Russia and appeared as a main witness against Trotsky in the first Moscow Trial in 1936. Together with the other witnesses he was condemned to death and shot in August 1936. The younger brother, Pavel, was arrested and executed in October of the same year. Valentin's wife Betty was sent to the Gulag but was handed over as a result of the Molotov–Ribbentrop pact in 1940 to the German security service and disappeared without trace. His first wife Sulamith, stenographer and translator on the Comintern's executive committee, was shot in November 1937 (Bundesstiftung 2008; Nekropole 2013a; Nekropole 2013b).

Paul Olberg's position in respect of the internal struggles that, during the period leading up to the Second World War, split Menshevism was hardly unexpected. The Pact between Hitler and Stalin in the summer of 1939 convinced many socialists, the world over, that the Soviet state no longer represented, in any positive respect, the revolutionary development dating from 1917. Large parts of the political middle ground between the Comintern and the Socialist International, which despite the Stalinist repression defended the Soviet Union against both Fascism and Western Capitalism, then drew the conclusion that Stalin's Soviet system had now turned into a new type of imperialism and fascism. This was an approach that was wholly rejected by Fyodor Dan's *Novy Put* (The New Way) which within the Menshevik exile milieu did not only defend the Soviet Union's existence but also, despite its opposition, showed a certain understanding for Soviet foreign policy (Liebich 1997: 260–70). The Abramovitch line from 1940 sought, instead, to combine a socialist 'orthodox' Marxism with a furious resistance to communism and absolute opposition to the Soviet regime. Even Abramovitch followers came to defend the Soviet Union during the World War but, in the resistance to Soviet 'totalitarianism', to discount any hope in respect of the Soviet regime's views. For Olberg this was a self-evident attitude.

Anti-semitism, the Holocaust, and refugee relief

In Olberg's writing and engagement before the Second World War, Jewish issues and anti-semitism occupied no central position. A report trip to the Middle Eastern countries in the mid-1930s gave rise to several articles on social developments and political conditions in the Middle East, including the development of the *Yishuv*, the Jewish settlements. Here articles on the Arab political parties alternated with articles on Jerusalem's modernisation and issues surrounding the division of Palestine (Olberg 1936; 1937; 1938a; 1938b). Olberg was naturally interested in the labour movements and, for a period of time, was the Swedish correspondent for *Davar*, the newspaper of the Jewish trade union movement *Histadrut*.²¹ However, he did not regard the development primarily from the perspective of a Jewish state formation but rather as a general modernisation of the Middle East in a democratic direction. His idealised anthem to 'The modern Egypt' which was written after the trip expressed a very hopeful view of the region's future. Egypt found itself, in Olberg's judgement, on the threshold to the modern breakthrough with growing national awareness, economic development, democratic reforms, increasing freedom for women, and with the first signs of a modern labour movement. The many ethnic groups and being at the crossroads of world religions was, he believed, a source of strength not disruption and Egypt was free from totalitarian ideas and the European curse of anti-semitism (Olberg 1943: 26, 28, 46–8, 54).

Anti-semitism naturally belonged for Olberg to the crimes of German Nazism. But his journalism and writing during the war years were not dominated by his engagement for the persecuted Jews. It was, instead, in the examination of Soviet Communism that his great knowledge of Russian conditions found expression. In the book *Rysslands nya imperialism* (Russia's New Imperialism) from 1940 Olberg pointed out how Soviet expansionism had characterised Bolshevik policy ever since the early 1920s. The book, which was published after the Soviet attack on Finland, was for Swedish readers an uncommonly knowledgeable and detailed depiction of the Sovietisation of the Caucasus with Georgia and the Muslim areas in the former Tsarist Empire (Olberg 1940).

The presentation of the Soviet Union as imperialistic – and the Communist regime's continuity with Tsardom – was in line with the sharpened questioning of what the Soviet state really represented. Amongst the Mensheviks, the Soviet Union had for a long time, in economic terms, been characterised as a state capitalist system and the Stalin regime, during the 1930s, as 'totalitarian'. However, like other socialist currents, the Mensheviks constantly wrestled with the question what the social order under the 'new Tsar' really represented. Even on the outbreak of the new world war, the majority view in the Mensheviks' foreign bureau was that the Soviet state in key respects was a positive result of the great Revolution of 1917. The task was to democratise, not to dissolve, the new order. Olberg was not longer concerned by such distinctions.

Already, the following year, there was published in both Swedish and German, *Tragedin Balticum*, where Olberg examined in detail the com-

---

²¹ Olberg's press card for *Davar* issued in June 1940, ARAB, POA, vol. 1.

munist policies in relation to the Baltic states, from the time of the revolution after the First World War up to the annexation in 1940 (Olberg 1941). This work represented, according to Anders Örne in the foreword, an overview of "the practical implementation of Russian imperialism" (ibid. 7). Olberg's authorship, at least for the Swedish public, came thereby during the first war years to focus on Soviet excesses and become a powerful argument in the period's agitated anti-communism.

The years 1939 to 1942, in Sweden, were characterised by the internment of communists, police raids, transport bans on the communist press, and strong public condemnations. Zeth Höglund, who wrote the foreword to Olberg's *Rysslands nya imperialism,* had launched the epithet 'nazi communists' after the Molotov–Ribbentrop Pact and Social Democrats, Syndicalists, and Left Socialists encouraged the purging of communists from trade unions and popular movements. The terror attack against the Communist newspaper *Norrskensflamman* in March 1940, which killed five people, represented a violent peak of the anti-communist mobilisation in the final phase of the Finnish Winter War.

Moreover, Olberg did not place the Jewish issue in the spotlight in the review of Poland's fate that he had long been working with (Olberg 1944). Instead, the unavoidable impression is that the book is aimed at a patriotic Polish and Polish-friendly opinion in line with the classic liberal nationalism that regarded Poland's liberation as a bulwark against the East.

"Every Pole is born a revolutionary", cited Olberg approvingly the words of Karl Marx and conceived that Polish nationalism and democracy went hand-in-hand, not least where Tsarist Russia's Soviet heirs were concerned (ibid. 126). In his history nothing is found with regard to the extensive pogroms against the Jews, about the time of the Republic's formation in 1918, or the Jewish Labour Bund's struggles, during the 1930s, against an aggressive Polish anti-semitism.

It was, instead, the Soviet occupation methods that, according to Olberg, had been "of an anti-semitic nature" through deportations that hit the Jewish population hard. Nevertheless, he believed, it would be incorrect to equate the Russian and German occupation of Poland, above all owing to the "attitude to the Jewish question". Whereas the Russian regime, in principle, rejected anti-semitism as a policy, the Nazi occupation launched a war of extermination against the Jews with the object of "extinguishing the Polish nation as such" (ibid. 103–4). Olberg was thus careful not to separate the fate of the Jews from Polish suffering in general and, by way of introduction he designated the million victims of the German occupation as

"Polish citizens" and those wiped out communities as "Polish villages". Subsequently one becomes aware from reading the book that the figures, that already in 1944 were known, largely referred to the liquidation of the Jews. No Polish anti-semitism is highlighted in Olberg's history; only that the young Polish nation in 1918 had had minority problems "which were not easy to settle" (ibid. 56, 110). When Olberg, in the autumn of 1943, spoke before the Social Democratic association in Essingen on the subject "Poland and the Second World War" the focus was on the courageous military resistance to superior force. The awful terror of the occupiers, according to the meeting minutes, had cost the lives of 3.5 million Poles, adding "of which 2.5 million Jews". But in Poland there were no Quislings and the Polish population stood united against the occupiers, was Olberg's conclusion.[22]

Nevertheless it was just here, in the final stages of the war and with the immense Jewish catastrophe in Europe that Olberg's engagement grew. Even before the war he had attempted to assist individual, persecuted comrades. The Kautsky family had fled from Austria after the 'Anschlus's in 1938 and the 84-year old Karl Kautsky had died on arrival in the Netherlands. When Karl Kautsky's elderly widow Luise, in 1942, begged Olberg for help in coming to Sweden he contacted Zeth Höglund. Any operation there to assist appears to have ended in failure; Luise Kautsky, who was Jewish, was deported two years later to Auschwitz where she died after arrival.[23]

The Bund in Sweden

Through the US Jewish Labor Committee, Paul Olberg contributed during the last years of the war to provide contacts and help to Jewish camp prisoners and refugees.[24] From the autumn of 1945, and for the next couple of years, he was the Committee's paid representative in Sweden. He was responsible for establishing in Stockholm a committee to assist repatriation and transmigration of war refugees.[25] With LO Ombudsman Nils Goude a

---

[22] Essinge Social Democratic Association, meeting minutes 12 Oct. 1943, ARAB, ESFA.
[23] Postcard to Olberg from L. Kautsky, Amsterdam 16 July 1942. Copy of letter from Höglund to Foreign Minister Ch. Günther 1942, concerning L. Kautsky. For L. Kautsky's death in Auschwitz Birkenau, see letter to Olberg from fellow prisoner L. Adelsberger 13 Oct. 1945. All documents in ARAB, POA, vol. 23.
[24] Expense records 1943–45, YIVO, BA, ME18, vol. 205.
[25] Letter from Olberg to the Swedish European Relief in Stockholm, 15 May (no year given) ARAB, POA vol. 25. Olberg's tax declarations show income from the American Jewish Labor Committee amounting to SEK 1000 for Oct–Dec 1945, SEK 6000 for 1947

key figure, acting as a link to the trade union movement and thereby to central and local authorities, this committee arranged work and housing for Jewish refugees from camps in Poland, Germany, and Austria. It also helped in contacts with the public authorities, medical care, and educational issues, visas and all kinds of practical questions concerning finance, clothing, tickets, and not least contact with relatives and friends around the world. In practice, the committee comprised mainly Paul Olberg himself and Sara Mehr who once again, as after 1905, was engaged in helping Jewish socialists as refugees. In effect, the Jewish Labor Committee and Olberg's committee came to represent a support function for Jewish Bund followers among concentration camp victims and refugees.

Already in 1945 a group of Jewish refugees from Poland formed a Bundist group in Uppsala.[26] The following year saw the formation of the "Judiska Socialdemokratiska Förbundet 'Bund' i Sverige" (Jewish Social Democratic Association 'Bund' in Sweden) which over the following years organised local groups in almost a dozen Swedish towns and cities. Paul Olberg held membership card no. 1; the chairperson initially was Sara Mehr. The war's end thus meant for Olberg that membership of the Bund which, for him, had so long only involved correspondence with Abramovitch and other Russian Jewish Bundists scattered abroad, was reactivated again.

Now heading towards his seventieth birthday, Olberg initiated a febrile period of activity to receive, place, and assist hundreds of Bundist refugees in Swedish society – and help many on to the homes of friends, relatives, or party comrades in the USA, Canada, Argentina, Australia, and, in certain cases, Palestine.[27] In addition to the great practical assistance there was the political project to unite the separated Bundists again around their agenda on Swedish soil. This involved basic work on behalf of the association: forming local branches and working groups, choosing committees and designating responsibilities, holding meetings and conferences, and, not

---

and the same amount for 1948 as well as SEK 7200 for 1949, information for 1946 is lacking in the archive, ARAB, POA, vols 26 and 30.

[26] A report from Uppsala states that a Bund group was formed in Jan. 1945. Minutes from first national Bund conference in Sweden 14–15 Aug. 1948, handwritten notebook, YIVO, BA, ME18, 206.

[27] In the letter of 15 May to Swedish European Relief, ARAB, POA, vol. 25, which must have been written around 1948, it is asserted that the Committee provides help for purposes of repatriation and transmigration of refugees; it had helped five hundred families to Sweden, half of whom travelled onwards to other countries. *Sotsialistitcheskii Vestnik* maintained that this enabled around 2000 Bundists to travel onward to different countries in the world (Iz partii 1959).

least, running political work in the first place on behalf of the Jews in Sweden.

Most of the Bundists in Sweden arrived with the refugee transports from Poland, some from exile in the Soviet Union.[28] Besides supporting one another after difficult experiences and in the new country's unfamiliar surroundings the activities involved arranging discussion meetings and cultural events, marking May Day and celebrating Bund anniversaries as well as days of remembrance of the Warsaw Ghetto Uprising. Each Bundist would subscribe to *Unser Stimme*, the Bund's daily newspaper published in Yiddish from Paris. In addition, there was the more theoretical publication *Unser Tsait*, which after the war was issued by the Bund's international co-ordination committee in New York. A recurrent urge was that the local Bundist groups should seek collaboration with, and integration into, the ranks of Swedish Social Democracy. The Bund in Sweden presented itself as part of the Social Democratic Party, the design of the membership cards was copied, local contacts were established, Olberg was invited to the Social Democratic party congress and a small Bund column marching behind its own banner took part in the Social Democrats' May Day demonstration in Stockholm during the first post-war years. The language, however, represented a major obstacle. Only Paul Olberg and Sara Mehr mastered Swedish and toiled in their travel across Sweden to local events. Where no Swedish speaker was available the sphere of contact with local party organisations was reduced to a polite exchange of greetings.

In addition to the language obstacle, there was the deeper and more distant question: What should the Bundists in Sweden really do there? Their core tenet of *doykait* (hereness) referred to the struggle for a socialist Yiddishness 'in the here and now'. This would have been a natural approach in Poland with large, dynamic Jewish communities. Matters appeared differently in Swedish localities such as Alingsås, Vetlanda, or Eskilstuna with just a handful of Jewish families. The Swedish refugee policy did not permit those newly arrived to move to Stockholm or Malmö with their larger Jewish communities. During the first year in Sweden a self-evident starting point for several of the Bundists was their return to Poland where the Bund was seeking to reorganise itself amidst the ruins of the Holocaust.

---

[28] See question form for representatives at the Bund Conference in Stockholm 1948, where several of representatives indicate 'Soviet Union' or 'Russia' as answer to where they spent the war years. Minutes from the first national Bund conference in Sweden, 14–15 Aug. 1948, handwritten notebook, YIVO, BA, ME18, 206.

With the repatriation of hundreds of thousand Jews from exile in the Soviet Union, it appeared for a time as if Polish Jewish communities could be rebuilt once more. Pogroms in Kielce in 1946, and other anti-semitic outbursts, served to persuade most Jews that any return was inconceivable.

When the Bund in Poland in 1948 was faced with the ultimatum to join the ruling communist party, the history of the Bund in Poland came to an end. The once upon a time so mighty Jewish labour movement was now gone like the Jewish working class that constituted its mass base. At the same time, its Zionist rival had launched the struggle for Palestine with the goal of proclaiming a Jewish nation state. For the Bundists around Sweden and elsewhere in the world questions of an existential nature were being asked. What was the future for the Jewish socialist project for which their comrades in thousands had lost their lives? The question loomed up during those days when the world was gliding apart into the East and West of the Cold War.

When the Bund's international network of support groups, with around ten thousand members in some twenty or so countries, met for the World Congress in 1947, the previous opposition to Zionism was unchanged as well as the opposition to the formation of a Jewish state in Palestine (Slucki 2012: 24). The movement distanced itself from both Soviet Communism and American capitalism. Instead, what was essential, believed the international Bund, was to build a third Socialist force in world politics. This was represented, according to the Bundists, by international Social Democracy with the Labour Party's victory in Great Britain in 1945 as foremost example and Scandinavian Social Democracy as effective models. The international Bund also joined, as associated member organisation, the reorganised Socialist International in 1951.

The Bundists in Sweden participated in the movement's international debates and united themselves with the majority positions. At the national Bundist conference in Stockholm, in the summer of 1948, when the world situation had once again deteriorated and the state of Israel had been proclaimed a few months earlier, the assembled representatives of about three hundred members or so adopted the international line.[29] That Olberg was the self-evident key figure and the veteran, almost twice as old as most representatives, did not prevent him from being criticised for standing too close to the "Western side". On the other hand, he did not hear those re-

---

[29] Minutes from the first national Bund conference in Sweden, 14–15 Aug. 1948, handwritten notebook, YIVO, BA, ME18, 206.

presentatives who desired a more positive attitude towards the proclaimed Israel.[30] For those Bundists, who saw the British Labour government as the most important example of the socialist 'third way', the armed Zionist struggle in Palestine against the British mandate authorities represented an example of reactionary nationalism.

The rapid Soviet and American recognition of the Jewish state – the two big power blocs that the Bundists were opposed to – was also interpreted negatively as was the support of communist volunteers and arms from Czechoslovakia to the Israeli struggle. The murder of the UN mediator, Folke Bernadotte in 1948, was condemned by the Bund in Sweden as a crime of the "Fascist Stern gang" which had thereby lost any claim to be a civilised force and provided the worst example of the Zionist movement's nationalism.[31]

Menshevism, the Bund, and the Cold War

With the escalation of the Cold War and the loss of power by the British Labour Party in 1951, the socialist 'third way' between East and West melted away. In New York the last remnants of the foreign bureau of the Mensheviks were in process of disintegration. The split with Fyodor Dan's *Novy Put* had only been deepened during the World War and was unbridgeable by the early days of the Cold War. Or rather, when Dan died in January 1947 there was nothing really to hold the two wings together. Whereas *Novy Put* adopted a position in support of the Soviet Union in the growing conflicts between East and West, Abramovitch and *Vestnik* placed themselves, as increasingly anti-communist in outlook, on the side of the West.

The paradox, writes Liebich (1997: 288), was that the exile Mensheviks' great, new political opportunity also became their ruin. The opportunity offered by the moment involved the enormous Russian emigrant milieu which brought together Red Army soldiers from the prison camps, slave labourers, those driven into exile, and others who refused to return to the Soviet Union. The now elderly Mensheviks threw themselves into this environment, in rivalry with old supporters of tsarism and former Nazi collaborators, in an attempt to organise a democratic, Russian mass opposition. Their Marxist socialism, on the threshold of the 1950s and the escala-

---

[30] Ibid.
[31] Declaration from the Social Democratic Bund in Sweden, YIVO, BA, ME18, 206.

tion in the Cold War, was clearly not an asset amongst the Russian exiles who shunned everything that could be associated with the term 'socialism'.

Facing the immense problem of building alliances in the new exile milieu – who could be regarded as friend and foe? – and the pressure to renounce socialism, at least the terminology, the Foreign Committee was dissolved in 1953. Abramovitch continued to issue *Vestnik* for a further ten years, together with his closest comrades up to his death, in an imagined continuity with the Russian Revolution's Menshevik Social Democracy. The combination of a furious anti-communism which placed *Vestnik* amongst the Cold War hawks, with its profession of a socialist vision of the future, had during the intensive years of McCarthyism an extremely limited political space both in the USA as elsewhere. For the last Mensheviks who had been fighting Bolshevism ever since 1917, indeed since the split that divided Russian Social Democracy in 1903, the socialist vision subsequently faded out to be replaced by the warnings against any compromise at all with the Soviet regime. Like Olberg, many of these had suffered great personal losses. Abramovitch's son, for example, had headed for Spain as a volunteer in the Civil War but was apparently kidnapped by Soviet agents and never seen again.[32]

The international Bund too, like the Mensheviks, subsequently joined the Western side against Soviet communism in the Cold War. For Paul Olberg, this position did not represent any dilemma. Since 1917, he had belonged to the hardest critics within the Menshevik ranks of the Soviet system and communism in general. For almost forty years, as a writer, he had fought to establish the anti-communist credentials of social democracy, not least in the Swedish party. In particular, he had been involved in the resistance of the Baltic States against annexation by the Soviet Union and participated in the ceremonial occasions held by the Latvian Social Democrats in Swedish exile.[33] At the same time as the last Mensheviks in New York attempted to bring together what – they hoped – constituted

---

[32] Abramovitch never gave up trying to find the truth about the disappearance of his son, Mark Rein (Liebich 1997: 261–2). S.D. Erlich, the widow of the Bundist leader H. Erlich, executed in the Soviet Union, also belonged to the Mensheviks in New York but followed the line of *Novy Put* (ibid. 275).

[33] On, for example, Latvian Social Democracy's fiftieth anniversary in Stockholm 1954, the Bund was represented by Olberg (Lettiska 1954) as in the case of the first May Day celebration in 1953 of the *Östeuropeiska Socialistiska Samarbetskommittén*. For the Baltic Committee in Stockholm, together with T. Nerman's brother, B. Nerman, he issued the booklet *Balticum: Fantasi och verklighet* (The Baltics: Fantasy and Reality) (Olberg and Nerman 1946) and, on his death, condolences were sent by the Estonian National Council and other Baltic organisations, ARAB, POA, vol. 28.

democratic elements of the Russian exile community into a US supported anti-communist movement for Russia's freedom, he himself became a member of the Swedish department of the CIA funded *Congress for Cultural Freedom*.[34] The movement whose purpose was to bring together intellectuals behind the West in the Cold War had been formed in Berlin under the leadership of leading Mensheviks, among others.[35] In presentations of the Jewish Labor Committee it was underlined where the Committee stood in world politics and Olberg was welcomed at the US embassy.[36]

Within the Bund, the Swedish Social Democratic project could be seen as a model, or perhaps rather as a last socialist example. Olberg himself was keen to present Sweden as a genuine socialist social development for the exiled Bundists he attempted to integrate into the Swedish labour movement. Swedish socialism was slow but sure, he explained for countless refugees in cold barracks while awaiting transit onwards. And the Bund's international coordination committee in New York sent greetings to the Swedish Social Democrats' party congress in 1952, in the form of a telegram:

> Our best wishes to the delegates of your party congress in their relentless effort to create a genuine socialist welfare state – STOP – During the cruel years of the Second World War your country shined as a haven for all persecuted by the Nazi-hangmen – STOP – May the spirit of international brotherhood which distinguished your great leader Hjalmar Branting lead you to further achievements for the cause of socialism, democracy and a lasting peace – STOP[37]

"I cannot sufficiently underline how happy I am to be a citizen in a free, democratic, and highly cultured country", explained Olberg in autumn 1953 for the Social Democratic *Morgon-Tidningen*, in response to the journalist's ingratiating question about his impressions of Sweden, after twenty

---

[34] Olberg had membership card no. 52 of the Swedish Committee for Cultural Freedom, issued 1955, ARAB, POA, vol. 1.

[35] It was B. Nicolaevsky and S. Schwarz who represented the Russian exile organisation Association for the Struggle for the Freedom of Peoples and the Mensheviks' foreign delegation (Liebich 1997: 298).

[36] See, for example, the letter of introduction for Olberg from A. Held, chairman of the Jewish Labor Committee in the USA to Honorable W.W. Butterworth, United States Ambassador to Sweden, 16 Oct. 1950, ARAB, POA, vol. 30.

[37] Telegram to the Party Executive Committee, Stockholm, Sweden, 4 June 1952 from E. Nowogrodsky, World Coordinating Committee of the Bund, YIVO, BA, ME18, vol. 207.

years in the country of which almost fifteen as Swedish citizen. "Here are the conditions of life which I dreamed of in my youth" (75-årige 1953).

The same year Olberg, at the age of 75, represented the Bund during the re-instituted Socialist International congress in Stockholm. In actual fact, most Bundists in Sweden had by then travelled onwards to family members and comrades in other countries and only a handful then remained. Even if those remaining continued to maintain contact and follow the Bundist press, coherent activities had now dwindled. Olberg himself continued to maintain contact with the international Bund – and to long use its letter head – but his resurrection as a leading Bundist comprised a relatively short-lived experience in the late 1940s and early 1950s.

Soviet anti-semitism

Even if Olberg did not publicly turn against Sweden's neutrality policy, he criticised the accommodation towards the Soviet Union and belonged to the Swedish party's most anti-Soviet circles. With the publication of his book *Antisemitismen i Sovjet* (Anti-semitism in the Soviet Union) which branded Stalin's anti-semitism, his opposition to those he considered communist fellow-travellers came to the surface (Olberg 1953a). In the Social Democratic newspaper *Morgon-Tidningen*, Nils Lindh (1953) criticised the book for being too propagandistic and based on partly dubious source material. In a furious rejoinder, Olberg (1953b) accused Lindh of using communist polemical methods to confuse public opinion and, with the review of his book, to have performed "a service for Moscow-inspired anti-semitism". Lindh, who was a contemporary of Olberg's, had worked during the inter-war years as press attaché at the Swedish embassy in Moscow and was a member of *Sällskapet Sverige–Ryssland* (Swedish–Russian Society). During the 1920s he wrote about the revolution and Soviet developments in *Social-Demokraten* under the pseudonym Strannikov and was regarded as the Social Democratic expert on the Soviet Union (Björlin 2003: 55). Olberg was to complain to Hugo Valentin, the leading Swedish scholar on Jewish history, about the fact that "the Social Democratic Party's main organ had been used to defend Stalin's anti-semitic policy".[38]

During his final years, Olberg had acquired a clear profile as the friend of Jewish refugees and a bitter critic of anti-semitism in the Soviet Union – even if his personal friend and principal of Brunnsvik Folk High School

---

[38] Letter to Valentin from Olberg of 5 May [in error, should be June] 1953, ARAB, POA, vol. 22.

(Dalarna), Alf Ahlberg, feared that in this respect his was a "voice crying in the desert".[39] In actual fact, as we have seen, the issue of anti-semitism had not previously dominated Olberg's political involvement; at least where his public profile was concerned. He had in his writings about, for example, Poland and the Baltic States almost downplayed the domestic anti-semitism there or referred to Russian "foreign rule" (Olberg 1944: 57). His irritated reply to the Bund's European office, which after the war sought information on how the Swedish Bundists were responding to anti-semitism in Sweden, was as follows: "I do not think we should look for anti-semitism where it does not exist."[40]

Without questioning Olberg's sincere engagement on behalf of the Soviet Union's Jews, it is a short step to connect it with the more strategic struggle against Communism. Ever since the Russian Revolution, Soviet power in a broad anti-Bolshevik opinion had been associated with the Jews. And for many Jews, the Red Army and Soviet power had represented a lesser evil, both during the Civil War 1918 to 1920 and in relation to Nazism and the Holocaust. However, with the Slansky show trial in Czechoslovakia, the trial of the Jewish doctors (Doctors' Plot) in Moscow, and the repression of Jewish culture, Soviet Communism also played the anti-semitic card, as Olberg saw it, as a way of attracting popular support in the East.

He was not alone. The Jewish Labor Committee in the USA, the international Bund, and other Jewish organisations openly attacked the same development. Hereby the issue of anti-semitism in the Soviet bloc came to be one of the Cold War's interfaces. At the same time as it constituted a way for Jewish organisations to win support from niggardly authorities in Europe and the USA, it could also serve as a tool for the West in the Cold War for winning support amongst the Jewish population.

That Israel's position in world politics during this period shifted from having a degree of support, at least for a time, from the Eastern bloc to getting closer to the West was also significant for both the Bund and for Olberg. In 1955 the International Bund finally adopted the position that Israel "constituted a positive factor in the Jewish world community" (Slucki 2012: 173). Behind this change lay not least the American Jewish Labor Committee which spoke out for Israel at an early stage. Rather than the leading Bundists prompting the American mass organisation to follow the Bund's course, the pressure from the American workers finally came to

---

[39] Letter from Ahlberg to Olberg, Brunnsvik 26 Sept. 1958, ARAB, POA, vol. 20.
[40] Letter from Olberg to R. Ryba, 7 Apr. 1949, YIVO, BA, ME 18, vol. 206.

change the Bund's attitude. Even though the Bund in this way came to accept Israel, its negative view of Zionism was not changed.

After three quarters of a century of endeavour, under tumultuous political circumstances, the once so revolutionary socialism of Olberg, the Jewish Labour Bund, and the last Mensheviks had now morphed into a strong loyalty to the capitalist West side in the Cold War against communism. For Paul Olberg, in particular, the social democratic welfare project he experienced in Sweden constituted the real and possible socialism. For his old Menshevik comrades in the USA, Abramovitch, Nikolaevsky, Held, Schwartz, and others, the struggle for socialism had been transformed into the struggle against totalitarian communism where they were welcomed as uncompromising ideologues. Several of the last, elderly Menshevik leaders finally achieved successful, individual careers as writers and lecturers amongst other hawks of the Cold War. Abramovitch even went so far as to regret the American reticence to using the atomic bomb (Liebich 1997: 300).

Epilogue

"Do you remember?" Indeed yes. In the flow of letters to Olberg's widow from the worlds of Menshevism and Bundism there were still those who could answer Angelica Balabanoff's question affirmatively, those who could associate Olberg with Balabanoff's words about "a good and faithful socialist" who remained attached to the "cause of socialism".[41] When Essinge Social Democratic association held its members' meeting in May 1960, the new times however had begun to wipe away the traces of what had been. The cheers for socialism at the close of the local association meetings had fallen silent already at the beginning of the 1950s; roughly at the time when meeting participants started to complain of lack of interest amongst young people and show films from the US embassy.

So when the meeting – which the local party association chairman opened by reporting on Olberg's decease – drew to a close, it was not with any memorial sketch of the political cosmos which, with the figure of the aged Jewish Socialist, had now faded away. It was with the American cartoon film "Woody Woodpecker Heralds Spring".[42]

---

[41] "Vid gravsättningen av Paul Olbergs aska den 29 maj 1960", manuscript by T. Nerman, ARAB, POA, vol. 25.
[42] Essinge Social Democratic Association, meeting minutes 18 May 1960, ARAB, ESFA.

The young Olberg (Labour Movement Archives and Library, Stockholm / photo: 22111878-05051960)

Olberg in his mature years (Labour Movement Archives and Library, Stockholm)

(Above) "Welcome – Long live socialism". Paul Olberg with bundists in Sweden, 1946 (Labour Movement Archives and Library, Stockholm / Photographer: Bäckstrand)

(Left) 'Bund' at the First of May demonstration in Stockholm, 1946 (Labour Movement Archives and Library, Stockholm)

References

"75-årige Paul Olberg är glad att aldrig ha varit bolsjevik." (1953) *Morgon-Tidningen* (21 Nov.).

Ascher, A. (1972) *Pavel Axelrod and the Development of Menshevism*. Cambridge, Ma.: Harvard University Press.

Bauer, O. (1907) *Die Nationalitätenfrage und die Sozialdemokratie*. Wien: Brand.

Björk, K. (1984) *Ett 30-tal*. Stockholm: Tidens förlag.

Björkegren, H. (1985) *Ryska posten: De ryska revolutionärerna i Norden 1906–1917*. Stockholm: Bonniers.

Björlin, L. (2003) "Kultur och politik: Kommunistiska frontorganisationer i Sverige." *Kommunismens hot och löfte: Arbetarrörelsen i skuggan av Sovjetunionen 1917–1991*, ed. by Blomqvist, H. and Ekdahl, L. Stockholm: Carlssons, 39–76.

Blatman, D. (2003) *For Our Freedom and Yours: The Jewish Labour Bund in Poland 1939–1949*. London and Portland: Vallentine Mitchell.

Blomqvist, H. and Ekdahl, L. (eds) (2003) *Kommunismens hot och löfte: Arbetarrörelsen i skuggan av Sovjetunionen 1917–1991*. Stockholm: Carlssons.

Brovkin, V.N. (1987) *The Mensheviks after October: Socialist Opposition and the Rise of the Bolshevik Dictatorship*. Ithaca and London: Cornell University Press.

Bundesstiftung Aufarbeitung (2008) "Olberg, Valentin." Biographische Datenbanken [online]. Available from http://www.bundesstiftung-aufarbeitung-.de/wer-war-wer-in-der-ddr-%2363%3B-1424.html?ID=4855 [13 Feb. 2014].

"Demokrati eller diktatur." (1919) *Social-Demokraten* (29 Oct.).

Elmbrant, B. (2010) *Stockholmskärlek: En bok om Hjalmar Mehr*. Stockholm: Atlas.

"En flyktingarnas vän fyller 80 år." (1958) *Stockholms-Tidningen* (21 Nov.).

"Fult streck av nazispion i Stockholm." (1934) *Arbetaren* (17 Aug.).

Gitelman, Z.Y. (1972) *Jewish Nationality and Soviet Politics: The Jewish Sections of the CPSU, 1917–1930*. Princeton: Princeton University Press.

Haimson, L.H. (ed.) (1974) *The Mensheviks: From the Revolution of 1917 to the Second World War*. Chicago and London: The University of Chicago Press.

Hudis, K. and Anderson, B. (eds) (2004) *The Rosa Luxemburg Reader*. New York: Monthly Review Press.

"Hyllningar." (1938) *Social-Demokraten* (24 Nov.).

"Iz partii: 80-letie P.K. Olberg." (1959) *Sotsialistitcheskij Vestnik* (No. 1, Jan).

Jacobs, J. (ed.) (2001) *Jewish Politics in Eastern Europe: The Bund at 100.* New York: New York University Press.

Kan, A. (2005) *Hemmabolsjevikerna: Den svenska socialdemokratin, ryska bolsjeviker och mensjeviker under världskriget och revolutionsåren 1914–1920.* Stockholm: Carlssons.

"Lettiska socialdemokrater firade sitt 50-årsjubileum." (1954) *Morgon-Tidningen* (20 June).

Liebich, A. (1997) *From the Other Shore: Russian Social Democracy after 1921.* Cambridge, Ma. and London: Harvard University Press.

Liebich, A. (1992) *Tables de la Revue Russe Le Messager Socialist 1921–1963.* Paris: La Bibliotèque Russe Tourguénev, Institut d'Études Slaves.

Lind, N. (1953) "Antisemitism i Ryssland." *Morgon-Tidningen* (8 May).

M., V. (1919) "Råds-Ryssland i verkligheten." *Folkets Dagblad Politiken* (6 Nov.).

Minczeles, H. (1999) *Histoire générale du BUND: Un mouvement révolutionnaire juif.* Paris: Denoël.

"Nazistspionen Glienke åter i farten här. " (1934) *Arbetaren* (24 Nov.).

Nekropole (2013a) "Pavel Olberg" [online]. Available from http://nekropole.info/lv/Pavel-Olberg [13 Feb. 2014].

Nekropole (2013b) "Valentin Olberg" [online]. Available from http://nekropole.info/lv/Valentin-Olberg [13 Feb. 2014].

Olausson, L. (1987) *Demokrati och socialism: Austromarxismen under mellankrigstiden.* Lund: Arkiv.

Olberg, P. (1917) "Den ryska socialdemokratin och det nuvarande historiska ögonblicket." *Social-Demokraten* (I: 2 May, II: 10 May, III: 26 May).

Olberg, P. (1919a) "Sovjet-Ryssland i verkligheten: Brev till Social-Demokraten från P. Olberg." *Social-Demokraten* (I: 25 Oct., II: 28 Oct., III: 29 Oct.).

Olberg, P. (1919b) *Briefe aus Sowjet-Russland.* Stuttgart: J.H.W. Dietz Nachf.

Olberg, P. (1928) *Sovjet-Rysslands internationella fackföreningspolitik.* Stockholm: Tidens förlag.

Olberg, P. (1930) *Die Rote Gewerkschafts-Internationale und die Europäische Gewerkschafts-Bewegung.* Stuttgart: Verlagsgesellschaft des Deutschen Metallarbeiter-Verbandes.

Olberg, P. (1936) "Jerusalems omvälvning." *Jorden Runt* (Sept.).

Olberg, P. (1937) "De arabiska politiska partierna i Palestina." *Statsvetenskaplig Tidskrift* 40 (3), 255–60.

Olberg, P. (1938a) "Palestinas delning." *Mellanfolkligt Samarbete* 8 (3).

Olberg, P. (1938b) "Moderna strömningar i Nillandet." *Jorden runt* (April).

Olberg, P. (1940) *Rysslands nya imperialism: De små nationernas drama i diktaturstaten.* Stockholm: Natur och Kultur.

Olberg, P. (1941) *Tragedin Balticum: Annektionen av de fria republikerna Estland, Lettland och Litauen*. Stockholm: Natur och kultur.

Olberg, P. (1943) *Det moderna Egypten i det andra världskriget*. Stockholm: Natur och kultur.

Olberg, P. (1944) *Polens öde: Ett europeiskt kardinalproblem*. Stockholm: Wahlström & Widstrand.

Olberg, P. (1953a) *Antisemitismen i Sovjet*. Stockholm: Natur och kultur.

Olberg, P. (1953b) "Rysk antisemitism i skottgluggen." *Morgon-Tidningen* (23 May).

Olberg, P. and Nerman, B. (1946) *Balticum: Fantasi och verklighet*. Stockholm: Baltiska kommittén.

"Old Yiddish Cultural Activist, Paul Olberg, Dead in Sweden." (1960) *Jewish Daily Forward* (7 May).

"Paul Olberg 80 Jahre alt." (1958) *Volksrecht* (22 Nov.).

"Paul Olberg död." (1960) *Stockholms-Tidningen* (6 May).

"Paul Olberg gestorben." (1960) *Neue Zürcher Zeitung* (9 May).

"Paul Olberg: Zum 80. Geburtstag." (1958) *Neue Zürcher Zeitung* (22 Nov.).

"Pavel Karlovich Olberg." (1960) *Sotsialistitcheskij Vestnik* (No. 5, May).

Sapir, B. (1974) "Notes and Reflections on the History of Menshevism." *The Mensheviks: From the Revolution of 1917 to the Second World War*, ed. by Haimson, L.H. Chicago and London: The University of Chicago Press, 349–89.

"Sitzung des Holländisch–skandinavischen Komitees mit Pavel Akselrod und Paul Olberg, 15. Mai 1917" (1917) [online]. Available from http://www.socialhistoryportal.org/stockholm1917/documents/111548 [12 Feb. 2014].

Slucki, D. (2012) *The International Jewish Labor Bund after 1945: Toward a Global History*. New Brunswick, N.J. and London: Rutger University Press.

"Socialdemokratiska flyktingskommittén understödjer spion! " (1934) *Ny Dag* (24 Nov.).

Traverso, E. (1997) *Les marxistes et la question juive*. Paris: Éditions Kimé.

Weinstock, N. (2002) *Le pain de misère: Histoire du mouvement ouvrier juif en Europe, vol. 1: L'Empire russe jusqu'en 1914*, and *vol. II: L'Europe centrale et occidental jusqu'en 1945*. Paris: La Découverte.

Wolin, S. (1974) "The Mensheviks under the NEP and in Emigration." *The Mensheviks: From the Revolution of 1917 to the Second World War*, ed. by Haimson, L.H. Chicago and London: The University of Chicago Press, 241–349.

7. From Fordism to High-Tech Capitalism: A Political Economy of the Labour Movement in the Baltic Sea Region

Werner Schmidt

The research project "The Labour Movement in the Baltic Sea Region" (*Arioso*) has worked in a close-knit research environment at Södertörn University since 1997. In different constellations but with a constant inner circle, the project systematically has sought since then to understand the outlines of the social development in the Baltic Sea region during 'the short twentieth century' by examining the two competing branches of the labour movement – social democracy and communism – and their endeavour to gain influence and power over this development.

The project started the same year that the Swedish translation of Eric Hobsbawm's book *Age of Extremes* was published. The researchers affiliated with *Arioso* did not yet have a common theoretical framework at the time, but could all agree with Hobsbawm's general characterisation of the twentieth century. It corresponded fairly well with the results of their own research. Hobsbawm described "the Short Twentieth Century" (1914–91) as a triptych. 'The Age of Catastrophe' (1914–45), with its two world wars, its economic world crisis, and the advance of fascist and totalitarian regimes, was followed by about 25 years "of extraordinary economic growth and social transformation", which he called 'the Golden Age'. The final period, the one we still live in, is "a new era of decomposition, uncertainty and crisis" (Hobsbawm 1994: 6) – accentuated by the economic world crisis that started in 2007.

According to Hobsbawm (1994: 55), one of the constitutive factors of the short twentieth century – especially during the catastrophic years 1914 to 1945 – was the conviction, the vague feeling or fear that "the old society, the old economy, the old political systems had, as the Chinese phrase put it, 'lost the mandate of heaven'", and that humanity waited for a better alternative. Up to the First World War such an alternative was mainly associated with the social democratic labour movement. After the October Revolution of 1917 – and failed revolutionary attempts in the West – the Soviet Union claimed to be the embodiment of the one and only alternative. It is this aspect of the 'Age of Catastrophe' on which the first phase of the project mainly focused. Out of this research grew a common set of problems, which found its condensed expression in the title of one of the books resulting from this project, the anthology *Kommunism – hot och löfte: Arbetarrrörelsen i skuggan av Sovjetunionen* (Communism – Threat and Promise: The Labour Movement in the Shadow of the Soviet Union) (Blomqvist and Ekdahl 2003). The book treated different aspects of the ideologies and the practices of the labour movement in their interplay with the power emanating from Soviet communism.

The second period (1950–75) was the era of both the global confrontation of systems in the Cold War and different welfare regimes. The vital impulse for the formation of the welfare regimes in the West was the specific balance between different social and political forces – nationally and internationally – that arose out of the victory over Hitler-Germany and its allies. With the economic, social, and political crises of the 1930s still fresh in people's minds, there was a general consensus at the end of the Second World War that, for social and political reasons, mass unemployment was not to be allowed to emerge again and that "a return to *laissez-faire* and the unreconstructed free market was out of the question" (Hobsbawm 1994: 272). Although this approach was transformed into a material force through strong demands from below, an even more significant factor for the willingness to reform was the fear that the influence of the Soviet Union would spread westward. Partly because of the competition between the two major political and economic systems during the Cold War, mass consumption and the welfare state were elevated to hallmarks of the bourgeois-capitalist system in the West. Hobsbawm (1994: 286) characterised this period, the 'Golden Age', with good reason as the time when "the most dramatic, rapid and profound revolution in human affairs of which history has record" was initiated and "largely achieved".

The project's research on this period resulted in, among other publications, three biographies that attracted much attention in Sweden. They dealt with representatives of different wings of the Swedish labour movement who contributed to the creation of its Golden Age: The communist leader C-H Hermansson (Schmidt 2005), the trade union economist

Rudolf Meidner (Ekdahl 2001 and 2005), and the social democratic prime minister Olof Palme (Östberg 2008 and 2009). The *Arioso* project resulted furthermore in the anthology *Efter guldåldern: Arbetarrörelsen och fordismens slut* (After the Golden Age: The Labour Movement and the End of Fordism) (Blomqvist and Schmidt 2012).

This chapter provides an analysis of the 25-year period of the Golden Age by means of certain regulation and hegemonial theoretical tools. These are the result of the analysis of Fordism; the latter are inspired by the theoretical work of Antonio Gramsci. With hindsight, the short period 1950–75, the middle panel of Hobsbawm's triptych, represents an exceptional historical period in the transition from one era of crises to another. This article asks how the process can be explained that led from the golden age of the post-war era to the present world of crises and insecurity. It also examines how the labour movement acted and how it was affected in this process. With the ongoing third phase of the *Arioso* project, "The Labour Movement in the Baltic Sea Region – in a New World of Crises and Insecurity" we intend to contribute to an understanding of this process. This article revolves around this question, too.

Fordism – an international phenomenon with a Swedish variant

From a global perspective the period 1950–75 was characterised by the Cold War, that is, the global confrontation and competition between the capitalist system in the West and the state-socialist system in the East (cf. Schmidt 2008). During this period, as Samir Amin (1999: 121) explained, development became the most important goal of all regimes. Amin distinguished between three different projects: (a) the capitalist Fordist development type in the West, (b) the Soviet system in the East with a special type of Fordism (cf. Busch 2009), and (c) the rapid modernisation in parts of the Third World ('developmentalism').

The following figures on the annual increase of the gross domestic product (GDP) in different world regions (Table 1) confirm the notion of a golden age and show that development was not only a high priority, but also an achievement across the world:

Table 1: Annual increase of GDP per capita in per cent, different world regions (Bladh 1995: 336)

	1913–50	1950–73	1973–89
Western Europe	1.0	4.2	2.0
Eastern Europe*	2.2	3.6	1.2
Latin America**	1.5	3.3	0.9

* Czechoslovakia, Hungary, and the Soviet Union.
** Argentina, Brazil, Chile, and Mexico.

A common trait in the Swedish historiography of the post-war era is that it exaggerates national uniqueness or – in other words – it underestimates the over-determining importance of the international context.[1] In fact, the development in Sweden is a variation on an international phenomenon, a variation with distinctive national features.[2]

As in the other capitalist industrialised countries, the period from the end of the Second World War to the early 1970s was an exceptionally successful era for the Swedish economy (see Magnusson 1996: part IV). Although the annual increase of the gross domestic product (GDP) from 1870 to 1980 was on average 2.5 per cent, it climbed to 4 per cent during the Fordist period, reaching its peak during the 'record years' 1960–65, when the increase was on average 5.3 per cent annually. Industrial production increased by more than 6 per cent each year and tripled in inflation-adjusted real value during the Fordist period. Workforce productivity within the industrial sector increased annually by 6.5 per cent, that is, faster than production. The industrialisation of Sweden was completed during this period. In 1950 about one-fifth of the population earned its livelihood from agriculture; by the 1970s this number had dropped to 5 per cent. The number of industrial workers reached a maximum of almost one million during the 1960s and then slowly started to decline, losing workers mainly to the service sector. Because of rapidly increasing productivity, the value of the total industrial production continued to grow nevertheless, increasing threefold in real value between 1950 and 1974.

Unemployment decreased rapidly in Sweden after the end of the Second World War and remained steady at about 2 per cent until the 1970s –

---

[1] This is to some extent also true for the rest of Scandinavia (cf. Torfing 1997: 227).
[2] In Swedish research the term Fordism is mainly used by economic historians in the sense of a technical-economic paradigm. Here it is used as a tool to analyse society as a whole, encompassing its different spheres and their internal relations (cf. Tanner 1999).

despite a growing population (which increased by 15,000 per year through net immigration) and a vastly increasing number of women in the workforce. In the interwar period it was mainly unmarried women who worked outside the home. Among married women, only one out of ten was in paid employment in 1930; the number more than doubled (from 15 to 36 per cent) between 1950 and 1964. In the 1960s and 1970s half a million women entered the workforce. From the 1960s the expanding public sector played a decisive part in the increasing number of women in paid employment, because the number of women working in the industrial sector did not grow at all after the mid-1960s.[3]

The exceptional and sustained economic growth both enabled and, in turn, was enabled by a consumption that doubled between 1950 and 1970. Private consumption increased by just under 2 per cent annually during the 1950s and by 3 per cent annually during the 1960s. A characteristic trait during this period was that private consumption increased at the same time as public spending expanded rapidly, growing even faster than the former. An increasing part of the newly created resources was reserved for redistribution to the economically and socially less fortunate. The revenues of the state almost tripled in the ten years following the Second World War. The public sector, defined as the part of the GDP that passes through any public budget, reached one-quarter in the beginning of the 1950s. Twenty-five years later it had increased to one-half. Of this, 20 percentage points were used for the redistribution of resources between different social and demographic groups through public budgets.

In 1945 half the Swedish population lived in rural areas. Many did not yet have access to electricity. A majority of families in towns and urban areas lived in one or two rooms with a kitchen. They did not have access to indoor toilets or warm water. In the 1946 fifteen-year plan for housing construction, quantitative goals were set: two rooms and a kitchen (meeting strictly specified standards) for every family with two children. With the help of municipal planning and the regulation of the capital market, the building rate was propelled from 40,000 apartments annually to double that

---

[3] As Lars Magnusson (1996: 444) has emphasised, although it is correct that the equal pay principle took effect during the 1950s and 1960s, "women were mainly given low paid jobs – thus becoming overrepresented among low-income earners. [...] Similarly the proportion of women was higher in industries with lower wage levels, e.g. the textile and food industries. The percentage of women within the badly paid sector of national or municipal health care was also very high. [...] All in all the 1950s and 1960s saw a huge step towards better conditions for women. But there was a long way left to a more equal position in working life and in society."

by the mid-1960s, two-thirds of which were multi-unit homes. Housing standards had improved dramatically.

The Fordist period became the so-called 'harvest time' of publicly administered welfare. The national and municipal welfare sector afforded comprehensive social services from cradle to grave. In 1946 all political parties endorsed a state retirement pension raise. The strictly means-tested child benefit, which had existed for ten years, was replaced in 1947 by a universal benefit. The Annual Leave Act of 1951 increased statutory vacation from two to three weeks a year. Working hours decreased gradually to 40 hours a week, and Saturday became a day of rest. The school system was extended and modernised: in 1950 comprehensive schools replaced the old parallel school system, and in 1962 a nine-year compulsory school was introduced. In 1955 a mandatory publicly financed health insurance was established, and Parliament agreed to a more comprehensive insurance for accidents at work. To replace the old poverty relief laws, a new social security act was passed in 1957. Gradually a complex system of building subsidies and housing benefits was created. In the early 1970s reforms of part-time pensions along with more comprehensive health insurance and parental leave completed the picture.

As Lars Magnusson has emphasised, most of these reforms were almost unanimously supported in Parliament. When it came to the introduction of occupational pensions, however, a conflict erupted between the labour movement and the bourgeoisie. The contention was the future of the universal, as opposed to the selective, welfare system (Magnusson 1996: 459).

The rapid increase in private and public consumption formed a new Sweden and a new Swede. The subsistence of the wage labourers, which earlier had been precarious and at the mercy of recessions, became more secure and more long-term. The nuclear family, the spatial separation of work, home, and shopping, the standardised home, mass consumption of cars, electric household machines, and other capitalistically produced lasting consumer goods became the hallmarks of the new way of life. This led to not only a marked rise in the wage labourers' living standards but also to a complete transformation of their socialisation pattern, that is, to the formation of a specific "Fordist social character" (cf. Lüscher 1985). Gender relations were determined by the dominance of the male industrial worker at the same time as women's unpaid domestic work was of central importance for the reproduction of the workforce, "for its psycho-physical balance, for leisure, health, child raising" (Haug, F. 2003: 616).

Social regulation and hegemony

Regulation theory assumes that the economic reproduction process is not self-regulating but politically mediated. Only with the help of the state can the rival groups dominating the economy enforce relatively consistent politico-economic strategies to shape the social reproduction process. Political regulation (though not necessarily by the state) is a prerequisite for a relatively crisis-free reproduction process. Institutions, social norms, and forms of individuality shape individual and collective conduct to become compatible with the conditions of the economic accumulation process. This regulation consists of a combination of force and necessity, contract and social control, internalised values and patterns of conduct – it is an actor-driven process, but without a ruling subject. The transmission and articulation of different interests and strategies are finally condensed into a hegemonic project.

In contrast to the state socialist regimes, the political power in the bourgeois capitalist system does not rest mainly on dominance through violence but rather on social hegemony or – as Gramsci expressed it – on consensus armoured with force. We understand social hegemony as economically, politically, ethically, culturally, and intellectually leading and creating influence. Established social hegemony does not mean that conflicts are eradicated but that they are given a certain form, a form that rarely resembles a stable, unchanging order. Social hegemony is a general consensus on a certain direction of development in order to come to terms with existing or emerging conflicts.

The hegemony is materially rooted in certain ways of production, work, and living and in corresponding socialisation patterns, social characters, and gender relations. Thus, a mutual and relatively coherent connection between these material elements, on the one hand, and political consent and ideological accord, on the other, is created. Through economic, social, and political practices a sort of "social concrete" (Poulantzas) is mixed out of ideas and conceptions, customs, and lifestyles. A hegemony created in such a comprehensive way and rooted in the everyday life of the people can rest confidently on the popular 'common sense'.

For modern societies the economic sphere together with the civil and political society are woven into a hegemonic historical bloc. Such a bloc achieves an always contradictory yet functioning social unity, an active and activating interplay of different social groups that drives society into a certain direction. A historical bloc always has to be "based on the decisive function exercised by the leading group in the decisive nucleus of economic activity" (Gramsci 1971: 161). During the Fordist period industrial capital groups were this nucleus. However, into the bloc of these capital fractions and other leading groups some subordinate, dominated groups were also incorporated, mainly the industrial workers. The historical bloc of Fordism is therefore a bourgeois–proletarian industry bloc. This compromise between the classes took the institutionalised form of the corporatist triangle of state – capital – trade unions.

The increasingly homogenous working conditions of the industrial wage labourers led to a growing awareness of their shared problems and common living conditions. The relatively strong trade unions could use this 'organic' form of working-class awareness to gain a crucial influence over the formation of social labour during the Fordist industrialisation process. The correlation between productivity gains and raised wages constituted the basis for the Fordist class compromise. The labour movement, building on this compromise, succeeded in combining conflict strategies on the company level with regional and national regulation of social labour. Through the extension of welfare state arrangements, a partial decommodificiation of the workforce was achieved.

The third panel of the triptych opens

What at first looked merely like an economic crisis in the mid-1970s in actual fact started a profound process of change in all areas of society. The Fordist development type dissolved and with it eroded also, as Frigga Haug put it, "the protest potential, which we had up to then recognised as solidarity, labour movement, the community of male workers, risen from Fordism, Taylorism, mass production" (cited in Tanner 1999: 586).

The new development type that arose out of the eroding Fordism has not yet taken its final shape, something that also explains the difficulty of finding an adequate term for it. It has become increasingly common to identify the main traits of the predominant politics as neoliberal, but these politics are still disputed and their long-term hegemonic potential is questionable. Regarding a general characterisation of present-day society, there is so far only a consensus as to what it is not or is not any more. We seem to live in a *post*-society: in a post-Fordist, postmodern, post-democratic, post-national, or post-industrial society. I prefer as a provisional term 'high-tech capitalism' (cf. Ohm and Haug, F. 2004; see also Haug, W.F. 2003a). The choice of this term is based on the understanding that the new development type requires that we take the starting point in an analysis of the relationship between the changing capitalist means of production and the new material and human productive forces.

The erosion of the capitalist Fordist development type started with the economic world crisis of 1974/75. Like the depression in the 1930s, this was no ordinary crisis following a recession, but an 'organic' or structural one (Gramsci). In this kind of crisis different critical processes are condensed and interwoven, leading to conflicts and obstructions in the existing historical bloc and eventually to a rearrangement of this bloc. Thus, an organic crisis cannot be solved within the framework of the existing development type; instead it triggers a longer period of economic and social restructuring and results in a complete transformation of the mode of production and living.

Within the bourgeois capitalist social system, the political transformation process that the crisis results in always takes the form of what Gramsci termed 'passive revolution'. *Passive* refers to the transformation and integration of the interests and aspirations of the subaltern groups in such a way that they remain dominated while their intellectual and leading groups are absorbed into a new hegemonic historical bloc. According to Gramsci, a passive revolution does not consist of a strategic frontal assault on the subaltern groups and their organisations. Instead it takes place 'behind their backs' in a process of silent undermining of the existing power structures.

Such a transformation process moves through several phases and at different speeds, depending on specific national or regional conditions. Although an organic crisis always has its epicentre in economic conflicts, the nature and course of the crisis can be shaped by political disputes and phenomena. Examples are the protests of 1968 with their criticism of certain aspects of the Fordist development and civilisation type and their individualistic tendencies (that were later rearticulated and then integrated into the neoliberal project), Pinochet's coup d'état in Chile which resulted in a neoliberal social experiment, Thatcherism, and Reaganomics, and, last but not least, the implosion of state socialism.

As Gramsci (1971: 184) emphasised, organic crises in themselves cannot "produce fundamental historical events; they can simply create a terrain more favourable to the dissemination of certain modes of thought, and certain ways of posing and resolving questions involving the entire subsequent development of national life". The transition from the Fordist to the neoliberally influenced development type is therefore not the replacing of the old type by a new and completely developed social type in its final form. Out of the crisis process itself and as a complex result of certain crisis resolution measures and methods, a new social development type eventually evolves. An important aspect of this transformation method, which Bob Jessop terms "conservation-dissolution effects" (2001: 12), is that earlier social relations, institutions, and discourses are transformed and sublated into a new context through the incorporation of selected parts thereof into different relations, institutions, and discourses.

The petrification of the communist labour movement

According to Hegel, the owl of Minerva spreads its wings only with the falling of dusk – history must have completed its work before it can be judged wisely. Gramsci (1999: 2191) expressed a similar thought about the labour movement. In his view it is not until "the end of a historical cycle" that its actions can be judged. This cycle, the historical period during which the labour movement developed and proved its emancipatory potential, seems to have reached its end with the crisis and erosion of Fordism.

It is quite obvious that the implosion of state-socialism in the years 1989–91 marked the end of the historical cycle of the communist labour movement. Whereas the bourgeois capitalist systems succeeded in dealing with the crisis by self-transformation (with the passive revolution as a method), the crisis in the East proved insoluble within the framework of the repressive political system. It imploded and along with it went the communist labour movement.

In the German Democratic Republic (GDR), starting in the early 1960s, several attempts were made to reform the socio-economic system in order to make it compatible with the changes that were there called the 'scientific-technological revolution'. However, to break the command structure that resulted in passivity, irresponsibility, and a general atmosphere of suspicion, not only economic but also political and cultural reforms would have been necessary – a complete change of the intellectual climate in society.

The fundamental problem for the ruling power bloc in the GDR was its hegemonic weakness. Since the 'workers' rising' of 17 June 1953 – a traumatic experience for the workers' party – the power of the SED rested on a kind of compromise between the party officials, the 'new class' (Djilas 1983[1957]), and the class of manual labourers. Through this compromise, construction and factory workers gained a privileged position in the socio-economic system, with social security and a reduced workload.

This favoured position was accentuated furthermore, as the sociologist Wolfgang Engler (1999: 173–208) has pointed out, by the fact that the East German society was culturally and socially marked by the workers; he calls the East German society *arbeiterlich* (workerly). But the price the workers had to pay for their social advancement was the surrender of their political self-determination to the party bureaucracy and ultimately to its highest leadership: the *Politbüro* (the executive committee of the ruling party, the *Sozialistische Einheitspartei Deutschlands* [Socialist Unity Party of Germany], SED). Analogous with the Fordist historical bloc in the West, the state-centred Fordist historical bloc in the GDR was therefore a Politbürocratic-proletarian-industrial bloc.

The result of this compromise was ambiguous: On the one hand, it led to a relatively high material living standard for the working masses; on the other, it restrained innovation and slowed the increase in productivity and efficiency. The hindrance of innovation and the repressive hostility towards the emerging 'cultural left' (the new cultural, environmental, civil rights, and peace movements) were crucial elements in the inability of the state-socialist system to self-transform.

The 'de-Fordisation' of the reformist labour movement

In the mid-1970s a book was published containing letters and conversations by three leading European social democrats: Willy Brandt, Bruno Kreisky, and Olof Palme. The book documents the labour movement's lack at the time of a plausible concept for how to transform the crisis-ridden Fordist development type and a widening credibility gap the social democratic parties faced. Kreisky pointed out, almost unintentionally satirically:

> As long as everything went swimmingly this capitalist order was termed social market economy [*soziale Marktwirtschaft*], and the social democratic parties, too, were quick to take refuge under the roof of this social market economy (Brandt, Kreisky, and Palme 1975: 121).

But now that the capitalist market economy grew less and less 'social', the leaders of the social democratic labour movement no longer knew where to turn.

As Mario Candeias has pointed out, the transition of the German Social Democratic Party to neoliberal positions, "has to be seen in the context of profound structural transformations of the party's class and social structure" (2004: 22–3). He focused in this connection on the salient point for a Marxist or materialist understanding of both the ideological impact of neoliberalism and the adaptation of the social democratic movement to it. There is a danger of 'structural idealism', that is, of viewing society upside-down, formed and regulated by ideas or ideals, when the latter are really a consequence of the existing material conditions. It is insufficient to ridicule neoliberalism as merely a set of beliefs that are out of touch with reality, cherished by the 'seriously rich', to explain the neoliberal conversion of social democracy as the result of a 'coup' or to portray the return to the Swedish welfare state as a simple act of volition (see e.g. Josefsson 2005: 12–21). Rather, a scientific analysis needs to focus on the actual transformation of social conditions and has to take as its starting point the alteration of the productive forces and the means of production. Although it is true, as W.F. Haug has pointed out, that with such an approach we still do not understand everything, "without it we certainly understand nothing" (2003b: 173).

The long period of full employment and the wage labourers' faith in Keynesian growth and employment policies gave them in the early 1970s – in a general climate of radicalisation – an unusually strong position in relation to capital. Capitalists perceived a wave of strikes and other actions – not only for higher wages but also for better working conditions and participative decision-making – as a threat to their own position of power. In connection with this labour offensive, the capital accumulation problems that had arisen some years earlier became increasingly apparent. Capital intensity had increased, and full employment had driven up wage costs. But the key reason for the crisis of Fordism was that, under the existing conditions (that is, with the means of regulation of the Keynesian welfare-state), the productivity reserve within the Fordist accumulation model was insufficient to guarantee the long-term stability of capital profits. The Fordist-Taylorist work process rested heavily on the separation of living labour from the knowledge of production and its incorporation into the machine system. This type of work process had exhausted its potential by the late 1960s. The increase in productivity slowed, the organic composition of capital rose, and profits declined (see, e.g., Röttger 2010).

The crisis of Fordism became apparent. Its resolution did not follow a predetermined plan, but the measures taken followed a certain direction of development. The productivity problem was solved partly through the implementation of a new technology: the automation and computerisation of production. This demanded a greater 'responsible autonomy' for the direct producers, the incorporation of their intellectual capacities and their voluntary cooperation with management and engineers. The flexibility necessary for this led to the individualisation of work tasks and demanded adaptability and mobility.

During the last third of the twentieth century, automated work penetrated almost all parts of the production and reproduction process. Thus monotonous-repetitive, standardised mass work was reduced to a subordinate position, while work relations characterised by communication skills and independent thought and group work became increasingly important. The combative power of the workers fell during that period, victim to mass unemployment. The destructive side of this crisis claimed the attention of the left to such an extent that the constructive aspects and possibilities of the transformation process were left almost exclusively to the organic intellectuals of capital. The political and trade union branches of the labour movement let themselves be all but overwhelmed by this development, especially as they concentrated on the illusory defence of the status quo. The consequence was a passive revolution in the world of labour. Just as industrialisation had crushed the power of the qualified craftsmen, automation and computerisation crushed the force of the Fordist mass workers.

The Fordist work organisation had an essential feedback function for the formation of a political consensus. The organisational strength, internal unity, and political impact of the trade unions and the social democratic party rested on the large number of members who volunteered and sacrificed parts of their leisure time, energy, and intelligence to trade union or party work. With the erosion of the Fordist work organisation and the transition to a more flexible organisation this political resource disappeared. Furthermore, the strictly hierarchically structured trade unions did not correspond to the expectations of new groups of workers, who were used to relative autonomy in the work process and to self-organisation in the lifeworld.

From the mid-1970s the partly deliberately produced mass unemployment constituted a form of structural violence which undermined the negotiating power of the workers and the trade unions: the fear of unemployment demobilised them. In that situation working conditions and terms of employment that used to be general and standardised started to become individualised. Collective interest representation yielded to competition within the company, to individual strategies of resistance, adaptation, and submission. The creation of mass unemployment and precarious forms of employment constituted the material foundation for the transition to neoliberal means of production and life.

These phenomena were diverse but connected steps in a capitalist solution of the crisis, ultimately aiming at a fundamental restructuring of the global means of production and thereby at an alteration of the power balance on the national level in favour of capital. Globally, the liberalisation of currencies, capital, and commodity markets was a prerequisite for the creation of transnational production networks. New communication and information technologies overcame geographic boundaries and significantly lowered the transaction costs of decentralised production. Transnational production – which followed the inclined plane of global wage levels – constituted yet another way of undermining wage negotiations and gaining acceptance for new forms of employment.

The increase of precarious employment and the loss of collective bargaining power do not lead to a complete cessation of collective representation of interests but transform it into a competitive corporatism; that is, it accepts the supremacy of company interests in a time of globalisation. The trade unions have thus ceased to fill the strategic role that they had during the era of Fordism: to function as the transmission belt of social democracy.

The fundamental requirement for the breakthrough of neoliberalism was the transnationalisation of production and financial markets beginning in the mid-1970s. But that was not the only requirement. The crisis of Fordism and the implosion of state socialism led to the discrediting of not only state socialist economic planning but also its Keynesian variant. Neoliberals succeeded in blaming the crisis on 'overregulation' and portrayed it as a general crisis of state regulation, which necessitated extensive deregulation and 'state slimming'. The latter did not mean a smaller state in general but rather a dismantling of public welfare. This process incorporated earlier criticism (dating back to 1968) of the hierarchical and centralistic structures of the Fordist state that did not allow radical democratic influence from below.

From the Golden Age to strategic paralysation – a tentative conclusion

The changes sketched above contributed to the weakening of the conditions the reformist labour movement rested on and – lacking alternatives of its own – facilitated its adaptation to the dominating neoliberal frame of reference. Thus the social democratic labour movement contributed considerably to the hegemonic position of neoliberalism.

In conclusion, the labour movement that for some decades after the Second World War experienced its golden age suffered a "strategic paralysation" (Deppe 2009: 19). The question is, whether it will recover. On the one hand, the historian can, in Eduardo Galeano's (1988[1971]: 11) word, be compared to a prophet looking back; on the other, the historian must, as Karl Marx pointed out, be wary of "writing recipes […] for the cook-shops of the future" without knowing which ingredients will be available (Marx 2007[1867]: 21). Thus, historians – including researchers of contemporary history – need to be careful when making predictions about the future. Yet, I hazard to state – against the backdrop of the process described here – that the type of labour movement that once helped to form the Golden Age of the post-war era belongs to history and will never again arise as historical subject – at least not in our part of the world.

Welding job at a generator, AEG turbine plant, West Berlin, 9 July 1955 (Bundesarchiv, B 145 Bild-F002761-0001 / Photographer: Brodde)

Computer-based steering of a robot at a youth event, Germany 1988 (Bundesarchiv, B 145 Bild-F077869-0023 / Photographer: Engelbert Reinecke)

References

Adolphi, W. (2010) "Über Hegemonie und Gewalt in der DDR." *Das Argument* 52 (4/5 = no. 288), 103–23.

Amin, Samir (1997) *Capitalism in the Age of Globalization: The Management of Temporary Society*. London: Zed Books.

Bladh, M. (1995) *Ekonomisk historia: Europa och Amerika 1500–1990*. Lund: Studentlitteratur.

Blomqvist, H. and Ekdahl, L., eds (2003) *Kommunismen hot och löfte: Arbetarrörelsen i skuggan av Sovjetunionen*. Stockholm: Carlsson.

Blomqvist, H. and Schmidt, W., eds (2012) *Efter guldåldern: Arbetarrörelsen och fordismens slut*. Stockholm: Carlsson.

Brandt, W., Kreisky, B., and Palme, O. (1975) *Briefe und Gespräche*. Frankfurt/Main: Europäische Verlagsanstalt.

Busch, U. (2009) "Die DDR als staatssozialistische Variante des Fordismus." *Jahrbuch für Forschungen zur Geschichte der Arbeiterbewegung* 8 (3), 34–56.

Candeias, M. (2004) *Neoliberalismus – Hochtechnologie – Hegemonie: Grundrisse einer transnationalen kapitalistischen Produktions- und Lebensweise: Eine Kritik*. Hamburg: Argument.

Deppe, F. (2009) "Die 'Große Krise' und die Gewerkschaften." *Die Große Krise und die Lähmung der Gewerkschaften*, ed. by Deppe, F., Müller, W., and Riexinger, B. München: Institut für Sozial-Ökologische Wirtschaftsforschung, 3–19.

Djilas, M. (1983[1957]) *The New Class: An Analysis of the Communist System*. San Diego: Harcourt Brace Jovanovich.

Ekdahl, L. (2001) *Mot en tredje väg: En biografi över Rudolf Meidner, vol. 1: Tysk flykting och svensk modell*. Lund: Arkiv.

Ekdahl, L. (2005) *Mot en tredje väg: En biografi över Rudolf Meidner, vol. 2: Facklig expert och demokratisk socialist*. Lund: Arkiv.

Eklund, K. (1995) *Vår ekonomi: En introduktion till samhällsekonomin*. 5th rev. edn. Stockholm: Tiden.

Engler, W. (1999) *Die Ostdeutschen: Kunde von einem verlorenen Land*. Berlin: Aufbau.

Galeano, E. (1988[1971]) *Las venas abiertas de America Latina*. 8th edn. Madrid: Siglo Veintiuno.

Gramsci, A. (1971) *Selections from the Prison Notebooks of Antonio Gramsci*. New York: International Publishers.

Gramsci, A. (1999) *Gefängnishefte*, vol. 9. Hamburg: Argument.

Haug, F. (2003) "'Schaffen wir einen neuen Menschentyp': Von Henry Ford zu Peter Hartz." *Das Argument* 45 (4/5 = no. 252), 606–17.

Haug, W.F. (2003a) *High-Tech-Kapitalismus: Analysen zu Produktionsweise, Arbeit, Sexualität, Krieg und Hegemonie*. Hamburg: Argument.

Haug, W.F. (2003b) "Warum sich Sozialkonflikte nicht mehr politisch ausdrücken – Thesen." *Klassen und soziale Bewegungen: Strukturen im modernen Kapitalismus*, ed. by Bischoff, J. et al. Hamburg: VSA, 169–73.

Hobsbawm, E. (1994) *Age of Extremes: The Short Twentieth Century 1914–1991*. London: Joseph.

Jessop, B. (2001) "Nach dem Fordismus: Das Zusammenspiel von Struktur und Strategie." *Das Argument* 43 (1 = no. 239), 9–22.

Josefsson, D. (2005) "Korståget mot välfärden eller Den svenska elitens våldsamma revolt." *Ordfront Magasin* (no. 10), 12–21.

Lüscher, R.M. (1985) *Henry und die Krümelmonster: Versuch über den fordistischen Sozialcharakter*. Tübingen: Gehrke.

Magnusson, L. (1996) *Sveriges ekonomiska historia*. Stockholm: Tiden.

Marx, K. (2007[1867]) *Capital: A Critique of Political Economy, vol. 1, part 1: The Process of Capitalist Production*. New York: Cosimo.

Ohm, Ch. and Haug, F. (2004) "Hochtechnologische Produktionsweise." *Historisch-kritisches Wörterbuch des Marxismus*, vol. 6/1. Hamburg: Argument, 435–50.

Östberg, K. (2008) *I takt med tiden: Olof Palme 1927–1969*. Stockholm: Leopard.

Östberg, K. (2009) *När vinden vände: Olof Palme 1969–1986*. Stockholm: Leopard.

Röttger, B. (2010) "Krise des Fordismus." *Historisch-kritisches Wörterbuch des Marxismus*, vol. 7/2. Hamburg: Argument, 2147–60.

Schmidt, W. (2002) *Antikommunism och kommunism under det korta nittonhundratalet*. Lund: Nordic Academic Press.

Schmidt, W. (2005) *C-H Hermansson: En politik biografi*. Stockholm: Leopard.

Schmidt, W. (2008) "Kalter Krieg." *Historisch-kritisches Wörterbuch des Marxismus*, vol. 7/1. Hamburg: Argument, 21–32.

Tanner, J. (1999) "Fordismus." *Historisch-kritisches Wörterbuch des Marxismus*, vol. 4. Hamburg: Argument, 580–587.

Torfing, J. (1997) "Die Zukunft des skandinavischen Wohlfahrtskapitalismus: Der Fall Dänemark." *Jenseits der Nationalökonomie? Weltwirtschaft und Nationalstaat zwischen Globalisierung und Regionalisierung*, ed. by Becker, S., Sablowski, T., and Schumm, W. Hamburg: Argument, 214–31.

8. Solidarity and Diplomacy: Sweden and the Democratisation of Poland, 1980–1989

Klaus Misgeld and Karl Molin

How do you relate to a dictatorship? In the Cold War context this general question took the shape of how Western democracies should approach the communist Soviet Union and its satellite states. An influential answer emerged in the 1960s with the 'Eastern Policy' (*Ostpolitik*) as it was defined during the leadership of Willy Brandt, foreign minister (1966–69) and chancellor (1969–74) of the Federal Republic of Germany (FRG). The objective of this policy was to combine stability and security with trustful relations, open the boundaries to informal contacts and the exchange of information. Its aim was to focus on areas of consensus, conclude mutually beneficial agreements, and work for détente in the relations between the superpowers. The *Ostpolitik* was manifested in the agreements concluded by the FRG in Moscow, Berlin, and Warsaw, which confirmed the inviolability of existing borders but also opened up opportunities for increased relations. It was a policy which, in a period of looming nuclear apocalypse, was based on the paramount importance of preserving peace. "Peace is not everything," said Brandt, "but without peace everything is nothing" (*Frieden ist nicht alles, aber ohne Frieden ist alles nichts*) (Geis and Lau 2013; Snyder 2011; Brier 2014).

However, being goals in their own right, peace and stability were also a prerequisite for change. Contacts with the West would lead to insight in the East – both among regular citizens and the ruling elite – about the inefficiency and repressiveness of 'real socialism'. This realisation was to lead to liberal and democratic reform, which countries in the West would endorse. The new policy was encapsulated in 1963 by Egon Bahr in three words: Change Through Rapprochement (*Wandel durch Annäherung*). It was a perhaps cunningly subversive strategy, but above all it was a strategy for peaceful change – for peace *and* change (Schmidt 2014).

The *Ostpolitik* of West Germany helped to increase international détente in the 1970s and laid the foundations for the 1975 Helsinki Final Act, which brought together all European countries (except Albania) as well as the USA and Canada. The Final Act was an attempt, in the spirit of *Ostpolitik,* to combine stability with change: the signatories recognised the inviolability of frontiers and also committed to respecting human and political rights and promoting the free exchange of information across national borders.

But the climate of the late 1970s was conducive to neither peace nor change. The arms race continued and the military tensions escalated. At the end of 1979, the Soviet Union invaded Afghanistan and deployed medium-range ballistic missiles in Europe, something the USA also threatened to do. The new US president Ronald Reagan labelled the Soviet Union an 'empire of evil' and pledged to fight communism wherever it appeared.

In this situation, it became necessary to re-evaluate the way in which the two dimensions of *Ostpolitik* were inter-balanced. When the risk of war escalates, prioritising stability at the expense of change may seem like the right choice. But if, meanwhile, the forces of change voice their demands and expect support, it may nevertheless be the wrong choice. It was such a climate of uncertainty that the events in Poland in autumn 1980 brought about. The fact that the new social movement Solidarity (*Solidarność*) unexpectedly managed to establish itself and to challenge not only the Polish government but all 'real socialist' regimes, increased the risk of military entanglements but also fuelled hopes for reform.

Balancing the line between stability and change was a key concern in Sweden's policy towards Poland. Sweden's Social Democratic Party had close connections with its West German sister party and had followed the emergence of the *Ostpolitik* with approval. This policy was also accepted by the Swedish centre-right governments of 1976–1982 when assessing relations with the Soviet Union and its satellite states (Bjereld, Johansson, and Molin 2008).

However, foreign policy was not shaped only in the corridors of power. In the 1980s, a strong popular movement emerged in Sweden, firmly committed to supporting Solidarity and the Polish opposition. This Swedish activism was multi-layered, embracing trade union and political as well as church and humanitarian organisations. Strong and sustained help came from the trade union movement directly and via the International Centre of the Swedish Labour Movement (AIC). Solidarity activism was a force that profoundly influenced Sweden's official relations with Poland. In addition to the Swedish foreign service and foreign ministry, it played a crucial role in the events examined in this chapter.[1]

Solidarity and hopes for a new Poland: August 1980 to December 1981

In summer 1980 the Polish government introduced a major increase in the price of meat. During the 1970s it had financed a relatively high level of prosperity with sizeable overseas loans, but now believed that it was necessary to raise the prices on heavily subsidised food to keep up with rapidly rising interest payments, among other things. Workers all over the country reacted to the rising cost of living with strikes and demonstrations. In the majority of cases, they went back to work after receiving promises of a pay increase.

But when the wave of strikes reached Gdańsk on 14 August, the strikers would not be appeased by pay increases. Workers at the Lenin Shipyard and other workplaces in the region drew up a list of 21 demands, the most important of which was the right to form free, independent trade unions. Under pressure from 70,000 striking workers, the communist party yielded to most of the demands including free trade unions and on 31 August signed the Gdańsk Agreement which laid the foundations for the new Poland. The new trade union movement, named Solidarity, was led by Lech Wałęsa, an electrician from Gdańsk. It grew at an explosive rate and soon accumulated some 10 million members. Censorship was relaxed and an open public debate became possible. Journalists from all over the world flocked to Warsaw and Gdańsk to cover the Polish miracle (Kemp-Welch 2008; Kubik 2009; Linch 2009; Meszmann 2009; Paczkowski 2003).[2]

However, the sixteen months leading up to 13 December 1981, when martial law was declared, was also a period marked by continuous confrontations between Solidarity, which demanded that the agreement be respected, and the regime, which was under pressure from Moscow to stop the 'counter-revolution'. The threat of Warsaw Pact troops intervening to restore order was constantly in the background. Tensions grew in 1981 with two dramatic congresses: the Communist Party's in July and secondly Solidarity's national congress in September–October. At the former, the

---

[1] This article is based on an upcoming book written by Klaus Misgeld and Karl Molin in collaboration with Stefan Ekecrantz and Paweł Jaworski. More detailed analysis, sources, and literature can be found in the book which is scheduled for publishing in 2014.
[2] The following accounts of developments in Poland are also based on these works.

reformist communists hated by Moscow threatened to seize power; at the latter, the new movement presented radical political ambitions.

*

The fact that the Polish regime had sensationally recognised Solidarity as a legal trade union movement and paved the way for reform meant that it was no longer a clear-cut dictatorship in the eyes of the world. Instead, the predominant anti-democratisation force in the Polish drama was the Kremlin, which threateningly showed its displeasure with current events. The burning question was how much change Moscow could accept before intervening with military means and if Solidarity should reflect on the risk that its campaign might lead to a devastating war, a bloodbath at the centre of Europe. Solidarity also repeatedly stressed that its ambitions were limited and that its goal was a "self-limiting revolution" within the framework of the existing socialist system and the alliance with the Soviet Union (Ascherson 1987 [1981]). A key component in this self-imposed restraint was that its function was defined as a non-political trade union organisation. Solidarity contacted the International Confederation of Free Trade Unions (ICFTU) and referenced the International Labour Organisation's (ILO) convention – which Poland had ratified – as validation for its activities (Müller 1988). Solidarity was also careful to emphasise that it operated independently of sympathisers in the West. It was essential to disprove any allegations that it was a West-led political movement.[3]

The Swedish trade union movement made a similar assessment of the situation and took equivalent precautionary measures in expressing its support for Solidarity. Firstly, the Swedish Trade Union Confederation (LO) was consequent in insisting that Solidarity was simply a trade union movement. It realised, of course, that this was an illusion – an independent trade union movement was by its nature a challenge to the existing political system of Poland. But in LO's view, this was a useful illusion that suggested that it would not meddle in politics in its contacts with Solidarity but was devoted exclusively to trade union solidarity. For this reason, LO also declined the offer of a closer collaboration with representatives of the Polish

---

[3] This was the motivation for Solidarity declining the Swedish foreign minister's proposal of a meeting with leading Solidarity representatives, see Cryptogram, 3 June 1981, folder 147, Hp 1 Ep, Swedish Ministry of Foreign Affairs, Government Offices archives (hereinafter FM).

Workers' Defence Committee's (KOR, founded in 1976) which they regarded as a political organisation (Misgeld 2009).

Secondly, LO underlined the necessity of fighting the perception that Solidarity depended on foreign organisations and international support. The ICFTU's supporting role was to be downplayed to prevent Solidarity being perceived as a West-controlled movement.[4] Collaboration with Polish activists living in Sweden and other western countries was to be avoided if their assets could be construed as coming from LO's US counterpart, the American Federation of Labor and Congress of Industrial Organizations (AFL-CIO) and thereby in practice from the US government (which supported AFL-CIO's international activities). When it came to specific arrangements, the ICFTU had to toe the LO line, which was also supported by other Nordic trade union confederations as well as by the Confederation of German Trade Unions (DGB). Lech Wałęsa also expressly adopted the same line.

LO's third strategy of caution was to remain in the background or, as it was phrased in the minutes of the international committee meeting on 29 October 1980: "... this measure shall be communicated in Sweden in a manner that makes it clear that we are transferring funds that have flowed in spontaneously", which was also the message to the ICFTU.[5] LO's approach was reminiscent of the DGB's in this respect. But LO also wanted the ICFTU and the International Trade Secretariats (ITS) to keep a low profile. The high-profile players would be individual trade unions such as the Swedish Union of Graphical Workers (GF), local trade union organisations in Sweden, and *i-fonden* (the Labour Movement's International Fund for Solidarity), that is, the fund that the labour movement had set up to fund trade union and democratic movements around the world. In a circular issued on 15 January 1981, the LO leadership appealed to all trade union organisations to support Solidarity but observe "great caution" and be restrictive with disseminating information about it given the sensitivity of the situation in Poland. Any major fundraising campaigns would have to wait. In the meantime local organisations and single trade unions should deposit funds into *i-fonden*.[6]

---

[4] U. Asp to G. Nilsson, 10 Dec. 1980: "Överläggning med FFI [ICFTU] om formerna för stöd till Solidaritet i Polen", F23:92; F26B:4, LO archives (hereinafter LO), Labour Movement Archive and Library, Stockholm (hereinafter ARAB).
[5] LO's International Committees minutes, 29 Oct. 1980, A06:7, LO, ARAB; Communiqué to the ICFTU, 31 Oct. 1980, copy/U. Asp, annex, ibid.
[6] F26B:2, LO, ARAB.

Protected by these precautionary strategies, LO built up an extensive organisation for supporting Solidarity. In mid-September 1980, LO received the first trade union report about the movement that would become Solidarity. It was written by Charles Kassman, editor-in-chief of the International Centre of the Swedish Labour Movement's (AIC) magazine *aic-bulletinen*. In mid-September he had been dispatched by the AIC, LO, and ICFTU. He had previously visited the Lenin Shipyard in Gdańsk and met the former strike leaders. But now it was first and foremost his talks with Lech Wałęsa and Jacek Kuroń, one of KOR's founders, that were of interest. They clearly demonstrated the scale of the help that was needed and the size of practical obstacles that needed to be overcome in order to build up the strikers' organisation (Misgeld 2010; Misgeld 2013; Misgeld and Molin 2010).

Other Swedish trade union representatives soon also travelled to Poland and provided detailed reports about the structure of the new trade union movement and its help needs. The reports were summarised in articles in the trade union press. The LO's leadership and the committee for international affairs, which was led by LO's secretary Rune Molin, frequently discussed the situation in Poland and the help that it could provide. LO decided to supply printing equipment for disseminating information within and via Solidarity, something that was absolutely essential at a time when the possibilities of digital information technology did not exist. The task of overseeing the Poland project went to the GF and the person appointed to coordinate its execution was technical ombudsman Ture Mattsson, who was put on the LO payroll. From 1980 to 1981 he made around twenty visits in Poland while building up the Solidarity's printing technology. This was his chief task and LO's primary undertaking.[7]

The printing presses that were delivered were relatively small compared with the equipment used by the Swedish trade union movement. But this was in accordance with the recipients' express requirements. "We need printing equipment but it must be simple to begin with", Lech Wałęsa had explained to Swedish graphical workers when they met him in Gdańsk in November 1980. A few weeks later, when the deliveries had begun, he expressed his satisfaction and gratitude: Sweden was the first country to help Solidarity and it would not be forgotten.[8]

---

[7] Press release "LOs kontakter med Solidaritet i Polen", doc. no. 1981-int-133, F09A:3, LO, ARAB.
[8] "Rapport från GF:s andra besök hos 'SOLIDARNOSC' i Polen den 3-10/12 1980", F26B:1, LO, ARAB. See also Wałęsa's telegram before the LO congress in 1986: "We will never forget that the Trade Union Confederation of Sweden was among the first to give

In all, LO's initiative ranked as one of the largest undertaken by any trade union organisation on behalf of Solidarity (Goddeeris 2013; Domber 2008). LO paid Ture Mattsson a salary for almost a year, employed a Polish-speaking secretary, provided premises and funded administrative expenses. The combined amount of the Swedish initiatives in the LO group up until December 1981 was in excess of SEK 2 million. It consisted mainly of funds paid directly by LO and its international solidarity fund.[9] The amount can be compared with other measures during the same period. According to LO's administration report for 1981, the organisation's combined revenue for 1981 was SEK 252 million, of which 19 million was paid to the LO-funded or LO-owned daily press, two million went "to LO's closely-related international organisations" and 11.6 million to "closely-related Swedish organisations" (including the Social Democratic Party).[10]

After reaching an agreement with Lech Wałęsa and the ICFTU's secretary general Otto Kersten in November 1980, LO also undertook to coordinate the help to Solidarity from the ICFTU and its affiliated organisations.

For Swedish diplomatic relations, the trade unions' commitment to Solidarity was both encouraging and troubling in a volatile and precarious situation. The rich abundance of material about the Polish crisis contains no evidence that the Swedish foreign ministry and embassy in Warsaw were anything but sympathetic to the trade union involvement. But it does indicate that there were misgivings about some of the more enthusiastic union activists not being aware of the risks they were running.

Just before Christmas 1980, when the apprehension of a Soviet invasion reached a critical point, Ambassador Knut Thyberg in Warsaw discussed Solidarity's international contacts with one of the Polish Communist Party's foreign policy experts. The latter knew all about Solidarity's contacts with LO and had observed that the first aid consignments from outside the country had come from Sweden. But while he did not object to these contacts, he insinuated that they might play into Moscow's hands (i.e. giving the Kremlin a pretext to intervene), particularly as there was "a German dimension to the picture". According to Thyberg, his message was

---

us their support and help both during our successes and the persecutions we were subjected to on 13 December 1981" (Landsorganisationen i Sverige s.d. [1987], 495).
[9] In 2013 monetary value this corresponds to approximately SEK 5.6 million (*Statistics Sweden*/KPI/Price converter). In the LO archive's Poland volumes (F26B:1-8, LO, ARAB) there are a number of different summaries.
[10] LO (1982), 187, Income Statement, note 11.

that the trade union relations should draw the least possible attention and trade union organisations in the larger NATO countries should preferably be kept out of the picture altogether. Thyberg wanted this message to be relayed to LO. Poland's situation, he wrote, hung on "a very fine thread" (cf. Molin 2011).[11]

The Polish Communist Party's message did not contain anything that the LO leadership did not already know, in particular that supporting Solidarity could be a problem both from the perspective of international détente and for the Polish opposition. The Swedish trade unions were aware of the risks that the embassy warned about. Despite this, there were misgivings at the foreign ministry and the Swedish embassy in Warsaw that Swedish trade union representatives would neither understand nor respect the "political realities". The foreign ministry's line in the discussions with the Poles was that 'LO had the freedom to determine its own international contacts'. However, during the turbulent times in the late autumn of 1980, when the threat of invasion was seen as imminent, there were several discussions about whether the Swedish foreign ministry should warn LO activists and it did so on at least two occasions.[12]

Both LO and the foreign ministry agreed that support for Solidarity should be drawn up with great caution to avoid giving the Russians cause to intervene. But the need for caution also applied to Solidarity. After the agreement in Gdańsk many commentators, including the Swedish embassy, believed the time had come for the organisation to consolidate its gains and try to find a *modus vivendi* with the regime. The LO leadership's view of Solidarity as a non-political trade union movement coincided with hopes for finding a new balancing point in Polish society. Moderation and caution were also prescribed by Solidarity's leaders in the spring and summer of 1981.

However, Solidarity presented a new, more radical profile in September 1981. At the first of its two-part congress, the organisation adopted a series of subversive proposals, including free elections to the Sejm and worker self-determination at companies. The delegates also agreed to send an official greeting to all workers of Eastern Europe who struggled for free trade unions. Leading Western politicians shared the view that Solidarity had gone too far. In Willy Brandt's view, the greeting to Eastern Europe's

---

[11] Cryptogram, 22 Dec. 1980, folder 140, Hp 1 Ep, FM.
[12] Cryptogram Stockholm – Warszawa, 5 Sept. 1980, folder 135, Hp 1 Ep, FM; Cryptogram, 15 Sept. 1980, Thyberg, folder 136; memo 16 Sept. 1980, Engdahl, folder 136, Hp 1 Ep, FM; Cryptogram, 7 Nov. 1980, folder 137, Hp 1 Ep, FM; Cipher Stockholm – Warszawa, 2 Dec. 1980, folder 138, Hp 1 Ep, FM.

workers was an act of provocation and meddling in other countries' internal affairs. The Danish foreign minister, social democrat Kjeld Olesen, explained that it was in the West's interests to prevent Solidarity from continuing down the beaten path, while Austrian chancellor Bruno Kreisky appealed to Poland's workers to stop striking and return to work so that Austria could receive the deliveries of coal that had been ordered (Johansson 1981:7f; cf. Boll and Świder 2013; Lorenz 2012:213ff; Rathkolb 2013; Boel 2013).

The critical view of Solidarity's political move also received some sympathy at the foreign ministry in Stockholm. In a conversation with the Canadian ambassador the head of the political department, Lennart Eckerberg, remarked that "Solidarity should, for its own sake as well as Poland's, have stopped and consolidated its gains" instead of making a number of "purely political demands and proclamations which, in Poland and Eastern Europe, was very risky". According to the Canadian representative, the outlooks of Stockholm and Ottawa were very much in harmony.[13]

However, from the embassy in Warsaw the critics received no support whatsoever. In autumn 1980, Ambassador Thyberg was among those who hoped for compromise and moderation and that the parties in the Polish struggle would find a new balancing point. But in spring 1981 he began to accept the movement's political nature. In May, he described Solidarity as being "more than a trade union", namely "a powerful popular movement, a virtually irresistible protest against an entire system, a political opposition".[14] After Solidarity's congress he defended the organisation's new radical profile. He argued that, in addition to foreign loans, power-sharing reforms were necessary to get the country on its feet. The rights that Solidarity had forced into existence were a step in the right direction and the congress's demands for further reforms sparked hopes for the future.[15] Thyberg's view was that Solidarity was not the problem, but rather the solution.

Within the Swedish labour movement, too, there were those who disapproved of the idea that Solidarity should conform to the principle of caution. One of them was Professor Sten Johansson at the Swedish Institute for Social Research at Stockholm University, who had close contacts with KOR representatives. In autumn 1981 he and KOR activist Maria Borowska,

---

[13] Memo 1 Oct 1981, folder 151, Hp 1 Ep, FM.
[14] Cryptogram, 4 May 1981, folder 145, Hp 1 Ep, FM.
[15] Cryptogram, 9 Oct. 1981, folder 151, Hp 1 Ep, FM.

who operated out of Sweden, published a brochure in which Brandt's, Olesen's, and Kreisky's magisterial comments after the congress were described as "something of a propaganda victory for the Polish government" (Johansson 1981: 7–8). Like the Polish emigrant groups, Johansson distanced himself from those who argued that the opposition must restrain itself, given the risk of the Soviet Union restoring order in Poland with military force.[16] As he saw it, out of pure opportunism the western countries had, "in a manner bordering on the perverse", adopted a stance of "relative tolerance" towards the Polish regime (Johansson 1981: 40; cf. *Tiden* 1982:2: 74–7).

*

In a sense, those who argued in favour of Solidarity continuing to drive new reforms had history on their side. Previous periods of liberalisation had been short-lived; the orthodox forces gradually retook lost ground and the old repressive system was soon back in place. A possible conclusion was that this time one should not stop until the reforms had come so far that they were irreversible. But this strategy also increased the risk that those, who were in a position to lose their privileges would resort to violence and initiate a bloodbath, which could lead to all-out war. There was no simple answer to how Solidarity should act: put on the brakes and consolidate its gains or continue the struggle for new goals. Observers who shared the same fundamental values arrived at completely different conclusions.

Martial law and isolation: December 1981 to September 1986

At 6 a.m. on 13 December, Wojciech Jaruzelski, supreme commander, prime minister, and party leader, appeared on TV in his general's uniform and announced the imposition of martial law and that a military council had seized power until further notice. The country, he said, was close to collapse because of the extensive undermining activity by extremists in Solidarity and other opposition groups. With the Polish society now standing on the brink of the abyss, martial law was an unavoidable necessity.

With the coup, General Jaruzelski placed power in the hands of the force that he knew best and trusted, namely the army. With the assistance of the security forces, it detained numerous leaders and activists in Solidarity and other independent organisations. Wałęsa was taken to an unknown location

---

[16] Johansson to R. Molin/LO (copies to the Social Democratic politicians O. Palme and P. Schori, B. Säve-Söderbergh/AIC and *Tiden* magazine): "Rapport från resa till Warszawa 6–10 mars 1981", F26B:3, LO, ARAB.

and put under house arrest. Censorship was tightened and TV stations and other media were put under surveillance. A number of major firms were made subject to military law and key positions were given to entrusted officers. The new order was completed by a trade union act which the Sejm passed on 8 October 1982. It abolished both Solidarity and the old Communist-controlled trade union organisation, and made Solidarity an outlawed organisation.

Resistance to the coup was not as strong as many had anticipated, but there were demonstrations and strikes. The workers at the Wujek coalmine in the province of Śląsk (Silesia) were among those who held out the longest, refusing to give up until the security forces intervened. Eleven workers had been killed by the time the strike was broken.

*

Irrespective of the motives behind Jaruzelski's coup, the threat of a Soviet intervention appeared to be averted, at least for the time being. There was also a tone of relief in the initial reactions from the West, but virtually no one expressed support for the coup. With varying degrees of forcefulness governments condemned the coup. They proclaimed that fundamental human rights had been violated, provisions of the Helsinki Final Act had been broken, and a promising change process had been stopped in its tracks. In terms of *Ostpolitik*, this could be interpreted as a failure of the strategy of 'change through rapprochement'. Instead, most western governments adopted a stance more along the lines of 'change through isolation', that is, the opposite of *Ostpolitik*. Virtually unanimously, they formulated three demands on the Polish regime: repeal martial law, free the prisoners, and re-establish a dialogue with the opposition. They severed relations with Poland and made it clear that they would not resume them until their demands were met. The USA under President Reagan did not stop at freezing diplomatic relations, but also introduced a number of economic sanctions against both the Soviet Union and Poland (cf. Sjursen 2003; Domber 2008).

In this situation, Western diplomats faced new problems regarding what would be required to thaw frozen relations. For Solidarity's supporters in western civil societies, the coup meant that an old problem had been removed. The question of whether Solidarity went too far in its radicalism was no longer significant. Rather, the issue now was providing as much support as possible to a movement that had been deprived of its freedoms of speech and association. On 23 December, Prime Minister Thorbjörn Fälldin called the Swedish population to give "sizeable contributions" to the aid programmes organised across the country. The response was strong and gifts to Poland flooded into the aid stations. SEK 25 million had been donated before Christmas and the Christmas collection in many churches went to Polish children. A government order was issued decreeing that from 29 December, all packages to Poland by post would be sent free of charge. This increased the aid immediately. From Halmstad, for example, consignments with a combined weight of more than 50 tonnes arrived on the first day. The Swedish government placed SEK 10 million at the disposal of individual organisations' aid work in Poland. Not since the Second World War had the country been so strongly involved in helping a neighbouring country (*Anno [19]81* 1982: 187–9).[17]

In addition to humanitarian aid, the Polish opposition needed help to resume its political activities. It duly arrived, thanks largely to groups of Polish exiles living in Sweden. They worked up opinion, established channels to the underground Solidarity, and carried out their own direct actions. They could rely on the self-sacrifice of volunteers but still needed the support of Swedish society, which they received mainly from the trade union movement.

The Solidarity Information Office in Sweden functioned as the hub of the Polish opposition. It was housed inside premises provided by LO in Stockholm and funded mainly by LO and AIC/*i-fonden*, and other organisations such as the Swedish Confederation of Professional Employees (TCO). LO, which clung to the delusion that Solidarity was exclusively a trade union movement, saw the information office as its sister organisation's representative in Sweden. The office began activities on 27 December 1981, two weeks after the coup, and devoted the following years to spreading information about the situation in Poland, arranging meetings and demonstrations, drawing up lists of imprisoned activists, organising humanitarian aid, and even smuggling material to the underground Solidarity movement. The office's activities ceased officially at the turn of 1989/90 (Jaworski 2011).

---

[17] Other examples of solidarity action: On 9 January 1982, artists at the Royal Opera House in Stockholm gave a gala performance for Poland. Before the concert, Anders Wijkman from the Red Cross read out the preliminary collection results for the day: 60,000 sacks of children's clothes, 4500 with blankets, more than 200,000 pairs of children's shoes, and SEK 8.5 million in cash (Cable Warszawa to Stockholm 1 Feb. 1982, folder 159, Hp 1 Ep, FM).

The information office conveyed a substantial portion of the aid to the Polish opposition, but not all. The AIC conducted its own extensive aid programme. It consisted of purchases of food, clothes, and other goods for private use, which were shipped into Poland in trucks. Until the end of 1983, AIC sent 50 fully-loaded trucks.[18] While humanitarian aid was completely legal and acceptable to the Polish regime, deliveries to the underground Solidarity like printing equipment, small radio transmitters, and literature which began in the spring 1982, were treated as illegally smuggled goods. Solidarity's information office played an important role in this context, but many other organisations and individuals in Sweden and abroad were also involved, some in collaboration with AIC, others independently. The contraband reached Poland in trucks or in small motor or sailing boats (Jacobsson 2006; Lundström 2011).

The AIC and the information office jointly organised an extensive 'adoption programme'.[19] This meant that associations and individuals took direct contact with Poles, mainly Solidarity activists' families, wrote letters (with no political content), and sent packages. The Swedish postal administration paid the postage until 1 October 1982, and *i-fonden* (AIC) paid it until the end of 1989.[20] Addresses in Poland were collected both by the Catholic Church in Poland and by Solidarity's information office in Stockholm. In October 1982 around 250 Polish families had a sponsor in Sweden via the AIC and *i-fonden*.

But the AIC and LO were not involved in all the Polish support projects. The LO leadership maintained its distance from initiatives that it regarded as 'political'. This applied particularly to the Poland Solidarity Committee which had Trotskyist elements, and other '*Solidarność* committees'.[21] Relations with the Swedish Solidarity Support Committee in Lund were not particularly close, and the largely secret Independent Polish Agency (IPA) which devoted itself mainly to smuggling literature and equipment into Poland (Heino and Plewa 2007) was kept at even greater distance. The IPA

---

[18] Bengt Colling/AIC "till redaktionen", Dec. 1983, vol. 11, International Centre of the Swedish Labour Movement (AIC), ARAB.
[19] B. Säve-Söderbergh/AIC, "Rapport från besök i Polen" (17–24 februari 1982), 9 March 1982, F26B:6, LO, ARAB.
[20] Letter by AIC: "Adoption of Polish family", undated (June 1982), F26B:6, LO, ARAB; message about the programme's conclusion by J. Hodann/AIC in Dec. 1989, vol. 43, AIC, ARAB.
[21] Material about *Polen-Solidaritet* (which disbanded in 1984) in the Socialist Party's archive, ARAB; Solidarity's Information Office in Stockholm (hereinafter SIKiS), ARAB, vol. 149.

was funded by the National Endowment for Democracy and was suspected of collaborating with US government agencies including the CIA (cf. Domber 2008: 199 ff).[22] Its extensive activities were singled out by the Polish intelligence service for special attention, something that later led to diplomatic complications.

Like the Social Democratic opposition, the Swedish government expressed its disgust with the Polish regime's martial law. It used fairly abrasive tones and paid no heed to Jaruzelski's motives for the coup. It had been conducted, said Ola Ullsten at the Conference on Security and Co-operation in Europe in Madrid in February 1982, "not to save the nation but to preserve the privilege of power". A "genuine revolt of the people" had been crushed in order to save "a discredited and bankrupt system" (*Documents on Swedish Foreign Policy* 1982 [1985]: 14, 15).

It is questionable whether such outright condemnation was consistent with the bridge-building spirit of *Ostpolitik*. This question was encapsulated by the Finnish diplomat Max Jacobson in a column in the Swedish daily newspaper *Svenska Dagbladet*. Jacobson argued that while the "policy of protests and boycotts" had appeased the protesters' consciences, it had little impact on the reality that prevailed in Eastern Europe. As he saw it, "only a policy of continued cooperation can push developments in Eastern Europe in the direction favoured by western opinion". Jacobson's column provoked a memo at the foreign ministry which, although highly critical of his view, agreed that Jacobson's collaborative philosophy was justifiable when it came to long-term policy. In the short-term, however, it would be treasonous for western countries not to express their disgust at the way that the Polish freedom movement had been crushed. To show any understanding for the military regime would, it was reasoned, break the spirit of Polish resistance.[23]

Most people within and outside the foreign ministry seemed to agree in the condemnation of Jaruzelski's coup. Initially, Swedish policy was fairly self-evident. Sweden followed the same line as the other western European countries: no economic sanctions but a dramatic reduction in diplomatic contacts. In the first eighteen months after the coup, diplomatic relations were limited to the routine contacts of embassy officials with the Polish foreign ministry. There were no visits by cabinet ministers or other pro-

---

[22] The National Endowment has been labelled by Heino and Törnquist-Plewa (2007: 35) as "an independent American institution", which was formally correct but hardly in touch with reality – Discussion with Ture Mattsson, 1 Sept. 2009 (Misgeld).
[23] Memo 14 Jan. 1982, Pol 1, S. Ottosson, folder 158, Hp 1 Ep, FM. The article was published on 13 Jan.

minent politicians. Meanwhile, all the Swedish ambassadors in the 1980s enjoyed healthy contacts with what they occasionally referred to as 'the other Poland', which included the Catholic Church, groups of catholic intellectuals, Solidarity and other independent groups. Solidarity activists such as Bronisław Geremek, Jacek Kuroń, and Adam Michnik were regular guests and discussion partners at the Swedish embassy.

The question of whether to relax the visiting boycott was raised for the first time at the foreign ministry in summer 1983 after the Polish government had repealed martial law. But there was no decisive change as the regime had passed other laws giving itself similar powers. Far more importantly, particularly in the long-term, was that the regime threatened to put eleven known Solidarity leaders and former KOR members on trial. That same autumn when it became known that three security police officers had murdered father Jerzy Popiełuszko, an outspoken, controversial priest and a strong supporter of Solidarity, interest in normalising relations cooled even further.

In the following years the Swedish foreign service closely monitored the Polish government's policy towards the opposition and calibrated its visiting policy accordingly. In July 1984 the regime proclaimed a general amnesty and the imprisoned people were released, and the same year, a Polish minister was allowed to visit Stockholm for the first time since the coup. In the summer of 1985 there were signs that the regime had resumed its harassments of the opposition. This did not prevent the Swedish trade minister's planned visit to Poland from going ahead, but the visitors were encouraged to express the Swedish government's concern over these developments.[24] Polish proposals about foreign minister's visits – which would have been a sign that relations had normalised – met with evasive replies. However, when the regime proclaimed a general amnesty in September 1986 and explained that no one would be punished for their political activities, the road to normalisation opened once more. In November 1986 the state secretary for foreign affairs, Pierre Schori, travelled to Warsaw to prepare for a visit and in June 1987 the Polish foreign minister, Marian Orzechowski, came to Stockholm.

The adopted visiting policy was comparatively restrained. Sweden had traditionally played the role of bridge-builder to the East but now lagged behind several western countries when it came to high-level contacts with Poland. Within the foreign ministry, the question was raised whether the

---

[24] Memo 18 July 1985, S. Carlsson, folder 182, Hp 1 Ep, FM.

Swedish line was too strict. Ambassador Thyberg had in October 1983 pleaded the case for normalising relations and was supported by the foreign ministry. In December 1984 his successor Örjan Berner pointed out to the foreign minister that it would not be in Sweden's interests to be the last country to resume normal relations. One year later the foreign ministry noted that Sweden risked slipping into "an increasingly isolated position among western countries when it came to resuming the exchange of visits at foreign minister level."[25] One key argument in favour of normalisation was that the Polish regime had, despite everything, been heading in the right direction. Jaruzelski was seen as a reformer whose intention was to liberalise society and enhance economic efficiency within the existing system's framework. Moreover, in comparison with other eastern countries that Sweden had normal relations with, Poland was positively exemplary. One reporter quoted a common expression at the time: "As bad as the Poles currently have it, this good will the Russians or Czechs never have it."[26] Another argument, presented in December 1984, was that the Polish opposition no longer saw any advantages in isolation.[27]

Despite these repeated proposals for resuming contacts, rapprochement had to wait. The main reason was Swedish Solidarity activism. In the internal foreign ministry correspondence, the boycott policy was said to have the strong support of public opinion and this was also emphasised to Poles who wished to speed up the normalisation process.

The Polish government was familiar with Sweden's support for Solidarity and also complained that it was an illegal organisation which could use the information office to spread propaganda and arrange demonstrations in Sweden – with the government's consent and with funding from the Social Democratic party and LO. The Poles' complaints did not prevent them from demanding diplomatic normalisation, but Solidarity activism made it harder for the Swedes to accommodate them. In July 1984 Swedish Foreign Minister Bodström explained to the Polish ambassador that a premature foreign minister's visit would provoke a discussion that no one would profit from.[28] In December 1985 and April 1986, various foreign ministry memos show that the exchange of visits was to a "not inconsiderable extent"

---

[25] Personal letter Berner – Bodström, 6 Dec. 1984, folder 180, Hp 1 Ep, FM.
[26] Cryptogram Bonn – Stockholm, 25 Nov. 1982, Backlund, folder 166, Hp 1 Ep, FM.
[27] Personal letter Berner – Bodström, 6 Dec. 1984, folder 180, Hp 1 Ep, FM.
[28] Memo 2 July 1984, V. Tham, folder 177, Hp 1 Ep, FM.

influenced by the strong commitment that Swedish opinion and Swedish trade union and other organisations felt for Solidarity.[29]

*

After the imposition of martial law Poland was stable insofar as the risk of a Soviet military intervention – and thereby an international crisis – was small. The situation was simply less precarious than it had been before the coup. Western governments and organisations could now voice their criticism of the regime and express sympathies for the opposition without jeopardising peace and stability. This possibility was also seized upon by the Swedish government which froze the exchange of visits with Poland, and by Solidarity sympathisers who, in varying forms, gave extensive support to the Polish opposition. However, there were limits: the government did not take part in the Reagan administration's economic sanctions and LO continued to distance itself from aid projects in which US involvement was suspected.

For both the foreign office and the activists, the intention was to support the processes that helped to bring change in 'real socialist' Poland. For the foreign office the aim was also – in the spirit of *Ostpolitik* – to combine isolation at ministerial level with continued contacts at civil service level. Sweden was able to clarify its position through routine diplomatic channels; it could now bring home the point that isolation was linked to its demands for the cessation of martial law, the release of prisoners, and renewal of dialogues with the opposition. Problems arose when the Polish government began to meet these demands. As the regime grew increasingly liberal and change-oriented in its tone, people began to question whether isolation served any real purpose. It also became increasingly difficult to justify why the Swedish prime and foreign ministers visited countries like Yugoslavia, China, the GDR, Hungary, and the Soviet Union, but refused to set their feet in the far more liberal Poland.

Solidarity's return and victory: September 1986 to autumn 1989

In the year after the September 1986 amnesty, General Jaruzelski's image as a communist reformist in the spirit of Gorbatjov's perestroika was confirmed. In May 1987 the Polish government presented a comprehensive package of reforms aimed at streamlining bureaucracy, enhancing enter-

---

[29] Memo 6 Dec. 1985, Westerlind, folder 183, Hp 1 Ep, FM; quoted from memo 23 April 1986, Westerlind, folder 185, Hp 1 Ep, FM.

prise efficiency, adapting pricing policy to the market, and democratising the country's political life. According to a Swedish embassy report, the regime now aimed at dismantling the socialist command economy. A major problem was, however, that the initial phase of the programme included strong austerity measures that brought new tribulations on the already hard-hit Polish people.

The government failed to win popular support for the programme in a referendum but nevertheless began to implement it, albeit at a slower pace. But lack of public confidence impeded all the reform work. The only political force that the people trusted was Solidarity, which although no longer threatened with detention, was still fighting to regain its legal status. All demands for the legalisation of independent unions were rejected on the grounds that such a union already existed, namely the All-Poland Alliance of Trade Unions (*Ogólnopolskie Porozumienie Związków Zawodowych*, OPZZ) founded in 1986. Government representatives stressed that 'trade union pluralism' was out of the question.[30]

When strikes broke out in spring 1988 the strikers' demands included Solidarity's legalisation, and a long period of tug-of-war began. A solution was not reached until January 1989, when the Polish Communist Party's reformist leadership succeeded in convincing the conservatives of the necessity of accepting trade union pluralism. This opened the door for roundtable discussions which in April culminated in an agreement that allowed partially free democratic elections to the Sejm in June, and the establishment of a presidential office. Solidarity regained its legal status in April 1989.

The elections were held as planned and Solidarity won practically all the available seats. The opposition's success was greater than expected and this caused problems for the newly elected parliament. A major challenge was putting together a majority that was prepared to appoint General Jaruzelski as president, something the parties had agreed on at the roundtable discussions. On 19 July he was elected with the narrowest possible margin. On 24 August, the longstanding Solidarity advisor Tadeusz Mazowiecki was elected prime minister with an overwhelming majority.

---

[30] Cryptogram Warszawa – Stockholm, 4 May 1988, Öberg, folder 198; letter Warszawa – Stockholm, 20 June 1988, Anderman, folder 199; see e.g. Cryptogram Warszawa – Stockholm, 20 Aug. 1988, folder 201, Hp 1 Ep, FM.

*

The amnesty in 1986 simplified contacts between LO, AIC, and Solidarity. Solidarity now needed help to solve the new tasks that confronted it; mainly the fight for legalisation and preparations for its existence as a legal organisation. LO helped preparing Solidarity for competition with the 'official' trade union OPZZ by providing funding to Solidarity's 'initiative committees' (which were similar to the plant unions in Sweden) at ten workplaces. Discussions were held by *i-fonden's* executive committee about continuing the aid programmes to Poland, "which could be expected to total SEK 650,000–700,000 on an annual basis" (February 1988), but no immediate limitations were as yet prescribed.[31] TCO again provided additional support funding.[32]

One way to increase the contact network and to help with training and information was to invite Polish trade union activists on a study visit to Sweden. In June 1987, the trade union secretariat funded a two-week visit for ten Solidarity members via the Solidarity Information Office in Sweden. The guests were to receive training for roles as advisors in social and economic affairs, including tax issues.[33] The group visited the LO, TCO, local associations, and various companies.[34] Wałęsa was also informed and expressed his gratitude to LO in a letter.[35] Several similar courses were arranged after Solidarity's legalisation. In spring 1989, LO also allocated SEK 1 million from *i-fonden* to fund a new printing press for Solidarity. Moreover, LO provided an additional SEK 500,000 from its own international solidarity fund for the training of Polish graphical workers.[36]

The work of Swedish diplomats in Poland changed too as a result of the 1986 amnesty. If contacts with the regime had previously been on a low level and contacts with the opposition had been erratic due to its harassment, the goal now was to establish stable contacts with both sides. When State Secretary Schori announced in Warsaw in November 1986 that

---

[31] *I-fonden's* executive committee (*styrelse*), minutes, 16 Feb. 1988, vol. 2, *i-fonden*, ARAB.
[32] TCO's executive committee decided on 22 Feb. 1988 to provide SEK 150,000 to Solidarity; note to Solidarity's information office, 26 Feb. 1988, SIKiS vol.121, ARAB.
[33] LO secretariat minutes 15 June 1987, the LO doc. no. 1987-int-187, LO, ARAB.
[34] Programme, lists of names and budget, doc. no. 1987-int-187 (340), F09A:60,63, LO, ARAB.
[35] Gdańsk, 1 Sept. 1987; Swedish and Polish text and cover letter from the Swedish foreign ministry to the LO (22 Sept. 1987) and from the LO to the LO secretariat's members on 19 Oct. 1987, F09A:60, LO, ARAB.
[36] LO secretariat's, minutes 20 Nov. 1989, F09A:88, LO, ARAB.

Sweden would pursue a "parallel contact policy" his mission was to prepare the Polish foreign minister's visit to Stockholm but also to meet three Solidarity advisors: Geremek, Onyszkiewicz, and Sliwinski. He explained to them that resuming the exchange of government-level visits did not mean that they would break off contacts with Solidarity and other independent groups. Geremek commented that no one was interested in isolating Poland with its traditional ties with the west and with Sweden, which it did not wish to break. Geremek also expressed his appreciation for the fact that the Swedish ambassador and embassy had succeeded in maintaining close contacts with civil society without disrupting official relations.[37]

The Polish foreign minister did not appear to have any objection to Schori's contacts with the opposition and it can be noted that Jaruzelski later explained to the Swedish ambassador since 1987, J.-C. Öberg, that he recognised that a foreign emissary must listen to all the parties in a national crisis such as the one in Poland.[38] But despite this, complications arose and again they were rooted in Swedish Solidarity activism. The Support Committee for Poland and its semi-secret smuggling organisation, IPA, made the newspaper headlines in December 1986 when one of its truck consignments, fully loaded with equipment for Solidarity's underground printing presses, was stopped by Polish customs. The driver, Lennart Järn, was sentenced by a Polish court to two and a half years of imprisonment at the beginning of 1987. He was released on bail after a few months. But the 'truck affair' was not good for the thawing Swedish–Polish relations. When Ambassador Berner met General Jaruzelski at a New Year's reception in 1987, he had to suffer a minor chastisement. The General explained to him in "fairly impassioned" tones that neutral Sweden should be more accommodating than the NATO countries. To get a clearer picture of the cause of his dissatisfaction, Berner turned to the general's Chief of Cabinet who handed him a list of Swedish transgressions. Illegal goods smuggling to the opposition featured prominently on the list and Järn's confiscated truck cargo received special mention. Other complaints included the "overzealous trade embargo" (i.e., that an export ban would be imposed on goods to Poland if they contained even the tiniest American component) and – also attributable to Solidarity activism – "shallow and amateurish" reporting about Poland in the Swedish press (the journalist Richard Swartz was listed as an exception). Jaruzelski argued that while Sweden was a country that

---

[37] Cryptogram, 1 Dec. 1986, Berner, folder 188, Hp 1 Ep, FM.
[38] Cryptogram Warszawa – Stockholm, 30 Oct. 1988, Öberg, folder 203, Hp 1 Ep, FM.

should lead the way in improving relations with Poland, in reality it lagged far behind.[39]

Consequently, when foreign minister Orzechowski arrived in Stockholm six months later, the visit proceeded in a positive spirit but the guests also took the opportunity to voice the Polish complaints. According to them, the portrayal of Poland in the Swedish mass media had admittedly improved but was still unsatisfactory. "Poland was often presented in a one-dimensional manner which was inaccurate." The truck driver affair, he said, was the result of the illegal activities of emigrant circles which had put a strain on bilateral relations. The Swedish foreign minister replied that he did not support those who conducted subversive activities in other countries.[40]

When the Poles complained about the illegal smuggling, they said that they were aware that Järn's transport was part of a larger operation. They knew this because the Polish secret service had monitored the Swedish Support Committee's activities. Their informers in Malmö and Ystad provided information about what was being smuggled and by whom (Ekéus 2002: 117). But the Swedish intelligence service was also in place, supervising the activities of the Polish agents. As a result, two Poles, employees at the General Consulate in Malmö, were expelled in January 1988 due to unlawful intelligence activities. The Polish government responded by expelling the Swedish cultural attaché at the embassy in Warsaw, Hans Amberg.[41] The Polish criticism of the smuggling affair may have been the regime's way of establishing that even though it put up with its opponents receiving support from Sweden, there were still limits. The Swedish government could only agree.

The Polish regime's acceptance of the parallel contact policy was partly reflected in the fact that its own contacts with the opposition had improved, first through personal invitations to Wałęsa, then through promises of legalisation. But it was also an expression of the regime's interest in improving relations with all western countries, irrespective of whether they were in contact with the opposition. If there was specific interest in Sweden, it mainly concerned what was labelled the Swedish or Scandinavian model. It was an attractive alternative for those who wished to abolish the centralised socialist economy without ending up with unregulated capitalism (Misgeld 2011). In Öberg's reports from 1988–89, Jaruzelski appears

---

[39] Cryptogram, 23 Jan. 1987, Berner, folder 189, Hp 1 Ep, FM.
[40] Memo, 24 July 1987, Åhlander, folder 191, Hp 1 Ep, FM.
[41] See telegram Warszawa – Stockholm, 12 Dec. 1988, Öberg; Cryptogram Öberg, 13 Jan. 1988, and cipher Stockholm – Warszawa, 13 Jan. 1988, folder 194, Hp 1 Ep, FM.

as an admirer of Swedish domestic and foreign policy, and both the regime's representatives Mieczysław Rakowski and Józef Czyrek, and opponents Bronisław Geremek and Janusz Onyszkiewicz were described as social democrats of the Scandinavian kind.[42]

At any rate, the parallel contact policy appears to have been successful and enabled Swedish diplomacy to win the confidence of both the regime and the opposition. It reached its peak during the weeks following the sensational parliamentary elections in June when the embassy had frequent contact with both parties in the negotiations that were being held. Many of these contacts took place at the Swedish embassy, which is very close to the president's residence at Belweder castle. The embassy also served as a meeting place for the regime and Solidarity. On two occasions, 17 and 28 June, Czyrek, who was generally known to be the regime's second-in-command and Geremek, the top Solidarity advisor, held discreet meetings in the privacy of the Swedish embassy to discuss both the presidential election, and the formation of a government. At the former occasion, the discussion was mainly about how they could get a majority to vote for Jaruzelski as president despite the fact that Solidarity and even many in the agrarian United People's Party (*Zjednoczone Stronnictwo Ludowe*), one of the regime's supporting parties, were against him. According to Öberg's report, Geremek undertook to make sure that a number of members in Solidarity's parliamentary group would abstain from voting so that the necessary majority could be achieved.[43]

It is difficult to determine what actual significance these talks had on the solution of the political crisis in Poland after the parliamentary elections. Judging from Öberg's reports, however, this "technical aid"– to use his own term – was accepted with great gratitude. Jaruzelski, who like Wałęsa had approved the talks in advance, said that it should be remembered that in a critical situation, Sweden had shown Poland friendship and trust. He said that this was exactly how he envisaged the essence of Swedish foreign policy "to be available when it was needed the most".[44]

---

[42] Cryptogram Öberg, 17 June 1988, folder 199; Cryptogram Warszawa – Stockholm, 19 June 1989, Öberg, folder 210; Cryptogram Warszawa – Stockholm, 25 Aug. 1989, Öberg, folder 212, Hp1 Ep, FM.
[43] Cryptogram Warszawa – Stockholm, 19 June 1989, Öberg, folder 210; Cryptogram Warszawa – Stockholm, 29 June 1989, Öberg, folder 210; Cryptogram Warszawa – Stockholm, 1 July 1989, Öberg, folder 210, Hp1 Ep, FM.
[44] Cryptogram Warszawa – Stockholm, 29 June 1989, Öberg, folder 210, Hp 1 Ep, FM.

*

During the last few years leading up to Poland's systemic shift, Sweden sought good diplomatic relations with both parties in the Polish conflict and succeeded in getting them. The Swedish embassy had long enjoyed good personal relations with several leading Solidarity activists and held occasional discussions with Wałęsa. These ties were naturally strengthened by the concrete aid that Solidarity still received from Sweden, not least from the trade union movement. Its relations to the regime went through a slight crisis after the smuggling affair but both parties were reticent to let it damage their cooperation in the long-term. Reports from the Swedish embassy indicate that there were close contacts in a friendly atmosphere. Sweden's diplomacy in Poland represents an example of successful bridge-building, although the question, how important this bridge was for Poland's development more exactly, is difficult to answer on the basis of the current state of research.

Sweden's path

There were strong ties between Sweden's and West Germany's social democrats and the Swedes whole-heartedly endorsed the new *Ostpolitik*. However, during Poland's democratisation in the 1980s, Sweden and West Germany went separate ways. The main difference arose out of their relations to the Polish opposition.

West Germany's *Ostpolitik*, which promoted both stability and change, met with early scepticism in Polish dissident circles, who wanted the communist regime to be put under as much pressure as possible by the outside world. Their misgivings increased in the years after Jaruzelski's coup in December 1981. They wondered why Willy Brandt and the Social Democratic Party of Germany (SPD) were so tolerant of martial law and so quick to normalise relations with the regime, and why they had so little contact with Solidarity. This criticism reached its peak in conjunction with Brandt's visit to Poland in December 1985 where he held respectful discussions with Jaruzelski but did not meet Wałęsa. The fact that the SPD had exerted pressure on the regime behind the scenes did not appease the critics. Many of the dissidents preferred the policy of Reagan's USA with aggressive rhetoric, economic sanctions, and frozen diplomatic relations (Brier 2014; Rother 2010).

From the outset, Sweden's policy was characterised by the trade union movement's contacts, first with the striking workers in Gdańsk and then the

Solidarity movement. Even after the strong popular support for Poland had died down LO and AIC continued supporting the Polish opposition in different ways. Swedish diplomats in Warsaw followed a similar path; they quickly established contacts with Solidarity and other anti-regime groups. In their reports they declared that they viewed contacts with 'the other Poland' as a key part of the embassy's mission. As opposed to Brandt and the SPD, the Swedish line entailed significantly more contacts with Solidarity and other opposition groups.

The Polish opposition hoped for Sweden to help mend the broken relationship to the SPD. Representatives of Solidarity made overtures to the Swedish Social Democratic Party, the LO, and the foreign ministry on several occasions for this purpose. In January 1986, shortly after Brandt's visit to Poland, an emissary from the underground Solidarity movement found himself at the foreign ministry in Stockholm and talked about the "infinite disappointment" that the visit had caused. He now wanted Sweden's help to organise the long-awaited dialogue with the SPD.[45] But what these and other similar talks resulted in is unclear.

As opposed to their US colleagues, Swedish diplomats also had regular contact with the regime's officials in the years after the coup. One ingredient that recurred in contacts with the Poles was their wish to improve relations in the form of the exchange of visits at the political level. Occasionally they held up neutral Austria as an example that Sweden should follow; its government had quickly resumed normal diplomatic relations. Sweden's reply consisted of the same three component parts: that it shared Poland's hopes about improved relations, that the Swedish criticism of martial law, imprisonments, and suppressed dialogue with the opposition was well-known, and that it was too early to return to normal. The tone of these talks, as they are described in the reports, was frank but not ill-natured.

However, the boycott on visits could not continue forever and in the autumn of 1984 the Swedish foreign ministry and the embassy began to consider a cautious normalisation of relations. It happened, although slowly, and when the Poles complained, the foreign minister and foreign ministry officials referred them to Swedish opinion's strong commitment

---

[45] Memo 30 Jan. 1986, M. Westerlind, folder 184, Hp 1 Ep, FM. Solidarity also requested O. Palme for mediation assistance for Brandt and the SPD, see S. Johansson and M. Borowska to Palme (et al.), "Rapport i tio punkter från Polenbesök den 1–4 nov. 1985", undated, 3.2:439, Olof Palme's archive, ARAB.

for Solidarity. When the exchange of visits at top-level were finally prepared in autumn 1986 it took the form of the state secretary's trip to Warsaw where he visited both the foreign ministry and leading Solidarity activists.

The Swedish line of striving for trustful relations with both parties in the Polish drama received high recognition from Jaruzelski's and Wałęsa's emissaries when they met at the Swedish embassy for discrete talks. Even if the actual significance of these talks is difficult to assess, they nevertheless stand as a solid expression of a policy that, in the spirit of *Ostpolitik*, paved the way for peaceful change.

(Top) Demonstration outside the Lenin Shipyard, 13 Dec. 1981 (Labour Movement Archives and Library / photo: Solidarity Information Office in Stockholm)

(Bottom) Solidarność activists in the internment camp in Strzebielinek, Aug. 1982 (Labour Movement Archives and Library / photo: Solidarity Information Office in Stockholm)

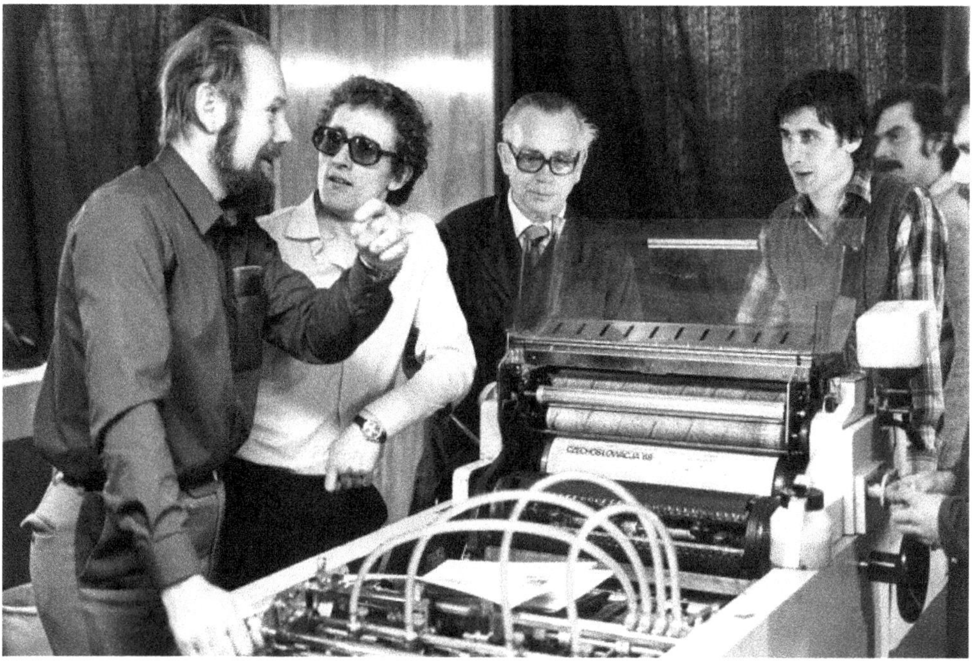

(Top) Ture Mattsson of the Graphics Industry Union demonstrates a printing press donated by the Swedish Trade Union Confederation to Polish colleagues, 1981 (Labour Movement Archives and Library / photo: Grafia 21–22 / 1981)

(Bottom) Pro-Solidarność demonstration in Sweden (Labour Movement Archives and Library / photo: Solidarity Information Office in Stockholm)

References

Anno [19]81 (1982). Malmö: Corona.

Ascherson, N. (1987[1981]) *The Polish August: The Self-Limiting Revolution.* New York: Random House.

Bjereld, U., Johansson, A.W., and Molin, K. (2008) *Sveriges säkerhet och världens fred: Svensk utrikespolitik under kalla kriget.* Stockholm: Santérus.

Boel, B. (2013) "Denmark: International Solidarity and Trade Union Multilateralism." *Solidarity with Solidarity: Western European Trade Unions and the Polish Crisis, 1980–1982*, ed. by Goddeeris, I. 2nd edn. Lanham, MD: Lexington Books, 219–42.

Boll, F. and Świder, M. (2013) "The FRG: Humanitarian Support without Big Publicity." *Solidarity with Solidarity: Western European Trade Unions and the Polish Crisis, 1980–1982*, ed. by Goddeeris, I. 2nd edn. Lanham, MD: Lexington Books, 159–89.

Brier, R. (2014) "The Helsinki Final Act, the Second Stage of Ostpolitik, and Human Rights in Eastern Europe." *Human Rights in Europe during the Cold War*, ed. by Brathagen, K., Mariager, R., and Molin, K. London: Routledge.

Documents on Swedish Foreign Policy 1982 (1983). Stockholm: Allmänna förlaget.

Domber, F. (2008) "Supporting the Revolution: America, Democracy, and the End of the Cold War in Poland, 1981–1989." Diss. George Washington University, USA.

Ekéus, R. (2002) "Samtal med Jaruzelski." [18 Oct. 2002] *Fred och säkerhet: Svensk säkerhetspolitik 1969–1989: Bilagedel.* SOU 2002:108. Stockholm: Fritzes.

Geis, M. and Lau, J. (2013) "Annnäherung ohne Wandel." *Die Zeit* (8 May).

Goddeeris, I., ed. (2013) *Solidarity with Solidarity: Western European Trade Unions and the Polish Crisis, 1980–1982.* 2nd edn. Lanham, MD: Lexington Books.

Heino, M. and Törnquist-Plewa, B. (2007) "Svenska Stödkommittén för Solidaritet – The Swedish Solidarity Support Committee and Independent Polish Agency in Lund." *Skandinavien och Polen: Möten, relationer och ömsesidig påverkan*, ed. by Törnquist-Plewa, B. Lund: Lunds universitet, 25–61.

Jacobsson, G. (2006) "De hittade lönnfacket: För Solidarnosc i polskt fängelse." *Arbetarhistoria* 30 (4), 18–23.

Jaworski, P. (2011) "Sverige och polska Solidaritet 1980–1982." *Kriget som aldrig kom: 12 forskare om kalla kriget.* Stockholm: Marinmuseum/Statens maritima museer.

Johansson, S. with Borowska, M. (1981) *Polens sak är vår: Om övergången till demokrati under kommunismen*. Stockholm: Tiden.

Kemp-Welch, A. (2008) *Poland under Communism: A Cold War History*. Cambridge, New York: Cambridge University Press.

Kubik, J. (2009) "Solidarność (Solidarity)." *The International Encyclopedia of Revolution and Protest: 1500 to the Present*, vol. 6, ed. by Ness, I. Chichester: Wiley-Blackwell, 3072–80.

Landsorganisationen i Sverige (1982), *Landssekretariatets verksamhetsberättelse för 1981*. Stockholm: [LO].

Landsorganisationen i Sverige (s.d. [1987]) *21:e ordinarie kongress 20–27 september 1986: Protokoll, del 1*. Stockholm: LO.

Linch, A. (2009) "Poland, Committee for Workers (KOR)." *The International Encyclopedia of Revolution and Protest: 1500 to the Present*, vol. 6, ed. by Ness, I. Chichester: Wiley-Blackwell, 2694–98.

Lorenz, E. (2012) *Willy Brandt: Deutscher, Europäer, Weltbürger*. Stuttgart: Kohlhammer.

Lundström, L. (2011) "Åren med arbete för stöd åt polska Solidarnosc: Smuggling av tryckeriutrustning och trycksaker till Polen via Valleviken och Sjaustar 1985 och några år framåt." *Haimdagar* (153–154), 3–6.

Meszmann, T.T. (2009) "Poland, Trade Unions and Protest, 1988–1993." *The International Encyclopedia of Revolution and Protest: 1500 to the Present*, vol. 6, ed. by Ness, I. Chichester: Wiley-Blackwell, 2707–10.

Misgeld, K. (2009) "Samarbete och missförstånd: Anteckningar kring ett samtal mellan Landsorganisationen i Sverige och polska Solidaritet 1981." *I politikkens irrganger: Festskrift til Knut Einar Eriksen*, ed. by Halvorsen, S. [et al.]. Oslo: LO Media, 208–23.

Misgeld, K. (2010) "A Complicated Solidarity: The Swedish Labour Movement and Solidarność." Amsterdam: International Institute of Social History. Available from http://www.iisg.nl/publications/respap45.pdf [22 July 2010].

Misgeld, K. (2011) "En 'svensk modell' för Polen? Diplomatiska sidospår under det demokratiska genombrottet i Polen 1988–1989." *Utenfor det etablerte: Aspekter ved Einhart Lorenz' forskning*, ed. by Kopperud, Ø., Moe, V., and Kieding Banik, V. Oslo: HL-senteret, 181–203.

Misgeld, K. (2013) "Sweden: Focus on Fundamental Trade Union Rights." *Solidarity with Solidarity: Western European Trade Unions and the Polish Crisis, 1980–1982*, ed. by Goddeeris, I. 2nd edn. Lanham, MD: Lexington Books, 19–50.

Misgeld, K. and Molin, K. (2010) "Solidarity despite Reservations." *Baltic Worlds* 3 (3), 10–16.

Molin, K. (2011) "The Admonitory Authorities and the Foolish Subalterns: The CPSU Politburo and the Polish Crisis 1980–1981." *Baltic Worlds* 4 (2), 15–21.

Müller, D.H. (1988) "Gewerkschaft und 'Selbstverwaltete Republik': Die 'Solidarität' und die Tradition der europäischen Arbeiterbewegung." *Gesellschaft und Staat in Polen: Historische Aspekte der polnischen Krise*, ed. by Hahn, H.H. and Müller, M.G. Berlin/West: Spitz, 119–35.

Paczkowski, A. (2003) *The Spring Will Be Ours: Poland and the Poles from Occupation to Freedom.* University Park, PA: Pennsylvania University Press.

Rathkolb, O. (2013) "Austria: An Ambivalent Attitude of Trade Unions and Political Parties." *Solidarity with Solidarity: Western European Trade Unions and the Polish Crisis, 1980–1982*, ed. by Goddeeris, I. 2nd edn. Lanham, MD: Lexington Books, 269–88.

Rother, B. (2010) "Zwischen Solidarität und Friedenssicherung: Willy Brandt und Polen in den 1980er Jahren." *"Nie mehr eine Politik über Polen hinweg": Willy Brandt und Polen*, ed. by Boll, F. and Buchniewicz, K. Bonn: J.H.W. Dietz Nachf., 220–64.

Schmidt, W. (2014) "Willy Brandts Ost- und Deutschlandpolitik." *Willy Brandts Aussenpolitik*, ed. by Rother, B. Wiesbaden: Springer VS, 161–257.

Sjursen, H. (2003) *The United States, Western Europe and the Polish Crisis: International Relations in the Second Cold War.* New York: Palgrave Macmillan.

Snyder, S. B. (2011) *Human Rights Activism and the End of the Cold War: A Transnational History of the Helsinki Network.* Cambridge, New York: Cambridge University Press.

Part 3: Gendered Identities

9. Gender Equality Policies: Swedish and Lithuanian Experiences of Nordic Ideas

Eva Blomberg, Ylva Waldemarson & Alina Žvinklienė

The issue of human rights has been discussed and institutionalised ever since its origins in the political philosophy of Enlightenment. In the early days, this concerned the rights of a small, well-educated group, but gradually came to comprise an increasing number of individuals. Researchers use the term 'expanding circle' (Singer 2011; Hunt 2007: 16–21; Ishay 2004).[1] Since 1948, when the United Nations adopted the Universal Declaration of Human Rights, both the concept of rights and the UN have often been addressed by social movements and when people experienced injustice (Donnelly 2013: ch. 1; Hunt 2007: 207–8; Young 2000). The concept of 'human rights' has gradually become accepted in global politics, at least on the level of principles, and has attained a prominent position in official rhetoric. This change in political discourse has given individuals new formal means for holding states, collectives, and perpetrators accountable for violations of human rights, that is, discrimination or infringement (Gellhorn 1966; Roth 2007). The global institutionalisation of human rights has thus on the one hand created an international context in which politics and legal practice are kept apart from each other while on the other hand human rights have acquired greater legitimacy and improved the living conditions of many people (Hafner-Burton and Tsutsui 2005).

Today, gender equality is considered to be one of the democratic values that constitute the human rights discourse. Gender equality has thereby been transformed from a controversial, and sometimes rejected, claim to a

---

[1] For a discussion about the different definitions and use of the concept of human rights see, for example, Robertsson and Khondker 1998; Therborn 1998; Thörn 2000.

meta-concept endorsed in global political discourse, if not necessarily in equal measure in practical policy making.

Theoretical and empirical starting points

The present widespread discourse of human rights has been analysed through theories addressing the complicated relationship between rights, their infringement, and acknowledgement. According to the philosopher Axel Honneth, individuals who feel their rights are violated because they are different from others signal alienation, non-citizenship, and a crisis in democracy. The institutional management of rights is therefore of particular significance to democratic states, collectives, and, not least, individuals themselves (Honneth 2007).

The philosopher Nancy Fraser, for her part, maintains that insisting on the acknowledgement of various forms of diversity has fuelled the struggle for group identity, a process by which established class interests have been replaced by multifarious group identities as a basis for political mobilisation. According to Fraser, concepts such as interests, exploitation, and redistribution therefore disappear from the political agenda. Instead of experiencing discrimination and infringement collectively and channelling the response into political movements, as in the late 1800s, reactions are now channelled into individual feelings. The problem that this shift gives rise to concerns whether rights should be interpreted socially or culturally, and the political measures that this implies. With regard to social conflicts, solutions are to be sought in the field of redistributive politics; when moral conflicts arise, however, the solution might be acknowledgement politics (Fraser 2003).

Gender equality policy and its implementation and institutionalisation are highly significant to these theoretical discussions. A study of equal opportunity ombudsman institutions and of gender equality politics in a wider sense provides a good starting point to analyse the dilemmas that arise with altered bases for discrimination from the perspective of interests, identities, collectives, and gender. It is also a good starting point for analyses of the influence of the human rights discourse on the understanding, use, and change of gender equality policies (Krizsan, Skjeie, and Squires 2012; Squires 2007; Young 2000; Scott 1988/1996).

As the sociologist Håkan Thörn (2000: 22) suggests, a question of vital importance for the human rights discourse is by whom these rights are defined and who it is that interprets their application once stipulated and institutionalised. The only way to give a proper answer is by means of empirical studies. Such studies must also take into consideration the impact of the historical, political, and economical contexts in which human rights are applied and institutionalised (ibid. 23).

This chapter addresses two major issues by means of three case studies. The first issue is how the Nordic Council and the Nordic Council of Ministers spread ideas and institutions in the field of gender equality to the Baltic States and by doing this also promote a 'Nordic gender equality model'. The other issue concerns how gender equality is institutionalised; here examined in two case studies on the establishment of equal opportunities ombudsmen in Sweden and Lithuania, respectively. The ombudsman institution itself has become a Nordic model for conflict resolution that is lacking in countries relying only on legislation (Nielsen 1990) and the Nordic equal opportunities ombudsman model has also been copied elsewhere.[2]

Case study 1: Gender equality the Nordic way

By having been incorporated in the idea of human rights, gender equality is nowadays counted among the democratic values that put states under pressure of political reform. While there are a large number of international actors who wish to influence the field of gender equality, there is no consensus about how to define it. Rather, there is an on-going struggle for the power to determine the content of the concept. In this struggle, the Nordic countries try to convince international audiences to practise gender equality according to their standards. This mission is part of the political agenda of the Nordic Council and the Nordic Council of Ministers.[3]

Both organisations often refer to a joint Nordic political model and from the late 1960s this model gradually began to include gender equality politics. However, despite similarities in the gender equality policies pursued by individual Nordic countries, there are also significant differences. Moreover, there is no national consensus as political parties have different agendas with regard to gender equality. The model of gender equality as pre-

---

[2] As regards the Nordic Council and Nordic Council of Ministers, the ombudsman institution is seen as one component in a more comprehensive Nordic gender equality model.

[3] The members of both institutions are Denmark, Finland, Iceland, Norway, and Sweden. The autonomous territories Faroe Islands, Greenland, and Åland are also represented. The Nordic Council is an inter-parliamentary body. The Nordic Council of Ministers is a forum for governmental cooperation.

sented by the Nordic Council and the Nordic Council of Ministers is thus an outcome of political discussions and compromises. Furthermore, this model has changed, for instance through the shift from a collectively designed gender equality policy that aimed for general implementation to a liberal policy that views gender equality as an option that individuals may realise. Another apparent change is the expansion of topics embraced by the model. Over the last decade, gender, together with categories such as ethnicity, race, and sexuality, has been incorporated in the concept of multi-discrimination.[4] This illustrates that gender equality politics is the result of a political struggle over the power to define its content.

Since the late 1980s the Baltic States have undergone various economic experiments, and countless projects have been designed to emulate western institutions and strengthen democracy. Although there has always been a Nordic interest in this region, the collapse of the Soviet Union and the independence of the Baltic States brought a revival. According to the Nordic Council and the Nordic Council of Ministers, one incentive behind the co-operation that emerged was to support democratisation and the development of a civic society as well as to support the institutionalisation of human rights.[5] Since then, the cooperation has expanded and it is now institutionalised in numerous international, national, regional, and local bodies, organisations, and networks. Moreover, the Nordic Council of Ministers maintains offices in Tallinn, Riga, and Vilnius in order to facilitate the implementation of this cooperation (*Nordic–Baltic* 2001; 2004a; 2004b; *Guidelines* 2010a; Kütt 2008; Peltonen 2012; Kharkina 2013: 75; *International Co-operation* 2013).

Despite stressing that the cooperation with the Baltic States should be characterised by mutuality, the Nordic Council and the Nordic Council of Ministers often act as if they alone are aware of solutions to various political problems (*Nordic–Baltic* 2001; 2004a; 2004b; *Guidelines* 2010a; Kütt 2008; *Gender Equality – the Nordic Way* 2010; *International Nordic Region* 2013).

---

[4] The conclusions in this paragraph are mainly based on the annual sector programmes for cooperation on gender equality that are produced by the Nordic Council of Ministers, available from: http://www.norden.org/sv/publikationer/publikationer. For a broader discussion, see Bergqvist 1999; Bergqvist et al. 1999; Bergqvist and Jungar 2000; Bergqvist, Adman, and Jungar 2008; Kütt 2008; *Kön och makt i Norden I* 2009; Melby, Ravn, and Carlsson Wetterberg 2009; *Kön och makt i Norden II* 2010; *Gender Equality – the Nordic Way* 2010; Blomberg, Waldemarson, and Wottle 2011.

[5] Other reasons for the interest in this region were linked to security, defence, and financial reasons, see Aylott, Johansson, and Simm 2011/12; Harvard 2011/12; Piirimäe 2011/12; Strang 2012; Kharkina 2013: 75; Björkman, Fjæstad, and Harvard 2011/12; Peltonen 2012.

Statements that the Nordic countries and the Baltic States shall jointly promote the northern dimension of gender equality do not rule out the former being regarded as more equal than the latter to determine the political content of this dimension. A publication by the Nordic Council of Ministers illustrates the asymmetric relationship:

> Singled out as the most gender-equal societies in the world, the Nordic countries have contributed essentially to developing their Baltic neighbours' understanding of the goal of gender equality so we can truly work together to achieve it (Kütt 2008: 7).

Furthermore, Nordic representatives' expectation to determine the political definition of gender equality is often based on ideas about a specific Nordic identity. Statements about a joint Nordic identity, based on shared values, deeply rooted in a common history, has always characterised the Nordic Council and the Nordic Council of Ministers. However, such statements have become increasingly entrenched over the last decade. The value par excellence is referred to as a common understanding of democracy, but shared social values, or, more vaguely, a set of shared values are also mentioned. Gender equality is pointed out as one of the democratic values that characterise the Nordic countries (*Copyright Norden* 2008; Kütt 2008; *Gender Equality – the Nordic Way* 2010; *Nordic Co-operation* 2011; Burch 2011/12; Harvard 2011/12; Strang 2012: 87–9; *Nordic Council – Our Council* 2012; Kharkina 2013). Therefore the affiliation with the Nordic identity discourse has severe consequences for how gender equality is discussed, legitimised, and presented to the world.

The two Nordic councils' cooperation with the Baltic States in the field of gender equality aims to achieve several political goals. First, it is intended to inspire these countries to implement gender equality the Nordic way. Second, once this goal is achieved, a more ambitious goal is to strengthen the position of the policy in Northern Europe at large. A third aim is to extend its influence to global political arenas (Guidelines 2010b). These aspirations can be interpreted in two ways. One is to understand them as resulting from a sincere wish to make the world a more democratic place, based on the conviction that Nordic gender equality politics may contribute to such a change. The other is that the Nordic commitment in this field is prompted by the expectation that gender equality might also serve as a door opener for other goals such as strengthening Nordic influence in international arenas. These interpretations represent complementary aspects of the Nordic interest in the Baltic States.

On the one hand, an examination of activities initiated by the Nordic Council and the Nordic Council of Ministers shows that gender equality is a political field of vital interest. This is to a large extent the merit of individual politicians in this field, many of whom have a genuine concern for gender equality (Kütt 2008). It is also evident that official Nordic cooperation has a considerable influence on the policy field of gender equality, especially with regard to the spread of ideas. Conferences, workshops, and seminars funded by the Nordic Council and the Nordic Council of Ministers function as arenas for politicians, civil servants, scholars, experts, feminist activists, trade unions, lobby groups, various networks, and non-governmental organisations (NGOs). The conferences arranged within the framework of Nordic–Baltic gender equality cooperation since 1998 have contributed to the exchange of ideas on gender equality (Nordic–Baltic 2001; 2004a; 2004b; Kütt 2008; Peltonen 2012).

However, on the other hand gender equality may also be used as a means for other political goals, in particular the strengthening of the international influence of the Nordic countries. The frequent assertion that gender equality is a vital part of Nordic identity suggests that this is sometimes the case.

During the last decade 'globalisation' has held a prominent position on the political agenda of the Nordic Council and the Nordic Council of Ministers and it is evident that this phenomenon is seen as a challenge to Nordic international influence (*Meeting Change* 2008). As Nordic co-operation is built on transnational principles, the present process of Europeanisation, with its transfer of political power from the national and inter-governmental level to the supranational level of the European Union (EU), is regarded as another challenge. This has been reinforced by Estonian, Latvian, and Lithuanian EU accession in 2004 (*Meeting Change* 2008; Kütt 2008; *Globaliseringsredogörelse* 2008; Ketels 2009; *Nordic Council – Our Council* 2012; Peltonen 2012; *International Nordic Region* 2013).

As the EU has generally perceived the Nordic countries as political models as regards gender equality, Baltic EU-membership might have been expected to strengthen Nordic influence. Nevertheless, it is questionable whether the Nordic understanding of gender equality is currently accepted as the main inspiration of EU policy. As matters stand today, there is a considerable gap in opinions among EU members concerning gender equality – a gap that has widened with the entrance of some of the newer members (Harvard 2011/12).

The Nordic Council and Nordic Council of Ministers discuss a number of ways to meet the experienced threats to Nordic international influence. One is to strengthen the already existing Nordic cooperation (Harvard 2011/12: 17; Wetterberg 2010), another to support a political development that contributes to growth and stability in Northern Europe at large. In this respect, cooperation with the Baltic States is given a prominent role (Harvard 2011/12: 19). A third way is to exert influence by assuming the role of international political actors within the present process of a global institutionalisation of human rights. As gender equality is nowadays recognised as an essential part of human rights, any state that wishes to gain international respect and influence needs to endorse gender equality. If Nordic gender equality is associated with an advanced democratic position and an internationally admired standard, this might strengthen the Nordic position in international political arenas (Towns 2009; *Nordic Co-operation* 2011; Aylott, Johansson, and Simm 2011/12; Burch 2011/12; Kharkina 2013; *Nordic Model* 2013; for a general discussion of utilitarian policies see de los Reyes, Eduards, and Sundevall 2013). It is probably this intention that explains, at least partly, the frequent use of the notion of Nordic identity in the field of gender equality. The identity discourse is thus a way to convince the world of how deep-rooted gender equality is in the Nordic countries.

However, apparently self-evident talk about identity and shared values seems to imply that the struggle for gender equality has already been won, first in the Nordic countries and then, with their assistance, in the Baltic States. It communicates that gender equality has a given political content, thereby concealing that this policy is an outcome of political discussions, conflicts, and compromises. It also obscures the fact that the idea of gender equality has met resistance during a long period of time also in the Nordic countries. Consequently, the identity rhetoric disarms gender equality some of its political force. Instead of taking the Nordic identity in this respect for given, the discourse of gender identity needs to be re-examined, for example by asking to what extent the concept of gender equality can be associated with different political content and still claim to be a part of the Nordic model of gender equality.

Case study 2: The Swedish equal opportunities ombudsman

Traditionally, human rights have not played a major role in the consensus-oriented Nordic societies. In the 1930s, when the trade unions made agreements with employers to regulate the labour market and decide on the common rights and obligations, the emphasis was on the collective (Bruun 1990: 17; Nielsen and Halvorsen 1990: 261). All the Nordic states developed a system defining the obligations of the state, while little attention was paid to the rights of individuals (Staaf and Zanderin 2011). Therefore, when Sweden was asked to accept and incorporate international conventions on human rights, the process was often not entirely painless. The UN declared 1975 to be International Women's Year, and under its auspices the World Conference on Women was held in Mexico. The conference adopted a world action plan with recommendations to enhance gender equality between men and women. The Swedish delegation was active in this connection and proposed a number of provisions, all of which were adopted by the conference. Sweden was represented by all political parties and Prime Minister Olof Palme contributed to the general debate (Sandberg 1975: 79–81). Gender equality had been put on the global agenda and the process was begun by which the UN made gender a matter of international law (ibid.). In 1979, the General Assembly of the United Nations adopted the Convention on the Elimination of Discrimination Against Women and Sweden ratified it the following year.

Around the same time, the Swedish parliament passed an act against gender discrimination and in 1980 it set up an entirely new type of authority: the Equal Opportunity Ombudsman *(Jämställdhetsombudsmannen)*. With the establishment of this ombudsman, Sweden subscribed to an international legislative trend in which human rights for individuals are safeguarded in an increasing circle of prohibition of discrimination on grounds of identity (Ishay 2004). However, the activities of the Equal Opportunities Ombudsman were limited to the labour market and had to comply with existing labour legislation. This was not the only restriction as collective agreements applied to around 90 per cent of the labour market and the labour market parties were quick to include clauses that were not binding but which kept the ombudsman outside their sphere. The latter called this a policy of 'severed hands' *(Jämsides* 4/1988: 2; 2/1989: 4; 3/1990: 6).

Political scientist Katarina Tollin argues that the legislation was made innocuous and that the ombudsman lacked any real authority. The compromise for establishing the Gender Discrimination Act was that it was to be more or less voluntary. This situation changed in 1994, when the ombudsman was entitled to intervene in the labour market, and in 2001, when the authority of the ombudsman was expanded (Tollin 2011: 64–79).[6] In 2009, a new authority was created, the Equality Ombudsman (*Diskrimineringsombudsmannen*, literally 'Discrimination Ombudsman') with responsibility not only for discrimination on the grounds of gender but also ethnicity, religion or other belief, disability, sexual orientation, and age.

The Swedish Equal Opportunities Ombudsman has been continuously involved in Nordic cooperation via the Nordic Council, the Nordic Council of Ministers, and meetings with Nordic colleagues. The Norwegian and Swedish ombudsmen met every year to exchange experience and compare conditions. The Norwegian ombudsman had a broader portfolio than its Swedish colleague as its work was not limited to the workplace. When Finland established an ombudsman in 1987, all three ombudsmen met annually to compare legislation, working methods, and results and to advance gender equality efforts. In 1989, the Danish Gender Equality Council joined them, although it did not function in the same way as the ombudsmen (*Jämsides* 2/1988: 4–5; 2/1989: 15).

The Nordic Council, Nordic ministers, and the ombudsmen all worked in close contact with the Convention on the Elimination of Discrimination Against Women. This included meetings after UN conferences on women. It was at such Nordic gender equality conferences that joint action plans as the basis for gender equality work in the Nordic region were discussed. The aim was to integrate this work with other sectors within the framework of the Nordic Council of Ministers (*Jämsides* 3/1988: 3; 2/1988: 6–9; 2/1989: 14).

In Sweden, the Equal Opportunities Ombudsman was the institution to be approached by those who were or felt discriminated on the grounds of gender between 1980 and 2008.[7] When a complaint about discrimination was received, the Ombudsman would send an inquiry to the complainant's trade union. If the claimant was not a member of a trade union, the Ombudsman took care of the case itself. For an investigation to be initiated, the report needed to specify the individuals who were discriminated against or harassed, contain a description of the course of events, and if possible refer to evidence. If the claimant was unable to convincingly show that discrimination had occurred, the case was dropped. If sufficient evidence

---

[6] Complementary Act Ds 2001:37 removed the word "voluntary". See also Complementary Act SFS 1994:292.
[7] Swedish Equal Opportunities Ombudsman (1980–2008); Reports AO 1985, CH 1985, EB 1993, XD 1993, DE 1993, YC 1994, HA 1996, JD 1996, PC 2003, ÅA 2003, SD 2007. As parts of the source material are classified as secret and in accordance with standards of research ethics, no reference can be made to documents that may lead to the identification of individuals.

was found, a discussion on what had happened was started with the employer in order to resolve the issue and reach an agreement, and the claimant could claim damages.

The Equal Opportunities Ombudsman and the trade union were able to threaten legal action, such as taking the case to the labour court unless conciliation was reached and unless the employer agreed to some form of redress. Such threats usually sufficed to make employers realise the seriousness of the case. Under the act, the labour court had to be used restrictively, and this was also the prevailing practice. It was mainly cases of special interest that were heard in order to establish a legal precedent.

The reports to the ombudsman resulted in different forms of action. Approximately 40 to 70 per cent of all reports were dismissed because the complainant was not considered to be able to prove that discrimination had actually occurred. In approximately 10 to 20 per cent of cases some sort of conciliation was achieved. Recognition of their case and redress was considered as essential by claimants who felt that they had been treated unfairly. For example, it might be agreed that a complainant be given his or her job back, a higher salary, or a better reference. A third form of action was retraction, that is, complainants relinquished their reports more or less voluntarily. When conciliation was not achieved and the case was legally interesting it could also be taken to the labour court. Finally, some cases came to nothing because of limitation, when the claimant or the official institutions acted too late.

Case Study 3: The Lithuanian Equal Opportunities Ombudsman

Lithuania is the exemplary transmitter and user of western political and ideological instruments in the field of human rights and gender equality among post-socialist countries. Unlike Latvia and Estonia, which strove to demonstrate their continued nationhood by restoring pre-war constitutions upon independence in the early 1990s, Lithuania adopted a new document. The 1992 Constitution of the Republic of Lithuania declares the inborn rights and freedoms of individuals, secures the principle of legal equality of all people, and prohibits the violation of an individual's rights on the basis of his or her sex, race, nationality, language, origin, social status, religion, conviction, or opinions, and provides for the possibility to establish the ombudsman institution and specialised courts (Constitution 1992: §§ 18, 29, 73, and 111). The Lithuanian ombudsman 'family' comprises the parliamentary ombudsmen, established in 1994, the Ombudsman of Equal

Opportunities for Women and Men, created in 1999, and some later ombudsmen in other fields.

The establishment of the Lithuanian Ombudsman of Equal Opportunities for Women and Men is an example of how the permanent collective efforts of politically active women, notwithstanding their political affiliation, may enhance public reflection on gender (in)equality issues in a country undergoing transition, and stimulate politicians to adopt an anti-discrimination legislation. The Nordic Council of Ministers and the United Nations Development Program (UNDP) have played a significant role in bringing together Lithuanian women on gender equality issues and creating bridges between women's NGOs and authorities. According to the recollections of one female parliamentarian:

> With the assistance of Nordic experts we drafted the first law on [equal] opportunities ... But in 1996 the Conservatives obtained the absolute majority. So we strongly feared that this law would never pass. But it did.[8]

The occasional criticism of the ombudsman institution is related to the failure to establish a unified system monitoring the overall situation of human rights in Lithuania. Specific criticism aimed at the individual ombudsmen concern their specialisation, overlapping mandates, and the nature of their decisions or statements. Unlike the parliamentary ombudsmen, the Equal Opportunities Ombudsman is empowered not only to issue recommendations, but also to hear cases of administrative offences and impose sanctions (Žiobienė 2010). Criticism of the Lithuanian ombudsman institution suggests replacing the existing ombudsmen with a broad human rights agency based on the Paris Principles.[9] The proposed reform of the Lithuanian ombudsman institution has practical reasons: by assigning the supervision of all types of human rights to a single office, its authority might be strengthened because this also allows human and economic resources to be concentrated. However, dispersion of the legal basis for violation of

---

[8] In-depth interview A 2012. Homeland Union (*Tėvynės Sąjunga*), the Lithuanian conservative party, was the ruling party between 1996 and 2000. There were 25 women in the Lithuanian parliament, corresponding to 18 per cent of its members; a women's group with representatives from all parties was established.

[9] The Paris Principles relate to the status and functioning of national institutions for the protection and promotion of human rights. In terms of mandate, the Paris Principles require that such institutions have a broad mandate that extends to all human rights. They were adopted by the UN Human Rights Commission in Resolution 1992/54, and by the UN General Assembly in Resolution 48/134 (see Annex 1993).

human rights leads to the formal disappearance of gender equality as a matter in its own right.

The Ombudsman of Equal Opportunities for Women and Men (*Moterų ir vyrų lygių galimybių kontrolieriaus tarnyba*) was renamed the Office of Equal Opportunities Ombudsman (*Lygių galimybių kontrolieriaus tarnyba*, henceforth referred to as 'Office') in 2003. Today, the Office takes overall responsibility for the supervision and implementation of the Law on Equal Opportunities for Women and Men (1998) and the Law of Equal Treatment (2003) in Lithuania. Both laws deal with public life; they oblige state and municipal agencies, education, science and research institutions, employers, and conveyors of commodities and services to implement equal opportunities in their respective fields, but neither law applies to family and private life.

The ombudsman investigates individual complaints concerning direct and indirect discrimination on the grounds of gender, age, racial or ethnic origin, religion and beliefs, disability, sexual orientation, language, social status and harassment or sexual harassment. He or she submits recommendations and proposals to Parliament and governmental institutions on the priorities of gender equality policy, including recommendations on amendments to relevant legislation. The ombudsman also supervises mass media for use of discriminatory advertisements and the description of one social group as being superior or better than another.[10]

The Office dealt exclusively with gender equality matters in the years 1999 to 2004. The exclusion of the words 'women' and 'men' from the title of the Office was a sign of the diversification of the grounds for discrimination and signalled the disappearance of gender as a special issue of discrimination. However, in defence of grouping the various grounds of discrimination under the control of the Office, Aušrinė Burneikienė (2012), its first and re-elected ombudsperson, argued that expanding the list of the grounds of discrimination highlighted women's vulnerability in comparison to men, for instance age having a stronger impact on the social life of women than of men.

From a theoretical perspective, three conditions – naming, blaming, and claiming – need to be met before someone files a complaint with an ombudsman. As van Roosbroeck and van de Walle (2008: 293) put it: "The individual may *name* the problem and *blame* a person or organization that he believes is responsible, but if he does not know of the existence of an

---

[10] For more information on the Office of the Equal Opportunities Ombudsman, see http://www.lygybe.lt/en/titulinis_10_25.html [2 Feb. 2014].

ombudsman, he will not reach the *claiming* phase." Hence, it is difficult to estimate to what degree formal complaints represent the level of discrimination in Lithuanian society.[11] Since 1999, when the Office was established, the number of investigations of complaints has increased steadily. Gender discrimination complaints are still predominant compared to complaints with regard to other types of discrimination. Over the reporting period (1999–2012), on average men comprised 40 per cent of all complainants. The latest increase in men's complaints is usually explained by the expansion of the grounds of discrimination and by the on-going financial crisis that makes men complain. According to the opinion of the Ombudsperson: "I think about 90 per cent of our decisions are respected … And only if someone disagrees they go to court" (Burneikienė 2012). The majority of the disputed cases that are submitted to the court are won by the Office.

Looking at the variations in the number of individual complaints since the establishment of the Office, there is a connection between the selected grounds of discrimination (since 2005) divulged via the Office's mass media activity and international and local organisations addressing the respective issues. This has a twofold effect: it stimulates a social reflection on 'publicised' social issues and motivates individuals to approach the Office.

With the 2008 financial crisis, discrimination took on another connotation in popular discourse both in the labour market and at state level. People tended to interpret the closedown of enterprises, staff or payment cutbacks, and other unfavourable decisions to overcome the crisis as discrimination and complained to the Office. The adoption of many legal acts cutting public expenditure and worsening the economic situation of vulnerable social groups, especially of pensioners and disabled people, were considered to be discriminatory and brought before the Office.

An analysis of the Office's reports suggests that, despite its juridical limits, the Office contributes to the implementation of the idea of equality in Lithuanian society by raising legal awareness, establishing standards of political correctness, and creating gender sensitivity. For instance, there have been no discriminatory job requirements in advertisements published by the public sector since 2009.

---

[11] According to the findings of the latest European research on discrimination, 67 per cent of Lithuanians did not consider gender discrimination a social problem in 2009, see *Gender Equality in the EU* (2010).

The establishment of the ombudsman institution in Lithuania is considered to be a successful case of UNDP involvement in the processes of democratisation in Central and Eastern Europe and of Nordic cooperation with the Baltic States. Lithuania's Office of Equal Opportunities Ombudsman was the first office of its kind in a post-socialist country.[12] It not only conveyed the message that there was a strong women's agency in Lithuania, but also represented the 'woman's card', not for the first time played by Lithuanian leaders as proof of national progress towards modernisation and democratisation. The two anti-discrimination laws were also a political compromise between on the one hand traditional feminists aiming for gender equality in an unequal society and politicians wishing to demonstrate conformity to the current trend of EU equality policy of preventing injustice and promoting human rights on the other.

There is a widespread opinion that democratic changes in the central and east European countries, including the establishment of new political institutions, have been implemented under pressure from the EU and transnational agencies in exchange for EU and NATO membership. This impression is not entirely wrong. However, under the umbrella of the mandatory requirements for EU membership, local civil society organisations exploited the chance to promote the development of democratic institutions in their country, a process in which the collaboration with transnational agencies that provided a transfer of knowledge and financial support played a crucial role.

Conclusions: Gender equality policy as problem solving

Today, discussions about human rights and gender discrimination have become part of the global agenda, which means that all states are under pressure to adapt (Squires 2007; Donnelly 2003). Gender discrimination is tackled in an institutionalised problem-solving process throughout Europe. However, as shown in the three case studies, how this process is formulated, conceptualised, and implemented depends to a large extent on the social, political, and historical context.

Globalisation and, not least, Europeanisation were perceived as both a challenge and an opportunity for the Nordic countries to gain influence in international politics. This in turn contributed to the prominent role that the Nordic Council and the Nordic Council of Ministers assigned to gender

---

[12] Poland was the first and only socialist country to establish the ombudsman institution, the Commissioner for Civil Rights Protection (*Rzecznik Praw Obywatelskich*), in 1987.

equality politics in the international political context. The Nordic model of gender equality, in connection with the human rights discourse, was partly used as an instrument to gain international political influence. However, it is also evident that the ambition to promote Nordic gender equality was based on the will to contribute to a more equal and democratic world. From this perspective the opportunity to spread Nordic ideas of gender equality to the independent Baltic States was viewed as a 'window of opportunity'.

It is also evident that the historical contexts have influenced the establishment of the Equal Opportunities ombudsmen in both Sweden and Lithuania. In Sweden, the autonomy of the labour market made it rather difficult to handle discrimination. The Europeanisation processes strengthened the position of the ombudsman and diminished the impact of national peculiarities. In 1994, upon entering the EU, new Acts were implemented that allowed greater interference in the labour market. In Lithuania, Europeanisation was a constituent of the transitional process from the socialist system. The adoption of the new constitution in 1992 and the creation of the Equal Opportunities Ombudsman in 1999 was in line with EU membership. However, the EU was not the only international organisation to influence Lithuanians' disposition towards new signals and changes. The reconstruction of the ombudsman in 2003 was inspired and influenced by the UN, the global human rights discourse, and gender and diversity politics.

The state handles discrimination via a set of regulations, but this does not necessarily mean that a particular discriminated individual will be acknowledged. As Hans Ingvar Roth points out, in order to win a discrimination suit, one must possess expertise regarding the law's rules and processes, considerable sums of money, and a stubborn streak (Roth 2007: 63). We would like to add that one must also have convincing evidence, preferably be well educated, and in possession of social capital. In accordance with Fraser and Honneth recognition and identity politics has become a vital element in gender equality politics. The issue of recognition has, at least in Sweden, changed the conditions for gender equality politics and to some extent also diminished the impact of the redistribution policies.

The creation of the ombudsman institution as such is today regarded as an important tool in the endeavour for public trust in the nation state as being a true upholder of democracy, an endeavour that has become all the more important with the enlargement of the EU. The Equality Opportunities Ombudsman as an independent state institution offers individuals an opportunity to resolve issues of violation of human rights in individual cases, free of charge and in a relatively short time. Despite the variety of existing models and the subject matter to be dealt with, the main characteristic of the ombudsman is institutional independence in relation to the appointing authority and subordination to the courts. Another characteristic of the ombudsmen is the process of conciliation and negotiation of agreements.

Today gender equality constitutes a recognised principle in the global discourse of human rights. However, it is still an open question to what extent the idea of gender equality has transformed political thought and political action. Despite the common recognition of the significance of gender equality on the level of principles there is neither national nor international consensus about which policies it implies.

(Top) What step next? (norden.org / Photographer: Silje Bergum Kinsten)

(Bottom) The Nordic ministers for gender equality at a seminar in connection with the UN Commission on the Status of Women, New York, 23 Feb. 2011 (norden.org / Photographer: Cia Pak)

References

"Annex: Principles Relating to the Status of National Institutions" [The Paris Principles] (1993). New York: United Nations. Available from http://www.un.org/documents/ga/res/48/a48r134.htm [2 Feb. 2014].

Aylott, N., Johansson, K.M., and Simm, K. (2011/12) "Är nordisk demokrati en exportvara?" *RJ:s årsbok* 4, 136–141.

Bergqvist, C. (1999) "Norden: En modell eller flera?" *Likestilte demokratier? Kjönn og politikk i Norden*, ed. by Bergqvist, C. Oslo: Universitetsforlaget, 3–13.

Bergqvist, C. et al., eds (1999) *Equal Democracies? Gender and Politics in the Northern Countries*. Oslo: Scandinavian UP.

Bergqvist, C. and Jungar, A.C. (2000) "Adaption or Diffusion of the Swedish Gender Model." *Gendered Politics in Europe*, ed. by Hantrais, L. Basingstoke: Palgrave Macmillan, 160–179.

Bergqvist, C., Jungar, A.C., and Adman, P. (2008) *Kön och politik*. Stockholm: SNS.

Björkman, J., Fjæstad, B., and Harvard, J., eds (2011/12) "Ett Nordiskt rum: Historiska och framtida gemenskaper från Baltikum till Barents hav." [Theme Issue] *RJ:s årsbok* 4.

Blomberg, E., Waldemarson, Y., and Wottle, M. (2011) "Jämställt företagande 1990–2010." *Kvinnors företagande – mål eller medel?*, ed. by Blomberg, E. et al. Stockholm: SNS.

Bruun, N., Flodgren, B., Halvorsen, M., Hydén, H., and Nielsen, R. (1990) *Den nordiska modellen: Fackföreningarna och arbetsrätten i Norden – nu och i framtiden*. Malmö: Liber.

Burch, S. (2011/12) "Låt det nordiska komma in." *RJ:s årsbok* 4, 60–71.

Burneikienė, A. (2012) [Interview with Aušrinė Burneikienė, 4 Sept.].

"Constitution of the Republic of Lithuania" (1992) Available from http://www3.lrs.lt/home/Konstitucija/Constitution.htm [2 Feb. 2014].

"Copyright Norden: The Nordic Model – Fact or Fiction?" (2008) [Theme Issue] *Nordic Yearbook*. Available from http://www.norden.org/sv/publikationer/publikationer/2008-758 [2 Feb. 2014].

De los Reyes, P., Eduards, M. and Sundevall, F, eds (2013) *Internationella relationer: Könskritiska perspektiv*. Stockholm: Liber.

Donnelly, J. (2003) *Universal Human Rights in Theory and Practice*. Ithaca: Cornell UP.

Donnelly, J. (2013) *International Human Rights*. Boulder: Westview Press.

Fraser, N. (2003) *Den radikala fantasin – mellan omfördelning och erkännande*. Göteborg: Daidalos.

Gellhorn, W. (1966) *Ombudsmen and Others: Citizens' Protectors in Nine Countries*. Cambridge, Mass.: Harvard UP.

Gender Equality in the EU in 2009: Report (2010). Brussels: European Commission. Available from http://ec.europa.eu/public_opinion/archives/ebs/ebs_326_en.pdf [2 Feb. 2014].

Gender Equality – the Nordic Way (2010). Copenhagen: Nordic Council of Ministers. Available from http://www.norden.org/sv/publikationer/publikationer/2010-701 [2 Feb. 2014].

Globaliseringsredogörelse: De nordiska samarbetsministrarnas globaliseringsredogörelse till de nordiska statsministrarna, oktober 2008 (2008). Copenhagen: Nordic Council of Ministers. Available from http://www.norden.org/sv/publikationer/publikationer/2008-771 [2 Feb. 2014].

Guidelines [2010a] for the Nordic Council of Ministers' Co-operation with Estonia, Latvia and Lithuania 2009–2013 (2010). Copenhagen: Nordic Council of Ministers. Available from http://www.norden.org/en/publications/publikationer/2010-725 [2 Feb. 2014].

Guidelines [2010b] for the Nordic Council of Ministers' Co-operation with North-West Russia 2009–2013 (2010). Copenhagen: Nordic Council of Ministers. Available from http://www.norden.org/sv/publikationer/publikationer/2010-722 [2 Feb. 2014].

Hafner-Burton, E.M., and Tsutsui, K. 2005) "Human Rights in a Globalizing World: The Paradox of Empty Promises." *American Journal of Sociology* 110 (5), 1373–1411.

Harvard, J. (2011/12) "Det nya Norden – hårt eller mjukt?" *RJ:s årsbok* 4, 11–26.

Honneth, A. (2007) *Disrespect: The Normative Foundations of Critical Theory*. Cambridge: Polity.

Hunt, L. (2007) *Inventing Human Rights: A History*. New York: W.W. Norton.

In-depth interview A (2012) held on 6 September.

[The] International Nordic Region: The International Co-operation of the Nordic Council of Ministers (2013) Copenhagen: Nordic Council of Ministers. Available from http://www.norden.org/sv/publikationer/publikationer/2013-753 [2 Feb. 2014].

Ishay, M.R. (2004) *The History of Human Rights: From Ancient Times to the Globalization Era*. Berkeley: University of California Press.

Jämsides [Side by Side] 1988–1990.

Ketels, C. (2009) *Global Pressure – Nordic Solutions? The Nordic Globalization Barometer 2009*. Copenhagen: Nordic Council of Ministers. Available from http://www.norden.org/sv/publikationer/publikationer/2009-711 [2 Feb. 2014].

Kharkina, A. (2013) *From Kinship to Global Brand: The Discourse on Culture in Nordic Cooperation after World War II*. Stockholm: University, 2013.

Klinth, R. (2013) "Den svenska pappapolitiken i historisk belysning." *Arbete & jämställdhet: Förändringar under femtio år*, ed. by Blomberg, E. and Niskanen, K. Stockholm: SNS, 233–62.

Krizsan, A., Skjeie, H., and Squires, J. (2012) *Institutionalizing Intersectionality: The Changing Nature of European Equality Regimes*. Basingstoke: Palgrave MacMillan.

Kütt, Riina (2008) *Sharing a Common Goal: Nordic–Baltic Cooperation on Gender Equality 1997–2007*. Helsinki: Nordic Council of Ministers.

"[The] Law on Equal Opportunities for Women and Men" [Lithuania] (1998). *Official Gazette* No VIII-947.

"[The] Law on Equal Treatment" [Lithuania] (2003). *Official Gazette* No. IX – 1826.

Meeting Change: Nordic Council Programme (2008) Copenhagen: Nordic Council. Available from http://www.norden.org/sv/publikationer/publikationer/2007-753 [2 Feb. 2014].

Melby, K., Ravn, A.-B., and Carlsson Wetterberg, C., eds (2009) *Gender Equality and Welfare Politics in Scandinavia: The Limits of Political Ambition?* Bristol: Policy Press.

Nielsen, R. (1990) *En svensk jämställdhetslagstiftning i ett europeiskt perspektiv*. Stockholm: Allmänna förlaget.

Nielsen, R. and Halvorsen, M. (1990) "Jämställdhet." *Den nordiska modellen: Fackföreningarna och arbetsrätten i Norden – nu och i framtiden*, by Bruun, N., Flodgren, B., Halvorsen, M., Hydén, H., and Nielsen, R. Malmö: Liber, 259–294.

Niskanen, K. and Nyberg, A., eds (2009) *Kön och makt i Norden, vol. 1: Landsrapporter*. Copenhagen: Nordic Council of Ministers. Available from http://www.norden.org/da/publikationer/publikationer/2009-569 [2 Feb. 2014].

Niskanen, K. and Nyberg, A., eds (2010) *Kön och makt i Norden, vol. 2: Sammanfattande diskussion och analys*. Copenhagen: Nordic Council of Ministers. Available from http://www.norden.org/sv/publikationer/publikationer/2010-525 [2 Feb. 2014].

Nordic–Baltic Co-operation on Gender Equality 2001–2003 (2001). Copenhagen: Nordic Council of Ministers. Available from http://www.norden.org/sv/ publikationer/publikationer/2001-416 [2 Feb. 2014].

Nordic–Baltic Co-operation on Gender Equality 1998–2003 (2004a). Copenhagen: Nordic Council of Ministers. Available from http://www.norden.org/sv/publikationer/publikationer/2005-477 [2 Feb. 2014].

Nordic–Baltic Co-operation on Gender Equality 2004–2006 (2004b). Copenhagen: Nordic Council of Ministers. Available from http://www.norden.org/sv/publikationer/publikationer/2005-478 [2 Feb. 2014].

[The] *Nordic Council – Our Council* (2012) Copenhagen: Nordic Council of Ministers.

[The] *Nordic Model in a New Era: Programme for the Swedish Presidency of the Nordic Council of Ministers 2013*. Copenhagen: Nordic Council of Ministers. Available from http://www.norden.org/en/publications/publikationer/2012-749 [2 Feb. 2014].

Peltonen, C. (2012) [Interview with Carita Peltonen].

Piirimäe, P. (2011/12) "Baltiska provinser eller en del av Norden?" *RJ:s årsbok* 4, 111–20.

Roth, H.I. (2007) *Vad är mänskliga rättigheter?* Stockholm: Natur & Kultur.

Sandberg, E. (1975) *Målet är jämställdhet: En svensk rapport med anledning av FN:s kvinnoår*. SOU 1975:50. Stockholm: Liber.

Scott, J.W. (1988) *Gender and the Politics of History*. New York: Columbia UP.

Scott, J.W. (1996) *Only Paradoxes to Offer: French Feminists and the Rights of Man*. Cambridge, Mass.: Harvard UP 1996.

Singer, P. (2011) *The Expanding Circle: Ethics, Evolutions, and Moral Progress*. Princeton: Princeton UP.

Squires, J. (2007) *The New Politics of Gender Equality*. Basingstoke: Palgrave MacMillan.

Staaf, A. and Zanderin, L., eds (2011) *Mänskliga rättigheter i svensk belysning*. Malmö: Liber.

Strang, J. (2013) *Nordic Communities: A Vision for the Future*. Copenhagen: Nordic Council of Ministers.

[The] Swedish Equal Opportunities Ombudsman, Annual Reports 1980–2008; Reports to the Ombudsman 1980–2008.

Tollin, K. (2011) *Sida vid sida: En studie av jämställdhetspolitikens genealogi 1971–2006*. Stockholm: Atlas.

Towns, A. (2009) "The Status of Women as a Standard of 'Civilization'." *European Journal of International Relations* 15 (4), 681–706.

van Roosbroek, S. and Van de Walle, S. (2008) "The Relationship between Ombudsman, Government, and Citizens: A Survey Analysis." *Negotiation Journal* 24 (3), 287–302.

Wetterberg, G. (2010) *The United Nordic Federation*. Copenhagen: Nordic Council of Ministers.

Young, I.M. (2000) *Inclusion and Democracy*. Oxford: Oxford UP.

Žiobienė, E. (2010). "Reform of the Ombudsman Institutions in Lithuania." *Jurisprudencija* 1 (119), 29–42.

10. Group-Work on Gender Equality in Transnational Cooperation: Raising Feminist Consciousness or Diminishing Social Risks?

Yulia Gradskova

While the Nordic countries are frequently described as the most advanced in the world with respect to gender equality and the protection of women's rights, most recent research points to problems with the adoption of gender equality policies and notes the overall absence of feminist ways of thinking in the post-Soviet and post-Communist context (Salmenniemi 2008; Hemment 2007; Saarinen 2009; Johnson 2009; Gal and Kligman 2000; Einhorn 2000). The interpretation of such ideas and the forms of their institutionalisation in the capitalist and democratic 'West' did often not fit well into the 'post-equality' situation in the aftermath of state socialism.[1]

As for Russia, research on transnational cooperation around gender equality and rights for women shows that such cooperation dealt with many issues – from supporting women's representation in the power structures of the country to introducing gender courses into university curricula, from organising women's crisis centres to supporting feminist publications. At the same time, it was realised on different levels; cooperation partners included civil servants, NGOs and researchers (see, for example, Saarinen 2009; Brygalina and Temkina 2004; Hemment 2007). Women's organisations were expected to be the most significant partner, bringing change with respect to the situation of women's rights and opportunities in different spheres of social and political life. However, research on women's

---

[1] The equality of women and men was one of the major legal principles of the Soviet system – in the absence of many civil rights such 'mandatory equality' was frequently not experienced as particularly liberating (Suchland 2011).

rights activism and women's organisations also shows many problems with respect to both activists' communication with the wider Russian public and with donors (see, for example, McIntosh Sundstrom 2006; Hemment 2007: 50–1). After the Russian government took a more authoritarian course in the mid-2000s, the situation of women's organisations deteriorated and some achievements of previous cooperation projects were lost (Johnson and Saarinen 2012). Although women's organisations remained active and their transnational cooperation did not stop fully, they changed many of their forms and practices and the transfer of knowledge (Castells 2005) became more difficult.

This chapter analyses a trilateral cooperation project between Finnish, Lithuanian, and Russian organisations in the years 2006 to 2012 that aimed at the improvement of gender equality education through the method of group-work. With a focus on the Russian cooperation partner, the article explores the ways in which different agendas influenced how women's rights and gender equality were addressed in transnational cooperation.

Questions raised by previous research, such as how to interpret the ideology of organisations dealing with women's rights and how to define their social role, inform this study. While some researchers have seen women's organisations primarily as non-governmental organisations (NGOs), stressing that they were part of an emerging civil society (McIntosh Sundstrom 2006; Caiazza 2002), others classified them as primarily being a part of the women's movement, thus implying not only their commitment to democracy and human rights, but their adherence to the tradition of feminist collective learning about inequality and undertaking practical work to improve the situation of women (Hemment 2007; Azhgikhina 2008).

Unlike earlier publications, I look not only at Russian NGOs dealing with women's rights and gender equality issues and the aid they get from abroad, but explore the wider system of cooperation. At the centre of the analysis is the network that includes the organiser of the cooperation from the 'West' (in this case from Finland's autonomous and Swedish speaking region, Åland[2]), an NGO in the 'new West' (in Vilnius, the capital of one of the new members of the European Union, Lithuania) and an organisation

---

[2] According to Eurostat, the Åland Islands belong to the richest European regions with a gross domestic product (GDP) 25 per cent higher than the average EU-27 level – see http://epp.eurostat.ec.europa.eu/cache/ITY_OFFPUB/
KS-HA-12-001-01/EN/KS-HA-12-001-01-EN.PDF [19 Dec. 2013], 18.

in North-West Russia (in the region of Kaliningrad[3]) as well as several other cooperation partners from former post-Soviet states. The activities of this cooperation network were financed from various sources, the most substantial being the NGO-funding of the Nordic Council of Ministers.[4] The functioning of the network benefitted from the use of methods originally applied in two of the Nordic countries.[5] They were elaborated by Mia Hanström, a former school teacher and now freelance consultant who actively participated in the development of the network.

Thus, this chapter examines the effects and problems of transnational cooperation on issues connected to equal rights education and opportunities for women and men, with reference to a case from the Baltic Sea region. It explores questions like how the cooperation started and why it acquired its particular shape. Other questions are how the issues of women's rights and gender equality were approached by different agents in the cooperation process and what results this cooperation had for the involved organisations and, to some degree, also for individual recipients of the educational training.

Methodologically the research is based on the study of discourses as evident from various written sources, as well as of formal and less formal conversations with the adult members of the analysed organisations. Moreover, I apply a feminist anthropological approach to social reality, according to which the researcher is part of the study, influencing the field and being influenced by it (see, for example, Hemment, 2007; Ers, 2006).

---

[3] Kaliningrad and the Kaliningrad region (formerly Königsberg and East Prussia, part of the USSR since after the Second World War) are separated from the main territory of the Russian Federation and are surrounded by Poland, Lithuania, and Belarus. Different from the rest of Russia, most of the inhabitants of the Kaliningrad region have passports for travelling abroad and travel frequently. In 2007 the income of the population of the Kaliningrad region was lower than the average for Russia (16,881 RUB compared to 20,754 RUB per capita) – Denezhnye dokhody naseleniia, *Rossiskii statisticheskii ezhegodnik*, 2012. Available from: http://www.gks.ru/bgd/regl/b12_13/IssWWW.exe/Stg/d1/06-07.htm [19 Dec. 2013].

[4] On the Nordic Council website NGOs are defined as "non-profit, publicly anchored, civic organisations that are neither owned nor controlled by public authorities, nor by private companies, and which have an open and democratic structure" – see http://www.norden.ru/Article.aspx?id=100&lang=en [19 Dec. 2013]. The programme for support of NGOs in the Baltic Sea area has existed since 2006 and has funded approximately 60 cooperation projects up to 2012.

[5] For the purpose of this paper, I use 'Nordic' as a geographic term for the countries that constitute the Nordic Council of Ministers, regardless of the internal complexity and contradictions connected to the idea of a 'common Nordic identity' (see, for example, Ylva Waldemarson's presentation at the round table on gender equality at the 10th Nordic Conference on Women's History in Bergen, August 2012).

For this reason, some information about my position in the research field is relevant and helps to explain the character of my communication with the studied organisations and what kind of material they shared with me.

I myself was a member of a Russian women's NGO between 1998 and 2001. Once a week I answered phone calls on a hot-line for women in Moscow, regarding this as a significant part of my everyday life with repercussions on my self-conception. This aspect of my past has undoubtedly influenced my perception of the issues of identity, rights, and gender in the studied project and vice-versa – the perception of me by the members of the cooperation network. It was, most probably, this personal history that contributed to my relatively easy 'entrance' into the organisations I wanted to study. Different from Julie Hemment (2007), the US researcher who took part in the work of another women's organisation in Central Russia, my approach was not explicitly participatory. Nonetheless, my study includes some elements of such an approach. For instance, I shared my contacts and experiences or gave a talk about my dissertation topic at the meeting of representatives of the cooperation network.

I found the network to be analysed after having examined the list of organisations that received financial support in the framework of the Nordic Council of Minister's programme for cooperation of NGOs.[6] The initiator of the cooperation, the Åland Islands Peace Institute, twice received financial support for cooperation with NGOs in Eastern Europe and both times the project was connected to gender issues. The first instance concerned the project "Bridging experience: Prevention of gender based violence and trafficking in Finland and North-West Russia" that was active 2005 to 2009 with participants from Belarus, Russia (*Star of Hope* from Kaliningrad), and Lithuania (*Nendre* from Vilnius). In the second instance the project was named "Overcoming gender disparities as a tool for social change". This project worked between 2010 and 2012 and continued with the Lithuanian and Russian participants. In January 2012 I visited the Åland Islands Peace Institute and discussed cooperation with its coordinator, who offered me the opportunity to read reports and other documents about the realisation of the project in Vilnius and Kaliningrad that had been sent to the office on Åland. I visited Åland again in May 2012 on the occasion of a methodological symposium, where the representatives

---

[6] http://www.norden.org/en/nordic-council-of-ministers/ministers-for-co-operation-mr-sam/russia/apply-for-funding/list-of-approved-projects – this webpage is no longer available and has last been accessed in January 2012.

of women's and other civic organisations from five post-Soviet countries were present. During the three days of the symposium I had the chance to take part in discussions about running female and male groups, in particular on the formation of teenager groups and on methods of communication in the group dynamic. I also observed the communication between participants of the network from different countries and had individual conversations with some of the organisers of groups from Finland and from Kaliningrad. Finally, in autumn 2012 I visited both partner organisations in Vilnius and in Kaliningrad, where I had the opportunity to meet people organising educational activities in the framework of the project and to collect more material about the work of the organisations (including a more than one hour long documentary film made about *Nendre* by one of the foreign volunteers, see Brandoli 2012).

Thus, my analysis is based on the documents of cooperation collected through my mail and face-to-face contacts with involved organisations: reports, information pamphlets, as well as on information collected through organisations' websites and obtained in the process of personal observations and conversations with the cooperation participants.

Organisations and cooperation history

In 1991 the Nordic Council of Ministers defined support for initiatives developing civil society and gender equality in the countries of the former East Bloc as one of its goals. In 1995 the Council started to collect reports on NGOs dealing with women's issues in the Baltic countries and North-West Russia (Peltonen 1996). When it started a special programme for support of NGOs in 2005 some projects that received funding dealt with gender equality or sexual minorities' rights (10 out of 60).

The Åland Islands Peace Institute in Mariehamn was founded in 1992 as a politically and religiously independent institution situated in a demilitarised autonomous part of Finland (see http://www.peace.ax/). The institute focuses on research and practical work connected to conflict resolution, global and regional security, democracy and human rights, minorities, and prevention of human trafficking. The institute takes part in the global exchange of young volunteers (mainly students planning to work in international developmental agencies in the future). The cooperation of the Åland Islands Peace Institute with the Lithuanian NGO *Nendre* started in the late 1990s, at that time financially supported by the Finnish government. After Lithuania had become a member of the European Union, the cooperation was funded by the European Union and the Nordic Council of Ministers.

Nendre[7] was started by a number of women in Vilnius in 1998 (see http://www.nendre.org/en) with support of the Åland Islands Peace Institute and the Åland branch of the international charity *Emmaus*.[8] Originally, *Nendre* was a non-state kindergarten and from 2000 also an after-school centre for children. At the same time it functioned as a social and psychological support centre for mothers (mostly single parents) living in a poor neighbourhood in the Lithuanian capital. The centre also saw that it had a mission in preventing children from abandoning their homes and in preventing adolescents' delinquency. The centre brought together educators and child psychologists, but in addition to child care the work with the mothers was considered equally important. At the centre, mothers received psychological support and advice on employment and housing. The work of the centre is financed through foreign and international grants for particular programmes and through a network for the distribution of second hand clothes (*Emmaus*).[9] In a report to the Finnish government *Nendre* is presented as "one of the few preschool institutions in Lithuania that has introduced a gender equality approach in preschool education" (Final report 2009: 7).

The Star of Hope (Звезда Надежды) was founded in Kaliningrad in 2004 as a non-profit partnership (see http://www.zvezdanadezhdy.narod.ru/) on the basis of the local Centre for Social Support of Family and Children (see http://kcspsd.narod.ru/Cntr2.htm). This centre belongs to a national structure that was introduced in Russia in the 1990s as a post-Soviet attempt at improving social work with families classified as having special issues (including problems with children's or parents' asocial behaviour, families with adopted children, etc.). The centres' employees are mainly psychologists and social workers. In the case of Kaliningrad, however, those employed in the centre decided to also create an 'independent' organisation for after-work professional activities, *The Star of Hope*, which offered them more freedom with respect to financing and cooperation with other organisations, including NGOs. The Centre for Social Support (on its own

---

[7] The name of organisation is translated from Lithuanian as 'read'.
[8] *Emmaus* is an originally Catholic charity organisation founded in France in the 1950s that has branches around the world.
[9] *Emmaus* opened a second-hand clothes shop in the same neighbourhood as *Nendre*, thereby offering work to unemployed mothers and economic support to the organisation. It also helped mothers and children directly with clothing.

or through *The Star of Hope*) was involved in several cooperation programmes, which apart from the one analysed here included schemes for the support of families of people infected by AIDS (financed by UNICEF) and a project for the support of women-victims of domestic violence (supported by TACIS) (see *Otchet o resultatakh* 2011).

The collected documents show that the cooperation of the Finnish NGO from Åland with the Russian centre in Kaliningrad was organised through the mediating role of the Lithuanian NGO *Nendre*. The latter functioned as a translator of expertise from the 'Western' context to the 'Eastern' one. Thus, the personnel at *Nendre* participated in the planning of network meetings and in giving presentations to the representatives of the Russian partner organisation with regard to the model of social work carried out at *Nendre* (Final report 2009: 4). The Russian language, a remnant of the Soviet past, facilitated the development of the cooperation. Many materials produced in Vilnius were published not only in Lithuanian, but also in Russian and most of the participants of *Nendre* and *The Star of Hope* understood each other without translation into English.

From the promotion of 'girls space' to a gender equality project

The method of group work that was applied by the Lithuanian and Russian centres from the mid-2000s was adopted from a model used with teenage girls (and later boys) on Åland. Discussion of significant issues in groups has historically been the object of many organisations – from political and religious to self-help groups providing psychological support. Nevertheless, it is communication management, principles of leadership, and rules around meetings and discussions that to a large extent define the outcomes of meetings of different groups. The consciousness-raising groups of the 1960s and 1970s in Europe and North America saw their special mission in creating a space for exchange where women would be able to discuss their subordinate position in society and to start taking action for their emancipation (see, for example, Chicago Women's Liberation Union 1971). This model was also practiced in the Nordic countries, including Sweden (Petersen 1985). While most current so-called popular therapeutic groups (such as *Overeaters Anonymous*) do not follow a feminist agenda as such, popular group therapy is said to be partly traced (even if not always acknowledged) to the feminist movement of the 1960s and 1970s (for more see Elden 2009: 53–5). However, the development of psychological groups during more recent years has been criticised by feminist researchers for replacing a collective female identity with the individualism of 'choice'. Nevertheless, the group-method examined here straightforwardly states its aim as empowering girls and, even if not presenting itself as feminist, is connected to feminist thinking.

Despite the Scandinavian countries' good record on the way of overcoming the subordination of women since the 1970s, researchers and activists from these countries insist that many problems linger on (see, for example, Eduard 2012: 258–62; Skjeie and Teigen 2005; Tollin 2011: 168–9). Mia Hanström, who worked as an after-school teacher in Sweden in the early 1990s and later on Åland, developed a concept for the support and improvement of the situation of women through empowering the new generation of girls. She regarded the creation of 'own space' for the teenage girls she worked with as an important precondition for their command of power (Hanström 1997). Recalling the beginning of the girls' groups in a pamphlet published by the Finnish NGO *Folkhälsan* (Public health) that supported the realisation of the programme in the early 2000s, Hanström (2004: 5) explained her concern with the special groups for girls by the lack of interest in ordinary leisure activities among teenage girls in her school. Thus, she looked for a way of organising special groups for girls in order to give them space and time of their own to discuss topics of interest and to find answers to questions related to teenagers' opportunities and obstacles in the gendered society surrounding them.[10]

Despite consciousness-raising groups not being mentioned in Hanström's book on girls' groups or in the pamphlet, their reading suggests that the meetings proposed by her can easily be seen as such a kind of a group. Hanström (2004: 7) wrote that girls should feel involved and have a space to speak without boys evaluating them. According to the book on girls' groups, these should combine discussions about "difficult" topics usually connected to the spheres where gender hierarchies are most perceptible – love, beauty, sex, relations with parents – with some leisure activities, like group excursions and cooking together. Such a group (consisting of girls between 11 and 17 who joined it voluntarily) should have an adult female leader whose functions, however, were limited. For example, the group leader could propose topics for discussions, but it should be up to the teenage girls themselves to select the topics for the final agenda of the group meetings (Hanström 1997; 2004: 8). The analysis of the book on method shows that such groups are supposed to foster not only self-con-

---

[10] http://kumlinge.com/mia-hanstrom [2 Feb. 2014].

fidence and health, but also to develop skills of democratic participation and to give some knowledge about gender inequality and discrimination. The book indicates, that the concept of 'feminism' should be somehow brought up in the discussions and provides a short definition of it: "acknowledgement of the subordinated position of women in family, working life and society". Thus, those persons trying to change the situation and showing that men and women are equal, are characterised as 'feminists' (Hanström 1997: 61–74).

Later on, following developments in the public discussion of gender inequality and discrimination in Swedish and Finnish society, Hanström expanded her views on the method's application and in 2005 complemented the book on groups for girls by a book on groups for boys. In the introduction to the latter she confessed her initial doubts with respect to such a publication: "Do we need groups for boys? Is it not so that the boys in reality need to have more opportunities to hear about the experiences of girls and that they need to be trained in dialogue with them and each other?" (Hanström 2005: 1). Nevertheless, the author came to the conclusion that special groups for teenage boys were needed as well: such groups would complement groups for girls that by that time had become well-known in Åland for their democratic dialogue training skills and for explaining gendered power, discrimination, and its prevention (Hanström 2005: 1).

The method of organising sex-specific groups for teenagers where they are able to discuss problems of gender norms and individual choices were highly valued by the Åland Islands Peace Institute that found it to be an important practice of education directly connected to teaching gender equality. The Institute's flyer states that girls' and boys' groups are "a method in gender equality (*jämställdhet*) work and empowerment that helps to make visible, to develop, and to support teenage girls and boys. Through showing the connection between sex, sexuality, and power this method can contribute to girls and boys starting to question the structures that present the power of men over women as something obvious" (Åland Islands Peace Institute n.d.). Thus, the method was chosen for dissemination through the Institute's networks abroad.

Group-method between contextualisation and domestication

Bringing such ideas of groups for girls and boys to the post-Soviet space as a result of transnational cooperation, one can expect local circumstances to influence its content and practices. While the main interest in this chapter is with Russia, some attention will be paid to the contextualisation of the method in the post-Soviet space more generally.

The discussions between the organisers of teenage groups from Finland, Lithuania, Russia, Latvia, Belarus, and Azerbaijan at the method symposium in Åland in May 2012 showed many similarities in views on the groups' goals, problems, and ways of overcoming them in the process of the group work. The symposium participants were united in their stance against gender stereotypes, in their promotion of the further development of gender education and in their striving for recruitment of new organisers of groups among social workers, teachers, psychologists, and NGO-activists. At the same time, they were characterised by differences in age, professional qualifications, and views on particular issues. For example, participants from Lithuania and Russia were mainly older women with a background in education, psychology, and social work, while participants from Azerbaijan were young activists from women's NGOs. While the latter were enthusiastically discussing the progress of girls' groups in the context of civic activism, most of the Russian participants acted as professionals ready for discussions in more psychological terms. They spoke about women 'in a difficult life situation', thereby applying the official terminology used by social workers in Russia with respect to various kinds of problems – from poverty to domestic violence. My conversations with the participants from Kaliningrad showed that most of them considered groups to be a useful method. At the same time, they discussed the organisation of groups in terms of 'work' rather than activism and revealed a distance between themselves and the group participants they 'helped'. The first impression of differences between participants of the cooperation from various countries during the meeting in May 2012 was confirmed by the study of the organisations' documents and during visits in Vilnius and Kaliningrad in autumn 2012.

Documents from the Lithuanian organisation *Nendre* show that the understanding of gender stereotypes as an obstacle for the improvement of the situation of the women and children who were the initial target group of this organisation, was learned in the course of the close cooperation with Finnish partners starting from the beginning of the organisation. It occurred first of all through the educational staff programmes organised by the Finns. Elements of group work for teaching about gender stereotypes and rights for women were used for work with the single mothers before the groups of teenagers were organised. Questioning the dominant gender norms and work against gender stereotypes was included in everyday practices of the kindergarten and after-school group for teenagers. For example, the film on *Nendre* shows how boys attending the after-school programme do the dishes while teenage girls that have spent many years there discuss the significance of learning about gender stereotypes for their life (Brandoli 2012). Thus, the implementation of the project funded by the Nordic Council of Ministers in 2005 was not the first encounter of the members of the Lithuanian NGO with the method of group discussions and gender sensitivity training.

Nevertheless, material on the work of the centre indicates certain differences in applying the method of groups for girls and boys in Lithuania as compared to the Finnish approach.[11] *Nendre's* initial orientation towards children and families in the social risk zone and the international campaign against trafficking in women that was on the rise in the early 2000s (see, for example, Saarinen 2009: 523; Hemment 2007: 141) resulted in the method of groups being described primarily in terms of the 'risk of trafficking'. This risk was presented as a real danger: "1200 young women from Lithuania become victims of trafficking each year" (*Nendre* 2009: 38–9). Groups were presented as being aimed at teenagers who, due to their family situation with low income and other complications, were more likely to become subject to trafficking than others. While it is not clear how much the groups' participants were seen as potential victims of trafficking in the everyday work of the centre, this framing suggests a shift in the perception of the groups as such and draws attention away from other issues that could be significant for teenagers coming to *Nendre* – for instance, reflections on new gender inequalities, reproductive rights, or discrimination on the labour market. Moreover, when the main aim of teaching about gender equality to teenage girls is presented as connected to the prevention of trafficking, a reasonable question is whether gender equality education is less important for 'better-off' groups of teenagers who may become victim of gender discrimination of many other kinds.

Moving from Vilnius to Kaliningrad, however, the selective way of exporting and adopting 'global' knowledge on girls' and boys' groups and gender equality education becomes even more visible.

Similar to the case of Lithuania (or Azerbaijan in the later period), transnational cooperation and the need of funding was justified with reference to issues and problems that were vital to the 'Western' or 'Nordic'

---

[11] The analysis is based on documents published in Russian and English.

cooperation partner. When the girls' group method was chosen for international dissemination, a special methodological book for the group leaders titled "Girls' Groups: Girls, Gender Equality, and Democracy" was published in Russian (Hanström 2010). This publication was based on two earlier books by Mia Hanström, but the author modified the content for the Russian readers in accordance with the cooperation aims. Tellingly, the editing work and the publication were sponsored not only by the Åland Islands Peace Institute, but also by the Foreign Ministry of Finland and the International Organisation for Migration. In the introduction to the Russian edition, Hanström stated that the book was produced for work with girls belonging to the group with a high risk of getting involved in trafficking. In the following text, however, the risk group was defined differently, more in correspondence with the Russian political discourse on 'unfortunate families' (see Iarskaia-Smirnova 2011; Isola 2009). The book there refers to girls from "unfortunate families, incomplete families, or families living under difficult economic circumstances" and only in the last place to the families in which parents "do not pay enough attention to the upbringing of their children" (Hanström 2010: 15). Thus, again, the method initially aimed at 'ordinary' girls from 'normal' families, but living through the phase of life when one discovers gender hierarchies and stereotypes and shapes attitudes towards them, is applied to 'special' girls with particular problems and the need of special guidance. The book makes a direct connection between 'problematic families' and the risk of trafficking through several references, for example by dedicating one chapter to the discussion of *Lilya 4 Ever*, a film telling the tragic story of a young girl from one of the post-Soviet countries that is trafficked to Sweden (Moodisson 2002).

At the same time, the application of the group method to a specific setting and its realisation by a particular organisation in Russia also influenced its content and results. Three dimensions of domestication of the programme in Kaliningrad are particularly relevant.

The first is connected to the pronounced focus on family well-being as the major aim of the project. At first glance, the Kaliningrad experts seemed to follow *Nendre*'s contextualisation of the project as a substitute 'warm home' where adults and children would feel good and where they would learn how to make a similar home for themselves and their family.[12] However, in Kaliningrad group meetings usually took place in the premises of

---

[12] While showing me their premises – an old and well refurbished wooden house – the centre's personnel presented it as being a home for all the children and adults coming to it.

official agencies that were different from *Nendre*'s house with its atmosphere of a self-governed organisation. I was told by the organisers that the practice of group meetings included the possibility of several meetings where boys and girls met together, for example, to discuss the topic of family. The group work plans also included issues presented differently from how they were addressed in Hanström's book. For example, while the book for group meetings in Russian states that there could be different types of families (including "me and my grandmother", see Hanström 2010: 174), the programme in Kaliningrad worked for the "formation of the gender qualities that are necessary for the creation of an own family" and aimed at teaching "adequate gender behaviour" (*Materialy* 2011: 13–14). Obviously the local practice was deeply entangled with the model of the nuclear and heterosexual family.

Moreover, reports and other documents from Kaliningrad show a close connection between *The Star of Hope* interpretation of family problems and the political rhetoric of current Russian demographic discourse (see Rotkirch et al. 2007; Rivkin-Fish 2009). The teenagers participating in the programme were defined as coming from "problematic families", achievements being the "absence of teenage pregnancies and police records among the group participants" (*Otchet o rezultatakh* 2011: 15). The "lack of interest in the preservation of reproductive health" and the absence of "family values" among teenagers were claimed to be important social problems to be solved in the work of the groups (*Otchet o rezultatakh* 2011: 18, 3). Furthermore, the report about the realisation of the programme "Overcoming gender inequality as an instrument of social change" underlined – apart from such factors as growth of self-confidence and reflexivity with regard to domestic violence experienced by the groups' participants – the significance of learning "skills for successful family life" (*Otchet o deiatelnosti* 2011: 15–16).

The second dimension is connected to the organisation of training. The reports and other materials show that the non-governmental organisation *The Star of Hope* is almost inseparable from the official Centre for Social Support of Family and Children. Considering that the registration and functioning of NGOs has been severely restricted in Russia following a policy change in 2006 (Johnson 2009), this solution provides at least some space for self-reflection and discussions for girls. Two participants of the project proudly stated that the groups used the premises of the main centre and several of its branches in different cities of the wider Kaliningrad region, as well as the professional skills of those working in the family support system (mainly qualified psychologists). Moreover, according to them, the group meetings in the state organisation venues facilitated acceptance of the groups' activities by parents and school teachers, the lack of which might be an important obstacle in case of a fully independent organisation. Finally, the project also benefited from a well-established cooperation network of state organisations and NGOs, including clinics, police, city crisis centres for women, and women's organisations. This network was particularly helpful in the most difficult cases – for example, thanks to cooperation with medical institutions the centre had information about registered teenage pregnancies that facilitated invitations to the pregnant women to participate in the group. Even so, the coordinator of the project from the Åland Islands Peace Institute complained that such a way of organising the groups contributed to their over-psychologisation and more distinct hierarchies between leader and participants.

The third dimension is connected to the education of basic principles of gender equality as such. The documents of *The Star of Hope* suggest that the topics of gender and power in society, gender discrimination, and feminism are not much discussed as such in the groups (see, for example, *Osushchestvlenie* 2012). This corresponds to the overall lack of interest in feminist concepts in societies where women were previously forced into a double burden of work as professionals and at home under the slogan of the equality of men and women (see Gal and Kligman 2000). The analysis of the documents and conversations with those working at the centre show that the organisers of the groups regard the discussion about equality as a way to confront excessively polarised gender stereotypes. For example, the group leaders from Kaliningrad expressed the hope that, as a consequence of the group meetings, boys would understand that they were also supposed to do something in the family and with their children (not just bring home money and expect domestic service), while girls were expected to learn that they should also think about their education and profession and not plan their life with reliance on a 'good husband'.

Thus, while the Russian version of Hanström's book includes sections about the historical and social construction of men and women as well as the possibility of a critical approach to these categories (see Hanström 2010: 199–202), in the reports from Kaliningrad the idea of a critical approach to gender is blurred by the discussion on creation of the proper 'gender identity'. For example, the report from 2010 states that the work with teenagers should realise "principles of gender education for teenagers, applying a humanist and individualised approach to teenagers" (*Materialy* 2010: 3) and the report from 2011 highlights that the "formation of gender competence, adequate gender behaviour, and family values" was the aim of the groups (*Materialy* 2011: 4). Thus, while groups for teenagers in their Kaliningrad version aim at contributing to the development of useful communication skills as well as pondering over prevailing gender normativity, an amorphous language of 'gender identity' and 'adequate gender behaviour' tends to take the place of the language of anti-discrimination.

Contradictions and achievements of cooperation

Women's organisations from different communities and countries have a long history of helping each other with respect to issues assumed to be in the common interest of womankind – like justice, non-discrimination, and overcoming patriarchy. During the last thirty or forty years, however, the issues of women's rights and gender equality have been a concern of international cooperation, involving such partners as the United Nations and the European Union. Attempts at addressing problems at the global level obviously contributed to increased visibility of the problem of gender inequality, but the outcome of this globalisation of policies for gender equality is sometimes ambivalent (Hemment 2007: 83). The explored case about rights and gender equality education in the context of Nordic–Baltic cooperation is an example for such an ambiguity. Contrary to the neoliberal approach of democratic transition (assuming the free market as the most important condition for democracy in former Eastern Europe), the Nordic cooperation programmes were based on an understanding of transition to democracy that acknowledged gender equality as one of the important conditions for democratic development and for the prevention of insecurity and unrest.[13] The local visions of equality and interpretations of the existing problems and possible solutions do not always coincide with the visions and interpretations put forward on the global level.

Moreover, unlike many other countries in which popular education about personal, couple and group psychology is built around ideas of inherent gender differences, mainstream popular psychology in the Scandinavian countries sees gender equality "as a taken for granted point of departure" (Elden 2009: 224). However, ideas on gender equality and ways

---

[13] The countries that failed to demonstrate any affinity to principles of democracy were pushed out of the broader cooperation schemes as happened in the case of participants from Belarus. A report to the Foreign Ministry of Finland mentions "bureaucratic obstacles by the Belorussian authorities". Later, however, other forms of the cooperation with Belarus were found – the cooperation was reframed as a joint venture with a "developing country" (Final report 2009: 8).

of its achievement had to be accommodated and domesticated in the process of cooperation. In the case of the groups for girls and boys in Lithuania and Russia, the need for gender equality education was frequently justified with arguments instrumental to other causes like preventing trafficking, diminishing delinquency, and even contributing to the solution of the 'demographic crises' through the improvement of 'family values'. The utilitarian framing of the project contributed to its success in a politically different and sometimes socially hostile environment, including its implementation by a semi-state organisation of professional social workers in one of the Russian regions during a period of growing authoritarian tendencies in state politics. The implementation of the programme for the sake of 'family', 'welfare', and 'development' made it acceptable in a context where the ideas of 'sisterhood' and 'feminism' hardly would have worked. All this contributed to 'gender equality' being made an organic part of the cooperation programmes in the Baltic Sea region.

Still, the success of cooperation networks with former socialist states is rather limited with respect to both democracy and gender equality. In particular in the Russian case, the groups that were originally meant to create a space for ordinary teenagers to reflect on gender stereotypes and inequality were remade into instruments of adjustment to existing social norms rather than changing their normativity, at the same time as the group leader worked in the capacity of an 'expert' and 'professional'.

Nevertheless, while the larger cooperation network has much more balanced goals than many projects of international donors studied before: instead of supporting organisations with a clear human rights profile, the project analysed here involved "less outspokenly democratic organisations"[14] and sought to introduce gender equality as part of ordinary group meetings for teenagers in the framework of social work. The centre in Kaliningrad is an organisation associated with the Russian state and (similarly to *Nendre*) has moderate goals – to help girls and boys to become self-confident and to raise their awareness of existing forms of discrimination based on gender. Despite such modest goals the centre fulfils an important social function, facilitating group discussions on gendered social norms and on gender stereotypes. Even if it is not performed in feminist terms, such work provides – for individual teenagers – the possibility of a critical assessment of reality, including the review of the existing gender

---

[14] For more about criticism of earlier American donors' projects see McIntosh Sundstrom 2006: 176–9; Hemment, 2007: 52–3.

order. The cooperation also changes ordinary work patterns of social services and the individual social workers.

In June 2012, the Russian Parliament accepted a law declaring organisations dealing with democracy issues and receiving funding from abroad to be 'foreign agents'. In such a situation the cooperation examined in this text is probably even more beneficial, owing to its apparently 'apolitical' content (it has some similarity with the success of crisis centres in Russia, described in Johnson 2009). While the general information about rights and gender quotas is frequently perceived as abstract and annoying in the post-Soviet space, it is the connection between critical approaches to one's surrounding reality and one's own biography that makes this project particularly beneficial. At the same time, observations presented in this chapter give rise to further questions about hierarchies of organisations and limitations with regard to the cooperation for women's rights.

(Top) Psychologist Yelena Romanenko conducts training based on Mia Hanström's methodology, adapted for small children, Kaliningrad city, 21 June 2013 (Star of Hope / Photographer: Valentina Zherebtsova)

(Bottom) Training for young mothers on gender education in the family by Director of Star of Hope Nina Vorontsova, Bagrationovsk (Kaliningrad region), 15 Feb. 2014 (Star of Hope / Photographer: Valentina Zherebtsova)

References

Åland Islands Peace Institute (n.d.) Flyer. Mariehamn.

Azhgikhina, N. (2008) *Propushchennyi siuzhet: Istoria novogo nezavisimogo zhenskogo dvizhenia Rossii s nachala 1990-kh godov do nashikh dnei v zerkale SMI.* Moscow: Tsentr obshchestvennoi informatsii.

Brandoli, M. (2012) *Nendre: Fragments of Life* [film].

Caiazza, A. (2002) *Mothers and Soldiers: Gender, Citizenship and Civil Society in Contemporary Russia.* New York: Routledge.

Castells, M. (2005) "The Network Society." *The Network Society: From Knowledge to Policy*, ed. by Castells, M. and Cardoso, G. Washington, DC: John Hopkins Center for Transatlantic Relations.

Chicago Women's Liberation Union (1971) "How to Start Your Own Consciousness Raising Group." [Leaflet] Reprint available from http://www.uic.edu/orgs/cwluherstory/CWLUArchive/crcwlu.html [20 Dec. 2013].

Eduards, M. (2012) "Talibantalet." *Könpolitiska nyckeltexter*, vol. 2, ed. by Arnberg, K., Sundevall, F., and Tjeder, D. Göteborg: Makadam, 258–62.

Elden, S. (2009) *Konsten att lyckas som par: Populärterapeutiska berättelser, individualisering och kön.* Lund: Lund University.

Ers, A. (2006) *I mänsklighetens namn: En etnologisk studie av ett svenskt biståndsprojekt i Rumänien.* Stockholm: Gidlund.

Final report covering the years 2005–09 for project "Nendre – Lessons Learned" (Report by the Åland Islands Peace Institute to the Ministry for Foreign Affairs). Mariehamn: Åland Islands Peace Institute, 2009.

Gal, S. and Kligman, G. (2000) *The Politics of Gender after Socialism: A Comparative-Historical Essay.* Princeton: Princeton University Press.

Hanström, M. (1997) *Metodiken för tjejverksamhet.* Borlänge: Björnen.

Hanström, M. (2004) *Tjejgrupper – en fritidsverksamhet för flickor och en hälsofrämjande metod.* Åland: Folkshälsan.

Hanström, M. (2005) *Metodikbok för killverksamhet.* Borlänge: Björnen.

Hanström, M. (2010) *Gruppy dlia devushek: Devushki, ravenstvo polov i demokratiia* [Girls' groups: Girls, gender equality and democracy]. Mariehamn: Åland Island Peace Institute.

Hemment, J. (2007) *Empowering Women in Russia: Activism, Aid and NGOs.* Bloomington: Indiana University Press.

Iarskaia-Smirnova, E. (2011) *Class and Gender in Russian Welfare Policies: Soviet Legacies and Contemporary Challenges.* Gothenburg: University of Gothenburg.

Isola, A.-M. (2009) "Neblagopoluchnye semii: Ritorika rossiiskoi demograficheskoi politiki." *Novyi byt v sovremennoi Rossii: Gendernye issledovaniia povsednevnosti*, ed. by Zdravomyslova E., Rotkirch, A., and Temkina A. St. Petersburg: Evropeiskii universitet, 404–26.

Johnson, J. E. (2009) *Gender Violence in Russia: The Politics of Feminist Intervention*. Bloomington: Indiana University Press.

Johnson, J. E. and Saarinen, A. (2011) "Assessing Civil Society in Putin's Russia: The Plight of Women's Crisis Centers." *Communist and Post-Communist Studies* 44 (1), 41–52.

Lombardo, E. and Forest, M. (2012) *The Europeanization of Gender Equality Policies: A Discursive-Sociological Approach*. Basingstoke: Palgrave Macmillan.

Materialy o realizatsii programmy "Preodalenie gendernogo neravenstva kak instrument sotsialnykh izmenenii". Kaliningrad 2011.

McIntosh Sundstrom, L. (2006) *Funding Civil Society: Foreign Assistance and NGO Development in Russia*. Stanford: Stanford University Press.

Moodisson, L. (2002) *Lilya 4 Ever* [film]. Sweden.

Nendre: Dver v novoe nachalo (2009). Mariehamn: Åland Islands Peace Institute.

Osushchestvlenie proekta 'Preodolenie gendernogo neravenstva kak instrument sotsialnykh izmenenii' v Kaliningradskoi oblasti: Glavnye itogi (2012) [Presentation of the project for the final meeting of the project – word.doc and PPP]. Kaliningrad.

Otchet o deiatelnosti nekommercheskogo partnerstva Zvezda nadezhdy po realizatsii programmy 'Preodalenie gendernogo neravenstva kak instrument sotsialnykh izmenenii' v period s 1.09.2010 po 31.12.2010 (2010). Kaliningrad.

Otchet o rezultatakh i osnovnykh napravleniiakh deiatelnosti GBUCO 'Tsentr sotsialnoi pomoshchi semie i detiam' v 2011godu (2011). Kaliningrad. Available from http://kcspsd.narod.ru/Centr_11.htm [20 Dec. 2013].

Peltonen, C. (1996) *Norden och närområderna: Kartläggning av jämställdhetsamarbetet*. Copenhagen: Nordic Council of Ministers.

Petersson, A. (1985) "The New Women's Movement – Where Have All the Women Gone? Women and the Peace Movement in Sweden." *Women's Studies Forum,* 8 (6), 631–8.

Rivkin-Fish, M. (2010) "Pronatalism, Gender Politics, and the Renewal of Family Support in Russia: Towards a Feminist Anthropology of 'Maternity Capital'." *Slavic Review* 69 (3), 701–24.

Rotkirch, A., Temkina, A. and Zdravomyslova, E. (2007) "Who Helps the Degraded Housewife? Comments on Vladimir Putin's Demographic Speech." *European Journal of Women's Studies* 14 (4): 349–57.

Saarinen, A. (2009) "A Circumpolar Case: Networking against Gender Violence across the East–West Border in the European North." *Signs* 34 (3), 519–24.

Salmenniemi, S. (2008) *Democratization and Gender in Contemporary Russia*. London and New York: Routledge.

Skjeie, H. and Teigen, M. (2005) "Political Constructions of Gender Equality: Travelling towards … a Gender Balanced Society?" *NORA* 13 (3), 187–97.

Suchland, J. (2011) "Is Postsocialism Transnational?" *Signs* 36 (4), 837–62.

Temkina, A. (1997) *Gender in Russia in Transition: The Case of New Collective Actor and New Collective Actions*. Helsinki: Kikimora.

Tollin, K. (2011) *Sida vid sida: En studie av jämställdhetspolitikens genealogi, 1971–2006*. Stockholm: Atlas.

11. Young Moldovan Women at the Crossroads: Between Patriarchy and Transnational Labour Markets

Kristina Abiala

Post-Soviet Moldova is an emigration country and supplier of transnational labour markets. The narratives of young women from this country, asked about their dreams for the future, show how the creation of a gendered identity is based upon the coping behaviour of individuals. The present study explores the way migration and other determinants have an effect on gendered identity formation. Reflecting a construction of Moldovan women as mirrored in their own aspirations and quoting them in a text like this, it is hoped, makes their voices heard and provides a supportive frame of reference about their own situation that might be emancipatory. These women's stories are part of a worldwide narrative about inequality – in particular gender inequality – that has a bearing on the situation in Western countries. Making these Moldovan women invisible through a stereotypical account would mean obscuring the socio-economic conditions that constitute the foundation of inequality in other parts of the world as well. Thus, acknowledging the experiences of young Moldovan women is a way of reflecting back stereotyped projections and understanding general mechanisms of inequality.

Identity formation on the individual level is intrinsically interwoven with gender relations, and it is negotiated in specific societal contexts. The Republic of Moldova became independent in 1991, after having been one of the Soviet Union's Socialist Republics for 51 years. During that period women and men were discursively constructed as *tovarisch*, that is, as equal comrades. For Moldovan citizens of today traditional and patriarchal norms, as well as mass migration form the background of problem solving in everyday life, and for the construction of a gendered identity.

In the early 2000s, Moldovan women were often described as victims of sexual trafficking (cf. Abiala 2006). Perceptions circulated about them as deceived or even kidnapped, as naive and uninformed. Experts from abroad were engaged to help repatriated young women get back on their feet and find a job in Moldova. The prevalent stories contained a grain of truth, but they represented a minor part of the experiences of migrating women. Nevertheless, 'the Moldovan woman' became a projection surface representing poor victimised and sexualised women who were different from 'us' Western women. Against this backdrop, a second look was cast to facilitate a deeper understanding of the Moldovan 'other'.[1]

Doing gender and nation

Due to the weakness of the Moldovan state, women's protection by men in a classical family structure is often seen as essential in Moldova. In view of many women who emigrate to provide for their family, a complex or contrarious process of gender identity is conditioned on various levels.

Gender research has shown that men and women have obligations and rights that are deeply rooted in society, its history and culture. As pointed out by Yvonne Hirdman, a stereotypical, to some degree negotiable, gender contract codifies that the man is responsible for supporting the woman and that the woman given such support is tied to home and family. The man's obligations are mainly located outside the home, where he enjoys some freedom of action. The narratives about the stereotypical 'he' and 'she' have to be identified in order to understand how gender contracts are built, how they develop, and how they perhaps disappear in a particular context (Hirdman 2001: 26, 84–90). Another researcher to have addressed the issue of contracts, as expressed by classic contract theorists, is Carol Pateman. The latter viewed the social contract within society as dependent on a sexual contract – a story of submission: "Women must enter into the marriage contract. But the sexual contract requires that women are incorporated into civil society on a different basis from men" (Pateman 1988: 180–1). While the social contract includes patriarchal rights and gives men power over women, the sexual contract establishes men's systematic access to women's

---

[1] The first part of the study was based on field work conducted in 2003 and concerned prostitution and trafficking in Moldavian women (Abiala 2006). The second part dealt with women from Gagauzia in the south of Moldova who worked in Istanbul as domestics in 2007 (Abiala 2013a). The third part, based on interviews with young Moldovans carried out in March and April 2008, is partly reflected in Abiala (2013b) and partly in this chapter.

bodies. A husband may exploit his wife who has been established as subordinate through the marriage contract. In patriarchy, differences between women and men are seen as essential natural differences with far-reaching implications. Men's patriarchal power over women is presented as arising from the essential order of nature.[2]

Gender is also construed in terms of national identity, and how women's bodies are negotiated has consequences for the national project. According to Maud Eduards (2007: 14), a national frame of reference is crucial for what women are allowed to do and not to do. Generally believed to be controlled by their body and associated with gender and sexuality, women are made responsible for realising which man is trustworthy and whom they are to mistrust (Eduards 2007: 17, 22). In contrast, the male body is imagined as de-gendered and concealed, and at the same time elevated as universal. In such a gender construction men have the duty to protect the borders of the nation, women and children, freedom and honour. This protection appears both as an act of paternalism and patriotism (Eduards 2007: 17, 21). The nation's reliance on gendered categories of citizens appears as natural, and their conception is significant for how societies organise themselves morally, socially, and politically. Eduards (2007: 18) connects this to phenomena such as violence and sexual trafficking.

A particular question with regard to Moldova is how the fact that many women and men emigrate influences gender construction. Women show strength by travelling abroad, trying to find a job that will enable them to earn more than the salary that is offered in their country of origin. Many married women leave their family and the male head of the family behind, and their freedom will usually increase with emigration. The money they send home improves the situation of the family and they become (one of) the breadwinners, a circumstance that might change the gender contract in their case, as compared to more traditional ways of families staying in Moldova. However, going abroad also means being exposed to the stereotypical image of 'the Moldovan woman', being victimised and sexualised as a 'poor European other' (see also Augustin 2003; Cheng 2003; Demletiner 2001; Kapur 2002; Kofman et al. 2000; Lemish 2000; Ålund 1999).

---

[2] In addition Pateman and Shanley (1991) discriminate between the private (the domestic, the familial, the intimate), and the public (in terms of the economy and the state), thereby emphasising the political significance of differences among women (1991: 3).

Moldova in 2008 and later years: Poverty, migration, and gender

The interviews on which this chapter is based were held in 2008. The situation for people in Moldova has presumably changed since then and the question is whether the generated data can be assumed to have a bearing on the situation today.

A report on the realisation of the UN millenium development goals, published in 2010 by the Moldovan government with the assistance of UN agencies, targeted poverty and gender equality. As a background it referred to the first decade of transition, 1991–2000, when the country's economic recession caused increasing poverty. While the economy has grown by two thirds in the period 2000–08, the discrepancy between urban and rural areas that emerged after 1990 lingered on. In terms of consumption, income, and welfare the report maintained that, "as recent research suggests, Moldova displays one of the highest degrees of polarization of economic life in Europe" (Government of Moldova 2010: 14). Economic growth, based – to a substantial proportion – on remittances from emigrants, led to a fall in poverty rates in urban, but not in rural areas. Moldovans did not benefit equally from support from abroad, but rather "[f]amilies benefiting from remittances are least exposed to the risks of poverty" (2010: 27). The global financial crisis in 2009 translated into a decrease in Moldova's GDP. Repeated droughts, floods in rural areas, and export restrictions worsened the situation (Government of Moldova 2010: 14, 19). And "[t]he poverty rate in rural areas continued to grow in 2009, widening the gap between rural and urban areas" (2010: 8). While the Moldovan economy recovered in 2010 and 2011, the country slipped back into a recession in 2012 (World Bank 2013).

The current situation in Moldova is characterised by segregation into gendered spheres, similar to other countries. In the field of education a vertical segregation into different disciplines prevails. Female pupils and students tend to study social sciences while males prefer technical subjects. About 51 per cent of pupils and students are women, but their share in higher education is larger. The average marriage age is 24 years for women and 26 for men (National Bureau of Statistics n.d.). Women and men report that they spend their time differently with regard to work and household activities. Whereas men spend some more time in their working life than women, the latter spend substantially more time on household chores and with family care (National Bureau of Statistics 2013). Households headed by women are probably at greater risk of poverty. They tend to come from urban areas, are often formed by a single person with children, and frequently rely on social payments and remittances (National Bureau of Statistics n.d.).

Working life is another arena for the construction of gendered relations. In the interviews of this study the wish to get a higher salary – sufficient to support a family – is often mentioned.[3] The unemployment rate is an unreliable indicator in Moldova, where many of those not working are not registered as unemployed. In 2012 the unemployment rate was estimated to be 5 per cent for women and 7 per cent for men – however 54 per cent of the women were categorised as belonging to the 'inactive population' (National Bureau of Statistics n.d.).

The number of emigrants is difficult to estimate, as Moldovans tend to travel undocumented and become irregular migrants. Before 2009 there was "a mass exodus of people", with at least one-fourth of the active population leaving the country for abroad. Most of the migrants who returned home in 2009 made efforts to re-emigrate the same year or in 2010 (Government of Moldova 2010: 28). Table 1 shows that the emigration – out of a total population of approximately 3.5 million inhabitants – was high in the period 1995–2000 and even higher 2000–05, and that it decreased after that.

Table 1: Net number of migrants, both sexes (Source: UN Department of Economic and Social Affairs 2012)

	1985–90	1990–95	1995–2000	2000–05	2005–10
Moldova	-85,000	-132,000	-250,000	-317,000	-170,000

The Moldovan government report from 2010 claimed that migration "will in the long term have disastrous impact on the country's economy and demography" and suggested that issues "such as the so-called brain drain and the emigration of those with other skills will need to be addressed" (Government of Moldova 2010: 28). On a global scale the very young emigrate too, and it seems likely that a significant proportion of children and young people do this on their own (cf. McKenzie 2007, referred to in *World Migration Report* 2010: 117). There is also regional variation, and women are, in general, particularly represented among highly skilled

---

[3] In 2012 the average monthly salary in Moldova was 3478 MDL (the equivalent of 217 EUR or 1869 SEK); available from:
http://www.statistica.md/newsview.php?l=en&idc=168&id=3975 [12 Jan. 2014].

migrants (United Nations Development Fund for Women 2008, referred to in *World Migration Report* 2010: 117).

The persistence of gendered cultural models and socio-economic data like that presented above suggest that the interview survey of 2008 is still relevant to the current situation. The rural–urban development cleavage and the divide between poor and rich might have increased even further.

Fieldwork parameters

The present chapter is based on a study that was conducted during a seven-week stay in Moldova in the spring of 2008. The aim of the study was to investigate the dreams of young people in Moldova in the context of large-scale emigration. Particular concerns were the informants' situation, their expectations about the future, images about Moldovan women, and if and how their experience of migration was connected to the process of gender construction. Informants were meant to belong to the 16–25 years old age group and to represent varied levels of education, and both urban and rural backgrounds. Based on these criteria two local research assistants found informants and booked the interviews.

In practice, informants varied in age from 14 to 22, being somewhat younger than planned, and displayed an overrepresentation of the well-educated with an urban background. Most of the informants lived in the capital Chișinău. It proved difficult to find informants in the countryside, but a group interview was held in a village 30 kilometres from Chișinău. In all, 22 semi-structured interviews were conducted, of which four were with experts in the fields of gender, migration, national economy, and women in the labour market. Six interviews were carried out with groups of up to twenty pupils or students; one with four participants; four with two people and seven with a single informant. The interviewees responded to questions such as: Could you tell me something about yourself and your life? What is your special dream for the future? Can you describe 'Moldovan women'? Follow-up questions varied depending on the course taken in different interviews.

The interviews were held in English and Romanian, relying on the translation services of two female university students. A disadvantage of working with interpretation is that it changes the wording and to a degree the content of what has been said. Simultaneous translation from one language into another during an interview is a demanding task and the interview quotes in this chapter had to be edited in some cases so as to cite the informants at an adequate linguistic level. An advantage of working with native born interpreters was their familiarity with the Moldovan education system and their helpful eliciting of collective images in group interviews that the interviewer might not have noticed. The interpreters formed a significant part of a triangle of social interaction, in which the interviews were conducted with me as the 'skilled observer from outside' and them as 'insiders and cultural consultants'. Apart from informing them about my research questions and methodological guidelines, I also interviewed the interpreters. This helped me to understand their frames of reference, and it was an opportunity for them to reflect on the material they helped to gather (cf. Jentsch 1998: 287).

International designer or getting married

One of the group interviews was held with four female and three male social science students aged 20 to 22. Two of them started by setting the scene: The male student imagined himself as a national hero in a leading position in the Moldovan government, doing something to be remembered by. The female student explained how she felt subordinate in her discipline and that she was contemplating continuing her studies abroad.

Two other students had an argument about gender, based on the dreams of one of them. The female student described how she had studied abroad for several years to become a designer, something she liked very much. For family reasons she had to come back to Moldova, where she felt angry and did not know what to do. "I had to give up everything, my friends and my way of thinking, but after four years I am not sad. I got used to it." The interviewer asked her what she wanted to do now, triggering a dialogue between her and one of the male students. When the woman answered laughingly that she did not know, the man forcefully suggested "She is going to marry. Will marry." As if she did not hear him the female student continued her answer by saying that she might perhaps become an international designer and added, referring to the male student, "Yes, he is joking." His response was loud and clear: "Not a joke! Stop dreaming, get married!" Softly, but with some determination, the female student insisted that this was her dream and that she wanted to be an artist: "That is what I want. When I do something I want to do it will all my heart." On the interviewer's follow-up question she talked about painting and sculpting, but a bit resigned she proposed that it might be too late for her, being twenty-two years old – she had to finish university. However, she concluded: "No, it's not too late ... I would like to start painting again." During this conversation the male student remained determined as if he knew what she ought to do and would eventually do. Without explicitly going against him, the female student clearly stated her right to cherish her own dream and to make it happen.

A whole group discussion emanated from the interviewer's question about gender equality in Moldova. One female and two male students started a discussion on whether women in Moldova were treated as inferior or not. One of the male students stated "I don't think that Moldovan women have problems." A female student laughed, whereupon he argued that they had equal rights and that there was "no problem here". If a woman was unable to do something it was her own fault, not the fault of the society, he continued. "Or the fault of the man", another male student added. The female student maintained that women in Moldova were treated as inferior and made clear that "I respect that men are men, but they have to respect women and not say shut up because you're a girl or a woman." The relation between work and private life for women and men was exemplified by the different use of mobile phones. A male student suggested that men usually bought two, one for work and one for friends, whereas women were not used to having both work and home relationships.

Another theme was about who was the head of the family, the main rule being that the one who earns money is the boss. The son and not the mother was said to become the head of the family if there was no father. One of the female students disagreed in favour of the mother for being wiser and more experienced, continuing "Maybe I am wrong, but ..." A male student talked about the role of woman as housewife: "I don't see why she shouldn't be a housewife. She does everything she wants and everything for the family." Another male student added "She may even have her own money. For some women this is a very good position." "But", one female student argued, "there are different families. I know families where the woman is the breadwinner while her man's work is not so important for the family budget."

The question about gender equality was discussed in a societal context. A male student explained "our society is still a bit conservative. Men are, in some circles, considered superior. Women have their areas where they are superior." A female student related the view on gender and sexuality back to the Soviet times of Moldova.[4] She referred to "the communist mentality" with permanent fear, lack of education, and no talk about sex, "so we don't talk about that". At the same time, gender equality was taken for granted in the Soviet Union: "They said that there is no difference between men and women. We were all equal, 'tovarisch', on an equal scale." But she added, a girl was nevertheless educated how to cook and only later did a woman realise that she could do something else.

Both in this group and in another group of somewhat younger students the researcher mentioned an observation of a couple in the city, a pretty, slim woman with very short skirt, high heels, and long hair holding on to a big muscular man with shaven head and a black leather jacket. In the group of the younger students the following explanation was given: "This is the Moldovan ideal. A lot of girls envy that girl. Women in Moldova want to find this man who is a superhero who would take care of everything. Women will have to be beautiful, provided for or offered money, even [if it means losing] willpower, and self-initiative. People think that she is a happy woman, having found this man. Even women in villages … would like to be this girl."

Another student added that "the attention this young woman gets is believed to be lost later on in the relationship. Men show attention to women only at the beginning. In the end she is just like an object that remains in the kitchen or takes care of the children."

In the older group of students the topic was rather that of prostitution or escort services, and marital infidelity, although the way the couple's appearance reflected issues of money and safety – physically and financially – was also seen. A male student commented that the woman was dressed like a prostitute, and a female explained that she thought of how rich men in their forties go out with very young girls. A male student commented: "Something normal, they cheat on their wife." On the interviewer's question about prostitution in Moldova a female answered: "Here? I don't know." A male student replied "What do you mean by prostitution? We have prostitutes, it's normal and in a small country everybody knows, but it is forbidden, hidden."

---

[4] Moldova became independent in 1991 when these students where three to five years old. It is not likely they were much aware of the gender relations of Soviet times themselves except for the attitudes that were evident from their parents and grandparents, through stories or behaviour.

Potential victims of sexual trafficking or future academic professionals?

The youngest girls in this study were fourteen to fifteen years old, and were interviewed in groups both in a rural school,[5] and in a school in the capital city Chişinău.[6]

In 2007, Catholic Relief Services implemented a 'Jobs plus program' in Moldovan villages with young, unemployed female teenagers as beneficiaries, a group considered most at risk for forced labour migration and sexual trafficking. This course suggested rural women were more traditional and more at risk of sexual trafficking than city girls. While the course helped rural girls with labour market orientation, it also confirmed the image of them as more vulnerable than others. The teaching seemed to balance two different aims. On the one hand, it intended to open the girls' eyes to university studies, and on the other, it was meant to channel them into the blue-collar work available. The pupils were asked to think of different professions that they were interested in and to anticipate what kind of person an employer would want to hire. The teachers emphasised the 'external look'. The message was that those badly dressed and giving a not-so-clean impression would not be employed. Finding a job required getting references and good advice from people who were already working in the respective area. They were told that they could "go abroad with a degree and a profession". Migration after having obtained a degree was seen as something to counter the risks of trafficking.

In a group discussion with the researcher the pupils laughed when I asked how many wanted to travel, the answer being "Everybody!" To Italy, Spain, Egypt, the entire continent of Africa, Israel, the whole of Europe. One girl said she would like to go to Asia or Africa as a charity worker in order to help people in less developed countries. Another girl wanted to go to a professional school to learn cooking. The teacher added, "to be a good housewife" – a statement apparently positioning the girl in Moldova. She said she did not know where she wanted to work.

The topic of building a family came up. A woman in Moldova was believed to be "18 or 25" when marrying. "It's not like in Europe, where they get married at thirty years old." One of the respondents explained that in Moldova "women are not totally without rights, but in our society men are always superior to women. And females themselves accept this. In rural

---

[5] Where I attended a lecture, held a group discussion, and performed several group interviews.
[6] Where I perfomed one group interview.

areas the main point is becoming a housewife. The majority of women in Moldova are closer to family than to career." According to the girls, Moldovan women assumed a balancing role in their families and one fostering quality. Perhaps, it was believed, they made sacrifices for the family and for the happiness of the husband, or for the best of the children. The girls characterised Moldovan women as "friendly, elegant, simple, and modest." The latter point was explained as meaning that they would not claim they were better than someone else. However, there were limits to the modesty of Moldavian women: "They are beautiful, and everyone in the world knows it. For the woman it is very important that people are giving compliments to her. Girls and women care very much about their looks."

Dancing in Paris – some city girls' dreams

Another group interview was held at the Colegiul National de Coregrafie in Chișinău.[7] These city girls were not regarded as a conventional risk group in terms of trafficking. Compared to the group of rural girls, their education had a clear direction and their dreams appeared unfettered by worries about finding a good living, something that might also be a consequence of their social class background, a factor not investigated here.

Several girls expressed dreams about dancing and living abroad. Becoming a famous dancer was part of the plan for some of them. One example was a girl who wanted to dance "on a big stage in a faraway country like America, or Paris. Concerts all day long." Earning a fortune was mentioned, for example, in connection with wanting to "live in New York in my own house" or to "live in my own apartment with a few colleagues", feeling very happy. One girl wanted to travel to Egypt; another one said she would "try to see my family in Moldova every month". Becoming a dance teacher could also entail going abroad: "I want to teach children dancing in Rome."

---

[7] The future dancers also studied languages, mathematics, history, biology, and other subjects. According to the headmaster they could all be expected to find jobs and already performed at the opera, ballet houses, and clubs, both classical and traditional Moldovan dance (called Joc). They had visited numerous countries, including Sweden. A group of 13 girls was interviewed for one and a half hours at their school in the absence of a teacher. It was striking that no one was permitted to answer freely without suggestions being made from the group. To the researcher it felt like talking to a group mind. To get an idea of their dreams the girls were asked about how they imagined their situation in two years and also about emigration – something here referred to only when connected to issues of identity formation.

For other girls – often those involved in the traditional dance Joc – their future belonged to Moldova. Although they wanted to live there, they also mentioned travelling abroad. Thus, one girl explained she wanted to learn a foreign language and presented alternatives to the dancing profession, such as becoming an airline stewardess or running her own sports business. While wanting to "live in Chișinău with my parents, go to the sea, and the mountains", one girl also wanted to travel abroad. Another girl wanted to become a dance teacher and live in an apartment in the centre of Chișinău with her mother.

University students and 'the Moldovan woman'

A group of female university students had precise ideas of how Moldavian women were perceived abroad. They believed that people in Spain realised "that Moldovan women are very kind-hearted", in the sense of staying with the father of their children, regardless of circumstances. The female students were aware that the image of Moldovans held by people abroad was rather limited. For example, they pointed out that people did not expect to hear that their domestic helper had daughters enrolled in higher education. "My mum [told them] that she wants to see her girls with a university degree and that she needs to pay the tuition. People were very surprised about this."

Almost like a mantra, most of the girls and women used the words beautiful, hardworking, and courageous when describing Moldovan women. Other characteristics were perseverance and the pragmatic dealing with what life offered to them, knowing that they could not expect help from someone else. One student explained that being courageous was forced on Moldovan women by their living conditions. At the same time, descriptions also included a lack of will and power. According to this more self-critical picture, Moldovan women lost confidence quickly when confronted with a challenge and they lacked the ability to fight, something that was also related to the financial situation in Moldova. One student suggested a paradox: "Women of Moldova have dreams and ideals about staying at home and being provided for by their husbands. This contradicts the view of women as powerful, being the one who works and takes care of everything."

A difference between rural and urban women was described, the former being the general referent. Rural women were seen as the backbone of the family. In the villages women were believed to work more than men, without receiving the appreciation that they deserved. "The man is considered to be the leader of the family, but the woman works more." Women were also regarded as often being the ones heading abroad in order to earn money. In contrast to this ambiguous picture, the women of Chișinău were described as dependent on men, "so they are weaker". According to the students, urban women were to a higher degree out for attention and support from their husbands. "Here in Chișinău we have more young ladies with short skirts that search for a man with money", was one observation. According to another one, "women in the city know their price and they cherish themselves". City women were not believed to go abroad to an equal extent as rural women.

Emigrating women also met suspicion: "Migrate? Why does she need to go abroad? Why doesn't the money the man brings into the family suffice? She might meet an Italian man there and marry him, and forget about her family and husband." Another female student objected: "I don't consider it a problem that women go abroad. The state doesn't permit them to find a good job and build a better future here in Moldova."

Prostitution was a difficult issue for the interviewed women. "We must not destroy the image of Moldovan woman because of some women who work as prostitutes. My personal opinion is that they do this out of need, not for pleasure." The respondents tried to avoid being explicit about prostitution. One of them found it "very difficult to pronounce the words" and added "Yes, they offer sexual services abroad." One female student maintained that many women "step on their dignity to earn money", to provide for a better life for their children and for their entire family. Their work abroad was to "offer undignified services". One explanation for this was that they were forced to do this, however, they "didn't choose the safest way to go abroad". There they were believed to be controlled by men giving them strict orders that they were to "cheat on their husbands and even to sell themselves for work". The interviewer's question, whether this referred to prostitution, was answered in the affirmative. And it was explained that the bosses knew that the women could not go back to their country, because it had cost them a considerable sum to have left it illegally.

Gender equality or discrimination

According to the respondents, there were manifest differences in the view on gender at an early age. "A boy always says, I am a boy and you are a girl – whereas you are supposed to stay at home, I am supposed to go out and have fun. And the girls around him also believe that." Such attitudes were said to prevail into adult life. Even if women had plans for their lives, they tended to give them up out of a lack of courage and patience, students said. One woman gave the following explanation: "There is a stereotype that the man is the head of the family and whatever he will do, the wife will follow. And the woman will always say, he is my husband and I will need to help him with his plans. I will abandon my plans. And the man thinks that my wife should stay at home and take care of the children."

Some of the female students commented about the lack of equality in their country: "Here the first place is [reserved] for the husband. No law exists saying that men and women are equal. A woman must listen to her husband. In some cases men subordinate women and humiliate them." According to another view "women are a little bit discriminated against because they don't have the same rights as men, or these rights are not respected". At the same time women might long for 'a man in the house'. One student talked about her boyfriend who lived with his mother. "What I really like is that he understands that his mother has no husband, and he is like the man in the house. He understands that a man should never fight with a woman, beat her or doing anything aggressive." One student had come to the conclusion that she was equal to men: "I started having fears that I am not attractive or beautiful so I would have to wear a short skirt and high heels. But I don't like that. I don't see myself running up to my husband in high heel shoes and short skirt for him to give me money. I clearly see myself as equal to my husband." However, gaining employment was regarded as easier for men: "The boss fears that the woman will marry and have children". One student reminded us that there were some women in leadership positions in Moldova.

Being assaulted in the city at night, or in the family, is a problem, not only in Moldova. One student provided a intense overview of domestic violence: "Different cruel stuff happens like the killing of a wife, of the husband beating the wife, or divorce. A lot of problems. My father didn't actually beat my mother, but a little bit (demonstrates pinching). I know it is not good." Another story went as follows: "We have a family acquaintance, who is abused by her husband. She has three children and says 'How will I take care of them without my husband?' She is just like that." The students had heard that abroad Moldovan women were treated as subalterns: "They like Moldovan women a lot, but take them as slaves and treat them badly. And I can tell you why, because Moldovan women are beautiful and they think that since we are poor we will take any job to get some money."

These women interviewed were students and their dreams do, of course, encompass finding a job commensurate with their educational level. Becoming a social worker or an interpreter "would allow me to communicate with many people and to give them advice regarding someone's life". One female educational science student aimed at making a career and advancing to a position of responsibility. "I want to be a director of a lyceum or college, why not vice-chancellor of a university?" Another one wanted to work with fashion and "to have my own shop / atelier where I can sew the clothes".

One of the interviewees reflected on how both her parents' wishes for her future entailed different paths, one to a feminine coded work and one to the breaking of gender norms: "I haven't decided about university or the police academy. I think I will finish my education in pedagogy because mother wants me to do this for her."

However, the more enticing choice was the police academy favoured by the father. "There are some criteria, I don't know if they accept girls. It's very dangerous work." She did not believe that it was an advantage to be a woman in this job, but would nevertheless like to interact with many people and be able to defend her country.

The stereotypical image about Moldovans is one of poverty and migration. The interviews often expressed a wish to go abroad, but not necessarily a desire to migrate. "I want to go to Disneyland. I would also like to travel over the whole world and if I love a country, to stay there. I would like to go to Paris, with my family, and all my relatives." One student said "I would like to go to Brazil for the carnival. In Latin America there is a day of tomato fighting. I would like to go to Egypt or Turkey to see professional belly dancers." Travelling is also described as an element of future work. A student of psychology would like to do research abroad and help suffering people. Another student mentioned her wish to become part of a delegation and to travel a lot.

Many interviewees expressed love for Moldova with different connotations such as the countryside, flowers, and being with relatives. Often they considered remaining in Chișinău, in a big house, as the most attractive future. However, they regarded it as unaffordable and migration as a means, hopefully, to be able to build a home in Moldova. However, worries about difficulties and deprivation were also connected to the idea of staying in the country. "I have values and ideas about life that are not respected here in Moldova. They tell me that it only happens in movies: 'In real life you have to fight for it and have hardship like in Moldova.' I would like to go back to the US; here I begin to lose my self-confidence." There was also fear of migration reminiscent of the discourse on trafficking. "I hear of different stuff that happens, making me kind of worried a bit. The young girls that live abroad, some of them come back, and some don't. From what I hear it is not always good. I read different stuff. It worries me. I want to believe that this will not happen to me."

Another important theme was marrying and building a family. "I want to have a good family, good children, and a good husband." Migration might become necessary: "I think I would leave Moldova if I didn't have a job with a salary that would allow me to have a decent life, to provide for me and for my family." Here the extended family is included. Helping relatives is connected to a wish that Moldovan society, described as encompassing not only many poor people struggling for food, but also numerous rich people, would provide better welfare. Under the prevailing conditions it is regarded a necessity to support family members: "If something happens to a member of my family and I will need a big sum of money I will work abroad to do that, of course I will. If a member of my family will need an urgent operation that will cost tens of thousands of Euros or dollars …".

The description of a 'good husband' included him being somewhat older and a bit taller that the woman. Upon the interviewer asking why he was expected to be taller, everybody laughed and one of the women replied: "Maybe it is the mentality of women. When I go on a street I'd like my husband to be taller. It's not nice if I'm short and he is even shorter." Both appearance and personality were described: "He must be handsome, but not very handsome. Just to be able to go out with him without getting embarrassed." Another request was him having "not too dark skin, white skin, dark hair, and black eyes." The husband of the students' dreams was often respectful and understanding in the relationship. He was not jealous of other boys and friends, and had interests and values similar to the ones she had. The ideal husband would also care for the family, the children and help with the household chores. For him, family had to be the most important thing in life. Husbands could also be seen as compensating for one's own weaknesses: "He has to be freer than me, more courageous. Sometimes I'm shy, and I'd like him to be able to help me express myself." Having a university degree and a well-paid occupation was seen as desirable "so he can provide for me as well". The ultimate husband was the one who was "able to deal with any problem".

Having children was an obvious choice for these women, despite the low Moldavian birth rate. Two children was the norm, first a boy and then a girl. As the following statement shows, the proper sequence might sometimes be connected to a corresponding order of attention. "I want a boy and a girl. To be like a mother, carry him, educate him, and him being like a flower in my hands." A more traditional view of the adequate size of a family was also expressed: "I haven't thought about the number of children. Maybe two, four, six, or ten. Previous generations used to have twelve children, so if it is possible, why not. It is said that many pregnancies make a woman more beautiful."

Conclusion

This study on young Moldavians' narratives seeks to contribute to an improved understanding of the construction of gendered identities in the context of traditional and patriarchal norms, mass migration, and individual problem solving in everyday life. Its informants provided manifold examples of traditional ways of thinking and stereotypical gender contracts. The women and men interviewed did not seriously question the man's task to support and provide for his wife and family. The two sexes were assigned different life spheres starting with boyhood – going out to have fun – and girlhood – staying at home in the family. This was, apart from a few exceptions, apparently seen as the consequence of an essential natural difference. The prevalence of traditional norms was also highlighted in female students' description of the ideal husband: taller, protecting, and mentally and materially supportive of his family.

The question is whether there are indications that it is possible to negotiate the traditional gender contract. This is clearly the case in regard to women's participation in higher education and in the process of migration. Moldovan women are often stereotyped as naive and uninformed victims, but after independence in 1991 roughly half of the numerous emigrants from the country have been women, engaged in making a decent livelihood for their extended family. Thus, many of them have become (one of) the breadwinners of the family and that gives them an improved position from which to question and negotiate their gender role. Such material changes are likely to alter the situation of women in Moldova. The dispute between young men and women in one of the group interviews results, perhaps, from the male apprehension of women entering the educational arena and obtaining higher positions, both at home and abroad.

It is not so clear how the construction of a gendered identity is connected to the Moldovan national project of today. In the beginning of the 2000s, Moldova received much financial aid and practical support from experts and NGOs from other countries in order to stop trafficking, mostly of women. The government had the difficult task of balancing the national economy and welcomed this help. Human trafficking is still an issue, but remittances from migrants and the stabilisation of the economy have improved the Moldovan situation. At the same time, the reluctance to become overly dependent on foreign experts has led to increasing unwillingness to assume the role of 'the poor European other'.

Crossroads in Chişinău, 2006 (Photographer: Richard Fairbrother)

References

Abiala, K. (2006) "The Republic of Moldova: Prostitution and Trafficking in Women." *International Approaches to Prostitution: Law and Policy in Europe and Asia,* ed. by Gangoli, G. and Westmarland, N. Bristol: Policy Press, 91–111.

Abiala, K. (2013a) "'Som en i familjen': Invandrade kvinnor i turkiska hushåll." *Arbete & Jämställdhet. Förändringar under femtio år,* ed. by Blomberg, E. and Niskanen, K. Stockholm: SNS, 133–59.

Abiala, K. (2013b) "Longing and Hope: The Present and Future for Young Moldovan Women." *Post-Communist Transition and Women's Agency in Eastern Europe,* ed. by Simmons, C. Dordrecht: Republic of Letters, 121–37.

Ålund, A. (1999) "Feminsm, Multiculturalism, Essentialism." *Women, Citizenship and Difference,* ed. by Yuval-Davis, N. and Werbner, P. London: Zed, 147–61.

Augustin, L. (2003) "Forget Victimisation: Granting Agency to Migrants." *Development* 46 (3), 30–6.

Cheng, S.-J.A. (2003) "Rethinking the Globalization of Domestic Service: Foreign Domestics, State Control, and the Politics of Identity in Taiwan." *Gender and Society* 17 (2),   166–86.

Demleitner, N. V. (2001) "The Law at Crossroads: The Construction of Migrant Women Trafficked into Prostitution." *Global Human Smuggling,* ed. by Kyle, D. and Koslowski, R. Baltimore: John Hopkins University Press, 257–93.

Eduards, M. (2007) *Kroppspolitik: Om Moder Svea och andra kvinnor.* Stockholm: Atlas.

Government of Moldova (2010) *The Second Millennium Development Goals Report: Republic of Moldova.* Available from http://www.undp.md/presscentre/2010/MDG%20Report%20II/MDG2_RM.pdf [5 Jan. 2014].

Hirdman, Y. (2001) *Genus: Om det stabilas föränderliga former.* Malmö: Liber.

Jentsch, B. (1998) "The 'Interpreter Effect': Rendering Interpreter Visible in Cross-Cultural Research and Methodology." *Journal of European Social Policy* 8 (4), 275–89.

Kapur, R. (2002) "The Tragedy of Victimization Rhetoric: Resurrecting the 'Native' Subject in International/Post-Colonial Feminist Legal Politics." *Harvard Human Rights Journal* 15, 1–37.

Kofman, E., Phizackles, A., Raghuram, P., and Sales, R. (2000) *Gender and International Migration in Europe: Employment, Welfare and Politics.* London: Routledge.

Lemish, D. (2000) "The Whore and the Other: Israeli Images of Female Immigrants from the Former USSR." *Gender and Society* 14 (2), 333–49.

McKenzie, D.J. (2007) *A Profile of the World's Young Developing Country Migrants*. Bonn: Institute for the Study of Labor (IZA).

National Bureau of Statistics of the Republic of Moldova (n.d.) "Gender Statistics." Available from http://www.statistica.md/category.php?l=en&idc=264 [12 Jan. 2014].

National Bureau of Statistics of the Republic of Moldova (2013) "Utilizarea timpului în Republica Moldova: Principalele rezultate ale cercetării 'Utilizarea timpului'." [Time Use Survey.] Available from http://www.statistica.md/newsview.php?l=ro&idc=168&id=4055 [12 Jan. 2014].

Pateman, C. (1988) *The Sexual Contract*. Cambridge: Polity Press.

Pateman, C. and Shanley, M.L. (1991) "Introduction." *Feminist Interpretations and Political Theory*, ed. by . Pateman, C. and Shanley, M.L. Cambridge: Polity Press, 1–10.

United Nations, Department of Economic and Social Affairs, Population Division (2013) "World Population Prospects: The 2012 Revision." Available from http://esa.un.org/unpd/wpp/Excel-Data/migration.htm [12 Jan. 2014].

United Nations Development Fund for Women (2008) *Progress of the World's Women 2008/2009: Who Answers to Women? Gender and Accountability*. New York: UNIFEM.

World Bank (2013) "Moldova Economic Update." 10 April. Available from http://www.worldbank.org/content/dam/Worldbank/document/eca/Moldova-Economic-Update.pdf [12 Jan. 2014].

World Migration Report 2010: The Future of Migration: Building Capacities for Change (2010). Geneva: International Organization for Migration. Available from http://publications.iom.int/bookstore/free/WMR_2010_ENGLISH.pdf [12 Jan. 2014].

Part 4: Environmental Awareness

12. Waves of Laws and Institutions: The Emergence of National Awareness of Water Pollution and Protection in the Baltic Sea Region over the Twentieth Century

Simo Laakkonen

The Baltic Sea is often said to be the most polluted, the most researched, and the most protected sea in the world. Nonetheless, persistent environmental problems show that we do not sufficiently understand the temporal and spatial changes in societies and ecosystems in the region. The environmental history of Baltic Sea protection is still being written, and the lack of in-depth studies means that the interactions between societies and ecosystems in the region remain largely unknown. The environmental history of pollution and the protection of the seas and oceans in general is a poorly explored topic (Hughes 2006) despite the fact that water covers two-thirds of the surface of the globe.

Previous research has provided an empirical overview and analysis of the origins of water pollution and protection in the Baltic Sea region at the local level (Laakkonen et al. 1999; 2001; 2007). This is, however, not sufficient for understanding the complex socio-ecological processes that have transformed the Baltic Sea from a functioning natural resource into an environmental problem over the course of the twentieth century. Thus, there is a need to expand the research from local to national frameworks. Currently, most studies discussing these issues at the national level pertain almost exclusively to natural, scientific, or technical aspects and focus primarily on present-day problems and ignore the historical context.

In the social sciences and humanities, there is some work on certain aspects of the history (e.g., Kirby and Hinkkanen 2000; Maciejewski 2002; Bolin et al. 2005), environmental legislation, and the international power politics of Baltic Sea protection (e.g., Fitzmaurice 1992; Hjorth 1992; Vandeveer 2000). However, in this research the history of environmental issues has been largely neglected (an exception being the impact of pollution on fishing, see Holm et al. 2001). The problem is twofold; environmental history is not yet a firmly established academic discipline in the countries of the region, and practical research in the field struggles with the fact that publications and archival data are in many different languages and that there are significant geographical distances between research institutions in the region.

As a consequence only a few in-depth studies have explored the history of the pollution or protection of watercourses in the Baltic Sea region over the twentieth century. Denmark is the only country in the region for which the national debate concerning water pollution over the past century has been properly explored (Engberg 1999). In Sweden the long-term development of pollution paradigms has been studied (Löwgren, Hillmo, and Lohm 1989), while studies on the national debate have focused on the turn of the nineteenth and twentieth century (Lundgren 1974). In Finland national studies over the twentieth century have focused on towns and cities (Laakkonen, Laurila, and Rahikainen 1999) and wastewater treatment technology (Katko 1996). Scholars exploring the national history of water pollution and protection of the USSR have dealt with specific eras and themes (e.g., Goldman 1972; Peterson 1993; Kimstach, Mevbeck, and Baroudy 1998) and the Soviet period as a whole remains to be investigated. Studies concerning the Baltic Republics have examined the Soviet period and the history of environmental technology (Velner 1995; Cetkauskaité, Zharkov, and Stoskus 2001). Only a few studies have attempted to discuss the development of water protection in Poland from a national point of view (Roman and Tabernacki 1992; Carter 1993; Kowalik and Laakkonen 2007). In brief, studies that have explored national development in the aforementioned countries have generally focused on a relatively short and often recent time period (e.g., Joas, Jahn, and Kern 2008; Gilek et al. 2011). As a consequence we still lack a 'big picture' of the national development of water pollution and protection in the Baltic Sea Region over the twentieth century.

The study of the history of environmental problems has also been delayed by the prevailing assumption that modern environmental protection only emerged in the industrialised and democratic states in the late 1960s and early 1970s. According to this argument, there had earlier only been some forms of nature conservation that had emerged in the late nineteenth century. The hypothesis of the recent origin of environmental protection is generally accepted in the areas of environmental policy making, the media, and the sciences. While recognising the major expansion that took place in environmental concepts and practices in the late 1960s and early 1970s, I argue that the awareness of environmental problems emerged earlier than is generally believed. As the example of the Baltic Sea region illustrates, both nature conservation and environmental protection have their own history dating back to the late nineteenth century (Lundgren 1995).

The Baltic Sea catchment area is four times larger (over 1.7 million square kilometres) than the sea itself. Historical human-induced changes in the area and its numerous river basins have caused most of the environmental problems in the Baltic. This chapter seeks to provide an overall picture of how national awareness of water pollution and protection developed in four coastal states of the Baltic Sea region – Finland, Sweden, the Soviet Union, and Poland – until the end of the Cold War. It focuses on urban-industrial pollution because this has historically been the most problematic and most addressed environmental issue in the Baltic Sea region.

Although this essay is meant to explore how the awareness of water pollution and protection developed on the national level, a study of civil society in this respect is practically impossible due to its fragmentary character and the lack of previous historical studies. Therefore, this study examines governmental actors, legislation, and related institutions. The issues explored are when, why, and how ideas and practices related to water pollution began to be discussed in various official agencies and in the government. I consider both successful and unsuccessful efforts to develop nationwide institutional tools for controlling inland and coastal water pollution because they both indicate activities with the goal of improving the state of the aquatic environment in the region. Such a study has its limits because legislation neither guarantees that protective measures against water pollution are actually implemented nor does it necessarily reflect the severity of the environmental problems.

The pioneering era prior to the First World War

Sweden

In the nineteenth century, problems with urban and industrial pollution were both socially and spatially divided in Sweden because the majority of the urban population lived in the southern part of the country while most forest industries were established in the sparsely populated north. Polluting of urban watercourses was generally forbidden by municipal ordinances issued in 1868. This decree prohibited dumping of pig food, carcasses, garbage, and refuse from factories into urban watercourses. City governments were allowed to issue special decrees when needed, and the police had the power to impose fines and compensation for damages. The Public Health Act was passed in 1874, and this provided autonomy for towns and cities in terms of managing sanitary issues and codifying the existing regulations. Public health departments were established with their own laboratories and experts, and this gave them significant authority and power, especially in bigger towns. However, this did not stop the population and industries from increasingly contaminating urban watercourses.

Starting in the late nineteenth century, a growing number of factories were established by rivers and rapids in the Swedish countryside. Most of these factories were iron works, sugar factories, or pulp and paper mills that used local resources, raw materials, and energy. The pulp and paper factories were the most polluting of the air and water compared to other industries, and this led to problems for everyday household activities, agriculture, and fisheries. Local problems continued to increase during this time period, but there were hardly any regulations or authorities put in place to deal with pollution in the countryside. The scarce resources of the rural municipalities were mainly used for poor relief and basic education, and this led to the prevalence of a passive attitude in regard to pollution. National fisheries inspectors were, in principle, the only public authorities tasked with addressing industrial environmental problems in the countryside. Their number, activities, and powers increased significantly after the administrative reform of 1904. They were particularly concerned with the impact of fibre and lute on hatching areas (Lundgren 1974: 17, 210). The fisheries inspectors were entitled to investigate and intervene and, if needed, even temporarily close down polluting facilities.

The first time the question of water and air pollution was presented in the Swedish Parliament was in 1902. Five years later, the government ordered a committee – called the Ditching Law Committee (*Dikningslagskommittén*) – to prepare a bill addressing air and water pollution in Sweden. In 1915 the committee issued a white paper requiring the state to take action. The white paper and the associated bill were based on the concern for gaseous and liquid discharges from factories and their impacts on health. It was acknowledged that people had a right to healthy surroundings, including clean water and air, and the new industries were described as a risk to the purity of Sweden's watercourses. Based on reports from provincial medical doctors, the committee presented a gloomy overall picture of the state of watercourses in Sweden. The committee suggested that realistically a certain amount of pollution was unavoidable and had to be accepted due to related business interests. However, they stated that all possible protection measures were to be adopted as long as these were economically viable. The chemical industry resisted such demands and argued that a society that required expensive treatment facilities should also pay for them. Nevertheless, the committee suggested that the establishment of new factories be subject to licensing in order to take potential polluting impacts into account early in the planning process. The committee also proposed establishing a new organisation to oversee the implementation of the law. First, a water inspection office (*Vatteninspektion*) was to be established for research and law enforcement, and second a special water court (*Vattendomstol*) was to be set up to solve judicial problems related to water and wastewater issues both in municipalities and in industries (Dikningslagskommittén 1915).

The handling of the committee's white paper and the related bill was, however, delayed due to the First World War, which affected Sweden to some extent despite the country's neutrality. When the bill was finally introduced and debated in parliament in 1921 it was rejected. The economic interests of the growing industry were regarded as more important than the interests of people living by polluted watercourses. The situation in urban centres was not better than in the countryside. All towns and cities in Sweden had water works and municipal sewerage systems, but only one town had a wastewater treatment facility prior to the First World War (Lundgren 1974: 141, 187; Allmänna 1955).

Grand Duchy of Finland

From 1809 to 1917, Finland was a semi-autonomous part of the Russian Empire that was given ample opportunity to develop its industry. Export-orientated sawmills increased in number from the middle of the nineteenth century, and the forest industry acquired a more important role in Finland than in any other Nordic country. The mechanical wood processing industry also started to expand from the middle of the nineteenth century, and the chemical forest industry – along with the production of sulphite and sulphate cellulose – began to develop in the 1880s.

These changes did not go unnoticed, and just as in Sweden it was Finland's fisheries inspectors who were the first and most active governmental agency to pay attention to industrial water pollution. They played a major role in the various studies and committees that examined the environmental consequences of the forest industry on society as a whole and on fisheries in particular. Even as early as the 1870s, the first fisheries inspectors had called for regulations that would have completely prohibited detrimental discharges into the watercourses (*Fiskeritidskrift för Finland* 1897: 62). The inspectors were also the first authority to examine industrial water pollution and countermeasures in foreign countries and to initiate international cooperation in the field (Nordquist 1891). Moreover, they were active in establishing the Finnish Fisheries Association whose guidebook, published in 1895, addressed the harmful impact of pollution and the necessity to study it (Cederström 1894).

The development of legislation followed the same pattern as the development of the forest industry, although with some delay. Like other provisions from the time when Finland was still a part of Sweden, a Swedish law from 1734 remained in force that prohibited the dumping of sawdust into rivers. Sawmills were often obliged to prevent bark from ending up in watercourses and damaging fishing gear (Jaatinen 1965: 15). The prohibition of water pollution was included in the Imperial decree in 1868 concerning water pipes and water works as well as in the Water Act that became law in 1902. In 1891, the fisheries inspectors addressed pollution caused by the cellulose industry, but they considered that floating and sawmills still had a more detrimental impact on watercourses (Nordqvist 1891: 50). However, by 1898 a governmental fisheries committee described industrial pollution in its white paper in the following manner: "Cellulose mills, paper factories, and so on, the waste of which includes chemical products, discharge those directly into watercourses and have had a ruinous impact on fisheries" (Kalastuskomitealta 1898: 18).

At the beginning of the twentieth century, air and water pollution caused by the forest industry was widely acknowledged and a governmental Sulphate Committee studied the issue in 1907 and 1908. This committee demonstrated that the smell caused by a mill could be noted from a distance of 40 kilometres. Although a white paper published by the committee in 1909 asked whether the operations of the worst polluters should be closed down (KM 1909: 1, 105), the economic interests of the forest industry were given priority. However, Finnish towns and cities did not remain inactive, and by 1910 two towns had erected the first biological wastewater treatment plants.

Imperial Russia

The development of water pollution and protection issues in Imperial Russia has never been properly studied. It seems, however, that the country paid little attention to water pollution let alone spoke of water protection. According to Cherkinskii (1973: 9), the central tsarist government did not establish measures for the control of effluents or the protection of water resources despite numerous initiatives by experts. Watercourses and water protection were in a catastrophic state even in the Imperial capital of Saint Petersburg, which suffered from recurrent cholera epidemics long after such outbreaks ceased to occur in other European capitals (Krasnoborodko et al. 1999: 54–6). The Public Health Act did not give full autonomy to Russian towns and cities in sanitary issues. Due to the passive role of both the national government and municipalities, most towns and cities, including the Imperial capital, did not have proper water works or municipal sewer systems and the state of sanitary issues remained poor throughout the country (Filtzer 2010: 66–7). Hence after the October Revolution in 1917, the Bolshevik government inherited an exceptionally poor urban-industrial and administrative infrastructure.

The interwar period

Sweden

In Sweden, the bill for a water law had been rejected in parliament in 1921. However, industrial pollution, damage caused to fisheries, and lack of regulations in the countryside made the Board of Agriculture propose in the 1920s and 1930s that the legislative work be resumed (Lundgren 1974: 212). By 1935, the need to protect fisheries from pollution was readdressed in the Swedish Parliament. At the same time, progress was being made in the field of research and a governmental Fisheries Studies Institute (*Fiskeriundersökningsanstalt*) was founded in Stockholm in 1937 under the auspices of the Board of Fisheries that was tasked with investigating pollution problems. This institute – headed by Sten Wallin – initially consisted of only a few researchers and they carried a heavy load over the next few decades in terms of performing research, carrying out inspections, and preparing legislation in Sweden. A committee was established to renew existing legislation in the late 1930s. Its reports, published in 1939 and 1941, provided an updated overview of the state of watercourses in Sweden based again on provincial medical doctors' accounts of the dangers of increasing amounts of urban and industrial pollutants. The committee emphasised that the volume of the wastewater exceeded the carrying capacity of the watercourses and that the authorities lacked the resources to monitor the situation. The members of the committee, however, disagreed as to whether the state should make the adoption of effective wastewater treatment facilities mandatory or not. Hence the committee refrained from drafting a special 'pollution law' and recommended that, when necessary, existing regulations and administration should be renovated to improve control over wastewater discharges (Betänkande 1939).

The new water law that went into effect in 1942 allowed the fisheries studies institute to inspect and evaluate the risks of all new potentially polluting factories and other facilities. The right of water courts to supervise the situation in some industries before allowing wastewater to be discharged into watercourses was also a step forward. The separation of municipal and industrial issues was an important practical issue in the new water law. However, the overall lack of power to compel municipalities and industries to protect watercourses was a major weakness of the new law (Specialdomstolen 1940).

Finland

After the First World War had led to the independence of Finland, the office of fisheries inspectors was transformed into the National Board of Fisheries (*Kalastushallitus*) (Järvi 1941: 10). The work of the pre-war Sulphate Committee was accounted for in the Neighbour Infringement Law (*Naapuruussuhdelaki*) issued in 1920 that prohibited factories and other installations from causing excessive inconvenience by means of emitting noise, dust, gas, or bad smells (17 §, Finlex 26/1920). Furthermore, the statute on public health (*Terveydenhoitosääntö*) issued in 1927 determined that establishing a sulphate mill in a town or a city was subject to obtaining a license. However, another decree issued three years later annulled this statute (*Asetus* 1930).

In the 1930s, the Finnish forest industry was involved in several litigation processes because of water pollution issues. Pollution caused by forest industries was also discussed in parliament and in government in the late 1930s. The forest industry acknowledged the problems and in 1937 established its own Wastewater Committee that explored the issue in order to find cost-effective solutions. The work of this committee as well as governmental activities to establish a special supervisor for pollution caused by forest industries were, however, abruptly aborted in November 1939 when the Soviet Union attacked Finland and the Winter War and the Second World War started in northern Europe.

Soviet Union

There were altogether about 700,000 rivers in the Soviet Union that discharged into three oceans. The smallest drainage basin was that which emptied into the Atlantic Ocean and covered 8.4 per cent of the total area of the Soviet Union (Litvinov 1962: 441). The Baltic Sea was one part of this drainage basin. Thus in the following overview it is not sensible to try to separate activities addressing the Baltic Sea from the overall pan-Soviet water protection activities.

Despite the destruction caused by the First World War, the October Revolution, and the Civil War that raged until 1922, the new Bolshevik government did not waste time in attempting to improve the catastrophic sanitary conditions in the country. The administration of public health was, for the first time, centralised, and the needs of the working poor became a political priority (Solomon 1993: 184, 197). Already during the Civil War, in 1919, the Supreme Council of the National Economy established the Central Committee of Water Protection, which became the first government organ to oversee all water resources. A decree on "The Sanitary Protection of Conditions in Residential Areas" was issued in order to control sewage (Goldman 1972: 294, with reference to Kolbasov 1965: 212).

A decree of the Council of People's Commissars of the Russian Soviet Federative Socialist Republic (RSFSR) "On Sanitary Institutions of the Republic" that was issued in 1922 laid out the basic principles of the State Sanitary Inspection (Filatov, Leonard, and Shishkina 2009: 4–7). From its foundation that year, this agency maintained a central role in scientific pollution studies and policymaking. In addition, institutes of community hygiene, departments of community hygiene at medical schools, and sanitary-epidemiological stations were established in the 1920s and 1930s (Gabovich 1967: 54–5). These institutions considerably expanded the scientific base for investigations into water sanitation.

Attention was first given to the issue of healthy drinking water for urban populations. However, systematic surveys of the sanitary condition of the main rivers were also started early in the Soviet Union by various research institutes. These studies explored, among other things, the physiochemical and bacteriological features of rivers and the reasons behind the pollution. The main conclusions were published in two compilations, *Problems of Pollution and Self-Purification of Water Supply Sources*, published in 1937, and *The Pollution and Self-Purification of Water Supply Sources*, published in 1939 (Litvinov 1962: 444). In addition, the Central Institute of Community Hygiene arranged studies that focused on industrialised regions (Cherkinskii 1973: 10, 95; for chemical studies, see Zhulidov et al. 2003: 8–11).

Scientific study was accompanied by legislative work. The first government standards concerning minimum contents of dissolved oxygen in effluents were announced in 1929. A foundation for the planned protection of water resources was the decree of the Central Executive Committee and Council of People's Commissars of May 1937 "On the Sanitary Protection of Water Supply Systems and Sources of Water Supply against Pollution" (Litvinov 1962: 444; Kolbasov 1965: 104, 220). Thus, the first two decades of Soviet power showed notable legislative and administrative activity.

Poland

No studies are available about water pollution issues in Poland prior to the independence of the country in 1918. However, the collapse of the Tsarist regime was followed by notable sanitary reforms in Poland immediately after the First World War just as were seen in the USSR. The first national requirements concerning wastewater discharges into surface waters were introduced in 1922 when a new Water Law was issued. This law prohibited the pollution of waters in principle. It required that wastewater be registered and it entitled state authorities to stop discharges into rivers, lakes, and the sea when necessary. The law, which was modified several times over the following decades, remained binding in Poland until 1962. The second national regulation limiting pollution of watercourses was a decree issued for health resorts in 1923. This decree established sanitary protection zones in river catchment areas in cases where public health resorts took water from their respective rivers. In 1928, another law obliged all municipal authorities to take care of the discharge of pollutants. In 1932, the Fishery Law prohibited water pollution that was harmful for fishing and led to the establishment of criteria for permissible levels of pollutants in surface waters. The Fishery Law was also effective in Poland until 1962 when new regulations came into force. However, no specific institutions were established in the interwar period to enforce the implementation of this legislation (Kowalik and Laakkonen 2007: 222).

The Cold War era

Sweden

The Second World War created an unexpected hindrance to water protection efforts even in neutral Sweden. During and after the war, municipal autonomy was severely limited by state regulations. The Labour Market Board (*Arbetarmarknadsstyrelse*), which had no expertise in the field of water protection, was given the administrative power to decide whether a given municipality was granted permission to build a wastewater treatment plant or not. This agency regarded housing construction as a more important task than the reform of sewer networks, let alone the erection of wastewater treatment plants (Kloak 1947). The results of this administrative coup d'etat – or rather coup d'municipalité – were severe in terms of water protection, and yet this procedure continued until the 1950s (Vattenförorening 1952).

The press described another problem as the "unprecedented organisational fragmentation" that caused the waste of resources, a lack of information, and poor leadership and guidelines on the national level (Högrenat 1953). Experts counted altogether 14 different authorities – according to other calculation the number was 29 – that were involved in water protection issues (14 institutioner 1953; Tjugonio 1953). Inefficient state administration resulted in municipalities having poor guidance and a good excuse for not doing anything about water protection (Vattenföroreningar 1953).

The issue of water pollution was discussed in the Swedish Parliament again in the early 1950s, and the government called a Water Protection Committee (*Vattenvårdkommitte*) to reform existing regulations and administration. The committee worked from February 1953 until December 1954 and was described as being "exceptionally quick for being a Swedish committee" (Kraven 1956). The committee concluded that of the 3.2 million Swedes living in 116 towns and cities, 9 per cent had access to biological wastewater treatment methods and about 43 per cent had access to mechanical treatment methods. Hence, approximately 41 per cent of municipal wastewater was not treated at all. The situation was even worse in industries (Orena 1953). This committee also provided a gloomy national picture of the state of Sweden's watercourses, including rivers, lakes, and the coastline, on the basis of reports sent in by provincial medical doctors (Här 1957).

The legislation based on the committee's observations did not involve any major alterations to the existing laws. In 1954, the Water Protection Committee suggested integrating the two main governmental research organisations into "an independent organisation". Otherwise the administration was left almost unaltered except that the system of regional agricultural engineers was clarified and the institute of fisheries studies was provided with some additional resources and a new name, the Water Inspection Office (*Vatteninspektion*), which had already been proposed by the first committee in 1915 (Vattenfrågor 1957). Higher purification requirements, that is, the adoption of biological methods, were set for the municipalities with a transition period of five years. Some requirements concerning industry were tightened as well (Nya 1956). For the first time, agriculture was also taken into account and discharges of silage juice from silos and urea from animal sheds into watercourses were prohibited in the new water law. However, the most important issue – how to organise water protection on the national level – was not included in the new water law that went into effect on 1 January 1957 (Vattenvården 1955; Vattenvården 1957).

The new water law did not live up to expectations. There had been too much tug of war between different governmental institutions behind the scenes and this meant that each of the resulting three main organisations operated in too narrow a field to be efficient (Malmberg 1961). The establishment of a unified special national organisation (*Vattenvårdstyrelse*) for water protection issues was proposed by another committee in 1964. The government of Sweden under the social democrat Tage Erlander from 1946 to 1969 decided, however, not to establish such an organisation, but instead sought to integrate the various organisations responsible for the protection of water and air and those responsible for nature conservation into one independent and powerful organisation (Anonymous 1965).

The Swedish Environmental Protection Agency (*Naturvårdsverket*) began to operate in 1967 as the highest national organisation coordinating nature conservation and environmental protection, including water protection. Sweden established a holistic environmental administration and now every new facility that was potentially polluting had to apply regularly for an inspection and a license to function. At the time of the founding of the organisation, however, it was heavily criticised for its lack of resources. The total number of staff of the organisation was increased from 95 – the combined number of employees of the predecessor agencies – to not more than 104, thus the organisation did not gain significant additional resources (Anonymous 1966). Despite the establishment of a new governmental organisation, Swedish municipalities continued to carry the main responsibility for water protection, including the planning, financing, and construction of wastewater treatment plants. Of the 133 towns and cities in Sweden in 1960, 25 had biological treatment plants and 28 had mechanical treatment facilities leaving 80 with no treatment at all. Progress was made, but one problem was that the existing plants were often too small because of increasing populations and did not function properly because of poor maintenance. According to one report, "Unfortunately it seems that not a single purification plant in the country functions entirely well" (Nästan 1961). In 1964, a young scientist at the Water Inspection Office, Lars Karlgren, warned in several newspapers that "phosphorus is dangerous for our watercourses" and that its removal was both a complex and costly issue (Fosfor 1964). Thereupon, with some help from the government, Swedish municipalities invested heavily in phosphorus removal facilities. The total annual phosphorus load in Sweden's watercourses that had grown from 1000 tons in 1940 to 7000 tons in the late 1960s was reduced within a decade to approximately 2000 tons and by the mid-1980s to less than 1000 tons a year (Mundt 2006).

Finland

Finland participated in the Second World War, but managed to retain its democratic political and capitalist economic system. After post-war scarcity had passed, industrial production increased considerably and by 1955 the forest industries were using 77 per cent of the total volume of water that was consumed in Finland (Kaartotie 1977: 12). In that decade, the sulphite cellulose industry alone was responsible for 60 per cent of the total organic load in Finland. However, Finnish forest industries rejected all water protection measures despite an increase in their production that reached pre-war levels by the early 1950s. The municipalities continued to carry the main burden while governmental protection efforts were delegated to three administrative bodies that were engaged in unproductive rivalry (Katko 1996: 152–3). In practice, the National Board of Agriculture was the main agency responsible for enforcing water protection because it had its own water protection department and laboratory.

Systematic work to reform water laws was initiated by the Committee of Water Protection from 1954 to 1958. During these years, the committee studied numerous other nations' experiences with water pollution, formed the first national picture of water pollution in Finland, and prepared a bill for a new Water Act that was put into effect in 1962 (KM 1958: 13). It created Municipal Water Boards in towns, initiated the establishment of water protection associations in river watersheds, and founded water districts, three water courts at the district level, and the Supreme Water Court. A provisory Advisory Board for Water Matters coordinated water pollution issues at the national level until 1970 when a National Board of Water (*Vesihallitus*) was established to carry out water pollution control (FAO 1983: 43–9). It performed this task successfully until 1995 when it was substituted by the Finnish Environment Institute (*Suomen ympäristökeskus*, SYKE) that finally centralised the administration of governmental environmental protection and nature conservation.

Despite the aftermath of the war, the building of municipal wastewater treatment plants had begun again in Finland in the 1950s, accelerated in the 1960s, and peaked in the mid-1970s. By the mid-1980s, practically every town and city had a biological wastewater treatment plant. In Finland, the removal of phosphorus was taken care of by the 1970s when methods for the precipitation of copper sulphite were widely adopted in municipal treatment plants. However, the forest industry still resisted as long as possible demands to develop water protection measures. Mills adopted technical wastewater treatment methods in the 1960s and 1970s, and only introduced biological methods in the 1980s (Katko 1996: 254–63, 280–5). Thus both in Sweden and Finland municipalities were considerably more active in water protection than the forest industry.

Soviet Union

Despite the massive destruction of the Second World War, a lack of resources, and even famine, the Soviet Union acted rapidly to fight the widespread pollution of rivers after the war. In 1946, the Ministry of Agriculture of the RSFSR established the Main Department of Water Resources (*Glavnoe Vodnoe Khozyaystvo, i.e., Glavvodhoz*). In the following year, the State Sanitary Inspection was able to give a classified overall summary of the gloomy state of water pollution in the Soviet Union, including rivers, lakes, and coastlines (Filtzer 2010: 114–15). The Council of Ministers of the USSR issued a special decree "On Measures to Eliminate Pollution and to Provide Sanitary Protection of Water Resources" in the same year. Enforcing such a decree right after the devastating war would have been impossible without ample preparation in the inter-war period and the personal support of Josef Stalin. In the post-war period, attention was paid above all to industrial pollution. A special publication entitled "Industrial Waste Waters" was published bi-annually from 1948 (Litvinov 1962: 448; Kolbasov 1965: 214; Filtzer 2010: 116). Moreover, maximum permissible concentration standards for water (known by the Russian acronym

PDK (*predel'no dopustimye koncentratsii*) were established for the first time in the 1940s, and by 1954 no less than 30 substances were covered by these standards that were gradually adopted all over the USSR and in Eastern Europe (Goldman 1972: 295–6).

The next major wave of water protection legislation started in 1960, the year in which the USSR Council of Ministers issued a decree "Regulating the Use and Protection of Water Resources in the Soviet Union". It was the first act to provide specific sanitary norms for industries (Cherkinskii 1971: 4–5). Based on this work, the Council of Ministers issued another important decree on "Regulations for Protecting Surface Waters from Pollution by Wastewater". This provision divided water bodies into three categories according to their use (health and drinking water, fisheries, and agriculture), and the regulation of the volumes and the compositions of effluents was thereafter based on this classification (Cherkinskii 1973: 12).

In 1961, the RSFSR's Committee on State Water Management was established. In connection with the formation of this committee, economic and industrial undertakings and their respective ministries were made responsible for implementing measures to control surface water pollution. The State Sanitary Inspection of the Ministry of Health and the Fish Breeding Inspection were responsible for the implementation of protective measures against pollution and for regulating the conditions under which effluents were discharged into watercourses (Litvinov 1962: 447).

Different regulations published by various Soviet authorities in the 1960s were consolidated in 1970 in "The Principles of Water Legislation of the USSR and the Union Republics", which served for almost two decades as the principal legal act for water management and protection in the Soviet Union. The only amendment to the law was undertaken because the law did not allow for charging for the use of water resources, and in 1979 a new decree allowed for the billing of industrial users (but not agricultural or residential users) for excessive water consumption. Notably, the law of 1970 was only readopted by the Russian Federation in 2006.

In the 1970s, new administrative bodies were created. In 1972 the State Inspectorate for Protection of Water Bodies was established under the Ministry of Land Reclamation and Water Management – which was responsible for extensive irrigation and drainage programs – as a way to centralise the control of water quality and water management within the federal administration. In 1978, the State Hydrometeorological Service under the Ministry of Health was created along with a State Committee on Hydrometereology and Protection of the Environment to curb the power of industries and related ministries (Gustafson 1981: 51). However, the separation of use and protection functions did not take place until 1988 when the State Committee on Environmental Protection was established (DeBardeleben 1992: 65–70).

Based on this administrative and legislative work, water protection was improved in the Soviet Union. In 1959, a total of 687 Soviet cities had a sewerage system and 51 of these cities had wastewater treatment facilities, including 25 that provided biological purification. Thus, about ten per cent of the municipal wastewater was treated biologically, 30 per cent received mechanical treatment, and around 60 per cent was discharged directly into urban water bodies (Spyshnov 1960: 1–2). The building of wastewater treatment plants was accelerated by two decrees issued in 1972, and over the following years 110 cities established wastewater treatment plants. The next five-year plan allocated more funding for wastewater treatment plants, and 850 of the 1000 largest cities in Russia had built such treatment facilities by the end of 1980 (Zakharevksiy 1982: 3). Over the course of the 1980s, the total wastewater treatment capacity in the USSR increased by 53 per cent. Of the total volume of wastewater in the Soviet Union in 1989, 25 per cent was treated in compliance with the government standards, 51 per cent was treated but not complying with the standards, and 24 per cent remained untreated. Between 1976 and 1988, approximately 75 per cent of all government spending on environmental protection was targeted to water protection (Peterson 1993: 63). The obvious conclusion, therefore, is that water protection had become the highest environmental priority in the Soviet Union before the collapse of the communist regime.

Despite its immense size, the Soviet Union had undertaken a preliminary scientific assessment of the extent of national water pollution as early as the late 1930s. The development of water protection in the Soviet Union followed Western patterns with a delay of about ten to fifteen years. While mechanical and biological treatment advanced relatively rapidly, the slow adoption of chemical treatment to remove excess nutrients remained the main problem of water protection prior to the collapse of the Soviet Union.

People's Republic of Poland

During the Second World War, many Polish cities were destroyed and the urban water supply and sewerage services suffered considerably. Immediately after the war, the water quality of the Vistula, a river flowing through most of the major Polish towns, was considered to be in an almost pristine, natural condition – thus illustrating how badly the country and its industries had been devastated. However, surprisingly early after the war the new socialist government of Poland issued several statute laws concerning the protection of Polish waters. In the late 1940s, different ministries required industries to establish and maintain wastewater treatment plants and to protect surface waters and ports against pollution (Kowalik and Laakkonen 2007: 222).

The main authority in the Peoples' Republic of Poland responsible for the implementation of measures against surface water pollution was the State Sanitary Inspection under the Ministry of Health. This inspection agency was set up by a government decree in 1954 after which it established a network of sanitation and epidemiological stations throughout the country (Carter 1993: 122). At least since the late 1950s, the Institute of Hygiene and the aforementioned sanitation and epidemiological stations have surveyed the state of pollution of Polish rivers. Results of research were published regularly in such publications as the *Yearbook of the State Institute of Hygiene* (*Rocznik Państwowego Zakładu Higieny*); *Gas, Water, and Sanitation* (*Gaz, Woda i Technika Sanitarna*); and *Water Management* (*Gospodarka Wodna*) (Litvinov 1962: 458). Official statistics of the state of the environment have been included in the country's *Statistical Yearbook* since the 1970s (Carter 1993: 109).

The most important legal provision concerning conditions of wastewater discharge into surface waters was issued in 1950 by the Ministry of Communal Economy. The decree introduced the classification of surface waters into four categories related to the potential utilisation of the waters (category I designated water of the highest quality and category IV designated the lowest quality) and established related requirements for the quality of the treated wastewater discharged into surface waters. The parameters took into account the degree to which the wastewater was diluted in the open water and the consequences of the self-purification of open waters after the discharge of the wastewater (Roman and Tabernacki 1992: 127–30).

The government of socialist Poland issued a resolution in 1955 to reduce the pollution of surface waters and soils and to utilise wastewater as an economically useful resource. This resolution stressed the responsibility of the main sectors of the state economy to treat wastewater and the need to control how factories fulfilled these requirements. It strictly prohibited constructing, modernising, or reconstructing any factory without proper wastewater treatment. All permits concerning municipal or industrial discharge of wastewater were to be constantly evaluated to prevent further degradation of Poland's watercourses. In addition, this resolution took into account problems related to human resources, construction materials, research and technical documentation, and the locations of cities and new factories in terms of water protection. This pioneering government resolution, however, remained mainly on paper and was only partially implemented (Kowalik and Laakkonen 2007: 223). In all, by 1957 over a hundred minor regulations concerning water pollution were in effect, but only a few of these were actually enforced (Carter 1993: 122). One example of such a regulation was the government decision of August 1959 to confirm the sanitation requirements regarding the discharge of sewage into rivers (Litvinov 1962: 458).

By far the most significant legal provision on national water protection was prepared in the late 1950s and issued in 1961 (with amendments added in 1962). It concerned standards of permissible pollution levels of surface waters and the quality of treated wastewater, and it established five different types of utilisation of open waters based on quality classes. Since 1964, Poland's watercourses have been studied and classified by physicochemical methods and since 1980 by additional biological methods. Conditions related to the treatment of wastewater and the standards of such water were derived from the general rules of the quality of the water receiving the wastewater and of the self-purification processes of the water after the introduction of the wastewater. Special quality requirements for treated wastewater were also adopted in cases where the amount of wastewater was large and the volume of the recipient body of water was small (Kowalik and Laakkonen 2007: 223).

The new water law enacted in 1962 obliged the government to first establish quality classes for open waters as well as the conditions for treated wastewater. Nevertheless, the Council of Ministers of Poland only issued such regulations in 1970 and contrary to many other countries there were no general values for the permissible concentration of pollutants in the treated wastewater. Instead, the permissible concentration for particular factories and cities were calculated on an individual basis and allocated by administrative decisions case by case, which created an inefficient bureaucratic system. The regulations of 1970 introduced three quality classes for rivers, lakes, and the sea in terms of their potential use. For every one of these three classes, 49 indicators were established (Koblak-Kalinska 1992: 107–8).

Environmental protection amendments were introduced into the Polish Constitution in 1976. In 1980, a Statute on the Protection and Development of the Environment was issued to integrate legislation in different sectors of the field. In theory, this act was a model to solve environmental problems, but in practice its administration remained linked to innumerable ministries. The issue of fines remained unsolved as well. In 1981, the Office of Environmental Protection and Water Management was founded, followed a year later by the State Environmental Inspectorate, but these institutions were unable to solve the underlying problems (Carter 1993: 123).

Sufficient funding to finance the building of more than one thousand wastewater treatment plants was allocated in the 1971–75 Five-Year Plan, but in practice little was done. Problems started to accumulate further when the economic situation of the state worsened at the end of the 1970s. By 1989, a total of 459 Polish towns and cities maintained some kind of wastewater treatment facilities but 366 towns still had no municipal wastewater treatment plants at all. For example, the capital Warsaw – with about two million inhabitants at the time – had no wastewater treatment plant during the socialist era (Carter 1993: 114, 122–3).

The collapse of socialism was followed by notable changes in water quality and water protection legislation in Poland. In the years 1988 to 1993, the total nitrogen load from industrial sources was reduced by 11 per cent and the total phosphorus load was reduced by 39 per cent. The reduction in municipal wastewater load was even higher with a 37 per cent reduction in total nitrogen load and a 38 per cent reduction in total phosphorus load (Heybowicz, Bogacka, and Niemirycz 2001: 11–22). As a result, there had been a marked improvement in the water quality of the Vistula River in chemical and organic terms compared with the year 1987, but the water quality had deteriorated in terms of concentrations of salinity and nutrients. Generally speaking, water protection in Poland lagged behind other countries in Northeastern Europe (Kowalik and Laakkonen 2007: 227).

Conclusions

Environmental history is a new field of study and is not yet well established in the countries surrounding the Baltic Sea. This chapter is the first attempt to present an overview of the development of national awareness concerning water pollution and water protection in the Baltic Sea region from a long-term perspective.

Previous studies have highlighted the importance of civil society in general – and nature protection associations and popular movements in particular – in promoting nature conservation. This study strongly indicates, however, that the actors, arguments, and arenas in water protection have been markedly different than previously assumed. The role of governmental experts and civil servants has been constantly highlighted in water protection due to its complex urban-industrial and technical and scientific nature. Professional journals, as well as newspapers, have addressed water pollution and protection issues in the countries examined in this chapter and have shown that political parties and ministries representing agricultural interests and the countryside have generally been the first political spokesmen for water protection. In summary, governmental experts, civil servants, and politicians have undoubtedly constituted the *primus motor* behind water protection throughout the examined period and in all four countries studied here.

The development of governmental activities concerning water pollution and protection over the course of the twentieth century can be divided into five hypothetical eras. During the *initial stage* before the First World War, the earliest parliamentary debates on water pollution took place and pioneering governmental committees exploring national water pollution were established. All of this led to the first legislative efforts aiming to curb pollution. The *formative stage* in the interwar period was marked by the establishment of governmental committees to modernise national water protection legislation and by the creation of the first institutions dedicated to controlling industrial pollution. The *contradictory stage* during and after the Second World War was characterised by destruction and post-war scarcity. This was replaced in the 1950s by rapid economic growth that correlated with the establishment of committees tasked with preparing more effective national laws and regulatory institutions. The results of this work can be seen in the *institutionalising stage* that lasted from the late 1950s to the 1970s when national water protection legislation was enacted and regulatory institutions were established in all of the Baltic rim states examined here. The fall of the Soviet Union and the enlargement of the European Union (from 1995 to 2004) was naturally followed by a *harmonising phase*. With the exception of Russia, national and regional institutions were harmonised with those of the EU in the Baltic Sea region.

Further studies are needed to test the validity of these five stages of development. However, this study indicates that despite differences in socio-economic and political progress, the development of national awareness concerning water pollution and protection in the western and eastern halves of the Baltic Sea region has been marked by convergence rather than by divergence. The notion of a similar development in the eastern and western halves of the region helps to understand how it was possible that members of two mutually competing military alliances, the North Atlantic Treaty Organisation and the Warsaw Pact, were able to sign the Convention on the Protection of the Marine Environment of the Baltic Sea Area in 1974 in Helsinki. The converging development of awareness of water pollution in both parts of the Baltic Sea region has been a prerequisite for achieving results in water protection not only on the national level, but also in terms of international cooperation.

It can be argued that this century-long process of emerging environmental awareness and problem solving in the examined countries has generated a certain identity for the main groups of actors in the various fields of water protection. As water pollution problems expanded and related solutions were adopted, these processes involved a continuously growing number of people. This gradually developed into a national sense of the significance of water protection that represents a completely new dimension in traditional forms of national identities. As a result of this, environmental awareness is today a strong element in the national identities of the Baltic Sea region.

(Top) Researchers at work in the German Democratic Republic, 1948 (Bundesarchiv, Bild 183-M0719-509 / Photographer: Blunck)

(Bottom) New wastwater plant in the German Democratic Republic, 1974 (Bundesarchiv, Bild 183-N0807-014 / Photographer: Heinz Koch)

References

"14 institutioner vattenexperter: Pappren vandrar runt mellan dem." (1953) *Dagens Nyheter* (30 Aug.).

Aktuella (1955) "Aktuella problem inom vattenvården." *FKO-meddelande* (No. 19). Ingeniörsvetenskapsakademien: Stockholm.

Anonymous (1965) [Title missing] *Svenska Dagbladet* (26 March).

Anonymous (1966) [Title missing] *Dagens Nyheter* (20 Nov.).

Asetus (1930) *Asetus terveydenhoitosäännön muuttamisesta*, n:o 199 (23 May).

Betänkande (1939) *Betänkande angående åtgärder till motverkande av vattenförorening, vol. I: Förslag och motivering*. SOU 1939: 40. Stockholm: Justitiedepartementet.

Bolin, G., Hammer, M., Kirsch, F.-M., and Szrubka, W., eds (2005) *The Challenge of the Baltic Sea Region: Culture, Ecosystems, Democracy*. Huddinge: Södertörn University.

Carter, F.W. (1993) "Poland." *Environmental Problems in Eastern Europe*, ed. by Carter, F.W. and Turnock, D. London: Routledge, 107–34.

Cederström, C. (1894) *Neuvoja kalastuksen hoidossa pienempien kalavesien omistajille ja kalastajille*. Wiipuri: Suomen kalastusyhdistys.

Cetkauskaité, A., Zharkov, D., and Stoskus, L. (2001) "Water Quality Control, Monitoring and Waste Water Treatment in Lithuania from 1950 to 1999." *Ambio* 30 (4–5), 297–305.

Cherkinskii, S.N. (1971) "Obshchee gosudarstvennoe vodno-sanitarnoe zakonodatelstvo SSSR." *Gigiena i Sanitariia* 36 (12), 3–8.

Cherkinskii, S.N. (1973)"50 let gosudarstvennomu zakanodatel'stvu po sanitarnoi okhrane vodoemov v SSSR." *Gigiena i Sanitariia* 38 (11), 9–12.

Dikningslagskommittén (1915) *Betänkande med förslag till lag angående vatten- och luftförorening m.m.* Stockholm: Norstedt.

Engberg, J. (1999) *Det heles vel: Forureningsbekæmpelsen i Danmark fra loven om sundhedsvedtægter i 1850'erne til miljøloven 1974*. Copenhagen: Miljøkontrollen.

FAO (1983) *Water Law in Selected European Countries, vol. II (Cyprus, Finland, the Netherlands, Union of Soviet Socialist Republics, Yugoslavia)*. Rome: FAO. Available from http://www.fao.org/docrep/012/ak466E/ak466E.pdf [25 Nov. 2013].

Filatov, N.N., Leonard, N.V., and Shishkina, A.I. (2009) "Etapy stanovleniya i razvitiya gosudarstvennoi sanitarnoi inspektsii Moskvy." *Gigiena i Sanitariia* (6), 4–7.

Filtzer, D. (2010) *The Hazards of Urban Life in Late Stalinist Russia: Health, Hygiene, and Living Standards, 1943-1953.* Cambridge: Cambridge University Press.

Fitzmaurice, M. (1992) *International Legal Problems of the Environmental Protection of the Baltic Sea.* Boston, London, and Dordrecht: Graham & Trotman/Martinus Nijhoff.

"Fosfor i avloppsvattnet är farlig i våra sjöar." (1964) *Helsingborgs Dagblad* (17 Sept.).

Gabovich, R.D. (1967) "Osnovni napravlenia i etapi razvitie Sovetskoi gigieyenicheskoy nauki v sanitarno okhrane vodoyemov za 50 let Sovetskoy vlasti." *Gigiena i Sanitariia* 32 (4), 53–58.

Gilek, M. et al., eds (2011) Special Issue: Coping with Complexity in Baltic Sea Risk Governance. *Ambio* 40 (2), 109–246.

Goldman, M. (1972) *The Spoils of Progress: Environmental Pollution in the Soviet Union.* Cambridge: Cambridge University Press.

Gustafson, T. (1981) *Reform in Soviet Politics: Lessons in Recent Politics on Land and Water.* Cambridge: Cambridge University Press.

"Här har ni landets sämsta vatten." (1957) *Expressen* (27 Nov.).

Heybowicz, E., Bogacka, T., and Niemirycz, E. (2001) "Metody okreslania pochodzenia azotu i fosforu odprowadzanych rzekami do Morza Baltyckiego." *Wiadomości IMGW* 24 (1), 11–22.

Hjorth, R. (1992) *Building International Institutions for Environmental Protection: The Case of Baltic Sea Environmental Cooperation.* Linköping: Linköping University.

"Högrenat vatten för några ören per dag." (1953) *Dagens Nyheter* (19 July).

Holm, P., Smith, T. D., and Starkey, D. J., eds (2001) *The Exploited Seas: New Directions for Marine Environmental History.* St. John's: Census of Marine Life/International Maritime Economic History Association.

Hughes, D. J. (2006) *What is Environmental History?* Cambridge: Polity Press.

Jaatinen, S. (1956) *Vesien suojelun pääpiirteitä.* Helsinki: Tie- ja vesirakennushallituksen diplomi-insinöörien yhdistys r.y.

Järvi, K.H. (1941) *Suomen kalastusyhdistys 1891–1941.* Helsinki: Suomen kalastusyhdistys.

Joas, M., Jahn, D., and Kern, K., eds (2008) *Governing the Common Sea: Environmental Policies in the Baltic Sea Region.* London: Earthscan.

Kaartotie, T. (1972) *Vesiensuojelu.* Tapiola: Weiling & Göös.

Kalastuskomitealta (1898) *Alamainen mietintö kalastuskomitealta keisarilliselle majesteetille.* Helsinki: Edlund.

Katko, T. (1996) *Vettä! Suomen vesihuollon kehitys kaupungeissa ja maaseudulla*. Tampere: Vesi- ja viemärilaitosyhdistys.

Kimstach, V., Mevbeck, M., and Baroudy, E., eds (1998) *A Water Quality Assessment of the Former Soviet Union*. London: E and FN Spon.

Kirby, D. and Hinkkanen, M.-L. (2000) *The Baltic and the North Seas*. London: Routledge.

"Kloak får kanske byggas, men stopp för reningsverk." (1947) *Svenska Dagbladet* (27 Jan.).

KM 1909:1. Sulfatikomitean mietintö.

KM 1958: 13. Vesistönsuojelukomitean mietintö.

Koblak-Kalinska, E. (1992) "Wypowiedzi dyskusyjne." *Gaz, Woda i Technika Sanitarna* (5), 107–8.

Kolbasov, O. S. (1965) *Legislation on Water Use in the U.S.S.R*. Moscow: Iurisdat.

Kowalik, P. and Laakkonen, S. (2007) "Legal Requirements and Waste Water Discharges to Polish Water Bodies, 1945–2005." *Ambio* 36 (2–3), 214–22.

Krasnoborodko, K.I., Alexeev, A.M., Tsvetkova, L.I., Zhukova, L.I. (1999) "The Development of Water Supply and Sewerage Systems in St. Petersburg." *European Water Management* 2 (4), 51–61.

"Kraven på rent vatten skärpes." (1956) *Göteborgs Posten* (7 April).

Laakkonen, S. and Laurila, S., eds (1999) [Special issue] "The History of Urban Water Management in the Baltic Sea Region." *European Water Management* 2 (4), 29–76.

Laakkonen, S., Laurila, S., and Rahikainen, M., eds (1999) *Harmaat aallot: Ympäristönsuojelun tulo Suomeen*. Helsinki: Suomen Historiallinen Seura.

Laakkonen, S. and Laurila, S., eds (2001) [Special issue] "Man and the Baltic Sea." *Ambio* 30 (4–5), 263–326.

Laakkonen, S. et al., eds (2007) [Special issue] "Science and Governance of the Baltic Sea." *Ambio* 36 (2–3), 123–286.

Lundgren, L. (1974) V*attenförorening: Debatten i Sverige 1890–1921*. Lund: Gleerup.

Lundgren, L. (1995) "Sveriges gröna historia." *Människa och miljö: Om ekologi, ekonomi och politik*, ed. by Bolin, B. Stockholm: Tiden, 11–40.

Löwgren, M., Hillmo, T., and Lohm, U. (1989) "Water Pollution Perspectives: Problem Conceptualizations and Abatement Strategies in Sweden during the 20th Century." *GeoJournal* 19 (2), 161–71.

Maciejewski, W., ed. (2002) *The Baltic Sea Region: Cultures, Politics, Societies*. Uppsala: The Baltic University Press.

Malmberg, T. (1961) "Naturvårdsdepartament?" *Skånska Dagbladet* (19 Aug.).

Mundt, K. (2006) "Wastewater Treatment in Sweden." Available from http://www.docstoc.com/docs/2984080/Waste-Water-Treatment-in-Sweden [20 Nov. 2013].

"Nästan alla reningsverk i landet fungerar dåligt." (1961) *Stockholms Tidning* (14 April).

Nordquist, O. (1891) *Toimenpiteitä kalastuksen suojelemiseksi teollisuutta vastaan.* Helsinki: Suomen kalastuksentarkastajan tiedonantoja I.

"Nya lagar." (1956) *Länstidningen* (31 Dec.).

"Orena vattnet riksfara." (1953) *Dagens Nyheter* (19 July).

Peterson, D. J. (1993) *Troubled Lands: The Legacy of Soviet Environmental Destruction.* Boulder: Westview Press.

Roman, M. and Tabernacki, J. (1992) "Kierunki doskonalenia polskich przepisow dotyczacych ochrony wod przed zanieczyszczeniem." *Gaz Woda i Technika Sanitarna* (5), 127–30.

Solomon, S.G. (1993) "The Expert and the State in Russian Public Health: Continuities and Changes Across the Revolutionary Divide." *The History of Public Health and the Modern State,* ed. by Porter, M. Atlanta: Rodopi, 183–223.

"Specialdomstolen bör behandla vattenföroreningar: Förslag av dr Rosén." (1940) *Göteborgs Handelstidning* (18 March).

Spyshnov, P.A. (1960) "Razvitiye vodosnabzheniya i kanalisatsii v godakh SSSR." *Vodosnabzheniya i sanitarnaya tehnika* (6), 1–4.

"Tjugonio institutioner avgör vattenfrågorna! Ingen har huvudansvar." (1953) *Svenska Dagbladet* (4 Nov.).

"Vattenförorening investeringsfråga." (1952) *Svenska Dagbladet* (5 March).

"Vattenföroreningar och kommuner." (1953) *Dagens Nyheter* (2 Aug.).

"Vattenfrågor." (1957) *Uppsala Nya Tidning* (21 Nov.).

Vattenvården (1955) *Betänkande angående organisations- och lagstiftningsfrågor m.m. avgivet av vattenvårdskommittén.* SOU 1955: 6. Stockholm: Jordsbruksdepartementet.

"Vattenvården får ingen ny organisation." (1957) *Östersunds Posten* (28 Nov.).

Velner, H.-A. ed. (2004) *Veekaitse Eestis 1945–2002.* Tallinn: TTÜ.

Zakharevksiy, Y.V. (1982) "Smotret' vpered, videt' perspektivu." *Zhilishchnoye i kommunal'noye khozyaystvo* (July), 2–3.

Zhulidov, A., Robarts, R., Holmes, R., Peterson, B., Kämäri, J., Meriläinen, J., and Headley, J. (2003) *Water Quality Monitoring in the Former Soviet Union and the Russian Federation: Assessment of Analytical Methods.* Helsinki: Finnish Environment Institute.

List of Illustrations, Maps, and Tables

Chapter 1
1) The Berlin Wall at Zimmerstraße, 25 June 1984 (Bundesarchiv, Bild 210-0506 / Photographer: Philipp J. Bösel and Burkhard Maus)
2) Police from West- and East-Berlin at the Berlin Wall, improvised border crossing point at Potsdamer Platz, 15 Nov. 1989 (Bundesarchiv, B 145 Bild-00008581 / Photographer: Klaus Lehnartz)

Chapter 2
1) The Baltic Sea and its islands (Image: Janne Holmén)

Chapter 3
1) Diagram 1: Phases of ethnic violence
2) Map of Russian Lappland, St. Petersburg, 1745 (Photographer: Andrej Kotljarchuk)
3) Ethnographic map of the Murmansk region (Photographer: Andrej Kotljarchuk)
4) Front page of the Finnish-language newspaper *Polarnoin kollektivisti*, no. 92, 17 Dec. 1937 (Courtesy of Russian National Library in St. Petersburg / Photographer: Andrej Kotljarchuk)
5) Mourning ribbon in the Sami language over Petr G. Chaporov (executed in 1937 by the NKVD in Leningrad), Levashovo Memorial Cemetery, St. Petersburg 2000 (Photographer: Aleksandr Stepanenko)

Chapter 4
1) German solders passing hailing bystanders in the city of Aabenraa, Denmark, 12 April 1940 (Photo: Museum Sønderjylland, ISL / Photographer: Ludwig von Münchow)
2) Publications of the German minority in Denmark: The "Schulungsbrief" (Photographer: Steffen Werther)

3) Publications of the German minority in Denmark: "Der Nationalsozialismus … im Grenzland" (Photographer: Steffen Werther)

Chapter 5
1) Poster for the Polish science event in San Francisco, 7–8 Nov. 2013 (© USPTC)

Chapter 6
1) The young Olberg (Labour Movement Archives and Library, Stockholm / photo: 22111878-05051960)
2) Olberg in his mature years (Labour Movement Archives and Library, Stockholm)
3) "Welcome – Long live socialism". Paul Olberg with bundists in Sweden, 1946 (Labour Movement Archives and Library, Stockholm / Photographer: Bäckstrand)
4) 'Bund' at the First of May demonstration in Stockholm, 1946 (Labour Movement Archives and Library, Stockholm)

Chapter 7
1) Table 1: Annual increase of GDP per capita in per cent, different world regions
2) Welding job at a generator, AEG turbine plant, West Berlin, 9 July 1955 (Bundesarchiv, B 145 Bild-F002761-0001 / Photographer: Brodde)
3) Computer-based steering of a robot at a youth event, Germany 1988 (Bundesarchiv, B 145 Bild-F077869-0023/ Photographer: Engelbert Reinecke)

Chapter 8
1) Demonstration outside the Lenin Shipyard, 13 Dec. 1981 (Labour Movement Archives and Library / photo: Solidarity Information Office in Stockholm)
2) Solidarność activists in the internment camp in Strzebielinek, Aug. 1982 (Labour Movement Archives and Library / photo: Solidarity Information Office in Stockholm)
3) Ture Mattsson of the Graphics Industry Union demonstrates a printing press donated by the Swedish Trade Union Confederation to Polish colleagues, 1981 (Labour Movement Archives and Library / photo: Grafia 21–22 / 1981)
4) Pro-Solidarność demonstration in Sweden (Labour Movement Archives and Library / photo: Solidarity Information Office in Stockholm)

Chapter 9
1) What step next? (norden.org / Photographer: Silje Bergum Kinsten)
2) The Nordic ministers for gender equality at a seminar in connection with the UN Commission on the Status of Women, New York, 23 Feb. 2011 (norden.org / Photographer: Cia Pak)

Chapter 10
1) Psychologist Yelena Romanenko conducts training based on Mia Hanström's methodology, adapted for small children, Kaliningrad city, 21 June 2013 (Star of Hope / Photographer: Valentina Zherebtsova)
2) Training for young mothers on gender education in the family by Director of Star of Hope Nina Vorontsova, Bagrationovsk (Kaliningrad region), 15 Feb. 2014 (Star of Hope / Photographer: Valentina Zherebtsova)

Chapter 11
1) Table 1: Net number of migrants, both sexes
2) Crossroads in Chișinău, 2006 (Photographer: Richard Fairbrother)

Chapter 12
1) Researchers at work in the German Democratic Republic, 1948 (Bundesarchiv, Bild 183-M0719-509 / Photographer: Blunck)
2) New wastwater plant in the German Democratic Republic, 1974 (Bundesarchiv, Bild 183-N0807-014 / Photographer: Heinz Koch)

Contributors

Kristina Abiala is a senior lecturer at the Institute of Contemporary History at Södertörn University. She holds a PhD in sociology from Stockholm University. Her main interests are gender and intersectionality, stereotyping and indentity formation, and the complex relation between society and individual coping strategies.

Eva Blomberg is professor at the School of Historical and Contemporary Studies, and the School of Culture and Learning, at Södertörn University. She has earlier worked at Mälardalen University and Stockholm University, were she holds a PhD in history. Her main fields of research are political and contemporary history, gender equality, and labor market relations.

Håkan Blomqvist is associate professor in history and the director of the Institute of Contemporary History at Södertörn University. His main areas of research are the history of the labour movement, nationalism, and antisemitism.

Norbert Götz is professor of history at the Institute of Contemporary History at Södertörn University. He holds a PhD in political science from Humboldt University Berlin and has earlier worked at the University of Greifswald, the Swedish Institute of International Affairs, and the University of Helsinki. His main research interests are political culture, international history, and the history of global civil society.

Yulia Gradskova is an associate professor in history, working presently at Stockholm University. She is a graduate of the Baltic and East European Graduate School (BEEGS) and defended her dissertation at Södertörn University in 2007. Gradskova's interests include gender and social history, and a postcolonial approach to Soviet and post-Soviet history.

Janne Holmén is a senior lecturer at the Institute of Contemporary History at Södertörn University and at the Department of History at Uppsala University. He holds a PhD in history from Uppsala University. His main research interests are historiography, island studies, and educational history.

Andrej Kotljarchuk is an associate professor and senior researcher at the Institute of Contemporary History at Södertörn University; and a lecturer at Stockholm University. He is a graduate of the Baltic and East European Graduate School (BEEGS) and holds a PhD in history from Stockholm University. He has earlier worked at Uppsala University, Umeå University, and the Russian Academy of Sciences. His research focuses on ethnic minorities, epistemic communities, and the politics of memory.

Simo Laakkonen is an associate professor and works as a university lecturer of landscape studies at the University of Turku, Finland. He has a background in the study of the political history of Latin America and holds a PhD from the University of Helsinki. He has organized and directed several research projects that have examined the environmental history of the Baltic Sea, among others one based at Södertörn University. These studies have focused on the history of environmental science, media, policy, and technology in this region.

Klaus Misgeld, retired, PhD, professor (hon.) was a guest professor at the Institute of Contemporary History at Södertörn University in the years 2007 to 2010. He has earlier worked at the University of Uppsala and was from 1981 to 2007 responsible for historical research and publications at the Labour Movement Archives and Library in Stockholm. His main research interests are international history and labour history.

Karl Molin is emeritus professor of history. He has worked at Stockholm University, Uppsala University, and at the Institute of Contemporary History, Södertörn University. His main research interests are Swedish domestic and foreign policy in the twentieth century and international relations after the Second World War.

Sofia Norling is a research fellow at the Institute of Contemporary History and in Environmental Studies at Södertörn University. As a PhD candidate she was located at the Institute of Contemporary History, her PhD in political science being formally awarded from Linköping University. Her main research interests are the sociology of science, the history of science, and political history.

Werner Schmidt is professor at the Institute of Contemporary History at Södertörn University. His main research interests are Marxist theory of history, and the intellectuals of the communist and socialist movement. He is currently working on a biography of the writer and intellectual Peter Weiss.

Ylva Waldemarson is associate professor at the Institute of Contemporary History at Södertörn University. She holds a PhD in history from Stockhom University. Her main research interests are contemporary political history, oral history, and the history of the transnational diffusion of polical ideas and institutions.

Steffen Werther is a lecturer and researcher at the Institute of Contemporary History at Södertörn University. He is a graduate of the Baltic and East European Graduate School (BEEGS) and holds a PhD in history from Stockholm University. His research interests are modern German, Baltic, and Scandinavian history, with a focus on nationalism, right wing movements, racial theory, and Nazi ideology.

Alina Žvinklienė is a chief researcher at the Lithuanian Social Research Center. She holds a PhD in sociology from the Institute of Philosophy, Sociology, and Law at the Lithuanian Academy of Sciences and passed a habilitation in social sciences at the Institute for Social Research in 2006. Her main research fields are democratisation and social development, human rights, identities, and equality politics in multicultural societies from a gender perspective.

Södertörn Academic Studies

1. Helmut Müssener & Frank-Michael Kirsch (Hrsg.), *Nachbarn im Ostseeraum unter sich. Vorurteile, Klischees und Stereotypen in Texten*, 2000.
2. Jan Ekecrantz & Kerstin Olofsson (eds), *Russian Reports: Studies in Post-Communist Transformation of Media and Journalism*, 2000.
3. Kekke Stadin (ed.), *Society, Towns and Masculinity: Aspects on Early Modern Society in the Baltic Area*, 2000.
4. Bernd Henningsen et al. (eds), *Die Inszenierte Stadt. Zur Praxis und Theorie kultureller Konstruktionen*, 2001.
5. Michal Bron (ed.), *Jews and Christians in Dialogue II: Identity, Tolerance, Understanding*, 2001
6. Frank-Michael Kirsch et al. (Hrsg.), *Nachbarn im Ostseeraum über einander. Wandel der Bilder, Vorurteile und Stereotypen?*, 2001.
7. Birgitta Almgren, *Illusion und Wirklichkeit. Individuelle und kollektive Denkmusterin nationalsozialistischer Kulturpolitik und Germanistik in Schweden 1928–1945*, 2001.
8. Denny Vågerö (ed.), *The Unknown Sorokin: His Life in Russia and the Essay on Suicide*, 2002.
9. Kerstin W. Shands (ed.), *Collusion and Resistance: Women Writing in English*, 2002.
10. Elfar Loftsson & Yonhyok Choe (eds), *Political Representation and Participation in Transitional Democracies: Estonia, Latvia and Lithuania*, 2003.
11. Birgitta Almgren (Hrsg.), *Bilder des Nordens in der Germanistik 1929–1945: Wissenschaftliche Integrität oder politische Anpassung?*, 2002.
12. Christine Frisch, *Von Powerfrauen und Superweibern: Frauenpopulärliteratur der 90er Jahre in Deutschland und Schweden*, 2003.
13. Hans Ruin & Nicholas Smith (red.), *Hermeneutik och tradition. Gadamer och den grekiska filosofin*, 2003.
14. Mikael Lönnborg et al. (eds), *Money and Finance in Transition: Research in Contemporary and Historical Finance*, 2003.
15. Kerstin Shands et al. (eds.), *Notions of America: Swedish Perspectives*, 2004.
16. Karl-Olov Arnstberg & Thomas Borén (eds.), *Everyday Economy in Russia, Poland and Latvia*, 2003.
17. Johan Rönnby (ed.), *By the Water. Archeological Perspectives on Human Strategies around the Baltic Sea*, 2003.
18. Baiba Metuzale-Kangere (ed.), *The Ethnic Dimension in Politics and Culture in the Baltic Countries 1920–1945*, 2004.

19. Ulla Birgegård & Irina Sandomirskaja (eds), *In Search of an Order: Mutual Representations in Sweden and Russia during the Early Age of Reason*, 2004.
20. Ebba Witt-Brattström (ed.), *The New Woman and the Aesthetic Opening:Unlocking Gender in Twentieth-Century Texts*, 2004.
21. Michael Karlsson, *Transnational Relations in the Baltic Sea Region*, 2004.
22. Ali Hajighasemi, *The Transformation of the Swedish Welfare System: Fact or Fiction?: Globalisation, Institutions and Welfare State Change in a Social Democratic Regime*, 2004.
23. Erik A. Borg (ed.), *Globalization, Nations and Markets: Challenging Issues in Current Research on Globalization*, 2005.
24. Stina Bengtsson & Lars Lundgren, *The Don Quixote of Youth Culture: Media Use and Cultural Preferences Among Students in Estonia and Sweden*, 2005
25. Hans Ruin, *Kommentar till Heideggers Varat och tiden*, 2005.
26. Людмила Ферм, *Вариативное беспредложное глагольное управление в русском языке XVIII века*, 2005.
27. Christine Frisch, *Modernes Aschenputtel und Anti-James-Bond: Gender-Konzepte in deutschsprachigen Rezeptionstexten zu Liza Marklund und Henning Mankell*, 2005.
28. Ursula Naeve-Bucher, *Die Neue Frau tanzt: Die Rolle der tanzenden Frau in deutschen und schwedischen literarischen Texten aus der ersten Hälfte des 20. Jahrhunderts*, 2005.
29. Göran Bolin et al. (eds.), *The Challenge of the Baltic Sea Region: Culture,Ecosystems, Democracy*, 2005.
30. Marcia Sá Cavalcante Schuback & Hans Ruin (eds), *The Past's Presence: Essays on the Historicity of Philosophical Thought*, 2006.
31. María Borgström och Katrin Goldstein-Kyaga (red.), *Gränsöverskridande identiteter i globaliseringens tid: Ungdomar, migration och kampen för fred*, 2006.
32. Janusz Korek (ed.), *From Sovietology to Postcoloniality: Poland and Ukraine from a Postcolonial Perspective*, 2007.
33. Jonna Bornemark (red.), *Det främmande i det egna: filosofiska essäer om bildning och person*, 2007.
34. Sofia Johansson, *Reading Tabloids: Tabloid Newspapers and Their Readers*, 2007.
35. Patrik Åker, *Symboliska platser i kunskapssamhället: Internet, högre lärosäten och den gynnade geografin*, 2008.
36. Kerstin W. Shands (ed.), *Neither East Nor West: Postcolonial Essays on Literature, Culture and Religion*, 2008.
37. Rebecka Lettevall and My Klockar Linder (eds), *The Idea of Kosmopolis: History, philosophy and politics of world citizenship*, 2008.

38. Karl Gratzer and Dieter Stiefel (eds.), *History of Insolvency and Bankruptcy from an International Perspective*, 2008.
39. Katrin Goldstein-Kyaga och María Borgström, *Den tredje identiteten: Ungdomar och deras familjer i det mångkulturella, globala rummet*, 2009.
40. Christine Farhan, *Frühling für Mütter in der Literatur?: Mutterschaftskonzepte in deutschsprachiger und schwedischer Gegenwartsliteratur*, 2009.
41. Marcia Sá Cavalcante Schuback (ed.), *Att tänka smärtan*, 2009.
42. Heiko Droste (ed.), *Connecting the Baltic Area: The Swedish Postal System in the Seventeenth Century*, 2011.
43. Aleksandr Nemtsov, *A Contemporary History of Alcohol in Russia*, 2011.
44. Cecilia von Feilitzen and Peter Petrov (eds), *Use and Views of Media in Russia and Sweden: A Comparative Study of Media in St. Petersburg and Stockholm*, 2011.
45. Sven Lilja (red.), *Fiske, jordbruk och klimat i Östersjöregionen under förmodern tid*, 2012.
46. Leif Dahlberg och Hans Ruin (red.), *Fenomenologi, teknik och medialitet*, 2012.
47. Samuel Edquist, *I Ruriks fotspår: Om forntida svenska österledsfärder i modern historieskrivning*, 2012.
48. Jonna Bornemark (ed.), *Phenomenology of Eros*, 2012.
49. Jonna Bornemark and Hans Ruin (eds.), *Ambiguity of the Sacred: Phenomenology, Politics, Aesthetics*, 2012.
50. Håkan Nilsson, *Placing Art in the Public Realm*, 2012.
51. Per Bolin, *Between National and Academic Agendas: Ethnic Policies and 'National Disciplines' at Latvia's University, 1919–1940*, 2012.
52. Lars Kleberg and Aleksei Semenenko (eds.), *Aksenov and the Environs/Aksenov iokrestnosti*, 2012.
53. Sven-Olov Wallenstein and Brian Manning Delaney (eds.), *Translating Hegel: The Phenomenology of Spirit and Modern Philosophy*, 2012.
54. Sven-Olov Wallenstein and Jakob Nilsson (eds.), *Foucault, Biopolitics, and Governmentality*, 2013.
55. Jan Patočka, *Inledning till fenomenologisk filosofi*, 2013.
56. Jonathan Adams and Johan Rönnby (eds.), *Interpreting Shipwrecks: Maritime Archaeological Approaches*, 2013.
57. Charlotte Bydler, *Mondiality/Regionality: Perspectives on Art, Aesthetics and Globalization*, 2014.
58. Andrej Kotljarchuk, *In the Forge of Stalin: Swedish Colonists of Ukraine in Totalitarian Experiments of the Twentieth Century*, 2014.
59. Samuel Edquist, Janne Holmén and Erik Axelsson, *Islands of Identity*, 2014.

60. Norbert Götz (ed.), *The Sea of Identities: A Century of Baltic and East European Experiences with Nationality, Class, and Gender*, 2014.

Samtidshistoriska frågor

1. *Olof Palme i sin tid.* Red. Kjell Östberg (2001).
   (Finns endast elektroniskt i DiVA då den tryckta upplagan är slut.)
2. *Kvinnorörelsen och '68.* Red. Elisabeth Elgán (2001).
   (Finns endast elektroniskt i DiVA då den tryckta upplagan är slut.)
3. *Riva alla murar! Vittnesseminarier om sexliberalismen och om Pocket-tidningen R.* Red. Lena Lennerhed (2002).
4. *Löntagarfonderna – en missad möjlighet?* Red. Lars Ekdahl (2002).
5. *Dagens Nyheter: minnesseminarium över Sven-Erik Larsson. Vittnesseminarium om DN och '68.* Red. Alf W Johansson (2003).
6. *Kvinnorna skall göra det! Den kvinnliga medborgarskolan på Fogelstad – som idé, text och historia.* Red. Ebba Witt Brattström och Lena Lennerhed (2003).
7. *Moderaterna, marknaden och makten – svensk högerpolitik under avregleringens tid, 1976–1991.* Torbjörn Nilsson (2003).
8. *Upprorets estetik.* Lena Lennerhed (2005).
9. *Revolution på svenska – ett vittnesseminarium om jämställdhetens institutionalisering, politisering och expansion 1972–1976.* Red. Anja Hirdman (2005).
10. *En högskola av ny typ? Två seminarier kring Södertörns högskolas tillkomst och utveckling.* Red. Mari Gerdin och Kjell Östberg (2006).
11. *Hur rysk är den svenska kommunismen? Fyra bidrag om kommunism, nationalism och etnicitet.* Red. Mari Gerdin och Kjell Östberg (2006).
12. *Ropen skalla – daghem åt alla! Vittnesseminarium om daghemskampen på 70-talet.* Red. Mari Gerdin och Kajsa Ohrlander (2007).
13. *Makten i kanslihuset – ett vittnesseminarium om ett Regeringskansli i förändring.* Red. Emma Isaksson och Torbjörn Nilsson (2007).
14. *Partnerskapslagen – ett vittnesseminarium om partnerskapslagens tillkomst.* Red. Emma Isaksson och Lena Lennerhed (2007).
15. *Vägar till makten – statsrådens och statssekreterarnas karriärvägar.* Anders Ivarsson Westerberg och Cajsa Niemann (2007).
16. *Sverige och Baltikums frigörelse. Två vittnesseminarier om storpolitik kring Östersjön 1991–1994.* Red. Thomas Lundén och Torbjörn Nilsson (2008).
17. *Makten och trafiken i Stadshuset. Två vittnesseminarier om Stockholms kommunalpolitik.* Red. Torbjörn Nilsson (2009).

18. *Norden runt i tvåhundra år. Jämförande studier om liberalism, konservatism och historiska myter.* Torbjörn Nilsson (2010).
19. *1989 med svenska ögon. Vittnesseminarium om Östeuropas omvandling.* Red. Torbjörn Nilsson och Thomas Lundén (2010).
20. *Statsminister Göran Persson i samtal med Erik Fichtelius (1996–2006).* Red. Werner Schmidt. DVD utgiven av SVT och Södertörns högskola (2011).
21. *Bortom rösträtten. Politik, kön och medborgarskap i Norden.* Lenita Freidenwall och Josefin Rönnbäck (2011).
22. *Borgerlig fyrklöver intog Rosenbad – regeringsskiftet 1991.* Red. Torbjörn Nilsson och Anders Ivarsson Westerberg (2011).
23. *Rivstart för Sverige – Alliansen och maktskiftet 2006.* Red. Fredrik Eriksson och Anders Ivarsson Westerberg (2012).
24. *Det började i Polen – Sverige och Solidaritet 1980–1981.* Red. Fredrik Eriksson (2013).
25. *Förnyelse eller förfall? Svenska försvaret efter kalla kriget.* Red. Fredrik Eriksson (2013).
26. *Staten och granskningssamhället.* Red. Bengt Jacobsson och Anders Ivarsson Westerberg (2013).
27. *Almedalen – Så skapades en politikens marknadsplats. Ett vittnesseminarium om Almedalsveckan som politisk arena.* Red. Kjell Östberg (2013).
28. *Anarkosyndikalismens återkomst i Spanien. SACs samarbete med CNT under övergången från diktatur till demokrati.* Red. Per Lindblom (2014).
29. *När blev vården marknad? Vittnesseminarium i Almedalen.* Red. Kristina Abiala (2014).
30. *Brinner "förorten"? Om sociala konflikter i Botkyrka och Huddinge.* Red. Kristina Abiala (2014).
31. The Sea of Identities: A Century of Baltic and East European Experiences with Nationality, Class, and Gender. Ed. Norbert Götz (2014).

www.ingramcontent.com/pod-product-compliance
Lightning Source LLC
Chambersburg PA
CBHW040745020526
44114CB00049B/2934